Power and Influence of Economists

Economists occupy leading positions in many different sectors, including central and private banks, multinational corporations, the state and the media, as well as serve as policy consultants on everything from health to the environment and security. *Power and Influence of Economists* explores the interconnected relationship between power, knowledge and influence which has led economics to be both a source and beneficiary of widespread power and influence.

The contributors to this book explore the complex and diverse methods and channels that economists have used to exert and expand their influence from different disciplinary and national perspectives. Four different analytical views on the role of power and economics are taken: first, the role of economic expert discourses as power devices for the formation of influential expertise; second, the logics and modalities of governmentality that produce power/knowledge apparatuses between science and society; third, economists as involved in networks between academia, politics and the media; and fourth, economics considered as a social field, including questions of legitimacy and unequal relations between economists based on the accumulation of various capitals. The volume includes case studies on a variety of national configurations of economics, such as the US, Germany, Italy, Switzerland, Greece, Mexico and Brazil, as well as international spaces and organisations such as the IMF.

This book provides innovative research perspectives for students and scholars of heterodox economics, cultural political economy, sociology of professions, network studies and the social studies of power, discourse and knowledge.

Jens Maesse is Assistant Professor at the Department of Sociology at the University of Giessen, Germany.

Stephan Pühringer is Postdoctoral Research Associate at the Institute for Comprehensive Analysis of the Economy (ICAE) at the University of Linz, Austria, and Research Fellow at the Institute of Economics at the Cusanus University of Bernkastel-Kues, Germany.

Thierry Rossier is Postdoctoral Research Fellow at the Department of Organization at the Copenhagen Business School, Denmark.

Pierre Benz is Postdoctoral Researcher at the University of Applied Sciences and Arts Western Switzerland, Faculté of Social Work (HETSL | HES-SO), Switzerland.

Routledge Frontiers of Political Economy

Markets, Community, and Just Infrastructures
Nancy Neiman

The Informal Economy
Measures, Causes, and Consequences
Ceyhun Elgin

Understanding Financial Crises
Ensar Yılmaz

The Political Economy of Populism
An Introduction
Petar Stankov

Capitalism, Institutions and Social Orders
The Case of Contemporary Spain
Pedro M. Rey-Araújo

Power and Influence of Economists
Contributions to the Social Studies of Economics
Edited by Jens Maesse, Stephan Pühringer, Thierry Rossier and Pierre Benz

Rent-Seeking and Human Capital
How the Hunt for Rents is Changing Our Economic and Political Landscape
Kurt von Seekamm Jr.

The Political Economy of State Intervention
Conserving Capital over the West's Long Depression
Gavin Poynter

For more information about this series, please visit: www.routledge.com/books/series/SE0345

Power and Influence of Economists

Contributions to the Social Studies of Economics

Edited by Jens Maesse, Stephan Pühringer, Thierry Rossier and Pierre Benz

LONDON AND NEW YORK

First published 2022
by Routledge
2 Park Square, Milton Park, Abingdon, Oxon OX14 4RN

and by Routledge
605 Third Avenue, New York, NY 10158

Routledge is an imprint of the Taylor & Francis Group, an informa business

© 2022 selection and editorial matter, Jens Maesse, Stephan Pühringer, Thierry Rossier and Pierre Benz; individual chapters, the contributors

The right of Jens Maesse, Stephan Pühringer, Thierry Rossier and Pierre Benz to be identified as the authors of the editorial material, and of the authors for their individual chapters, has been asserted in accordance with sections 77 and 78 of the Copyright, Designs and Patents Act 1988.

The Open Access version of this book, available at www.taylorfrancis.com, has been made available under a Creative Commons Attribution-Non Commercial-No Derivatives 4.0 license.

Trademark notice: Product or corporate names may be trademarks or registered trademarks, and are used only for identification and explanation without intent to infringe.

British Library Cataloguing-in-Publication Data
A catalogue record for this book is available from the British Library

Library of Congress Cataloging-in-Publication Data
A catalog record has been requested for this book

ISBN: 978-0-367-41984-4 (hbk)
ISBN: 978-0-367-56595-4 (pbk)
ISBN: 978-0-367-81708-4 (ebk)

DOI: 10.4324/9780367817084

The open access publication of this book has been published with the support of the Swiss National Science Foundation.

Contents

List of contributors	viii

1 The role of power in the social studies of economics: an introduction 1
JENS MAESSE, STEPHAN PÜHRINGER, THIERRY ROSSIER AND
PIERRE BENZ

PART 1
Economic knowledge and discursive power 17

2 Performative, imaginary and symbolic power: how economic expert discourses influence society 19
JENS MAESSE

3 Macroeconomics and monetary policy as autonomous domains of knowledge and power: rational expectations, monetarism and the Federal Reserve 36
JAN SPARSAM AND HANNO PAHL

4 The power of economics textbooks: shaping meaning and identity 53
LUKAS BÄUERLE

PART 2
Economic governmentalities 71

5 The constitution of neoliberal governmentality from early neoclassical economics to public choice theory 73
CEYHUN GÜRKAN

vi *Contents*

6 Competitive power: elements of Foucauldian economics   90
FLEMMING BJERKE

**7 Feelings in crisis: the emotional and affective
dimension of neoliberal economics in Greek crisis
prone society**   109
ELENA PSYLLAKOU

**8 Laboratories for economic expertise: lay perspectives
on Italian disciplinary economics**   126
GERARDO COSTABILE NICOLETTA

PART 3
Economists in networks   145

**9 Who are the economists Germany listens to?
The social structure of influential German economists**   147
STEPHAN PÜHRINGER AND KARL M. BEYER

**10 Global production and circulation of dominant
ideologies: Mexico from the default debt crisis to the
Brady Plan (1982–1989)**   170
JOHANNA GAUTIER MORIN

**11 Economists in public discourses: the case of wealth
and inheritance taxation in the German press**   188
HENDRIK THEINE

PART 4
Economics as a scientific field   207

**12 Are there institutionalized pathways to the Nobel
Prize in economics?**   209
PHILIPP KOROM

**13 Forms of social capital in economics: the importance
of heteronomous networks in the Swiss field of
economists (1980–2000)**   227
THIERRY ROSSIER AND PIERRE BENZ

Contents vii

14 Paths of international circulation: how do economists and economic knowledge flow? 248

ELISA KLÜGER

Index 266

Contributors

Lukas Bäuerle is Research Associate at the Institute of Economics at the Cusanus University Bernkastel-Kues and PhD candidate at the University of Flensburg, Germany.

Pierre Benz is Postdoctoral Researcher at the University of Applied Sciences and Arts Western Switzerland, Faculté of Social Work (HETSL | HES-SO), Switzerland.

Karl M. Beyer is Research Associate at the Institute for Comprehensive Analysis of the Economy (ICAE) at the University of Linz, Austria.

Flemming Bjerke is a retired scholar, Denmark.

Johanna Gautier Morin is Visiting Student Research Collaborator at Princeton University, US, and PhD candidate at the Graduate Institute of Geneva, Switzerland.

Ceyhun Gürkan is Associate Professor at the Department of Public Finance from the Faculty of Political Science at Ankara University, Turkey.

Elisa Klüger is Postdoctoral Researcher at the Centro Brasileiro de Análise e Planejamento (CEBRAP) in São Paulo, Brazil.

Philipp Korom is Principal Investigator of the Austrian Science Fund (FWF) Research Project "National and Regional Elites in Austrian Politics" at the University of Graz, Austria.

Jens Maesse is Assistant Professor at the Department of Sociology at the University of Giessen, Germany.

Gerardo Costabile Nicoletta is Teaching Fellow at the Department of Social Science at the University of Naples Federico II, Italy.

Hanno Pahl is Research Associate at the Department of Media Studies at the University of Bonn, Germany.

Stephan Pühringer is Postdoctoral Research Associate at the Institute for Comprehensive Analysis of the Economy (ICAE) at the University of Linz,

Austria, and Research Fellow at the Institute of Economics at the Cusanus University of Bernkastel-Kues, Germany.

Elena Psyllakou is Postdoctoral Research Fellow at the National Center for Social Research – EKKE, Greece.

Thierry Rossier is Postdoctoral Research Fellow at the Department of Organization at the Copenhagen Business School, Denmark.

Jan Sparsam is Research Associate at the Department of Sociology at the University of Giessen, Germany.

Hendrik Theine is Postdoctoral Researcher at the Institute for Heterodox Economics at the WU – Vienna University of Economics and Business, Austria.

1 The role of power in the social studies of economics[1]

An introduction

Jens Maesse, Stephan Pühringer, Thierry Rossier and Pierre Benz

1 Economics and power

The volume starts from the idea that economics as academic discipline and profession has enhanced influence and power during recent decades in many countries and in several social spheres. The forms of power, domination and authority that open up different channels of influence for economics are complex and diverse. But economics is not only a source of power, it is also product of power and domination through discourses, fields, networks and other means and tools. These discourses, fields and networks are controlled by different governmentalities and rules and they span different sectors of society. Thus, the study of economists, economics and economic expert discourse cannot be restricted to academia, as it involves a variety of domains of investigation (Maesse, 2015).

Accordingly, economists occupy positions at the top of institutional hierarchies in different sectors, such as banks and large firms, the state and the media, as well as within academia. They serve as consultants and advisors in several policy fields, ranging from fiscal to health and social security policy. Economists are appointed to the boards of big corporations, as governance experts, senior civil servants and central bankers. Economists are also members of consulting teams for newspapers and other media, regularly publish op-eds and leads, while acting as economic experts and translating their symbolic capital into policy by coining core "economic imaginaries" (Jessop, 2010). Actually, leading newspapers in the German-speaking area have started to establish their own economists' rankings based on their impact in several social spheres. Additionally, economists have become a dominant professional group, compared to traditional professions and other social science disciplines. At the international level, economists work in various influential organisations, such as the International Monetary Fund (IMF), the World Bank, the World Trade Organisation (WTO) and the European Central Bank (ECB) (Dezalay & Garth, 1998).

Furthermore, economists cannot act within society without a strong base in academia and science. Accordingly, economists constitute one of the most advanced examples of an *international* scientific field, resulting from a long process of standardisation of practices, careers and curricula, as well as the adoption

DOI: 10.4324/9780367817084-1

of external technical tools from mathematics and physics (Fourcade, 2006). Yet, economists do not form a homogeneous group, and their power is unequally distributed amongst members of the group. Strong hierarchies, compared to other academic disciplines and professions, characterise economics. There are only a few expressions for alternative approaches compared to the dominant orthodoxy in the field. This hierarchy, combined with a strong insularity in the field, helps to define a sentiment of self-confidence and superiority among group members (Fourcade et al., 2015). Economists face strong imbalances in the distribution of related capitals, and this stratification of the profession has implications for some features of their profiles. Economists are clearly under-feminised, and it can be hypothesised that, for the most part, they come from high social backgrounds. Women, individuals with a working-class background or with a particularly local profile are more or less excluded from resources in terms of chairs, research funds, grants and editorial board positions (Bayer & Rouse, 2016). Nonetheless, such individuals are sometimes able to offer real challenges to dominant actors in the field.

To sum up, several channels exist through which economists influence public policy issues; aside from analysing the traditional role of economic experts as policy advisors, there is also a strand of research focusing on the political power of economic ideas, as well as more recent literature on the performativity of economic models and the role of economists as "public intellectuals" (i.e. economists who are engaged and highly visible in political and public debates) (Mata & Medema, 2013). Consequently, aside from direct channels through which economic knowledge enters the political arena, there are also several indirect channels of impact that are mediated by intermediaries such as think tanks or media outlets (Hirschman & Berman, 2014; Plehwe et al., 2018). These institutions play a crucial role in the transmission of economic ideas.

Our volume reflects on these complex interrelationships between science and society, where economic experts act and have an impact on several levels. In this way, we present 13 contributions from four different methodological and theoretical domains. Each chapter takes a particular view on the multiple dimensions of power, action and impact. To sum up, this volume offers complex insights into the forms of power in economics and provides a broad overview of recent developments in the evolving field of social studies of economics (henceforth SSE).

2 Power as a complex phenomenon

SSE developed as a field for the analysis on the role of economists in society. The groundbreaking works of Coats, Hall, Mirowski, Morgan, Fourcade and Lebaron opened up a research field that is hardly manageable today (Coats, 1993; Fourcade, 2009; Hall, 1989; Lebaron, 2001; Mirowski, 1991; Morgan, 1990). Especially in recent decades, a huge array of young researchers started the endeavour to form a research field out of the canonical classics (Schmidt-Wellenburg & Lebaron, 2018a; Maesse et al., 2017; Mata & Medema, 2013;

Montecinos & Markoff, 2009; Hirschman & Popp Berman, 2014; Aistleitner et al., 2018). This work has developed in many national and disciplinary contexts, and it has shown how questions on the interrelation of power, discourse and knowledge have become important in this field. The contributions of this volume analyse the complex and widespread channels of influence as well as the mutual roles of economic experts in and on society from different disciplinary approaches and national contexts. It provides an overview of the diversity of perspectives and paradigms. Four different analytical views on the role of power and economics will be taken: first, the role of economic expert discourses as power devices for the formation of influential expertise; second, the logics and modalities of governmentality that produce power/knowledge apparatuses between science and society; third, economists as they are involved in networks between academia, politics and the media; and fourth, economics considered as a social field, including questions of legitimacy and unequal relations between economists based on the accumulation of various capitals.

In order to study economic expert knowledge, *discourse analytical* approaches became popular within SSE. Economic expert knowledge is mainly analysed from three perspectives. First, the production of economics knowledge is studied by economic historians and cultural sociologists (Coats, 1993; Morgan, 1990). In particular, different paradigms, hegemonic theories and marginalised forms of knowledge were analysed in order to understand how power relations influence the production of economic truths (Dobusch & Kapeller, 2009; Mirowski, 1991; Ötsch et al., 2017). In addition to this production-oriented research, the influence of economic expert knowledge on society became a major research field. Here, performativity studies have shown how economics as discursive tool impacts on the formation of markets and firms (Callon, 1998; MacKenzie et al., 2007; and critically Sparsam & Pahl in this volume). Other studies have taken into account the formation of legitimacy, argumentation strategies and speaker positions via economic expert discourses (Fitzgerald & O'Rourke, 2015; Maesse, 2015; Pühringer & Griesser, 2020; and Bäuerle in this volume). Both approaches – production and impact orientation – mostly interact by focusing on diverse forms of the circulation of knowledge and the various types of interpretative adoption by experts, professionals, politicians and the media (Maesse, 2017, and in this volume). Here, economic expertise is seen as a tool for exercising power through hegemonic discourses in different social contexts, such as politics, the business world and the media (Schmidt-Wellenburg, 2018). Finally, a third form of discourse analytical perspective considers diverse forms of informal knowledge (Maesse, 2018; Rossier & Bühlmann, 2018). This knowledge accounts for informal social rules in organisations, tacit knowledge in professional fields, institutional norms and values of politics and academia, as well as the social networks that control access to certain institutions and regulate official and unofficial membership categories.

Closely related to discourse approaches, *governmentality* studies analyse economics and economic expertise as a form of "soft power". Starting form Foucault's work on governmentality and "neoliberalisation" studies (Dean, 1999;

4   *Jens Maesse et al.*

Foucault, 2008; Miller, 2001), economics is seen as a governance tool for the creation of various forms of subjectivities. As Psyllakou shows in this volume, TV shows and certain forms of economic language can be analysed as mechanisms for producing and controlling the emotions of people. In addition to that, Nicoletta analyses in this volume how an economic governance apparatus in Italy emerged. Other studies have shown how neoliberal ideologies and economic theories interact in order to create certain political perceptions and interpretative frames (Zuidhof, 2012; and Gürkan in this volume). In addition, many studies have analysed how neoliberalism recruits economic experts and ideas in order to implement certain political programmes serving the interests of the ruling classes. In this volume, Bjerke shows how this works in the case of market theory. However, various other study areas have analysed the governmentality of neoliberalism, for example financialisation studies (Erturk et al., 2008). The main contribution of governmentality approaches to SSE can be seen in their ability to bring together critical views of knowledge use, connecting them to new approaches to power and domination and offering a new field for discourse analytical methods. Additionally, network and field approaches to economics are closely connected to the role of power/knowledge apparatuses considered by governmentality studies.

Another trend within SSE is the analysis of *network* structures in economics, either to investigate the transmission of economic knowledge into politics or to unveil social power structures inside academic economics. In the first case, a social network perspective enables highlighting the connections of economists to powerful elites and their involvement in policymaking processes, as well as the role of networks in spreading economic ideas in general. In this respect, recent approaches in SSE are related to critical policy studies (Mirowski & Plehwe, 2009) and the evolving field of think-tank network research (Salas-Porras & Murray, 2017). Thus, scholars are explicitly focusing on a sample of politically engaged economists and investigating personal (e.g. co-authorships, collaborations) and institutional (e.g. memberships, positions) networks between economic experts and advice bodies, as well as economic think tanks or initiatives (Grimm et al., 2018; Flickenschild & Afonso, 2019; Pühringer, 2020; and Theine and Pühringer & Beyer, in this volume). In this way, they are able to show the formative role of such personal-institutional networks in the process of the transmission of economic knowledge into policymaking (Helgadóttir, 2016; Plehwe et al., 2018; and Gautier Morin in this volume). In the second case, researchers are typically interested in hierarchies, stratification logics, path dependencies and network effects inside academia, and thus they often combine social network analysis (SNA) with bibliometric and/or biographical analyses (Beyer & Pühringer, 2019; Coman, 2019). While SNA as applied in SSE is rooted in early economic sociology (e.g. Granovetter, 1983), current approaches make use of the availability of huge databases and advanced analytical tools. In this vein, recent studies have investigated "citation cartels" between economic journals (Anauati et al., 2018) and authors (Önder & Terviö, 2015). On a more individual level, scholars also show that established social networks between economists and actors outside academic economics play a crucial role in shaping the prospects for successful academic careers (Rossier, 2020; and Rossier & Benz in this volume). This volume contributes to the debate on the public and political impact of economics by providing novel empirical analyses of social networks of economists both inside and outside academia.

A final approach conceptualises economics as a *field* (Bourdieu, 2005). Within this more or less autonomous social space, economists compete for the definition of both the field's boundaries and what (good) economics is (Lebaron, 2000). The distribution of capital, defined as a group of powerful resources involved in systemic processes allowing their garnering by those who possess them (Savage et al., 2005), and economists' individual dispositions shape their position in the field's structure and their scientific and political position-takings (Lebaron, 2001). This approach focuses on two particularities characterising this field. *First*, economics as a scientific discipline is subject to transnational processes of scientific recognition with, at the top of the hierarchy, a few US departments and scientific journals, as well as the Nobel and the "Nobel" prize, which shape academic careers and citations (Korom, 2020, and in this volume). The import of resources acquired in those departments provides economists with advantageous positions in their home countries (Dezalay & Garth, 2002; Gautier Morin & Rossier, 2021). *Second*, economics occupies a particularly central place within the field of power, i.e. the field of dominant individuals from all other fields (Bourdieu, 1996). Neoclassical economic theory contributes to spreading an "economic belief" that consolidates the production of a "dominant ideology", which reflects the interests of a capitalist class and legitimises the social order (Gautier Morin in this volume). Economists are not just a social group with increasing importance in the academic context but also most certainly the producers of some of the most important tools and perceptions to govern today's societies (Schmidt-Wellenburg & Lebaron, 2018b: 20). Consequently, they have a strong influence on policymaking and occupy positions among the public administration and private sector elites (Rossier et al., 2017; Klüger, 2018, and in this volume), whereas their internal debates often take place well beyond the field's borders, such as in the political arena (Schmidt-Wellenburg, 2018) and the media (Gautier Morin, 2019). More generally, when studying economics as part of a *field-analytical strategy* (Bourdieu & Wacquant, 1992), three interrelated dimensions are highlighted. First, economics is considered in relation to the field of power by stressing where economists are situated within this powerful space. Second, the objective structure of relations through the distribution of specific capital in economics is highlighted. This also includes a focus on economists' biographical and network-related resources. Third, processes related to economists' field-specific habitus, defined as a set of embodied dispositions that organise their ways of acting, thinking, feeling and perceiving (Lenger, 2018), are uncovered. Studying economists' habitus allows us to understand the relations between their position in the field and their theoretical, methodological and political position-takings. The chapters in this volume contribute, each in its own way, to the study of economics at those three levels, by focusing on original cases through the lens of different quantitative and qualitative descriptive methodologies.

6 *Jens Maesse et al.*

3 Fields of investigation

This book, through its four analytical dimensions, addresses the changes that economics underwent during recent decades, gaining influence and power in many countries and in several social contexts. The chapters of this book will help us to understand economics as it is involved in many power games. The relationship of power and knowledge production is complex and accounts for the special role of economics in current societies. This volume collects 13 contributions from different (qualitative and quantitative) methodological and theoretical fields. Each contribution takes a particular view on the multiple dimensions of power, knowledge and influence. The authors discuss various aspects related to economics as an academic discipline and profession from four main perspectives in SSE: discourse analysis, governmentality studies, network studies and field theory. Via these approaches we can understand several forms of power related to the profession, as well as various challenges that need to be analysed from a critical and interdisciplinary perspective. In order to represent different disciplines, the authors have backgrounds in sociology, history, political science, linguistics and economics. These studies cover a large historical period, mainly the second part of the 20th century, and focus on a variety of national cases (including the USA, Germany, Italy, Switzerland, Greece, Mexico, Brazil) and international institutions, such as the IMF. In addition, various qualitative and quantitative methodologies and research strategies are applied, such as interviews, content and documentary analyses, prosopography, historical and archival research, discourse analysis, text statistics, social network analysis, sequence analysis and geometric data analysis (multiple correspondence analysis). The main idea of the volume is to bring together different but interrelated analytical strategies in relation to a highly important phenomenon that is central to the formation of current globalised societies. The volume contributes to the formation and consolidation of SSE as a growing research field. It will help to make visible the diversity of research approaches that make this field attractive to scholars in political economy, economic sociology and beyond. Due to its methodologically and theoretically interdisciplinary perspective, this volume will serve furthermore as a reference point for future research avenues in the field of SSE. The book is organised into four sections. The first section deals with the relationship of discourse and power in economic expert knowledge production; the contributions of section two analyse practices of economic governmentality; section three will take into account networks of economic experts; and the final section analyses economics from a field angle.

4 Contributions to the social studies of economics

The chapters of the first part, *Economic Knowledge and Discursive Power*, analyse economic discourses from different methodological viewpoints. Jens Maesse's chapter, "Performative, imaginary and symbolic power: how economic expert

The role of power in SSE 7

discourses influence society", stresses different forms of discursive power. According to him, when economic experts start to speak, they do not simply enter into equal and non-coercive communications with other actors in the political economy. On the contrary, economic expert discourses have various impacts on the formation of societies. These discourses produce different forms of power and subjectivation. Starting from a Foucauldian approach to power and discourse, his contribution shows how economic expert discourses operate as power devices. Three different forms of discursive power are presented and illustrated, taking examples from the Brexit discourse and previous research on economics departments. First, he shows how the "performative power" of economic expert discourses contributes to the construction of institutional positions in European politico-economic relations. In a second step, he demonstrates how the polyphonic structure of controversies over the economic rationality of Brexit produces speaker positions. These positions are analysed as "imaginary power" that contributes to the formation of social identities. In a third step, his contribution analyses the role and logic of academic excellence discourses as "symbolic power" for the formation of superiority myths of expert positions in public discourses. By sketching out the complex field of discourse and power in economic expert communication, this contribution helps to understand the various forms and mechanisms of power that are at work beyond hierarchies, interests and domination practices.

The chapter by Jan Sparsam and Hanno Pahl, "Macroeconomics and monetary policy as autonomous domains of knowledge and power: rational expectations, monetarism and the Federal Reserve", investigates central bank policies. They start from the idea that academic macroeconomics and monetary policy in central banks share a strong connection. However, the practical needs and epistemic cultures in both domains differ significantly, so there is no straightforward dissemination of macroeconomic ideas into practical monetary policymaking. Instead, academic macroeconomics and central banks have to be understood as autonomous domains of knowledge and power. They refer to two case studies concerning the Federal Reserve, the central bank of the USA, to reveal the context conditions of action in the respective domains that are responsible for the transition of knowledge between them. The first case shows the imminent failure of the project to popularise rational expectations in the Federal Open Market Committee. Indeed, rational expectations revolutionised academic macroeconomics but not monetary policymaking. The second case shows how pragmatic needs when facing a crisis led the Federal Open Market Committee to selectively adopt monetarist ideas. Both case studies draw on verbatim transcripts of meetings of the Federal Open Market Committee.

Lukas Bäuerle, in "The power of economics textbooks: shaping meaning and identity", shows how textbook knowledge influences students of economics. By conducting a discourse analysis (SKAD) in the field of academic economics textbooks, this chapter aims to reconstruct the frames and identity options offered to undergraduate students relating to the questions of "Why study economics?" and "Who do I become by studying economics?"

8 *Jens Maesse et al.*

The analysis shows three major frames and respective identity offerings, all of which are contextualised theoretically. While a first frame promises that students will learn "eternal truths", thereby becoming "specialised knowers", a second frame encourages students to capitalise on their education by becoming self-entrepreneurs. A third frame combines the "Why?" of economic education directly with identity options by granting students insights into their "real" and "true" inner state. Taken together, economics textbooks appear as a total structure of actions brought to bear upon possible action, thus being a genuine example of Foucauldian power structures.

The second part, *Economic Governmentalities*, analyses economics as a governance tool. Ceyhun Gürkan, in "The constitution of neoliberal governmentality from early neoclassical economics to public choice theory", shows how neoliberalism emerged and changed over time. Drawing on Foucault, this chapter demonstrates the particular role of early neoclassical economics between the 1870s and the 1920s, and public choice theory throughout the second half of the 20th century in the constitution of neoliberal governmentality. Foucault examines how classical political economy and neoliberal economics developed two versions of liberalism. However, he mentions early neoclassical economics in a scattered and sparse manner and does not touch upon public choice theory as part of the developing neoliberal governmentality at all. The main argument is that an overall historical understanding of neoliberal governmentality can be achieved by pondering the radical modifications of classical liberalism by early neoclassical economics moving towards neoliberal governmentality and, by extension, the subsequent comprehensive modifications carried out based on public choice theory. The methodology of the chapter relies on Foucault's analytics of power/government, the nominalist method and the genealogical history of ideas. It concludes that governmentality-based analysis of early neoclassical economics and public choice theory concerning their related theoretical and discursive tools, and political reason, prove to complement the new lines of Foucauldian critique of neoliberal governmentality.

Flemming Bjerke, in "Competitive power: elements of Foucauldian economics", reflects on Foucauldian market theory. Economics generally excludes empirical analyses of how the soft power of marketing is exercised. Applying Foucault's concepts of power offers a fruitful way of analysing marketing as an exercise of power, which implies that *competition must be defined in terms of power*. In Foucauldian economics, business economists not only observe markets but also have to exercise power and must therefore acquire the rationalising skills of professional power technologies. Competitive firms participate in a *competition dispositive* which constitutes general principles for integrating a competing firm within its environment. Competition does not only spur differentiation and growth, it also expands throughout society, tending to become the dominant way of exercising power. This implies that the economy is basically irreversible and usually not in equilibrium.

In "Feelings in crisis: the emotional and affective dimension of neoliberal economics in Greek crisis prone society", Elena Psyllakou investigates the

The role of power in SSE 9

role of emotions in economic discourses. According to her, what is referred to as "neoliberalism" is often understood as a regime of emotional governance restricting, controlling and excluding emotions. Building a comparative framework between fragments of early "neoliberal" philosophical thought and critical work on current manifestations of neoliberal governance, the aim of this chapter is to track how interdiscursivities between neoliberal economics and socio-political practices largely rely on emotional and affective articulations that cannot be theorised in a singular way. She focuses on the neoliberal project pursued in Greece, as partly reflected in Greek bank advertising during the crucial years of imposed austerity policies and resistance (2009–2016). Employing critical discourse analysis, her chapter problematises the "negative" hypothesis of emotional exclusion and critically approaches the emotional and affective strategies of a specific form of culturally neoliberal governmentality.

In his chapter entitled "Laboratories for economic expertise: lay perspectives on Italian disciplinary economics", Gerardo Costabile Nicoletta analyses three Italian historical experiences as laboratories of transnational networks of disciplinary economics and deals with the contingent and (con)textual character of the power of economics, starting from its relationship with the object of its discursive and practical interventions: laypeople. This fundamental relational dimension, the source of economists' power in the global political economy, is often underestimated by current social studies on economics, which implicitly assume a self-referential and autopoietic foundation of this power. Conversely, combining discursive political economy, sociologies of expertise and transnational historical sociology, his contribution analyses economic expertise as a complex network of practices, discourses and institutions constantly and strategically deployed to deal with socio-political contingencies. His lay perspective on the Italian experience proposes a socio-historical understanding of economists' apparently neutral set of governmental practices. In this light, measurements, operative tools and conceptual apparatuses can be interpreted as practical and discursive interventions shaping strategically specific epistemic regimes and relational fields aiming to separate organisational and material issues from popular control and marginalising possible alternatives to get population and territories in line with socio-technical divisions of labour.

The third part, *Economists in Networks*, focuses on the circulation and network ties of economists and economic ideas in academia, national and transnational politics, the media and public discourses. In "Who are these economists Germany listens to? The social structure of influential German economists", Stephan Pühringer and Karl Beyer build on recent work on the political and societal impact of economics and distinct economists, respectively, to examine individual, research and institutional characteristics, as well as existing professional networks of what are considered to be "influential economists" in Germany. Through biographical research and the application of social network analysis, they show that most influential economists are involved in co-authorship and/or institutional networks, and that there are substantial connections to different levels of public governance. They find a tremendous

10   *Jens Maesse et al.*

gender bias within the sample as well as some hints for internationalisation and the division of labour. Their analysis, moreover, indicates a much less hierarchical structure of the German-speaking economics profession when compared to the US. However, they find that while a striking majority of media and policy advice economists have connections to (inter)national public governance bodies, only a minority of research economists have such connections. Furthermore, the ordoliberal bias, which is a crucial feature of the German economics profession, is mainly restricted to media and policy advice economists. Finally, their analysis indicates the central role of (also partly geographically organised) research hubs among influential research economists.

In her chapter "Global production and circulation of dominant ideologies: Mexico from the default debt crisis to the Brady Plan (1982–1989)", Johanna Gautier Morin provides a renewed understanding of multilateral financial cooperation and the role of economists in the ideological convergence that accompanied capital flows in the case of the Mexican default on external debt. According to this chapter, the core-periphery model has long distorted the study of multilateral cooperation. The 1970s–1980s marked a turning point in the transnational experimentation of economic policies, converting the Latin American sub-continent into a social laboratory. Most studies on the topic focused on the IMF's and the World Bank's methods, hegemonic business practices, or the international circulation of economic ideas. Few have explored the agency of the countries involved in such unbalanced situations and the central role they have played in the global financial revolution that has transformed markets over these two decades. In this chapter, she explores how negotiations were conducted in a context of financial dependency and transposes the theoretical proposals of Bourdieu and Boltanski on the production of the dominant ideology to the Mexican default on external debt in 1982. She analyses the crisis as a proxy for revealing the structural mechanisms of Mexican economic policies. This allows her to examine the global circulation of economic ideas at the heart of the negotiations between the Mexican government, the IMF, the US Treasury and investment banks involved in managing the crisis. The failures of the structural adjustment programmes tested the technocratic theories applied to the Mexican case and revealed the function of economic policy rhetoric in supporting the circulation of capital flows in the changing world of the 1980s.

In the final chapter of this part, entitled "Economists in public discourses: the case of wealth and inheritance taxation in the German press", Hendrik Theine investigates the role of economists in public discourses. Conceptually, he draws on the recent "cultural turns" in regulation theory and post-Marxist thinking, and in particular on the work of Bob Jessop and Antonio Gramsci in their discussion of intellectuals and their role in society. Empirically, the role of economists is investigated by drawing on the example of wealth and inheritance taxation in the German press at the beginning of the 21st century. The empirical analysis shows that well-known economists frequently occur in newspaper coverage. Furthermore, the stark dominance of economists associated with mainstream economics and ordoliberalism over post-Keynesian and other heterodox economists is revealed. Given the role of economists as organic intellectuals in the political economy, this points to a continuing legitimation and normalisation of the structural power of the capital class to assert their interests regarding low wealth and inheritance taxation.

The fourth part, *Economics as a Scientific Field*, centres on the social structure of the discipline, according to the distribution of its specific and external capitals among economists, along biographical and network dimensions. The chapter by Philipp Korom, "Are there institutionalized pathways to the Nobel Prize in economics?", proposes an empirical study of scientific careers in the field of economics. It focuses on the Nobel Prize, the single *ne plus ultra* award in economics, which has been awarded for half a century. Indeed, the preconditions for receiving the highest consecration of achievement are understudied. While the consideration of a few single cases, such as the life and work of Herbert Simon or John Nash, might suggest that the most successful scholars in economics are a rather varied collection of individuals, a prosopographical study of 81 Laureates reveals institutionalised pathways to the prize: The academic careers of Laureates nearly always lead to professorships in the top five departments of the discipline. Visiting professorships at the "big five" are another common characteristic. Similarly, publications of Laureates are concentrated in the top five journals. The academic profile of Laureates in economics mirrors the unitary macrostructure of the discipline, which is dominated by an elite subset of American universities, rather than by departments across the world.

Thierry Rossier and Pierre Benz, in "Forms of social capital in economics: the importance of heteronomous networks in the Swiss field of economists (1980–2000)", focus on the structure and evolution of social capital in the Swiss field of economists. They start from the fact that economists often argue that economics is a "pure" and "autonomous" discipline. In contrast, the relatively dense institutional and interpersonal networks owned by economists show how the discipline stands at the edge of several social fields, and thus can be particularly heteronomous. These networks provide a certain volume and form of social capital which strengthens the discipline, but they highlight its important porousness toward extra-academic powers. Very few studies have focused on the importance of social capital in fields and, according to Rossier and Benz, even less have systematically investigated the role of intra-disciplinary and extra-disciplinary social capital in economics. This chapter therefore aims to focus on the structure and evolution of social capital in the Swiss field of economists. It relies on an original prosopographical database of all economics professors at Swiss universities between 1980 and 2000 ($n = 200$). The authors exploit the data in two ways: First, through multiple correspondence analysis (MCA), they identify two structuring forces among economists. The main opposition is marked by the volume of extra-disciplinary social capital, and the volume of intra-disciplinarity capital only comes in second place. Second, they show, through class-specific MCA, that, despite the fact that intra-disciplinary social capital has gained in importance in the recent period, extra-disciplinary

12   *Jens Maesse et al.*

social capital remains the prime structuring logic across time. Despite the particularly strong cohesion and autonomy that characterise the discipline, this chapter points to the importance of heteronomous networks, which attest that economics is and remains much less autonomous than economists would argue.

Finally, in "Paths of international circulation: how do economists and economic knowledge flow?", Elisa Klüger investigates international circulation as a source of legitimacy and power for economists that distinguishes, technically and socially, those who have access to foreign institutions and cosmopolitan assets. These resources are particularly prized in peripheral nations, where connections with central areas are valuable capital for those aiming for prominent political/administrative positions. Moreover, going abroad has effects on the type of economic ideas diffused through peripheral areas. The questions addressed in this chapter are How do economists and economic ideas flow? and How do dissimilar ideas spread and (re)shape a structured space of economists? Klüger focuses on the Brazilian case, in which the space of economists is deeply amalgamated with external influences. After describing how international ties helped to shape the Brazilian space of economists, social network analysis is used to depict a polarised social space and reveal patterns of connections with foreign agents and institutions. The network illustrates that circulations towards the US, Europe and Latin America lie in dissimilar areas of the Brazilian space of economists, and that different streams of economic knowledge spread from each of these sources.

To conclude, this book addresses a large array of subjects and offers a variety of disciplinary perspectives. It contributes to study economics as an academic discipline and a professional occupation by extending conceptual and methodological frameworks for better understanding how economics, economic expert discourse and economists influence societies. Finally, this book provides important empirical data by focusing on discourses and networks in economics and considering economics as a governance tool and field. It therefore aims to consolidate SSE as a comprehensive and diversified research agenda rooted in various disciplines of the social sciences and humanities.

Note

1 Stephan Pühringer gratefully acknowledges funding by the Austrian Science Fund FWF (grant number ZK60-G27).

References

Aistleitner, M., Kapeller, J., & Steinerberger, S. (2018). The Power of Scientometrics and the Development of Economics. *Journal of Economic Issues*, 52(3), 816–834.

Anauati, M. V., Gálvez, R., & Galiani, S. (2018). Differences in Citation Patterns across Journal Tiers in Economics. NBER Working Paper Series. (25101).

Bayer, A., & Rouse, C. E. (2016). Diversity in the Economics Profession: A New Attack on an Old Problem. *Journal of Economic Perspectives*, 30(4), 221–242.

Beyer, K., & Pühringer, S. (2019). Divided We Stand? Professional Consensus and Political Conflict in Academic Economics. ICAE Working Paper Series (94).

Bourdieu, P. (1996). *The State Nobility: Elite Schools in the Field of Power*. Cambridge: Polity Press; Oxford: Blackwell Publishers Ltd.

Bourdieu, P. (2005). *The Social Structures of the Economy*. Cambridge: Polity Press.

Bourdieu, P., & Wacquant, L. J. D. (1992). *An Invitation to Reflexive Sociology*. Chicago: University of Chicago Press.

Callon, M. (Ed.). (1998). *The Laws of the Markets*. Oxford: Blackwell.

Coats, A. B. (1993). *The Sociology and Professionalization of Economics: British and American Economic Essays (Vol. 2)*. Abingdon-on-Thames: Routledge.

Coman, R. (2019). Transnational Economists in the Eurozone Crisis: Professional Structures, Networks and Ideas. *New Political Economy*, 93(3), 1–14.

Dean, M. (1999). *Governmentality: Power and Rule in Modern Society*. Thousand Oaks, CA: Sage.

Dezalay, Y., & Garth, B. (1998). Le "Washington Consensus". *Actes de la Recherche en Sciences Sociales*, 121(1), 3–22.

Dezalay, Y., & Garth, B. (2002). *The Internationalization of Palace Wars: Lawyers, Economists, and the Contest to Transform Latin American States*. Chicago: Chicago University Press.

Dobusch, L., & Kapeller, J. (2009). Why Is Economics Not an Evolutionary Science? New Answers to Veblen's Old Question. *Journal of Economic Issues*, 43(4), 867–898.

Erturk, I., Froud, J., Johal, A., Leaver, A., & Williams, K. (Eds.). (2008). *Financialization at Work: Key Texts and Commentary*. Abingdon-on-Thames: Routledge.

Fitzgerald, J., & O'Rourke, B. K. (2015). Performing Economics: How Economics Discourse Gets Enacted in Radio News Interviews. 10th international conference in interpretive policy analysis.

Flickenschild, M., & Afonso, A. (2019). Networks of Economic Policy Expertise in Germany and the United States in the Wake of the Great Recession. *Journal of European Public Policy*, 26(9), 1292–1311.

Foucault, M. (2008). *The Birth of Biopolitics. Lectures at the Collège de France, 1978–1979*. London: Palgrave Macmillan.

Fourcade, M. (2006). The Construction of a Global Profession: The Transnationalization of Economics. *American Journal of Sociology*, 112(1), 145–194.

Fourcade, M. (2009). *Economists and Societies: Discipline and profession in the United States, Britain, and France, 1890s to 1990s*. Princeton: Princeton University Press.

Fourcade, M., Ollion, E., & Algan, Y. (2015). The Superiority of Economists. *Journal of Economic Perspectives*, 29(1), 89–114.

Gautier Morin, J. (2019). The Keynesian-Monetarist Competition over Public Credibility. *The Tocqueville Review*, 40(2), 281–294.

Gautier Morin, J., & Rossier, T. (2021). The Interaction of Elite Networks in the Pinochet Regime's Macroeconomic Policies. *Global Networks*, online first. DOI: 10.1111/glob.12300.

Granovetter, M. (1983). The Strength of Weak Ties: A Network Theory Revisited. *Sociological Theory*, 1, 201–233.

Grimm, C., Kapeller, J., & Pühringer, S. (2018). Paradigms and Policies: The Current State of Economics in the German-speaking Countries. ICAE Working Paper Series (77).

Hall, P. A. (Ed.). (1989). *The Political Power of Economic Ideas: Keynesianism Across Nations*. Princeton: Princeton University Press.

14 *Jens Maesse et al.*

Helgadóttir, O. (2016). The Bocconi Boys Go to Brussels: Italian Economic Ideas, Professional Networks and European Austerity. *Journal of European Public Policy*, 23(3), 392–409.

Hirschman, D., & Popp Berman, E. (2014). Do Economists Make Policies? On the Political Effects of Economics. *Socio-Economic Review*, 12(4), 779–811.

Jessop, B. (2010). Cultural Political Economy and Critical Policy Studies. *Critical Policy Studies*, 3(3–4), 336–356.

Klüger, E. (2018). Mapping the Inflections in the Policies of the Brazilian National Economic and Social Development Bank during the 1990s and 2000s within Social Spaces and Networks. *Historical Social Research*, 43(3), 274–302.

Korom, P. (2020). How Do Academic Elites March Through Departments? A Comparison of the Most Eminent Economists and Sociologists' Career Trajectories. Minerva, online first. DOI: 10.1007/s11024-020-09399-1.

Lebaron, F. (2000). *La croyance économique. Les économistes entre science et politique*. Paris: Editions du Seuil.

Lebaron, F. (2001). Economists and the Economic Order. The Field of Economists and the Field of Power in France. *European Societies*, 3(1), 91–110.

Lenger, A. (2018). Socialization in the Academic and Professional Field: Revealing the Homo Oeconomicus Academicus. *Historical Social Research*, 43(3), 39–62.

MacKenzie, D. A., Muniesa, F., & Siu, L. (Eds.). (2007). *Do Economists Make Markets? On the Performativity of Economics*. Princeton: Princeton University Press.

Maesse, J. (2015). Economic Experts: A Discursive Political Economy of Economics. *Journal of Multicultural Discourses*, 10(3), 279–305.

Maesse, J. (2017). The Elitism Dispositif: Hierarchization, Discourses of Excellence and Organizational Change in European Economics. *Higher Education*, 73(6), 909–927.

Maesse, J. (2018). Opening the Black Box of the Elitism Dispositif: Graduate Schools in Economics. In R. Bloch, A. Mitterle, C. Paradeise, & T. Peter. *Universities and the Production of Elites: Discourses, Policies, and Strategies of Excellence and Stratification in Higher Education* (pp. 53–79). London: Palgrave Macmillan.

Maesse, J., Pahl, H., & Sparsam, J. (Eds.). (2017). *Die Innenwelt der Ökonomie: Wissen, Macht und Performativität in der Wirtschaftswissenschaft*. Berlin/Heidelberg: Springer.

Mata, T., & Medema, S. (Eds.). (2013). *The Economist as Public Intellectual*. Durham: Duke University Press.

Miller, P. (2001). Governing by Numbers: Why Calculative Practices Matter. *Social Research*, 68(2), 379–396.

Mirowski, P. (1991). *More Heat Than Light: Economics as Social Physics, Physics as Nature's Economics*. Cambridge: Cambridge University Press.

Mirowski, P., & Plehwe, D. (Eds.) (2009). *The Road from Mont Pèlerin: The Making of the Neoliberal Thought Collective*. Cambridge, MA: Harvard University Press.

Montecinos, V., & Markoff, J. (2009). *Economists in the Americas*. Cheltenham: Edward Elgar.

Morgan, M. S. (1990). *The History of Econometric Ideas*. Cambridge: Cambridge University Press.

Önder, A. S., & Terviö, M. (2015). Is Economics a House Divided? Analysis of Citation Networks. *Economic Inquiry*, 53(3), 1491–1505.

Ötsch, W. O., Pühringer, S., & Hirte, K. (2017). *Netzwerke des Marktes: Ordoliberalismus als Politische Ökonomie*. Berlin/Heidelberg: Springer.

Plehwe, D., Neujeffski, M., & Krämer, W. (2018). Saving the Dangerous Idea: Austerity Think Tank Networks in the European Union. *Policy and Society*, 37(2), 188–205.

Pühringer, S., & Griesser, M. (2020). From the 'Planning Euphoria' to the 'Bitter Economic Truth': The Transmission of Economic Ideas into German Labour Market Policies in the 1960s and 2000s. *Critical Discourse Studies*, online first. DOI: 10.1080/17405904.2019.1681283.

Rossier, T. (2020). Accumulation and Conversion of Capitals in Professorial Careers. The Importance of Scientific Reputation, Network Relations, and Internationality in Economics and Business Studies. *Higher Education*, online first. DOI: 10.1007/s10734-020-00508-3.

Rossier, T., & Bühlmann, F. (2018). The Internationalisation of Economics and Business Studies: Import of Excellence, Cosmopolitan Capital or American Dominance? *Historical Social Research*, 43(3), 189–215.

Rossier, T., Bühlmann, F., & Mach, A. (2017). The Rise of Professors of Economics and Business Studies in Switzerland: Between Scientific Reputation and Political Power. *European Journal of Sociology*, 58(2), 295–326.

Salas-Porras, A., & Murray, G. (Eds.). (2017). *Think Tanks and Global Politics: Key Spaces in the Structure of Power*. London: Macmillan.

Savage, M., Warde, A., & Devine, F. (2005). Capitals, Assets, and Resources: Some Critical Issues. *British Journal of Sociology*, 56(1), 31–47.

Schmidt-Wellenburg, C. (2018). Struggling Over Crisis. Discursive Positionings and Academic Positions in the Field of German-Speaking Economists. *Historical Social Research*, 43(3), 147–188.

Schmidt-Wellenburg, C., & Lebaron, F. (Eds.). (2018a). Economists, Politics, and Society. New Insights from Mapping Economic Practices Using Field-Analysis. *Historical Social Research, Special Issue*, 43(3).

Schmidt-Wellenburg, C., & Lebaron, F. (2018b). There Is No Such Thing as "the Economy". Economic Phenomena Analysed from a Field-Theoretical Perspective. *Historical Social Research*, 43(3), 7–38.

Zuidhof, P. W. (2012). *Imagining Markets: The Discursive Politics of Neoliberalism*. Rotterdam: Erasmus University Rotterdam.

Part 1

Economic knowledge and discursive power

2 Performative, imaginary and symbolic power

How economic expert discourses influence society

Jens Maesse

1 Introduction

Economic knowledge, ideas and concepts have a huge influence on society. The impact of economists extends across many institutions, realms and areas, such as banks and businesses, politics and administration, and it reaches (mediated by media and guidebooks) into people's daily lifestyles. However, to understand how the dissemination of expertise from science to society works is one of the main tasks of the social studies of economics. Whereas action-oriented approaches in the tradition of Max Weber highlight processes of persuasion, actors' interests and consensus among groups, as well as norms and values as devices for the transmission of economic expertise into society, structurally oriented approaches in the tradition of Marx and Bourdieu put their analytical focus on power, especially as it is represented by hierarchies, class structures, elite positions and other material constraints.

However, in order to understand the practical logic of power in economic expert discourses, a theory is needed that brings together the cultural as well as the structural dimension in these processes. Approaches in the vein of Michel Foucault and so-called performativity studies (inspired by the work of Callon, MacKenzie and others) took this challenge as a starting point for analysing how cultural and structural dynamics interact. Taking the Marxian and Bourdieusian traditions as a starting point and combining these with a Foucauldian approach, this chapter will ask how processes of *discursive power* can be analysed in economic expert communications as a way to overcome the culture/structure opposition. To this end, discursive power will be subdivided into *performative, imaginary and symbolic power*. In particular, I will show how and why performative, imaginary and symbolic power make visible different aspects of economic expert discourses. They are the key elements for analysing and understanding the different forms of an economic expert's impact on society.

The contribution is structured as follows. The first section (section 2) explains the idea of discursive power in the context of social studies of economics. Section 3 offers a definition of performative, imaginary and symbolic power in light of a Foucauldian conceptual framework. Section 4 takes examples from the Brexit discourse in order to illustrate each form of power. In addition, it

DOI: 10.4324/9780367817084-3

20   *Jens Maesse*

will be indicated how these different forms might interact. The general aim of this chapter is not only to sketch out how discursive power operates in the case of economic expert discourses, but also to present a methodological framework that can be used in further analyses to study the impact of economic expertise.

2 Forms of power in social studies of economics

The influence of economic expert knowledge is analysed at different levels of society. According to Hall, economic ideas become powerful when they are promoted by professional economists, adopted and implemented by certain actors within the administration, or find support among a majority of politicians and civil society (Hall, 1989). Hirschman and Popp Berman identify three different channels of influence, from the economics profession to state and politics: professional authority, the institutional position of economists in policymaking and the general cognitive infrastructure of polity (Hirschman & Popp Berman, 2014).

A deeper look at these three channels reveals that the first and third channels seem to be interlinked, because the authority of economists presupposes a certain cognitive infrastructure within society, politics and administration; and a preference for economics within the latter field will increase the probability of recruiting economic expertise as problem-solving knowledge. But, a distance between the economics profession and the state and society should be maintained. Otherwise, economists would directly rule society and the political economy. Against this backdrop, an open question in social studies of economics is how economic expertise is "transferred" through these channels.

One possible answer to grasp how the gap between economics knowledge and governance institutions can be bridged is "power". Many analyses, especially in the varieties of capitalism tradition, draw on Max Weber's theory of power and authority (Weber, 1972). Here, power (as authority) is analysed on the level of the formation of political values and norms through the construction of consent among actors. Accordingly, actors believe in the solution of social and political problems by applying certain economic concepts. The cultural sphere is of central importance here, because the influence of economic knowledge operates on the level of actors' opinions and perceptions. In contrast, Marxian and Bourdieusian approaches highlight the role of material power relations, hierarchies, political struggle and ideologies (Bourdieu, 1989). Here, power is understood as a means to move people's minds in a certain direction through symbolic coercion. In social studies of economics, many studies have analysed the impact of economics at the level of symbolic capital (Dezalay & Garth, 2009; Lebaron, 2008; Rossier, Bühlmann, & Mach, 2017; Schmidt-Wellenburg, 2017a). Symbolic capital does not operate on the level of actors' consciousness. Rather, it exercises different forms of coercion in the formation of governance institutions, policy programmes and worldviews, and it defines certain styles of thinking among ruling elites. Here, academic, administrative and political hierarchies and the role of certain elite actors within the

Performative, imaginary and symbolic power 21

field of economic power relations are much more influential when it comes to explaining why certain economic ideas take hold and others do not (Fitzgerald & O'Rourke, 2015; Maesse, 2015; Pühringer & Hirte, 2015).

Next to action-oriented (Weber) and structural (Marx/Bourdieu) theories, performativity theory has become established as a third type of approach to analyse the influence and power of economic expert knowledge (Callon, 2007). The original idea was to study economics as a meaning-making machine that does not analyse markets but reconstructs the economy according to a neoclassical worldview (MacKenzie & Millo, 2003). Initially, this approach was criticised for promoting naïve neoliberal worldviews and ignoring economic realities (Mirowski & Nik-Khah, 2008). Today, performativity studies no longer believe that economic theory is transformed into economic reality on a one-to-one basis. Rather, processes of performation are analysed as a complex process of adoption, translation, implementation and critique, taking place between economic science and society, politics and the political economy. Thus, when economic concepts are used to solve political and economic problems, the concepts will be transformed and translated into different contexts (Boldyrev & Svetlova, 2016). Performativity approaches have a deep relationship with the discursive character of the political economy (Maesse, 2018a).

Whereas action-oriented theories overestimate the interpretative capacity and cognitive sovereignty of actors in the course of the adoption of economic concepts, structural theories underestimate the interpretative and translational dynamics that are at work when economic ideas influence society. Furthermore, Weberian approaches reduce structural constraints, hierarchies and domination to merely institutional obstacles that can easily be overcome. They have a *structural deficit*. Marxian and Bourdieusian approaches pay too much attention to the rigidity of the structural level when analysing the influence of economic ideas. They very often have a *translational deficit*. Finally, performativity approaches can take into consideration the complex translational and discursive dynamics taking place between different social fields (such as science, politics, the economy and so forth). But they have a *conceptual deficit* since notions such as "power", "legitimacy" and "authority" are used very randomly and unsystematically.

An appropriate theory of power that is able to understand how economic expert knowledge influences society should keep the advantages of the aforementioned theories in mind but simultaneously find a solution for the disadvantages. It should meet the following criteria: first, it must take into account the structural constraints of heterogeneous social fields; second, it must be able to account for the translational and discursive logics that take place between various fields; third, it will analyse the diverse forms of use and adoption of economic concepts in non-academic and non-scientific contexts. Drawing on ideas inspired by the Foucauldian concept of dispositif (Foucault, 1980), the following chapter will outline a discourse-theoretical approach that is able to grasp processes of power in both its productive and coercive dimensions (Hamann, Maesse, Scholz, & Angermuller, 2019). According to such a

22 *Jens Maesse*

dispositif analytical understanding, power is always analysed according to its heterogeneous, transversal and heteroglossical character (Maesse, 2018b). The following chapter will explain in detail the scope and limitations of such a dispositif analytical approach for analysing economic expert discourses by sketching out three forms of discursive power.

3 Three forms of discursive power: performative, imaginary and symbolic power

Foucault's theory of power (Foucault, 2008) made important contributions to understanding what is going on in the formation of social and discursive relations based on structural constraints. Whereas Max Weber's sociology introduced the category of meaningful social action in order to analyse individuals' intentions and goals as forms of authority and legitimacy in contrast to Marxian and other structural approaches, Foucault's theory is still part of the structural camp in the social sciences. But in contrast to classical structuralism, Foucault's theory of power highlighted two important aspects of structural power dynamics: first, the fissures and fractures within structures that open up structured terrains for discursive conflicts over meaning; and second, the productive character of power which informs our view of social reality vis-à-vis oppressive as well as formative rules. Especially, the notion of governmentality has shown that exercising power is a decentralised phenomenon that cannot be reduced to one single mind (Weber's intention) and singular actors (Bourdieu's ruling classes). Rather, the discursive aspect of power always points to diverse modalities in the formation of power relations. It highlights the productive character of power and the biopolitical dimension of it, by showing how power strategies make things possible.

How can we grasp this often abstract and opaque poststructuralist theory with clear analytical units? I propose three different analytical categories that can help to understand how economic expert discourses influence societies as power devices: performative power, imaginary power and symbolic power.

Performative power can be defined as the possibility of economic expert discourses to create institutional infrastructures. Institutions will be understood, in a very broad sense, as often legally codified, but always socially fixed, fields of social action. These fields are hierarchically organised, as Bourdieu would claim, but they are at the same time open to other fields and in constant exchange with them. Networks and institutions usually fix these fields of economic expert action (Pühringer & Hirte, 2015; Rossier & Bühlmann, 2018). There is no single field logic, but each empirical field can be fixed in different ways. Despite this heterogeneity, fields are always the sedimented background for every discourse production, and they are themselves, simultaneously, a result of historical discourse formation. As Callon and others have shown for social studies of economics, and Bourdieu and his fellows have fully elaborated, fields are the manifestation and materialisation of language forms resulting from social struggles. Here, power is the possibility of discourses to produce

Performative, imaginary and symbolic power 23

Table 2.1 Performative, imaginary and symbolic power

Type	Performative power	Imaginary power	Symbolic power
Definition	The possibility of discourses to produce sedimented categories that are present in the background to future social action on the imaginary and symbolic levels	The ability of every discourse to create images of the speaker, the interlocutor and many other social roles	The ability of discourses to attribute respect, prestige, authority, fear and excitement to (an image of) a person, an institution or an object
Example	Institutional infrastructures such as contracts, money, offices, organisations, hierarchies	Images such as "expert", "racist", "Brexiteer", "Londoner", "neoclassic", "Keynesian"	Status positions such as "scientific elite", "Nobel Prize Award winner", "excellence"

sedimented categories that are present in the background to future social action on the imaginary and symbolic levels.

Imaginary power is the ability of every discourse to create images of the speaker, the interlocutor and many other social roles. Actors never exist only for themselves. Rather, they always speak and act in the name of a certain image (the image of the mother and father in family discourse; the image of socialism, environmental sustainability, conservativism etc. in political discourse; and so forth). These images are important because they define how speakers present themselves and how they see others according to the knowledge attached to the images. Lacanian discourse theory calls this aspect of discourse the "imaginary level", because it defines the fundamental categories for the formation of subjectivities (Lacan, 1991). What we are to other people and how we see others depends on our active and passive position within this imaginary register. Whereas Foucault presented the idea of discursive subject positions, Lacan fully elaborated this dimension of discourse (Žižek, 1989). Power, in the imaginary register, is the possibility to define others and to be defined in a certain way.

Symbolic power is the ability of discourses to attribute respect, prestige, authority, fear and excitement to (an image of) a person, an institution or an object. In economic expert discourses, the prestige of certain institutions is often used to equip certain speakers with powerful discourse positions. Symbolic capital is an important category in Bourdieu's sociology because it introduces a form of hierarchisation in the field that is not based on typical forms of exclusion, such as economic, cultural and social capital. It is important because this form of power is always misrecognised by actors involved in the production of symbolic capital (Rossier & Bühlmann, 2018). The "Nobel Prize Award" is a classic example (Lebaron, 2006). But the production and distribution of symbolic power cannot be detached from certain morphologies of social fields. In economic expert discourse, fields are always trans-epistemic and polycentric (Maesse, 2017b; Schmidt-Wellenburg, 2017b) because different fields and

24 *Jens Maesse*

field logics interact and transgress each other. For this reason, prestige can be produced in one field and must be transmitted to another one, where it can be attached to certain imaginary speaker positions (Fitzgerald & O'Rourke, 2015). Symbolic power is, therefore, the possibility of economic expert discourse to introduce hierarchies of perception in one field by importing "mythical capital" from another (Maesse, 2016).

4 Three cases from the Brexit discourse

This section will illustrate these three forms of discursive power with examples from the Brexit discourse. The empirical results are based on my sociological research on economic expert discourse. The data are collected by a multi-method research design consisting of capital analyses of academic fields (positions, publications, research grants based on economists' CV and homepage studies, analysis of data banks such as DFG and other sources), narrative-biographical interviews with economists, and discourse analyses of journal papers, policy papers, reports and media statements (see Maesse, 2015).

Brexit discourse is very much influenced by economic expert knowledge on very different levels. On the one hand, it is a discourse of critique of economic experts and the European Union (EU). On the other hand, "remainers" (people against the UK exiting the EU) as well as "leavers" (Brexit proponents) mobilise economic theory in order to support their position. Whereas remainers use a variety of new Keynesian, Keynesian, institutional and other economic arguments, the leavers align themselves with more or less classical and neoclassical free trade economics. Furthermore, even three years after the Brexit referendum in 2016, it is still not clear what it means to "leave" the EU. Thus, as this chapter will show, the UK is, with or without a deal, more or less part of the EU field that is highly influenced by economic expertise. This obscure situation is an interesting starting point for analysing what performative power means. This first subsection will illustrate the idea of performative power, taking the EU field and the British position in it as an example. The second subsection takes a conflict over economic policy to illustrate how imaginary power works. The third subsection will show how symbolic power is formed by examples from previous studies.

4.1 *Performative power: the economic formation of institutional relations and the place of the UK in the EU field*

Today, value chains, labour relations and economic services are no longer regulated by sovereign nation-states. They are rather organised on the basis of international agreements and rules. The European field is, for both internal and external relations, the most important playground for all the economic actors in Europe (EU, European Economic Area, European Free trade Association) (Jessop, 2012; Sweet, Sandholtz, & Fligstein, 2001). The European Union as an institutional field has been formed in a long historical process by translating economic language into governmentality apparatuses (Schmidt-Wellenburg, 2017a). As Mudge and Vauchez (2012) have demonstrated, language from the field of economics (and law) is used to make Europe calculable and manageable, even if (or because of) the original academic meaning of economic concepts changes in contexts of governance, finance, business and trade.

Against this backdrop, words from the economics discipline have always had a metaphorical character (Maesse, 2017a), otherwise they would not be transferable in non-academic contexts. In the course of the formation of the EU, starting with the Treaty of Rome in 1957 and leading to the never-ending reform of EU treaties, the so-called Four Freedoms have been established: the customs union, the common market, the capital union and the free movement of persons. But these Four Freedoms are not simply neoliberal concepts set in stone and functioning as authoritarian dogmas (Bruff, 2014). Most European policies are neoliberal, but the institutions and contracts as such are not. Rather, they regularly become an object of reform, interpretation and adoption to the diverse problems in the history of Europe (Miró, 2017). Performative power does not mean that content (as meaning) from economics is implemented in social reality. Rather, economic language, as discourse, can be used and applied in diverse contexts only if meaning changes. Therefore, the Four Freedoms have no singular content. On the contrary, their content was always subject to conflicting interpretations (see Nicoletta in this volume).

The studies by Seikel and Costantini demonstrate this interpretative flexibility and discursivity of economic language in the course of the ongoing institutionalisation of Europe as a field (Costantini, 2017; Seikel, 2016). Costantini shows how the most important institutional framework of the EU, the Stability and Growth Pact, was constantly changed after 1992. Furthermore, it was not only the legal framework that was reformed. The ways to implement this framework in different countries and in different historical and economic circumstances, by calculating national budgets through macro-economic valuations, have also constantly changed. For example, to qualify a certain measure, such as expenses for infrastructure or a tool for "increasing competitiveness", or to disqualify it as "budgetary expenses" results from expert interpretations by the EU administration. The meaning of a contract is not manifested in the paragraphs. Meaning results from the way these contracts are interpreted and applied. In line with this view, Seikel shows how austerity measures during the crisis were implemented completely differently in different crisis-ridden countries. Similar phenomena can be observed in the crisis policy of the European Central Bank. The statutes of the ECB do not determine social action. As an institution they rather provide actors (members of the board, staff members, other experts) with discursive material open to interpretation.

What we learn from these examples is that institutions, in light of performative power, are not closed entities, neither legally fixed contracts nor socially habitualised routines. They are rather material background and raw material for further discourses. This property becomes particularly important in the Brexit discourse. The UK became a member of the EEC/EU in 1973. Even if the UK

26   *Jens Maesse*

did not adopt the euro currency and did not sign the Schengen Agreement, almost all the activities on the state and economic levels take place within the European field. The UK is furthermore as deeply integrated as the average EU country into this field: 50% of all exports from and imports to the UK take place within the EU; the UK has a trade-balance deficit and does therefore depend on industrial production and services in other EU member states; and the economic heart of the UK, the City of London, depends on trading partners in the EU. The financial sector in the City of London is not an average sector of the national economy. It is rather a highly specialised sector that only can exist as part of the EU-wide division of labour. And even if the UK is not part of the Schengen Area, it nevertheless recruits approximately three million workers from other EU countries, appointed at all levels of income and qualifications. In exchange for that, British pensioners spend their sunset years in Spain. It is an illusion to believe that the UK stands outside the EU; it is rather part of the EU field produced by performative power.

However, what does "Brexit" mean against the backdrop of this deep involvement of the UK in the EU? Brexit means that old discursive-economic categories will be suspended and detached from diverse persons and economic activities. Capital transfers from the UK to the EU will no longer be easy; lorries will not easily cross the border to EU; aeroplanes may not take off and land. In order to avoid disruption, chaos and civil-war-like scenarios, a new contract must ensure that future social action is possible (within the UK and between UK and the rest of the world). An agreement between the EU and the UK was negotiated in 2018 for that reason: "the deal". In order to illustrate what I mean by the performative power of economics, I will briefly show how economics language can be used to create new institutional terrains. The following paragraph is part of the "deal" between the UK and the EU, ratified by EU institutions and member states and the UK.

Article 24 of the Brexit agreement regulates the rights and duties of people who fall under the category of "workers".

> Subject to the limitations set out in Article 45(3) and (4) TFEU, workers in the host State and frontier workers in the State or States of work shall enjoy the rights guaranteed by Article 45 TFEU and the rights granted by Regulation (EU) No 492/2011 of the European Parliament and of the Council. These rights include:
>
> (a) the right not to be discriminated against on grounds of nationality as regards employment, remuneration and other conditions of work and employment;
> (b) the right to take up and pursue an activity in accordance with the rules applicable to the nationals of the host State or the State of work;
> (c) the right to assistance afforded by the employment offices of the host State or the State of work as offered to own nationals;

Performative, imaginary and symbolic power 27

(d) the right to equal treatment in respect of conditions of employment and work, in particular as regards remuneration, dismissal and in case of unemployment, reinstatement or re-employment;

(e) the right to social and tax advantages;

(f) collective rights;

(g) the rights and benefits accorded to national workers in matters of housing;

(h) the right for their children to be admitted to the general educational, apprenticeship and vocational training courses under the same conditions as the nationals of the host State or the State of work, if such children are residing in the territory where the worker works.

Some people may doubt the underlying hypothesis that the category "worker" is a category from economic science. But, as studies on the history of scientific knowledge have shown, diverse labour-related categories such as "worker" became part of the economics discourse, especially in the 19th and 20th centuries, and from there they entered the political and administrative discourses of the emerging nation-state order (Desrosières, 1998; Wagner, 2001). Therefore, we follow those studies that presuppose that all categories related to the formation of the Four Freedoms, such as "worker", are somehow related to economics as a special realm of knowledge and language production. In the case of the worker category, this seems to be quite obvious, since alternatives for categorising persons come quickly to hand: "citizen", "human being", "person" etc. And all of them would probably impact on performative possibilities in a certain direction.

What makes an economic category such as "worker" performative is the fact that this category is not only used for a pure designation and description of people or other entities. It is also a category to be used as a legal entity. Special legal organisations are allowed and obliged to confer particular rights and duties on persons according to well-defined criteria. On the other hand, people can claim certain rights and duties when they rely on the category of "worker". For example, when a European citizen has a contract with a British organisation that is allowed to act as an employer, s/he can claim to be a "worker" and is now allowed to live in the UK, to bring his/her family to the UK, to use the British health system (NHS) and so forth. Generally speaking, the performative power of economic categories is only occasionally related to the original conceptual meaning of a word (in economic science). Rather, performative power implies that people can speak and act in the name of this category and start to produce further discourses, actions and artefacts.

Performative power provides human beings with a special status. In the production of this status, many people, institutions and organisations are involved because institutionalisation in the course of performative power formation is an ongoing process of permanent formulation, transformation and reformulation of that status. For example, what a "worker" is or can be is not only defined

28   *Jens Maesse*

by European acts, contracts and agreements. When such agreements are made, many other institutions start to interpret the diverse paragraphs and apply them to many different cases. In these processes of what I would call secondary institutionalisation/performations, European institutions will be changed and reformed, as we have seen in the aforementioned cases of the Stability and Growth Pact, austerity programmes and ECB policy. In the course of these permanent performations and transmutations, a European field constellation emerges as a contested and never fixed background for further discursive actions in all realms of European societies. The EU field cannot be reduced to the "Eurocracy" (Georgakakis & Rowell, 2013) in Brussels; rather it reaches across many levels of all European societies (Delanty & Rumford, 2005). Therefore, the performative power of economics means that social realities are produced by metaphorical uses of economic language.

Particularly interesting is what happens when certain performative categories are detached from people. This necessarily leads to the dissolution of diverse field belongings and can open up social fields to chaos and anarchy. The alternative to being a member of the EU (exiting the EU) is therefore not another positive state or another field belonging. It is probably furthermore a state of "pure negativity", the negation of institutional existence. This threat is at work during the ongoing Brexit discourse where an exit agreement is negotiated but a final deal not yet reached by EU and UK officials. This limbo leads to insecurity, anxiety, discursive chaos, hysteria and all the other psychotic states that can be observed in the UK since 2016. The next subsection will take this situation of psychotic field limbo that rules the UK discourse to look at the imaginary level of discourse production.

4.2   Imaginary power: the discursive formation of expert positions as political identities

To illustrate imaginary power, an example from economic expert discourses on the possible economic effects of Brexit on the UK economy will be selected. The following excerpt is taken from a response by one group of economists to another group called "Economists for Brexit". Patrick Minford, professor at Cardiff University and one of the "Economists for Brexit", predicts a welfare gain from Brexit of 4% GDP growth, provided by a "British Alone" strategy that would mean removing all barriers to world trade. The authors of the response, from which the following excerpt is taken, are appointed by the Centre for Economic Performance (a research centre at the London School of Economics) and reject Minford's expertise as follows:

> Minford's results stem from assuming that small changes in trade costs have tremendously large effects on trade volumes: according to his model, the falls in tariffs become enormously magnified because each country purchases only from the lowest cost supplier.

Performative, imaginary and symbolic power 29

In reality, everyone does not simply buy from the cheapest supplier

Products are different when made by different countries and trade is affected by the distance between countries, their size, history and wealth (the 'gravity relationship'). Trade costs are not just government-created trade barriers. Product differentiation and gravity is incorporated into modern trade models – these predict that after Brexit the UK will continue to trade more with the EU than other countries as it remains our geographically closest neighbour. Consequently, we will be worse off because we will face higher trade costs with the EU.

(*Economists for Brexit: A Critique* by Sampson et al., 2016)

In the following discourse analysis of the excerpt I want to show how enunciative markers form speaker positions which are a discursive precondition for social role and identity formation (Angermuller, 2014; Fløttum, 2005; Zienkowski, 2016). Enunciative markers evoke linguistic speaker roles that can be adopted by diverse social actors in order to create identity images. The image of "me" and the images of "others" are important parts of an actor's identity/image. They are created as discursive roles. The idea of this approach is that such discursive roles always operate with diverse images of the speaker and the other (Goffman, 1974). Based on Lacan's and Foucault's discourse theory (Foucault, 1972; Lacan, 1991), the following analysis shows how such images are formed by the textual use of deixis, negation, booster and hedges in the aforementioned discourse.

For illustrative reasons, I only take one sentence (in italics) which is of central importance in this process of identity and image formation. Whereas the first part presents Minford's thesis very quickly, the authors use this sentence to bridge the argumentation from Minford's argument to their own standpoint. The linguistic modalities that are at work in this sentence have nothing to do with the conceptual content of either expert statement (Minford's and their own). Rather, it works as a discursive-cognitive tool that directs the consciousness of any potential reader to certain images of opponent (Minford) and proponent (authors). Those discursive markers produce a certain ethos, as Maingueneau would put it (Maingueneau, 1999), and they introduce the dimension of political struggle into expert discourses (Maesse, 2017a; Pühringer & Hirte, 2015). Therefore, economic expert discourses are not simply representing ideas, concepts and arguments; they are also a tool in social conflicts over hegemony (O'Rourke & Hogan, 2014).

<u>In reality</u>, *everyone does* not <u>simply</u> *buy from the cheapest supplier*

In a first step, let's take a look at the formal level of this short utterance. The speaker's position is basically produced by antagonism to Minford's economic view. This antagonism is evoked by an operator of negation ("not"),

30   *Jens Maesse*

a presupposition booster ("in reality") and a hedger ("simply"). What does it mean for the production of certain images? In a first move, the authors create their own image by opposing Minford's position. In order to reject that image, an image of "Minford" (the other) must be produced first. Two discursive perspectives (points of view: pov) represent this image of the other (where (a) refers to the "other" of the discourse and (l) to the position of the speaker):

> $pov_1(a)$: "small changes in trade costs have tremendously large effects on trade volumes (since) the falls in tariffs become enormously magnified because each country purchases only from the lowest cost supplier" (presupposed here, taken from the aforementioned statement [in italics])

Point of view$_1$ introduces the voice of Minford in this sentence via implication in order to oppose it:

> $pov_2(l)$: NO pov_1, BECAUSE = "not real" (presupposition: true statements must be "real", evoked by "*in reality*")

Therefore, the formulation "in reality" evokes a two-step cognitive process: in a first step, the initial statement is reintroduced; and in a second step, the speaker goes on to distance themselves from it. But this second step is only made possible by making a positive reference to something that is "real". This comes in the statement: "everyone does *not simply* buy from the cheapest supplier". Thus, the solidarity with speaker 2 is represented by the (l) in pov_2, whereas opposition to the image of the opponent is indicated by the (a) in pov_1. Now, the discourse reaches its final moment because the image of the "me" position is developing:

> $pov_3(a)$: "everyone does buy from the cheapest supplier"

But before the speaker comes to their argument ("Products are different when made by different countries and trade is affected by the distance between countries, their size, history and wealth (the 'gravity relationship')") the opponent is again evoked by the discourse through negation ("not"):

> $pov_4(l)$: NO pov_3

This is even highlighted by a booster ("*simply*"):

> $pov_5(l)$: pov_4 IS OBVIOUSLY CORRECT BECAUSE pov_3 IS SO RIDICULOUS (implicit comment on pov_4, evoked by "*simply*")

What we can learn from this discourse is that the "me" image (all pov with (l)) cannot be produced without permanently repeating and reintroducing the

Performative, imaginary and symbolic power 31

image of the "other" (Minford, all pov with (a)). Furthermore, both discursive images are obviously the result of a certain polemical rhetoric. The other is not only presented twice (pov$_{1,3}$) but is three times rejected (pov$_{2,4,5}$). Strictly speaking, it can be said that the other has five images: two positive images and three rejections of them.

Depending on the emotional contexts in which those statements are read and used for further discourses, polemical modalities create huge gaps between political and professional counterparties. In this example, it is easily imaginable how "rational people" with "obvious and simple economic arguments" enter into strict opposition to a group of economists who have "lost contact with reality". On the other hand, in a situation where the institutional infrastructure of the UK reality becomes more and more precarious, people such as Minford can easily present "old-fashioned" economic arguments that are, in the eyes of many other experts, far away from the data and the current economic discussion. The moment of institutional disintegration might be when "zombies" (Zizek) enter the scene, because the Lacanian "real" suspends the "symbolic reality" (guaranteed by the institutional order).

However one reads this situation, depending on the standpoint and possible contexts of controversy, economic expert discourses can produce strong images of social actors. And these images can have a huge influence on how certain economic arguments are presented and perceived. This is basically the idea of imaginary power. Imaginary power cannot make certain things true or false. It is, rather, a way of producing images of real actors, and the potential reputation of these real social actors highly depends on the image that we have in mind when we listen to a speech, argumentation or an economic expert proposal. Discursive markers such as deixis, negation, boosters and hedges (and many more) can contribute to creating those identity images.

4.3 Symbolic power: how economic experts get reputation and legitimacy

In processes of formation and attribution of reputation, the image is only one aspect, even if this aspect is fundamentally important to construct social individuals as professional actors. In addition, symbolic power can support (or hinder) the formation of power connected to certain actors in discourses. Whereas the linguistic dimension forms images as power devices, symbolic power is not solely produced by ordinary speech acts. It rather presupposes the existence and operation of an institutionalised field that is not immediately involved in these politico-economic struggles. According to the sociology of professions, experts are always recognised by non-experts. For this reason, symbolic power must be produced in a place where it is *not used*, and it must be used in a place where it is *not directly produced*. The fields of production (the "factories of symbolic goods" as places of value creation) are not the fields of consumption ("the markets" as sites of price realisation). The structural condition for the possibility of legitimacy of expertise as such is based on the existence of a constellation of different sub-fields between academia and society (Hirschfeld & Gengnagel, 2017). The formation of reputation is finally the product of various discourses taking place at the interface of these sub-fields between academia and society.

Therefore, the world of economic experts is embedded in a *trans-epistemic field* that reaches across academia, politics, media and the economy (Maesse, 2015), and it produces diverse sources of legitimacy (Schmidt-Wellenburg, 2017b). Symbolic power is the product of discursive interplay between the academic field, the political field, the economic field and public discourses in the media. The possibility to confer respect, prestige and legitimacy on an economic expert in public political discourse is based on the production of "excellence" and "elite" labels as "mythical capital" in academia (Maesse, 2017b). According to this model, almost all economists who are involved in societal discourses on economic policy – such as the Minford debate presented earlier – can profit from "discourses of excellence" produced within academic daily life. Academia is like a "political production facility" for manufacturing symbolic capital to be used in political and media discourses.

In economics, discourses of excellence emerge within strong academic hierarchies that are formed by diverse concentric networks. The most important mechanism at work in these hierarchisations and elitisations is the mutual interaction of research rankings, excellence-oriented funding from the Research Excellence Framework (REF), the *de facto* dominance of only a few economics departments in the UK (such as the London School of Economics (LSE), Oxford, University College London, Warwick and a few others) and the role of exclusive clubs and networks such as the Centre for Economic Policy Research (CEPR) and other informal settings (Lee, Pham, & Gu, 2013; Maesse, 2018b). The detailed interplay of these technologies cannot be analysed here, but what can be said is that those elite networks do not simply produce academic elite positions. What they actually form is the idea of excellence, i.e. the material exemplification of the possibility that academic exceptionalism – as "excellence" – can exist.

Many economists from these elite networks obtain powerful positions within academia, and many of them move on to work in banks, international organisations, governments and central banks. Symbolic power is not attached to a single position in these kinds of networks. It is rather a structural effect of the entire network, and in discourses it can be easily attached to any sort of economic statement. For example, Patrick Minford is an economics professor at Cardiff University and simultaneously a Fellow of the CEPR network. The authors of the "response" to Minford's Brexit position are appointed by the LSE, which has a highly prestigious economics department. Therefore, both opponents and proponents of the previously analysed discourse may benefit from the institutional reputation of the very same elite structure. Symbolic power is therefore not connected to "true concepts" or "functioning ideas". Rather, it privileges, authorises and legitimises economic experts' speaker positions in discourses.

5 Conclusion

To conclude, all the different sorts of discursive power presented here interact with each other. Each form of power always presupposes all the other forms. There is no constitutive hierarchy between them. Rather, they are linked to each other like Lacan's rings. One sort builds on another, forming a network of power and knowledge that stretches across various fields in academia, politics, the economy and media. As this chapter argues, performative, imaginary and symbolic forms of power are key elements to understand the impact of economic expert knowledge on society. As discursive forms of power, these three forms can deal with certain problems in social studies of economics: first, we can understand how certain linguistic forms meld with socio-material relations on different levels resulting in structural constraints; second, we can grasp the translational character of economic experts' impact occurring between distinct social fields and mediated by discourses; third, we can analyse power on various levels and take into account the complexity of economic expert discourses.

This discourse analytical perspective on power opens up our analytical focus for the heterogeneity of the social that is evolving in the course of globalisation. With such an approach to hand, we are not obliged to assume a mysterious "global structure of meaning", as world polity approaches do (Meyer, Boli, Thomas, & Ramirez, 1997), and neither are we expected to reduce everything to the micro level of social interaction due to a lack of structuring terrains (Knorr Cetina & Bruegger, 2002). On the contrary, we can now grasp and analyse the diverse forms of social struggle taking place at various levels of globalised societies in-between the local and the global.

References

Angermuller, J. (2014). *Poststructuralist discourse analysis: Subjectivity in enunciative pragmatics.* London: Palgrave.

Boldyrev, I., & Svetlova, E. (Eds.). (2016). *Enacting dismal science: New perspectives on the performativity of economics.* London and New York: Palgrave Macmillan.

Bourdieu, P. (1989). *Distinction: A social critique of the judgement of taste.* London: Routledge.

Bruff, I. (2014). The rise of authoritarian neoliberalism. *Rethinking Marxism, 26*(1), 113–129.

Callon, M. (2007). What does it mean to say that economics is performative? In D. MacKenzie et al. (Eds.), *Do economists make markets? On the performativity of economics* (pp. 311–357). Princeton: Princeton University Press.

Costantini, O. (2017). Political economy of the Stability and Growth Pact. *European Journal of Economics and Economic Policies: Intervention* (14), 333–350.

Delanty, G., & Rumford, C. (2005). *Rethinking Europe: Social theory and the implications of Europeanization.* London and New York: Routledge.

Desrosières, A. (1998). *The politics of large numbers: A history of statistical reasoning.* Cambridge and London: Oxford University Press.

Dezalay, Y., & Garth, B. (2009). National usages for a "global" science: The dissemination of new economic paradigms as a strategy for the reproduction of governing elites. In G. Mallard, C. Paradeise, & A. Peerbaye (Eds.), *Global science and national sovereignty. Studies in historical sociology of science.* New York: Routledge.

34   Jens Maesse

Fitzgerald, J., & O'Rourke, B. K. (2015). *Performing economics: How economics discourse gets enacted in radio news interviews*. Presented at the 10th international conference in interpretive policy analysis.

Fløttum, K. (2005). The self and the others: Polyphonic visibility in research articles. *International Journal of Applied Linguistics, 15*(1), 29–44.

Foucault, M. (1972). *The archaeology of knowledge*. New York: Pantheon Book.

Foucault, M. (1980). *Power/knowledge: Selected interviews and other writings, 1972–1977*. New York: Pantheon.

Foucault, M. (2008). *The birth of biopolitics. Lectures at the Collège de France, 1978–1979*. New York: Palgrave Macmillan.

Georgakakis, D., & Rowell, J. (2013). *The field of Eurocracy: Mapping EU actors and professionals*. London: Palgrave.

Goffman, E. (1974). *Frame analysis: An essay on the organization of experience*. Cambridge: Harvard University Press.

Hall, P. A. (Ed.). (1989). *The political power of economic ideas: Keynesianism across nations*. Princeton: Princeton University Press.

Hamann, J., Maesse, J., Scholz, R., & Angermuller, J. (2019). The academic dispositif: Towards a context-centred discourse analysis. In R. Scholz (Ed.), *Quantifying approaches to discourse for social scientists* (pp. 51–87). London and New York: Palgrave Macmillan.

Hirschfeld, A., & Gengnagel, V. (2017). 'Das können wir nicht durchgehen lassen': Zur gesellschaftlichen Resonanz kritischer Interventionen. In J. Hamann, J. Maesse, V. Gengnagel, & A. Hirschfeld (Eds.), *Macht in Wissenschaft und Gesellscht: Diskurs- und feldanalytische Perspektiven* (pp. 425–452). Wiesbaden: Springer.

Hirschman, D., & Popp Berman, E. (2014). Do economists make policies? On the political effects of economics. *Socio-Economic Review, 12*, 779–811.

Jessop, B. (2012). The world market, variegated capitalism, and the crisis of European integration. In P. Nousios, H. Overbeek, & A. Tsolakis (Eds.), *Globalisation and European integration: Critical approaches to regional order and international relations* (pp. 91–111). London and New York: Routledge.

Knorr Cetina, K., & Bruegger, U. (2002). Global microstructures: The virtual societies of financial markets. *American Journal of Sociology, 107*(4), 905–950.

Lacan, J. (1991). *Das Seminar Buch 2, Das Ich in der Theorie Freuds und in der Technik der Psychoanalyse*. Weinheim: Quadriga.

Lebaron, F. (2006). 'Nobel' economists as public intellectuals: the circulation of symbolic capital. *International Journal of Contemporary Sociology, 43*(1), 88–101.

Lebaron, F. (2008). Central bankers in the contemporary global field of power: A 'social space' approach. *The Sociological Review, 56*(1), 121–144.

Lee, F. S., Pham, X., & Gu, G. (2013). The UK research assessment exercise and the narrowing of UK economics. *Cambridge Journal of Economics, 37*(4), 693–717.

MacKenzie, D., & Millo, Y. (2003). Constructing a market, performing theory: The historical sociology of a financial derivatives exchange. *American Journal of Sociology, 109*, 107–145.

Maesse, J. (2015). Economic experts: A discursive political economy of economics. *Journal of Multicultural Discourses, 10*(3), 279–305.

Maesse, J. (2016). The power of myth. The dialectics between 'elitism' and 'academism' in economic expert discourse. *European Journal of Cross-Cultural Competence and Management, 4*(1), 3–20.

Maesse, J. (2017a). Austerity discourses in Europe: How economic experts create identity projects. *Innovation: The European Journal of Social Science Research*, 1–17.

Maesse, J. (2017b). The elitism dispositif: Hierarchization, discourses of excellence and organizational change in European economics. *Higher Education, 73*(6), 909–927.

Maesse, J. (2018a). Discursive Marxism: How Marx treats the economy and what discourse studies contribute to it. *Critical Discourse Studies, 4*(15), 364–376.

Maesse, J. (2018b). Globalization strategies and the economics dispositif: Insights from Germany and the UK. *Historical Social Research, 43*(3), 120–146.

Maingueneau, D. (1999). Analysing self-constituting discourses. *Discourse Studies, 1*(2), 183–199.

Meyer, J. W., Boli, J., Thomas, G. M., & Ramirez, F. O. (1997). World society and the nation-state. *American Journal of Sociology, 103*(1), 144–181.

Miró, J. (2017). European integration, social democratic Europeanism and the competitiveness discourse: A neo-Poulantzian approach to discursive policy analysis. *Palgrave Communications* (4). DOI: 10.1057/palcomms.2017.60.

Mirowski, P., & Nik-Khah, E. (2008). Command performance: Exploring what STS thinks it takes to build a market. In T. Pinch & R. Swedberg (Eds.), *Living in a material world: Economic sociology meets science and technology studies* (pp. 89–128). Cambridge: MIT Press.

Mudge, S. L., & Vauchez, A. (2012). Building Europe on a weak field: Law, economics, and scholarly avatars in transnational politics. *American Journal of Sociology, 118*(2), 449–492.

O'Rourke, B. K., & Hogan, J. (2014). Guaranteeing failure: Neoliberal discourse in the Irish economic crisis. *Journal of Political Ideologies, 19*(1), 41–59.

Pühringer, S., & Hirte, K. (2015). The financial crisis as a heart attack: Discourse profiles of economists in the financial crisis. *Journal of Language and Politics, 14*(4), 599–625.

Rossier, T., & Bühlmann, F. (2018). The internationalisation of economics and business studies: Import of excellence, cosmopolitan capital, or American dominance? *Historical Social Research, 43*(3), 189–215.

Rossier, T., Bühlmann, F., & Mach, A. (2017). The rise of professors of economics and business studies in Switzerland: Between scientific reputation and political power. *European Journal of Sociology/Archives Européennes de Sociologie, 58*(2), 295–326.

Sampson, T., Dhingra, S., Ottaviano, G., & Van Reenen, J. (2016). *Economists for Brexit: A Critique.* CEP Brexit Analysis No. 6, Page 1. http://cep.lse.ac.uk/pubs/download/brexit06.pdf.

Schmidt-Wellenburg, C. (2017a). Europeanisation, stateness, and professions: What role do economic expertise and economic experts play in European political integration? *European Journal of Cultural and Political Sociology, 1*–27.

Schmidt-Wellenburg, C. (2017b). Wissenschaft, Politik und Profession als Quellen diskursiver Autorität. In *Macht in Wissenschaft und Gesellschaft* (pp. 477–504). Wiesbaden: Springer.

Seikel, D. (2016). Flexible austerity and supranational autonomy. The reformed excessive deficit procedure and the asymmetry between liberalization and social regulation in the EU. *Journal of Common Market Studies, 54*(6), 1398–1416.

Sweet, A. S., Sandholtz, W., & Fligstein, N. (Eds.). (2001). *The institutionalization of Europe.* Oxford: Oxford University Press.

Wagner, P. (2001). *A history and theory of the social sciences: Not all that is solid melts into air.* London and New York: Sage.

Weber, M. (1972). *Wirtschaft und Gesellschaft: Grundriss der verstehenden Soziologie.* Tübingen: Mohr Siebeck.

Zienkowski, J. (2016). *Articulations of self and politics in activist discourse: A discourse analysis of critical subjectivities in minority debates.* London: Palgrave.

Žižek, S. (1989). *The sublime object of ideology.* London and New York: Verso.

3 Macroeconomics and monetary policy as autonomous domains of knowledge and power

Rational expectations, monetarism and the Federal Reserve

Jan Sparsam and Hanno Pahl

1 Introduction: economic knowledge on planet academia and in central banks

In this chapter,[1] we argue that although practical monetary policy is strongly influenced by academic macroeconomics, this does not imply that developments in both domains run in parallel. As has been shown in numerous sociological works on the fabrication and application of scientific knowledge, especially in the so-called laboratory studies, knowledge production is always situated in social contexts that have an impact on the respective forms of knowledge (Knorr Cetina, 1981). Knowledge production in academic macroeconomics is also structured by a rather different social context than monetary policy. The main area of application of macroeconomics is supposed to be central banks. The power structure as well as the practical needs in both domains differ significantly, resulting in distinct epistemic cultures. Therefore, we pose the questions of what attempts to influence monetary policy with macroeconomic knowledge would actually look like and how macroeconomic ideas are conceived by practitioners.

The relevance of the questions stems not least from recent criticisms of mainstream macroeconomics as articulated by heterodox economists, the media, but also by central bankers themselves: Many different commentators have explained the outbreak of the crisis in 2008 as well as the initial helplessness of central banks at least partially with deficits of current mainstream macroeconomics. In particular, they criticized the merely rudimentary role of financial markets in the standard models of new Keynesian economics – currently the leading school of macroeconomics and the new mainstream (Leijonhufvud, 2009; Borio, 2012).

Focusing on the Federal Reserve, we argue that this diagnosis is not wrong but simplistic. Even though decision making in the Fed has been influenced by mainstream macroeconomics all along, the knowledge culture of the Federal Open Market Committee (FOMC), the Fed's highest decision-making

DOI: 10.4324/9780367817084-4

body, consists of more ingredients and actions than simply applying the actual standards of academic macroeconomics.[2] The existing literature tends to downplay the frictions that go along with knowledge transitioning from academia to practice. This is especially true for mainstream accounts of macroeconomics (e.g. Woodford, 2009), but also for their critical counterparts from global political economy (e.g. Grabel, 2000). Both assume a much too straightforward impact – praised by mainstream economists (suggesting monetary policy has become better due to technical expertise offered by academic macroeconomics), criticized by critical political economists (monetary policy as captured by neoliberal academic schools, c.f. Sparsam & Pahl, 2018). We argue that it is not predominantly the cognitive aspects of scientific knowledge and the criteria of success in academia that convince the practitioners to adopt macroeconomic concepts. In our opinion the context conditions of action in the respective domains are to a greater degree responsible for a – successful or failed – transition between them.

For our argument, we chose an episode that was historically crucial for the Fed and led to a paradigm change in monetary policy making. The transcripts of the meetings of the FOMC around 1978 and 1979 show that the politically critical situation for the Fed opened the deliberations of the FOMC for discursive interventions from its members that promoted specific macroeconomic ideas. The two cases we refer to are the absent impact of the so-called rational expectations revolution or, as it was labelled later, the rise of new classical macroeconomics and the adaption of monetarism in a practical way by the Fed under the chairmanship of Paul Volcker. Rational expectations macroeconomics emerged in the mid-1970s and led to a paradigm shift in academic macroeconomics within a few years (Mishkin, 1995; Hoover, 1992), with devastating effects for the credibility of the Keynesian mainstream. The influence of new classical macroeconomics on the Fed, however, remained rather modest for a long time. The reasons for this lag are quite opaque. In contrast, monetarism was allegedly adopted by the Fed with the debut of Volcker as chairman of the FOMC. The paradigm itself, however, did not revolutionize academic macroeconomics, and its main protagonist, Milton Friedman, is considered to be more of a political figure. But the history of macroeconomic thought is still struggling to answer the question in which way monetarism actually made an impact on the Fed's monetary policy.

Course of argument: The following section is divided into two subsections: We begin with sketching the broad support rational expectations macroeconomics received at one specific district of the Federal Reserve System, the Federal Reserve Bank of Minneapolis, as early as from the mid-1970s onwards (2.1). In the next subsection, we present empirical evidence to answer the question of why this support did not lead to a broader influence of new classical macroeconomics in the Fed, referring to the verbatim transcripts of the meetings of the FOMC. We discuss several examples from the late 1970s that shed some light on why the paradigm shift in academia did not have the same immediate impact on monetary policy (2.2). The following section deals with

38   *Jan Sparsam and Hanno Pahl*

the so-called practical monetarism of Paul Volcker's chairmanship. We will show how impulses from academic macroeconomics were picked up by the Fed in a selective and pragmatic way (3). In the discussion, we argue that both academic macroeconomics and monetary policy making encounter fundamentally different problems and therefore need distinct solutions that require translations between both domains. Because of that, they have to be understood as autonomous domains of knowledge and power (4). Our contribution thus combines empirical findings with insights from the relevant literature, spanning the history of economic ideas and the history of central banking.[3]

2 Why new classical macroeconomics has not taken the FOMC by storm

2.1 *The Minneapolis Fed as a breeding ground for rational expectations macroeconomics in the 1970s*

The Federal Reserve System consists of twelve regional Federal Reserve Banks that are jointly responsible for planning and implementing monetary policy measures in their respective districts (Hafer, 2005). The huge degree of independence of the districts supports quite some diversity within the Federal Reserve System, especially with regard to their research activities and monetary policy positions. For example, the Federal Reserve Bank of St. Louis is considered to have been a stronghold of monetarism from the late 1960s onwards (see Hafer & Wheelock, 2001). The same is true with respect to new classical macroeconomics for the Federal Reserve Bank of Minneapolis from the mid-1970s onwards.

Monetarism, especially represented by Friedman, renewed the quantity theory of money. The main argument concerning monetary policy was that central banks have to directly control the money supply. Even though Friedman challenged the Keynesian mainstream (of the so-called old neoclassical synthesis), the impact of monetarist thought on the academic profession was rather limited (De Vroey, 2016, p. 85). Instead, its influence is mainly supposed to be a political one, promoting the market against the Keynesian statism (c.f. Accocella et al., 2016, p. 51). The success of monetarism, therefore, can mainly be seen in the establishment of politico-economical tenets like inflation fighting as the main goal of monetary policy (c.f. De Long, 2000). In contrast, new classical macroeconomics, opposing monetarism but being not a bit less market-oriented than Friedman, radically changed the research landscape of macroeconomics. Initiated by Robert E. Lucas, it set a new theoretical standard for econometric modelling. The so-called Lucas Critique conveys that Keynesian models are not able to reproduce economic actors adjusting their preferences when they encounter changes in policy. As a solution, Lucas proposed basing models on rational expectations, which means that economic actors are able to anticipate the effects of policy changes. In such models, economic actors behave as if they knew the parameters of the model (Snowdon & Vane,

Macroeconomics and monetary policy 39

2005, p. 228; De Vroey, 2016, p. 167). Lucas's solution provided a micro-foundation for macroeconomic modelling and made it compatible with the microeconomic standard of general equilibrium theory (Sparsam et al., 2017). It also sparked the development towards building models as the main activity of macroeconomists and therefore providing new career opportunities (Colander, 1989, p. 33).[4]

At the Federal Reserve Bank of Minneapolis, during the directorships of Bruce MacLaury (1971–1977) and Mark H. Willes (1977–1980) the research focus shifted to the then brand-new theory of rational expectations, including an offensive proclamation of the market-affirmative and anti-Keynesian policy recommendations associated with this program. Regarding the propagation and popularization of this new theory and worldview, Willes stood out promi-nently. His predecessor remembers him in the following way:

> Mark Willes, who came in as president after I left, was very intrigued with this line of reasoning [rational expectations] within the research depart-ment at the Federal Reserve in Minneapolis and made it more of an official policy line of this bank, a symbol, if you will, of this bank within the Fed-eral Reserve System. So there became a voice for the rational expectation school coming out of Minneapolis. That grew out of work that was going on here while I was here, but I thought that it was a very interesting intel-lectual exercise, not a direct policy-related exercise while I was here.
>
> (MacLaury, 1992, n.p.)[5]

Economist Neil Wallace (in Hoover & Young, 2011, p. 27), one of the major contributors to new classical macroeconomics, who at that time belonged to the Bank's research staff, made similar comments:

> When Mark Willes came to the Minneapolis Federal Reserve as president, he decided to publicize some of the research on rational expectations. In particular, Mark had the view that some of the policy-ineffectiveness stuff was something that deserved a hearing within the system.[6]

The Bank's new research agenda, which quickly led to relevant publica-tions (such as Muench & Wallace, 1974; Sargent & Wallace, 1976), served as a multiplier effect that helped to spread Lucas's fundamental critique of the Keynesian paradigm in academic macroeconomics and stimulated research to make it more relevant for policy. Thomas Sargent (1995, p. 4), who also counts as a main protagonist of new classical macroeconomics today and worked in the research department of the Minneapolis Fed at the time, wrote about the influence of these interventions as follows:

> Neil Wallace and I had already written several papers about rational expec-tations in 1969–1972, and had read drafts of Lucas's JET paper [1972] as well as two key papers by Lucas and Prescott [1971, 1974]. But we didn't

40 *Jan Sparsam and Hanno Pahl*

understand what was going on until, upon reading Lucas's 'Econometric Policy Evaluation' in Spring of 1973,[7] we were stunned into terminating our long standing Minneapolis Fed research project to design, estimate and optimally control a Keynesian macroeconometric model.

Here, Sargent classifies Lucas's ideas as a crucial experience that radically redirected monetary policy research in Minneapolis. At the same time, the *Federal Reserve Bank of Minneapolis Quarterly Review*, launched in 1977, created a new series of publications at the intersection of academic discourse, monetary policy, and public relations, in which numerous articles proclaiming "radically different new directions" in theorizing as well as monetary policy (Lucas & Sargent, 1979, p. 15) were subsequently published.

Willes himself used his position as president[8] not only to readjust bank-internal research in Minneapolis but to attempt to popularize the new school of thought in the political field. In an interview he highlights this attempt as a main aspect of his presidential work:

I spent an enormous amount of time trying to help people be interested in public policy, help explain what public economic policy was, what kinds of effects it would have, what was possible, was what not possible. You take this last election discussion, and you could cry, because the general notion about what is possible is so far off the mark that people make really important decisions and then clamor for action, when often, if they get what they really ask for, they're going to be worse off, rather than better off.

(Willes, 1992, n.p.)[9]

These quotes show that Willes acted not only as a strong supporter of early new classical macroeconomics but also as a chaperone of its development. However, as will be subsequently shown, he was not able to establish the agenda of rational expectations at the power centre of the Fed, the FOMC, and we will examine some of the reasons of this failure.

2.2 Failed interventions: Mark Willes's efforts at persuading the FOMC to adopt rational expectations macroeconomics

The FOMC deliberates about and sets monetary policy and financial regulations. It comprises twelve voting members: seven members of the Board of Governors (BoG), nominated by the president of the USA and appointed by the Senate for a maximum term of fourteen years. Among these members are the respective chairs of the committee who, however, can only be appointed for consecutive four-year legislatures. The other five members of the FOMC are the presidents from the twelve Federal Reserve districts. The FOMC usually meets eight times a year to discuss and decide on the monetary policy stance of the Fed (see Meulendyke, 1998, pp. 121–138).

As president of the Minneapolis Fed, Willes also participated in the FOMC, first as a non-voting member and since March 1978 as a voting member. During this time, he firmly positioned himself as radical proponent of tight monetary policy: "Mark Willes . . . wanted to use a sledgehammer rather than a scalpel in tightening credit" (Silber, 2012, p. 138). A statistical evaluation of the voting behaviour of the members of the FOMC ranks him "among the most tightness-oriented members" (Chappell et al., 2005, p. 44). At the same time, his voting behaviour showed an unusually high degree of dissent, bringing some turmoil to this rather consensus-oriented committee.[10] Reminiscing, Willes (1992, n.p.) made the following remarks about his time at the FOMC:

> That was, of course, a time when there were some fairly sharply divergent views about how to manage things domestically. Even though I was president a relatively short period of time, I tended to get more than my share of attention, because I disagreed often with what the System was doing and how it was dealing with what I thought was a policy that was not going to deal with inflation as effectively as we ought to.

Willes did not only carry himself as a deviationist,[11] but he has also offensively brought the ideas of rational expectations macroeconomics into the FOMC. Surprisingly, he has not succeeded in arousing any interest of the other members of the FOMC for the policy-relevant implications of this new variety of academic macroeconomics. In his extensive history of the Federal Reserve, Meltzer (2010, p. 1017) concludes for the period of the late 1970s to the early 1980s: "Academic literature at the time was dominated by models with rational expectations. . . . President Mark Willes (Minneapolis) mentioned this work at times, but he did not get a response." It is instructive to take a closer look at some sequences of the verbatim transcripts of the meetings of the FOMC to investigate the main reasons for this failure.[12]

In the meetings of June and July 1978, Willes argued that the econometric models used by the Fed's scientific staff to inform the members of the FOMC fall short of properly including the expectations of economic actors (see June 20, 1978, p. 10; July 18, 1978, p. 16). In the September meeting of the same year, Willes refused to be regarded as an outsider concerning his preference for tight policy measures. He quoted a letter from the Fed to Congress that assures a long-run neutrality of monetary policy, criticizing that the Fed does not act the way it claims to do (September 8, 1978, p. 29). This did not lead to any kind of discussion, however. The first intervention by Willes that sparked a brief debate took place in the October meeting of 1978. He again emphasized the importance of including rational expectations, referring to the work done at the Minneapolis Fed. Incorporating rational expectations, he argued, could substantially change the perceived impacts of various policy alternatives. Since the voting members based their decisions to set the funds rate at least partially on models and econometric analyses offered by the Fed's scientific staff, using alternative model specifications or alternative models might

42   *Jan Sparsam and Hanno Pahl*

alter their perception of the economic situation. Staff member James L. Kichline admitted to Willes the need to improve the integration of expectations into their models,[13] demonstrating that he is fully aware of the methodological problems coming along with this missing variable. But he was also cautious to align himself with the work done at the Minneapolis Fed by emphasizing that the outputs of the models might be different:

> MR. KICHLINE. Yes. We have work going on now to try to incorporate in the various parts of the model a better expression of expectations than is now captured in the model. It's clearly a weak point of the model now. I guess my own judgment would be that perhaps we wouldn't get as strong a response as the results of your work in this area just looking at some of the early things we've done. But I think it's a quite valid comment that our model does not have in it as much of an "expectations" phenomenon throughout as [*your model] apparently. You're quite correct; I have no problem in saying that we have not progressed very far in putting that in the model.
>
> (October 17, 1978, p. 13)

However, as the further discussion reveals, Willes's colleagues at the FOMC were not that much convinced of the importance of his objections. J. Charles Partee, member of the Board of Governors, asked Kichline if the model incorporating expectations the staff is working on is "based on some new theory" or "on historical experience" which Kichline affirmed (October 17, 1978, p. 13). With this statement he, on the one side, emphasized the methodological difference between Willes's and the staff's approaches. On the other side, he thereby proclaimed a hierarchy in the validity of different forms of knowledge for the FOMC's concerns, valuating pure theoretical insights as inferior to more data-saturated information. This claim that was also supported by chairman G. William Miller, who stressed that rational expectations models still were not able to adequately reproduce time series data:

> MR. PARTEE [*Board of Governors]. But I still think, Mark, the test of the pudding is in the replication of the past. Again, no matter what your theory is, it has to be a model that –
>
> CHAIRMAN MILLER It's got to be proved throughout the cycle.
>
> MR. PARTEE To show it works, and this one is based on the past.
>
> (October 17, 1978, p. 13)

Although Willes tried to make clear that he was aiming at a qualitatively different "perception of policy impacts," (October 17, 1978, p. 13) the discussion quickly terminated because another member was called upon to comment on the economic situation.

This short episode is highly typical for Willes's failed interventions. The following meetings show similar sequences whenever Willes tried to bring his view to attention again. For instance, in the November meeting of the same

Macroeconomics and monetary policy   43

year, he repeated his claim about expectations, but nobody even picked up on his points (November 21, 1978, p. 17). In the December meeting, a somewhat humorous but also polemical verbal exchange took place. Willes tried to distinguish the rational expectations research agenda from monetarism, while Partee regards both schools of thought as mere variations of the same paradigm:

MR. WILLES I would like first to make a commercial, Mr. Chairman, and disavow that I am a monetarist. We hold a balanced portfolio in Minneapolis.
MR. PARTEE He's like an Episcopalian not being a Catholic.
MR. WILLES Someday when we have more time we will explain the substantive differences between the monetarist and what's even worse, I might say, and that's a rational expectations-ist. But that's another story.

(December 19, 1978, p. 28)

It is evident that Willes acted with the intention to single out the rational expectations school of thought as a new and independent stream of research in contrast to monetarism. His playful description of his intervention as advertising already shows that he was quite aware of the promotional character of his objections (and maybe their futility). His opponent played down his claim, by cracking a sarcastic joke, stealing Willes's thunder.

Later in the same meeting when the committee openly discussed the unavailability of different policy scenarios, Willes pointed out weaknesses in the models used by the Fed's staff again, arguing

> that there is no way we can say on the basis of those exercises [*simulations with the existing models] whether our proposed policy is consistent or inconsistent with the President's [*economic] programs. My fear is that we are going to mislead ourselves into thinking that we can determine with more precision than we can exactly what the options are that we face.
>
> (December 19, 1978, p. 58)

At this point, Willes seemed to be aware of the importance to not base his criticism only on general theoretical objections stemming from the rational expectations approach but to offer more data-saturated econometrical work to the committee and thereby a practical solution to the problems the FOMC identified in their mode of knowledge production. He continues:

> We hope to have for the Committee, in a few months, some simulation views in the MTS [*multivariate time series] model to indicate that there is really nothing we can say about the breakdown in nominal GNP between prices and real output, with any degree of confidence at all, based on the way that model is currently working. And that's not a criticism of that model any more than any other. It's just a fundamental difficulty we are having [in] how these things are being done.
>
> (December 19, 1978, p. 58)

44 *Jan Sparsam and Hanno Pahl*

Yet, it took Willes and his economic staff at Minneapolis much longer than expected to come up with econometric models (based on rational expectations) that would meet the needs of the FOMC. The first working models to adequately operationalize the Lucas Critique were the real business cycle models of the early 1980s (Kydland & Prescott, 1982). But these models left no place for monetary policy whatsoever (beneath keeping inflation low) because they explained business cycles exclusively as results of technology shocks or other real factors (c.f. Hoover, 2007, p. 423). This characteristic rendered them very unattractive for the needs of the FOMC and the Federal Reserve System in general. Willes's objections in the FOMC that monetary policy may be completely futile as a means of affecting the economy that were based on the "policy ineffectiveness proposition" (Sargent & Wallace, 1976) were also received as "very, very [specific]," (Partee, January 9, 1980, p. 59) but "very imprecise in terms of the numbers we come out with" (Schultz, vice chair Board of Governors, January 9, 1980, p. 59).

This interaction concerning rational expectations that took place between Willes and the FOMC almost like a ritual shows that the new paradigm that revolutionized macroeconomics did the very opposite in the FOMC. The transcripts reveal that in the committee it was conceived as a mere idiosyncrasy of one person. This also happened because the then crisis-ridden Fed referred to another academic paradigm to change its course: monetarism.

3 Muddling through: practical monetarism at the Fed as a pragmatic choice

Interestingly, in the beginning monetarism showed a similar fate in the Fed as rational expectations did. Before gaining influence in the FOMC, it was adopted in the Federal Reserve Bank of St. Louis. As Johnson shows (1998, p. 158), monetarism was explored by the staff at St. Louis concerning research and forecasts and had a significant impact on the respective president. However, similar to new classical macroeconomics in Minneapolis, the paradigm did not gain any influence in the FOMC's decisions in the early 1970s. According to Johnson (1998, p. 158), this was due to the pecking order that placed the staff of the FOMC above those of the districts. He also stresses that the presidents of St. Louis were ignored in the meetings.

But it was to turn out completely different: In August 1979 Paul Volcker became chairman of the FOMC.[14] When he took office, the economic situation in the US was quite precarious because the economy was ridden by a severe "stagflation" – high inflation and low growth – for a few years by then, for which the Fed took a lot of public and political blame. This made it necessary for the FOMC to finally come up with a solution. With Volcker, the period of so-called practical monetarism began. Although Volcker's rigid anti-inflation policy undoubtedly had greater common ground with Willes's policy preferences than with 1970s Keynesian economics, this rebuilding phase did

Macroeconomics and monetary policy 45

not lead to a breakthrough for rational expectations theory at the Fed either. To quote Meltzer again,

> Volcker did not take seriously the rational expectations claim that expectations would adjust quickly to his policy actions. . . . Both money growth and interest rates were highly variable, so it was difficult to hold firm expectations about future policy.
>
> (Meltzer, 2010, p. 1063)

Volcker acted as a technocrat as well as a pragmatist: "At the Fed, Volcker wasn't worrying about models. He was exercising the Fed's monetary muscle, raising interest rates to double-digit levels to bring down inflation at the cost of a severe recession" (Wessel, 2009, p. 72f.).

To get as much public attention as possible, Volcker chose not only to tighten monetary policy, but also to announce a fundamental change in policy. He used the label "monetarism" (targeting the money supply), which Friedman as one of the most prominent public critics invoked against the Fed, as a powerful signifier for the policy shift: Instead of halting inflation just by raising interest rates aggressively, "Volcker decreed that the Fed would henceforth target the supply of money in the banking system – he would switch from manipulating the price of credit to policing the quantity of it" (Mallaby, 2016, p. 232). The choice to announce a shift to an allegedly monetarist strategy reflects what the FOMC thought it had as room for maneuver under the given political circumstances and the power structure in the committee itself, not a confession to the academic paradigm. As Lindsey et al. (2013, p. 536) declare,

> The available record does not suggest that the FOMC was converted to monetarist ideology. The monetarist experiment of October 1979 was not really monetarist! Rather, the new techniques were conditionally adopted for pragmatic reasons – there was a good chance that they would succeed in restoring stability.

The decision to target the money supply in the October meeting was certainly not challenged by the Keynesians in the committee – they were just as helpless confronted with the phenomenon of stagflation, an occurrence that should have been impossible according to Keynesian thought.

This pragmatic turn to practical monetarism can be understood as a strategy to signal to public that the Fed was finally taking radical measures against soaring inflation (c.f. Mallaby, 2016, p. 232). Volcker represented to the outside that the new strategy was a long-term one (Axilrod, 2013, p. 79). On the inside, he urged the suspension of adverse inflation expectations to justify the policy shift (c.f. Hetzel, 2008, p. 150). He and the other members often used the term in the meetings of the FOMC. Practical monetarism was aimed at changing the "explosive inflationary psychology" (Balles, president Federal Reserve Bank of San Francisco, October 6, 1979, p. 16) that high inflation was a permanent feature of the economy: "We're going to have to break that psychology" (Teeters, Board of Governors, November 20, 1979, p. 24). It can be assumed that Volcker's emphasis on inflation expectations was less inspired by new classical macroeconomics than by an everyday philosophy of "market psychology" of economic actors, based on his experience at the trading desk at the New York Fed (see Volcker in Mehrling, 2007, p. 171). Therefore, practical monetarism did not follow the expectations of economic actors as new classical macroeconomics suggested but tried to shape the perception of what monetary policy is doing – with a highly uncertain outcome:

> There has been a great deal of discussion about the money supply and the feeling that so much of this psychology is related to the fact that the money supply is out of control. That's the comment we hear all the time. The virtue of a new approach, if it has one, is that we are accepting – with all its risks and dangers – more of a focus on the money supply.
>
> (Volcker, October 6, 1979, p. 15)[15]

Practical monetarism led to ambivalent results: On technical terms, the FOMC did not succeed in estimating the correct growth of the money supply. Therefore, it terminated the experiment in 1982 (c.f. Meltzer, 2010, p. 1229). However, on ideological terms, it was part of the broader shift to neoliberal politics that began in the late 1970s:

> [T]here is no doubt that the global ideological climate changed significantly, the Fed being part of these developments: For instance, from August 1979 onwards, until December 2008, the FOMC made no longer any references to employment in its policy directives, focusing exclusively on price-level stability.
>
> (Thornton, 2012, p. 117)

Ultimately, it was not a choice that followed academic recommendations and certainly not a technical precision coming along targeting the money supply that justified pursuing the overarching goal of monetarism – fighting inflation – but the economic and discursive success of monetary policy under Volcker.[16] It spread the impression that central banks can successfully intervene if they are independent and can fight inflation without instigating a recession (c.f. Goodfriend, 2007, p. 53). The new agenda, later supported by the conservative Reagan administration, "tipped America's balance of power much more in favor of those with dollars and against those with only votes" (Johnson, 1998, p. 147). Central banking – as it was framed from now on – should stay away from any attempts to support aggregate demand and a global management of the economy and should only care about keeping inflation low. Ironically, the success of the policy experiment that was called practical monetarism opened the doors for the successive paradigm of new classical macroeconomics that placed greater emphasis on the possible effects of monetary policy: new Keynesian economics.

4 Discussion: monetary policy making and academic macroeconomics as autonomous domains of knowledge and power

Our case studies show that the dissemination of academic macroeconomic ideas did not work in a straightforward way. What is convincing on planet academia does not have to be necessarily cogent for the practitioners in central banks. The failed intervention of Mark Willes reveals that even thorough local research and an aggressive propagation of the superiority of the paradigm did not nudge the committee into acknowledging its alleged benefits. The case reveals that new classical macroeconomics at that time was not prepared to fulfill the practical needs of the FOMC to work with models that suit and support the deliberation and decision-making process in the committee. In contrast, the implementation of practical monetarism demonstrates that the economic paradigm was used only in a pragmatic and selective manner by central bankers as part of their communication strategies as well as their operating procedures. It did not imply that central bankers necessarily stuck to the technical and ideological details of the respective paradigm.

The cases principally show that, even though academic macroeconomics and monetary policy have a strong connection, they have to be characterized as autonomous domains of knowledge and power. This is foremost due to the different problems the actors have to solve in both domains and the related distinct epistemic cultures. To put it bluntly: Macroeconomists have to construct parsimonious models as artificial worlds that can claim scientific validity regarding the rigid rules in the academic domain (see Morgan, 2012). Solutions for monetary policy coming from macroeconomists, therefore, can be quite monocausal and reductionist. A crucial point is that macroeconomists do not have to care about the practical implementation of monetary policy. In contrast, central bankers in the Fed have to make decisions about monetary policy that can be realized with the available instruments and legitimized to the public and Congress. Therefore, they draw on a plethora of different kinds of information and knowledge – the more, the better, not on models and their outcomes alone. Also, macroeconomic knowledge has to be translated into a practicable format the FOMC can use to make a decision confronting the complexity of the real-world economy. The transformations of knowledge in the FOMC proceed more incrementally than the scientific revolutions in macroeconomics (c.f. Sparsam & Pahl, forthcoming).

The cases suggest that the organizational structure of the Fed permits it to focus on specific macroeconomic paradigms in the districts, but that the FOMC is hierarchically superior in its routine as well as its rationale for decision making. It holds the prerogative of interpretation of the economic situation and the adequacy of actions the Fed can take, and this is interestingly based in the tenet that macroeconomic paradigms must not override the autonomy of the deliberations in the FOMC (c.f. Blinder, 1998, p. 7). This autonomy is partially based on the role of the chair "as an agenda setter and as a consensus builder" (McGregor & Young, 2014, p. 169). They have to channel the individual preferences and lead the meetings to a decision, with the relative freedom to divert the agenda of the meeting (and possibly taking the blame for a bad decision). But it is also established in a persistent organizational routine: The structure of the meetings of the FOMC has not substantially changed from the 1970s to today. The meetings guarantee that every participant has the freedom to say whatever they think is important, but that a decision can be made even if preferences diverge substantially.

The autonomy of monetary policy even stays intact in times of a tighter relation between both domains. As is well known today, some of the theoretical standards as well as some of the policy recommendations from new classical macroeconomics were established since the 1990s. This influence occurred mainly through the mediation of new Keynesian economics, a paradigm that merged some ideas of new classical macroeconomics with features of the older Keynesian economics. Leading figures in the Fed, most notably Ben Bernanke and Janet Yellen, had some affinity for new Keynesian economics. Before becoming chairs, both already had significant influence on the Federal Reserve System: Bernanke as member of the Academic Advisory Panel of the New York Fed, and Yellen as member of the Board of Governors. Since 1995, the FOMC has increasingly discussed inflation targeting, the new Keynesian variant of a rule-based monetary policy that explicitly includes the formation of expectations by market actors in order to achieve monetary policy goals (cf. Gavin, 1996). Concerning models, new Keynesian discourse first enters the FOMC in 1996, when the FRB/US model was introduced. Although still in the tradition of older Keynesian models, it is already altered by new Keynesian specifications. But the aforementioned also applies in these cases: The extreme approach of the new classical economists has not fully removed Keynesian stabilization policies from the agenda of the central banks and presumably never will in an absolute fashion. To blame new Keynesian economics for the crisis denies the autonomy of the domains of knowledge and power that central banks are. Instead of searching for technical similarities between both domains, it would be more fruitful to see if their modes of operation are different – maybe even opposed – variants of a pro-market belief system.

Notes

1 This chapter is based on the research project "From Modelling to Governance." In the project we analyzed the verbatim transcripts of the meetings of the Federal Open Market Committee (FOMC). The meetings of the FOMC are taped and transcribed afterwards. Since 1994 the transcripts are available to the public with a lag of five years (online: www.federalreserve.gov/monetarypolicy/fomc_historical_year.htm). The transcripts document the entire official proceedings of each of the FOMC's eight annual meetings and comprise around 60 to 120 pages. Our main focus was the problem of

Macroeconomics and monetary policy　49

how the committee refers to macroeconomic ideas and econometric models for deliberating and deciding on monetary policy. Our approach is based on grounded theory analysis (Corbin & Strauss, 2008). It was chosen because our analysis does not aim at the mere identification of economics terms or aspects of knowledge from academic macroeconomics but at the specific utilization of this knowledge in the FOMC, also considering ambivalences, translations, or the like. We explicitly do not offer a rational reconstruction of the FOMC's decision-making process (as most economic analyses do, e.g. Romer & Romer, 2002; Chappell et al., 2005) but an interpretative reconstruction of knowledge production in the committee. The project was supported by the Bundesministerium für Bildung und Forschung [Federal Ministry of Education and Research] of Germany under Grant 01UF1503.

2　See the extensive case study in Sparsam and Pahl (forthcoming) for an in-depth microsociological analysis of the FOMC's knowledge culture.

3　Two qualifications have to be made: First, it is beyond the scope of this chapter to introduce the respective economic schools of thought that are of relevance for the development of macroeconomics in detail. One may refer here to the pertinent nontechnical literature (e.g. Snowdon & Vane, 2005; De Vroey, 2016). Second, as we focus on knowledge utilization in central banks, we limit our discussion to aspects that can be shown empirically, avoiding too much guesswork. It is our aim to contest accounts that suggest causal and too straightforward linkages between academic economic ideas and practical monetary policy without looking at the level of concrete deliberations.

4　"Funding for rational expectations research rose rapidly in the late seventies as support for large-scale macromodels declined" (Newlon, 1989, p. 207).

5　See also Mishkin's (1995, p. 3) assessment: "The rational expectations paradigm was then wholeheartedly adopted by the research staff of the Federal Reserve Bank of Minneapolis, who then became the most active advocates for rational expectations within the Federal Reserve System."

6　Wallace, together with Thomas Sargent (1976), proposed that considering rational expectations in Lucas's sense, policy can have no systematic effect on the economy.

7　This paper was only published in 1976 but was made available earlier as a draft.

8　"Federal Reserve Bank presidents give many speeches and author policy-oriented articles that receive wide attention and sometimes advocate policy positions opposed by the Fed chairman and/or a majority of FOMC members" (Wheelock, 2000, p. 267).

9　See Willes (1979) as an example for promoting the policy assumptions of rational expectations, including a very polemical stance towards Keynesian economics.

10　Chappell et al. (2005, p. 82f.) offer the following details: "[H]e did vote at eleven meetings and cast dissenting votes six times. As we have noted, a dissent frequency of this magnitude is unusual."

11　Willes often played the role of the dissenter in the committee quite dramatically: "My wife made me promise that I would be more agreeable in the new year, so I would like to say that I agree with everything that has been said. I'd like to say it, but the fact is that I don't agree" (January 8, 1980).

12　The following discussion is limited to selected empirical evidence. It is beyond the scope of this chapter to present a full-fledged account of the style and procedure of FOMC deliberations. See the aforementioned paper by Sparsam and Pahl (forthcoming) for such an account. We are citing from the transcripts of the FOMC stating name, position first time the name occurs, date of the meeting, and page of the transcript. Remarks in square brackets are in the original; our own additions are denoted with [★].

13　Interpreting this passage requires keeping in mind that the staff usually replies approbatively to inquiries of the members of the FOMC.

14　In early 1979, under chairman Miller, the FOMC showed serious signs of disunity, ultimately leading to the chairman's dismissal (see Bailey & Schonhardt-Bailey, 2008).

15　The necessary operations coming along with practical monetarism were very vague for the FOMC. The staff of the FOMC had to answer a lot of technical questions in the

50 *Jan Sparsam and Hanno Pahl*

beginning (see especially the transcript of January 8 and 9, 1980). Quite uncommon, the meetings turned into events to acquire basic knowledge in technical terms.

16 After a peak in the rate of inflation in 1980, it steadily declined (see Goodfriend & King, 2005, pp. 982–983).

References

Accocella, N., Di Bartolomeo, G., & Hughes Hallet, A. (2016). *Macroeconomic Paradigms and Economic Policy: From the Great Depression to the Great Recession.* Cambridge: Cambridge University Press.

Axilrod, S. H. (2013). *The Federal Reserve: What Everyone Needs to Know.* Oxford: Oxford University Press.

Bailey, A., & Schonhardt-Bailey, C. (2008). Does Deliberation Matter in FOMC Monetary Policymaking? The Volcker Revolution in 1979. In: *Political Analysis,* 16 (4), 404–427.

Blinder, A. S. (1998). *Central Banking in Theory and Practice. Lionel Robbins Lectures.* Cambridge, MA: MIT Press.

Borio, C. (2012). *The Financial Cycle and Macroeconomics: What Have We Learnt?* (BIS Working Papers, 395). www.bis.org/publ/work395.pdf.

Chappell, H. W., McGregor, R. R., & Vermilyea, T. (2005). *Committee Decisions on Monetary Policy. Evidence from Historical Records of the Federal Open Market Committee.* Cambridge, MA: MIT Press.

Corbin, J., & Strauss, A. (2008). *Basics of Qualitative Research. Techniques and Procedures for Developing Grounded Theory.* Thousand Oaks: Sage Publications.

De Long, B. (2000). The Triumph of Monetarism? In: *Journal of Economic Perspectives,* 14 (1), 83–94.

Gavin, W. T. (1996). The FOMC in 1995: A Step Closer to Inflation Targeting? In: *Federal Reserve Bank of St. Louis Review,* September–October. https://files.stlouisfed.org/files/htdocs/publications/review/96/09/9609wg.pdf.

Goodfriend, M. (2007). How the World Achieved Consensus on Monetary Policy. In: *Journal of Economic Perspectives,* 21 (4), 47–68.

Goodfriend, M., & King, R. G. (2005). The Incredible Volcker Disinflation. In: *Journal of Monetary Economics,* 52 (5), 981–1015.

Grabel, I. (2000). The Political Economy of 'Policy Credibility': The New-Classical Macroeconomics and the Remaking of Emerging Economies. In: *Cambridge Journal of Economics,* 24 (1), 1–19.

Hafer, R. W. (2005): *The Federal Reserve System. An Encyclopedia.* Westport, CT: Greenwood Press.

Hafer, R. W., & Wheelock, D. C. (2001). The Rise and Fall of a Policy Rule: Monetarism at the St. Louis Fed, 1968–1986. In: *Federal Reserve Bank of St. Louis Review,* January–February, 1–24. https://research.stlouisfed.org/publications/review/01/0101rh.pdf.

Hetzel, R. L. (2008). *The Monetary Policy of the Federal Reserve: A History. Studies in Macroeconomic History.* Cambridge and New York: Cambridge University Press.

Hoover, K. D. (1992). The Rational Expectations Revolution: An Assessment. In: *Cato Journal,* 12 (1), 81–106.

Hoover, K. D. (2007). A History of Postwar Monetary Economics and Macroeconomics. In: W. J. Samuels, J. Biddle, & J. B. Davis (Eds.): *A companion to the History of Economic Thought.* Malden, MA: Blackwell, 411–427.

Hoover, K. D., & Young, W. (2011). Rational Expectations: Retrospect and Prospect. A Panel Discussion with Michael Lovell, Robert Lucas, Dale Mortensen, Robert Shiller,

Macroeconomics and monetary policy   51

Neil Wallace. Moderated by Kevin Hoover and Warren Young. (*CHOPE Working Paper*, 2011–10). www.dklevine.com/archive/refs4786969000000000227.pdf.

Johnson, Peter A. (1998). *The Government of Money: Monetarism in Germany and the United States*. Ithaca and London: Cornell University Press.

Knorr Cetina, K. D. (1981). *The Manufacture of Knowledge. An Essay on the Constructivist and Contextual Nature of Science*. Oxford: Pergamon Press.

Kydland, F. E., & Prescott, E. C. (1982). Time to Build and Aggregate Fluctuations. In: *Econometrica*, 50 (6), 1345–1370.

Leijonhufvud, A. (2009). *Macroeconomics and the Crisis: A Personal Appraisal* (ARC 2009 Opening Lecture, Crisis and Reform, Brussels). http://ec.europa.eu/economy_finance/events/2009/20091015/0-leijonhufvud_en.pdf.

Lindsey, D. E., Orphanides, A., & Rasche, R. H. (2013). The Reform of October 1979: How It Happened and Why. In: *Federal Reserve Bank of St. Louis Review*, November–December, 487–542.

Lucas, R. E., & Sargent, T. J. (1979). After Keynesian Macroeconomics. In: *Federal Reserve Bank of Minneapolis Quarterly Review*, 3 (2), 1–16.

MacLaury, B. K. (1992). Interview with Bruce K. MacLaury. Interview conducted by James E. Fogerty. www.minneapolisfed.org/about/more-about-the-fed/history-of-the-fed/interview-with-bruce-k-maclaury.

Mallaby, S. (2016). *The Man Who Knew. The Life and Times of Alan Greenspan*. London: Bloomsbury Publishing.

McGregor, R. R., & Young, W. (2014). Federal Reserve Bank Presidents as Public Intellectuals. In: *History of Political Economy*, 45 (Supplement 1), 166–190.

Mehrling, P. (2007). An Interview with Paul A. Volcker. In: P. A. Samuelson & W. A. Barnett (Eds.): *Inside the Economists Mind: The History of Modern Economic Thought, as Explained by Those Who Produced It*. Malden, MA: Blackwell, 165–191.

Meltzer, A. H. (2010). *A History of the Federal Reserve*. Volume 2, Book 2, 1970–1986. Chicago: University of Chicago Press.

Meulendyke, A.-M. (1998). *U.S. Monetary Policy and Financial Markets*. New York: Federal Reserve Bank of New York.

Mishkin, F. S. (1995). The Rational Expectations Revolution: A Review Article of: Preston J. Miller, Ed.: The Rational Expectations Revolution, Readings from the Front Line (*NBER Working Paper Series*, 5043). www.nber.org/papers/w5043.pdf.

Morgan, M. S. (2012). *The World in the Model. How Economists Work and Think*. Cambridge: Cambridge University Press.

Muench, T., & Wallace, N. (1974). On Stabilization Policy: Goals and Models. In: *The American Economic Review*, 64 (2), 330–337.

Newlon, D. H. (1989). The Role of the NSF in the Spread of Economic Ideas. In: D. Colander & A. Coats (Eds.): *The Spread of Economic Ideas*. Cambridge: Cambridge University Press, 195–228.

Romer, C. D., & Romer, D. H. (2002). The Evolution of Economic Understanding and Postwar Stabilization Policy. In: Federal Reserve Bank of Kansas (Ed.): *Proceedings – Economic Policy Symposium – Jackson Hole*. Kansas: Federal Reserve Bank of Kansas, 11–78.

Sargent, T. J. (1995). *Adaptation of Macro Theory to Rational Expectations* (Manuscript). http://minneapolisfed.contentdm.oclc.org/cdm/ref/collection/p16030coll1/id/32.

Sargent, T. J., & Wallace, N. (1976). Rational Expectations and the Theory of Economic Policy. In: *Journal of Monetary Economics*, 2 (2), 169–183.

Silber, W. L. (2012). *Volcker. The Triumph of Persistence*. New York: Bloomsbury Press.

52   *Jan Sparsam and Hanno Pahl*

Snowdon, B., & Vane, H. R. (2005). *Modern Macroeconomics. Its Origins, Development and Current State*. Cheltenham, UK and Northampton, MA: E. Elgar.

Sparsam, J., Nies, S., & Pahl, H. (2017). Der Aufstieg der New Classical Macroeconomics: Zum (un-)gleich-zeitigen Wandel von Steuerungsparadigmen in der Makroökonomik und in Zentralbanken. In: S. Lessenich (Ed.): *Geschlossene Gesellschaften. Verhandlungen des 38. Kongresses der Deutschen Gesellschaft für Soziologie in Bamberg 2016*. http://publika tionen.soziologie.de/index.php/kongressband_2016.

Sparsam, J., & Pahl, H. (2018). Soziologie der Zentralbanken. Makroökonomisches Wissen und Geldpolitik. In: C. Trampusch & J. Beyer (Eds.): *Finanzmarkt, Demokratie und Gesellschaft. 58. Sonderheft der Kölner Zeitschrift für Soziologie und Sozialpsychologie*. Wiesbaden: Springer VS, 343–366.

Sparsam, J., & Pahl, H. (forthcoming). *Central Banking as Scenario Building: The Utilization of Macroeconomic Knowledge in the Federal Open Market Committee* (Manuscript, under review).

Thornton, D. L. (2012). The Dual Mandate: Has the Fed Changed Its Objective? In: *Federal Reserve Bank of St. Louis Review*, 94 (2), 117–133.

Vroey, M. de (2016). *A History of Macroeconomics from Keynes to Lucas and Beyond*. New York: Cambridge University Press.

Wessel, D. (2009). *In Fed We Trust. Ben Bernanke's War on the Great Panic*. New York: Crown Business.

Wheelock, D. C. (2000). National Monetary Policy by Regional Design: The Evolving Role of the Federal Reserve Banks in Federal Reserve System Policy. In: J. von Hagen & C. J. Waller (Eds.): *Regional Aspects of Monetary Policy in Europe*. New York: Springer Science and Business Media, 241–274.

Willes, M. H. (1979). *Rational Expectations as a Counterrevolution*. Manuscript. https://fraser. stlouisfed.org/title/?id=1115#!1480.

Willes, M. H. (1992). *Interview with Mark H Willes, President of the Federal Reserve Bank of Minneapolis, 1977–1980*. Interview conducted by James E. Fogerty, Minnesota Historical Society. December 8, 1992. www.minneapolisfed.org/about/more-about-the-fed/ history-of-the-fed/interview-with-mark-h-willes.

Woodford, M. (2009). Convergence in Macroeconomics: Elements of the New Synthesis. In: *American Economic Journal*, 1 (1), 267–279.

4 The power of economics textbooks
Shaping meaning and identity

Lukas Bäuerle

1 Introduction

According to Gregory Mankiw, Mark Taylor and other important textbook authors in economics, any economic question can be subsumed under one of the following questions: (a) What is being produced? (b) How? (c) For whom? (Mankiw/Taylor 2014, 1; Samuelson/Nordhaus 2010, 7–8; Schiller 2008, 2, 12). Irrespective of the further elaboration upon these key economic problems, it seems remarkable that the 'Why?' of economic production is ignored within this set of questions. Hence, the specific *meaning* of economic production has to remain disregarded in the mentioned textbook literature.

Against this background, it becomes plausible that economic science does not foster a reflection upon *its own* existence and meaning either. At least in the context of higher education, future economists do not typically become confronted with reflexive subjects, such as the philosophy, history or methodology of their discipline. That is to say that although students become highly involved with the curriculums' requirements, the reason and deeper meaning of these requirements remain unquestioned. This void certainly leaves open self-reflexive questions concerning the identity of future economists themselves as well. In other words, the question 'Why study economics?' bears a strong connection to a second question, 'Who do I become by studying economics?' and both typically remain unaddressed.

This chapter aims at making sense of economics, concentrating on economic education and more specifically on economics textbooks. As will be shown, the discipline's most important textbooks do contain answers to both questions – although in most cases only posed implicitly and generally without any further elaborations. The explication of these answers is the main task of this chapter. I did not ask for *possible* meanings and identity offerings but rather collected, typified and elaborated upon fragments of economics textbook literature that correspond to the questions posed.

To this end I worked with means of the sociology of knowledge approach to discourse (SKAD) (Keller 2011a, 2011b). The specific subjects of analysis were (1) fundamental frames (*Deutungsmuster*) of economics textbooks relating to the question 'Why study economics?' and furthermore (2) subject positions

DOI: 10.4324/9780367817084-5

54   *Lukas Bäuerle*

or identity offerings that bear answers to the question of 'Who do I become by studying economics?' By focusing on the deep layers producing meaning in the economics textbooks discourse I strike up with sociology of knowledge and linguistic research of economics (see a review of the literature in Maesse 2013, chap. 4). Pioneering but rare contributions to a discourse analysis of economics textbook literature do exist with Klamer (1990), Pahl (2011), Zuidhof (2014), Graupe (2019), Graupe/Steffestun (2018), and Maesse (2019), but none address the fundamental motivational frame ('Why study economics?') and related identity offerings as analyzed in this chapter.

The analysis showed that the textbook discourse offers three different rationales in order to cope with the discipline's meaning, all of them bringing along subject positions, offering concepts to the students to identify with. Every frame and identity offering could be found in at least three of the overall eight cases taken into account. Alongside a scientifically orientated frame centered on the term 'truth' (section 3), there could also be reconstructed a second frame focusing on the pecuniary return of studying economics (section 4). A last frame offers a sense of self-empowerment for the student, integrating the former cases to a coherent and obligatory identity option (section 5). After having reconstructed frames and identity offerings from the empirical material, I will contextualize each of them theoretically. To begin, I will sketch out the economics textbook discourse and the dimensions of the analysis.

2 The economics textbook discourse

2.1 Overview

Academic economic education reveals an enormous degree of standardization in form and content across institutional and national borders (Graupe 2019). Regarding content, economics textbooks almost exclusively introduce students to a fixed and narrow corpus of theoretical and methodological considerations, mostly identified with neoclassical theory (Fullbrook 2009, 18 f.). Hence, the textbook discourse normally does not contain any discourse coalitions, insofar as it presents itself as a univocal discourse lacking any opposition. Furthermore, the structural and didactical design of economics textbooks rarely differs from one another (Smith 2000, 42–44). Nevertheless, for my analysis I chose the following eight international textbooks that could be identified as most influential in terms of market shares (Lopus/Paringer 2012), sales probability on amazon. com (Zuidhof 2014, 159), historical impact and number of editions.

The heavily standardized aspect of economics textbooks can be linked to the fact that the genre itself was developed around the 'archetype' of Paul A. Samuelson's *Economics* (first published in 1948) during the course of the second half of the 20th century (Klamer 1990, 130; Gottesman/Ramrattan/Szenberg 2005, 98, 101). Following its subsequent translation into over 40 languages (Skousen 1997, 137), it became the self-declared "international benchmark of macro- and microeconomics". Concerning market shares, it was topped by Campbell McConnell's *Economics* during the 1970s (Elzinga 1992, 874). A third and today predominant textbook author is Gregory Mankiw (2015: *Principles of Economics*[1]). By 2012 the textbooks by McConnell (now publishing together with Stanley Brue and Sean Flynn) and Mankiw together held 40% of the market share for English language introductory economics textbook literature (Lopus/Paringer 2012, 298). For these reasons the three textbooks may qualify as 'key documents' within the discourse of introductory economics textbooks.[2] Based on the aforementioned criteria, the following five textbooks could also be identified as dominant: Miller (2012): *Economics Today*; Schiller (2008): *The Economy Today*; Gwartney et al. (2006): *Economics: Private and Public Choice*; Krugman/Wells (2015): *Economics*; and Frank/Bernanke/Johnston (2013): *Principles of Economics*.

2.2 Introduction of the economics textbook discourse

Two aspects of the economics textbook discourse shall be pointed out here regarding its context and reach: firstly, it can be identified as a specialized *scientific* discourse that not only addresses beginners but furthermore lays out a paradigmatic ground on which subsequent levels of training and finally the discipline as a whole relies on. In the context of a typical Kuhnian 'textbook science', the economics textbook discourse can be attributed to a fundamental function for the discipline's coherent development. So while first-year students can be called its narrow academic audience, the discipline as a whole can be called as the discourse's wider academic audience.

Secondly, it can be labelled a *semi-public* if not *public* discourse insofar as it not only addresses future or present economists but a wide range of all kinds of academics. Pahl (2011, 369) estimates that other-than-economics students in academic US introductory economics courses outnumber 'purely' economics students by a factor of 50. Hence, the discourse reaches an audience far beyond the discipline's borders. This also accounts for economics graduates, who exert a significant impact on non-scientific discourses, e.g. in politics or media (Christensen 2017). Taken together, the reach of fundamentals in economics clearly goes beyond the discipline's borders, insofar as "theoretical ideas or models, expert interpretations of reality respectively seep into common knowledge of individuals, thereby shaping their actions more or less pragmatically" (Keller 2011a, 183; transl. by the author). The knowledge resources of this highly standardized and institutionalized discourse can be assumed at least in present public economy-related discourses. In this sense, the economics textbook could be labelled as *public mass media*.

Despite this reach of the economics textbook discourse, the modes and means of its production remain widely uncertain. This can partly be explained by referring to the powerful position of only four major remaining publishers that do not publish any detailed information regarding the history and production of their textbooks.[3] Furthermore, economics textbook research so far mostly concentrates on its *contents* (e.g. Aslanbeigui/Naples 1996), thereby

56 *Lukas Bäuerle*

leaving (political, institutional or economical) questions of discourse *production* uncovered. Recent network analysis (Giraud 2014) and a brief review of the acknowledgements of the textbook literature mentioned indicate that this discourse is not being established merely by textbook authors alone but by a rather large network of actors from within and outside the academic sphere.

2.3 Method and research strategy

This chapter continues to ignore the "personnel of discourse production" (Keller 2013, 38; transl. by the author) and its "institutional infrastructures" (ibid.) but focuses on rarely analyzed frames that relate to either of the central questions of this discourse analysis: 'Why study economics?' and 'Who do I become by studying economics?'[4] These questions were addressed in the introductory chapters[5] of the selected textbooks.

A frame is a discursive element that "depicts fundamental meaning and action-generating schemata, which are circulated through discourses and make it possible to understand what a phenomenon is all about" (Keller 2011b, 57). The German term *Deutungsmuster* points out that frames refer to typical and constitutive layers of a discourse. The analysis pursued in this article at first focused on the frame giving meaning to the entire context of economics textbooks – hence, economics education – as such. Why would this study program be of any interest? What do the textbooks promise their readers in terms of meaningful ends of studying them? Secondly, the analysis aimed at reconstructing subject positions or identity offerings presented to textbook readers. They "depict positioning processes and 'patterns of subjectivation' which are generated in discourses and which refer to (fields of) addressees. Technologies of the self are understood as exemplary elaborated, applicable and available instructions for subjectivation" (Keller 2011b, 55). Hence, identity offerings may introduce and guide a transformation of self-understanding of the addressees. As will be shown, frames and identity offerings bear a close relationship within this sample: with every frame there goes along a certain subject position that corresponds to a meaningful study of economics. The link between frames and identity offerings therefore is always being elaborated conjunctively.

My analysis consisted of a continuous questioning on a sentence-to-sentence basis of the sample given with the two questions at hand. What could one learn about the aim of studying economics (or the self one could become) from every single sentence of the sample? In doing so, not only the 'What?' of given answers but also the characteristics of the 'How?' of their introduction were noted. For instance, where frames and identity options alike were introduced in antagonistic ways, the analysis also considered the relatedness of 'positive' frames to their 'negative' counterparts (as indicated in both sections 3 and 5). Where no connection at all could be established between sentences and questions, these non-answers were not further progressed in the analysis. All of the reconstructed answers were subsequently subjected to a comparative analysis, aiming at typifiable 'meta-answers' bearing fundamental similarities in terms of addressing the two questions posed (as reflected in the headings of the three following sections). It was only after this empirical part of the research that possible theoretical interpretation schemes were taken into account in order to saturate and contextualize the findings.

2.4 The power of economics textbooks

It is precisely the already mentioned interrelatedness of meaningful frames and identity options offered where I locate the specific power and influence of economists in the given example. By classifying the 'Why?' and 'Who?' (along with other questions concerning the 'What?' or 'How?', for instance) of economic reasoning and practice, introductory textbooks set the field of relevant knowledge that possibly becomes the 'intellectual infrastructure' of students. The magnitude of this power grows with the opaqueness or even absence of the explicit formulation of the aforementioned questions and answers to the questions alike. If overtaken and embodied uncritically by students, frames and identity options gain an influence that reaches, as mentioned, presumably far beyond the academic field (for the theoretical foundations of this understanding of power see section 5).

3 First frame: learn the truth!

Why study economics? In the seventh edition of his *Principles of Economics*, Gregory Mankiw devotes the entire preface to this question of a possible meaning of studying the subject:

> Why should you, as a student at the beginning of the 21st century, embark on the study of economics? There are three reasons.
>
> The first reason to study economics is that it will help you *understand the world in which you live*. . . . The second reason to study economics is that it will make you a *more astute participant in the economy*. . . . The third reason to study economics is that it will give you a better understanding of both the potential and the limits of economic policy. *Economic questions are always on the minds of policymakers in mayors' offices, governors' mansions, and the White House.*
>
> (Mankiw 2015, xi; emphasis added)

The discussion of 'economics principles' is being introduced as inevitable for someone who (1) wants to understand 'the world', (2) is an active participant of the economy and finally (3) is a policymaker in this (economic) world. Although Mankiw introduces a plurality of identities to which the study of economics seems suitable,[6] he limits the reason for this manifold suitability to only one: "principles of economics can be applied in many of life's situations" (ibid.). In other words, 'principles of economics' take effect on any level of

58   *Lukas Bäuerle*

human engagement. Therefore knowing them will be relevant for any participant of society irrespective of her special purpose.

Samuelson/Nordhaus consistently and most clearly limit the reasons to engage with their textbook to only one: "as we have come to realize, there is one overriding reason to learn the basic lessons of economics: All your life – from cradle to grave and beyond – you will run up against the brutal truths of economics" (Samuelson/Nordhaus 2010, 3). And furthermore: "Of course, studying economics will not make you a genius. But without economics the dice of life are loaded against you" (ibid.). Irrespective of time and space, 'brutal truths of economics' constitute the inevitable foundation of human action. In the most distinctive situations of their lives, people find themselves confronted with a sphere of truths they can ignore or forget but which under any circumstances will never cease to exist. Paralleled by the natural laws known to natural scientists, the social domain is controlled by economic laws known to the economist (Frank/Bernanke/Johnston 2013, 7). Any decision we take in life is in fact a "calculation of costs and benefits" (ibid.). Knowing the laws that govern these calculations will therefore yield a significant advantage in tackling daily life. By referring to another natural science (biology) a few pages later, Frank/Bernanke/Johnston introduce a specific subject that possesses this kind of knowledge about the fundamental aspects of 'human existence':

> Learning a few simple economic principles . . . enables us to see the mundane details of ordinary human existence in a new light. Whereas the uninitiated often fail even to notice these details, the economic naturalist not only sees them, but becomes actively engaged in the attempt to understand them.
>
> (ibid., 17)

The 'economic naturalist' is a figure that knows about economic principles or at least tries to 'understand' them. This figure is to be sharply contrasted to the 'uninitiated', who is not able to notice the 'mundane details of human existence'. Along with the introduction of a sphere of economic laws or principles, all of the cited textbooks introduce specific subject positions that correspond to these laws. The genuine feature of these figures consists in *knowing* economic laws or principles. As seen in the last quotation, this knowledge constitutes a figure or even a group: it is the economist or the discipline of economics that governs and preserves the specific type of knowledge. This figure and group are, as in this case, often sharply separated from the non-knowers, the 'uninitiated'. In obtaining the decisive knowledge and thereby becoming an economist consists the first meaning of studying economics.

In his lectures on the 'Birth of Biopolitics' (1978–79), Michel Foucault carved out that a hidden world of laws governing human action served as the ultimate legitimizing foundation of a *science* called 'political economy'. In the early stages of this new science in late 18th century, economists suggested themselves as advisers to and constrainers of governments. Their actions and decisions, the former claimed, were limited by laws, binding and undeceivable in character. Upon these laws economists developed a field of knowledge that – from then on – came to be the primary domain and resource of economic science (Foucault 2010 [1978–79], 15–16).

Political economy knows a second sphere behind or underneath anything called 'governmental action' by which the latter is determined. One cannot see or touch this second sphere, but one can grasp it by the means and tools developed by economic scientists. In being able to grasp economic truth, economists were soon endowed with the capacity to distinguish right from wrong and, most precisely, right action from wrong action; 'right action' meaning that it corresponded to the fundamental laws it was bound up to (ibid.). Hence, truth became the central criterion of governmental action and the specific domain where this truth was continuously uncovered was the science of political economy.

Having developed to a state of textbook science, present economics still lives within this powerful and long-lasting self-conception. Today not only governments are offered economic knowledge and advice but, according to textbook authors, *anyone* seeking a fundamental understanding of human action can approach the laws of economics: "Generations of students, often to their surprise, have discovered how stimulating it is to look *beneath the surface* and understand the fundamental laws of economics" (Samuelson/Nordhaus 2010, 3; emphasis added).

The specific meaning of economic education, according to this frame, originates from the existence of economic laws that govern daily human action. It is a strong classificatory frame that discursively produces a sphere of phenomena. It profoundly changes the experience (and research) of reality: any daily experience is now predominated by a causal, law-like reason, which is valid independently from space and time (in China or the US, yesterday or tomorrow). Economists have discovered and studied these laws in a tradition lasting 250 years. The distilled core of this alleged knowledge is now being presented to students of the subject in the form of textbooks. Studying the textbook and the subject is meaningful since it promises insights into this knowledge. In the end, only 'the knowing' will be able to live a conscious and truthful life. And 'the knowing' are identified with the economists: only they possess this knowledge, whose acquisition marks the target of economic education.

4 Second frame: capitalize your education!

The second frame does not refer merely to the *contents* of economics textbooks but is also mirrored in their *forms* (their composition, design, etc.). In this respect it demonstrates a structural familiarity with other formal elements of contemporary economic education (curricular design, assessment modalities, etc.). In the following section, this dual character of the frame (content *and* form) will be elaborated upon by referring to explicit textbook quotes (and not, for example, by means of a structural analysis of the considered textbooks).

60 *Lukas Bäuerle*

To better understand the institutional roots of formal elements, this section also contains an excursus about the Bologna reform and its intellectual underpinning: human capital theory.

The textbook of Gwartney et al. contains a separate chapter called 'Economics as a Career' that nourishes the expectation of an annual income between US $75,000 and $90,000 for economics graduates (Gwartney et al. 2006, 2; see also Miller 2012, 2). According to this chapter, studying economics becomes meaningful due to its potentially high reimbursement measured in monetary income. The twin thought to this income-orientated perspective is more frequently found in textbooks: studying economics prevents negative income, that is costs. Schiller introduces this thought by closely referring to the daily decisions (and its omnipresent opportunity costs) of students:

> The more time you spend reading this book, the less time you have available for that alternative use of your time. The opportunity cost of reading this text is the best alternative use of your scarce time. . . . Hopefully, the benefits you get from studying will outweigh that cost. Otherwise this wouldn't be the best way to use your scarce time.
>
> (Schiller 2008, 6)

According to Schiller, in educational affairs, as well as in any other affairs, there exists the possibility to decide rationally[7] and unambiguously. This stems from the fact that educational decisions are governed by the same laws and truths that govern any other activity (see section 2). Since rational decisions are possible, and the economics curriculum is offering tools to thoughtfully realize such decisions, studying the subject will yield its payoff. Even more than that, anyone not applying economic tools and knowledge properly will not be using her time in 'the best way'. Hence, maximizing behavior is being elevated to the rank of a norm. According to this frame, the meaning of studying economics does not exhaust itself in the apprehension or understanding of economic knowledge, but in its *profitable application*. What is true for the engineering sciences is also true for economics: if the world is governed by (economic) laws that cannot be changed in space and time, one can at least work with them profitably.

But reading the textbook is not only profitable due to the valuable knowledge offered by it. In a broader sense it is profitable because textbooks themselves have been designed according to maximizing principles in the first place:

> Our textbook grew out of our conviction that students will learn far more if we attempt to cover much less. Our basic premise is that a small number of basic principles do most of the heavy lifting in economics, and that if we focus narrowly and repeatedly on those principles, students can actually master them in just a single semester.
>
> (Frank/Bernanke/Johnston 2013, vii)

The textbook of Frank/Bernanke/Johnston is efficient because it sticks to the most important lessons, therefore being able to convey the essential in less time. The field of economic education *itself* is being structured by a specific economic reasoning way beyond the contents of economics textbooks. For example, the production process of textbooks itself can be described as efficient (Pinto 2007, 108 ff.). Furthermore, the transfer of their knowledge is being supported by the supply of ready-to-use slide sets that do not have to be developed by the teachers, therefore gaining valuable time for research (Grimes 2009, 98). The economic order of the field also applies to its assessment modalities. The reason why economic education traditionally sticks to written multiple-choice exams is found in "cost considerations" (Becker 2000, 116). Consequentially, the cost factor – the magnitude of introductory courses – has itself been determined efficiently in the first place (Frank/Bernanke/Johnston 2013, 3–4). Students of economics learn that the educational setting they live and study in is being designed by the very same principles they get to know about in economics lectures. The study contents are being taught to the audience by referring to their own experiences in the educational context. The mode of discursive production, hence, conforms to the experiences made within the discursive setting and finally to the discursive contents. Forms and contents of economic education seem identical in character. Even more than that: the experiences of its form seem to *proof* the legitimacy of its contents.

This harmonization of economic forms and contents can certainly be contextualized if not explained by referring to the most popular economic theory about education: human capital theory.[8] The approach conceptualizes individuals as carriers and caretakers of their proper capital, which is formed by investing time and money in education, health, skills, etc. Do I opt for this or that study program? Does a bachelor's degree actually yield more income than a job training? Does it outweigh the costs to educate our child bilingually? Any decision individuals face on a daily basis can be brought down to only one single question: does the decision outcome yield an increase in income? Hence, human capital theory subsumes any educational consideration under the end of economic profitability. Thereby, human capital theorists implicitly state this one norm and imperative: 'Capitalize your education!' To put it in terms of this article: (economic) education is only meaningful if the educational process actually leads to increased future income. (Economic) education gains its legitimation in the economic profitability of the acquainted competences.

Human capital theory nowadays forms a core part of introductory economics literature.[9] Krugman/Wells describe the theory in a nutshell as follows: "Human capital is the improvement in labor created by education and knowledge that is embodied in the workforce" (Krugman/Wells 2015, 544). Gwartney et al. honor Gary Becker with an informational box ("outstanding economist") that highlights Becker's pioneering work in human capital theorizing (Gwartney et al. 2006, 532). Mankiw introduces the concept with direct

62   *Lukas Bäuerle*

reference to the educational context in which the student of economics gets to know about it:

> Education, training, and experience are less tangible than lathes, bull-dozers, and buildings, but human capital is like physical capital in many ways. . . . Producing human capital requires inputs in the form of teachers, libraries, and student time. Indeed, students can be viewed as 'workers' who have the important job of producing the human capital that will be used in future production.
>
> (Mankiw 2015, 530)

Students are addressed as 'workers' or 'producers' of their own capital stock, as human capitalists. Gwartney et al. explicitly remind their students of their being rational actors that face a cost/benefit trade-off when opting for different careers by stating, "A rational person will attend college only if the expected future benefits outweigh the current costs" (Gwartney et al. 2006, 532; see also Frank/Bernanke/Johnston 2013, 510).

The reconstruction of a second frame introduced by economics textbooks led us to a recapitulation of the structural context of contemporary higher education in Europe. From there, we came back to the economics profession and finally to economics textbooks by looking deeper into the theoretical background of the Bologna reform: human capital theory. What combines all of the considered discursive fragments is the subsumption of (economic) education under economic ends, understood as the maximization of pecuniary payoffs. Students of economics become acquainted with the frame of profitable studies not just through contents, but also by the forms of their training. Taking this correspondence of content and form seriously, the field could adequately be termed *economized economic education*. The corresponding identity offering to this frame is the 'entrepreneurial self' (Bröckling 2016), a rational subject that uses the economic rationale to invest in itself in order to finally capitalize these investments in terms of money. That this rationalizing is not just a *possible* (and indeed clever) way of thinking but actually the naturally embedded rationale of any subject is the final lesson of a third frame.

5 Third frame: become who you are!

Searching for the foundations of a capitalizing rationality in educational matters in section 4, we ended up in the very same science we started with: economics. From its beginning in the late 1950s onward, the theory carries along a decisive problem that shall finally lead to the clarification of a third frame found within the material.

The problem starts with the following early statement of human capital theorists: "Since it [human capital] becomes an integral part of a person, it cannot be bought or sold or treated as property under our institutions" (Schultz 1960, 571). An investment in this new sort of capital becomes inseparably 'embedded'

The power of economics textbooks   63

in a person. Hence, the investment is 'locked up' in that person and cannot be removed and sold again like physical capital (e.g. a machine). Third parties only dispose of this investment when living in a society that allows for slavery (this diagnosis is handed on in the textbook of Gwartney et al. 2006, 532). Ignoring the ethical implications of this problem, the main question for human capital theorizing can now be stated: Why should human beings invest in other human beings (or the youth of an entire country) if the legal context of this investment prohibits a direct disposition of it? This question is of enormous economic or, more specifically, entrepreneurial importance. The institutional constellation bears a gap of control for the investor (if he chooses not only to invest in himself). It is precisely this kind of gap − a lack of control − where Foucault locates questions of power. In the following section, I want to stress upon a frame found in economics textbooks that can be interpreted as 'textbook examples' of Foucauldian techniques and technologies of power.[10]

According to Foucault, power is foremost a *productive* phenomenon. It does not repress, exclude or censor, but it establishes spaces and rituals in which one can start living (see Foucault 1995 [1975], 194). For Foucault the most important of these spaces is the modern subject itself. The consideration of modern power phenomena for him is always constituted by the dispositif of selfhood: "Thus it is not power, but the subject, which is the general theme of my research" (Foucault 1983, 209). More specifically, Foucault's perspective focuses on the question of *production* of subjectivity (subjectivation). As he points out, this process starts with and relies upon a true knowledge of subjectivity: a knowledge of one's own truth, one's 'true character', 'true core', 'true nature', 'true self-image', 'true preferences' etc.

In section 3, we got to know economics as a science that presents itself as dedicated to eternal economic laws and truths. These truths and respective identity options now gain a productive character: they allow for specific and directive reference of subjects to themselves and the world around them. Powerful action is precisely the preconfiguration of these production processes of selfhood; it is 'action upon action'. An individual adopting given subject positions believes he is developing a genuine identity. Actually, she starts to govern herself on the basis of given options. Nevertheless, thereby the subject gains a feeling of certainty and self-consciousness. Therein lies the specific strength of modern power relations.

Now it is the science of political economy that Foucault identifies as the primary source of knowledge that developed this kind of power relations in modern times, simultaneously laying ground for the predominant identity offerings of modernity (Foucault 1991 [1978], 92, 102 f.). With reference to Friedrich A. Hayek, Foucault underlines a genuine facet of US-American (actually: Chicago) neoliberalism to have established economic reasoning as "general style of thought, analysis and imagination" within society (Foucault 2010 [1978−9], 219). Apart from the institutional preconditions of such claim, this development is intellectually grounded in a severe expansion of the scope of economic thinking. Taking into account this intellectual heritage, it seems plausible that

64   *Lukas Bäuerle*

common economics textbook literature today offers a purely economic, socially unbounded identity offering that – willingly or not – bears the possibility to influence its readers' actions. In this specific sense, economics textbooks can be looked at and analyzed as means of political communication.[11]

One precondition when aiming at governing them (*gouverner*) is the foundation of a specific mindset (*mentalité*) within the led or governed individuals. Mankiw/Taylor explicitly prepare their readers for such a shift of mindset:

> Many of the concepts you will come across in this book are abstract. Abstract concepts are ones which are not concrete or real – they have no tangible qualities. . . . – if you master these concepts they act as a portal which enables you to think like an economist. Once you have mastered these concepts you will never think in the same way again and you will never look at an issue in the same way.
>
> (Mankiw/Taylor 2014, 17)

According to Mankiw/Taylor, the world of economic knowledge is presented in 'abstract concepts' that trigger the experience of passing through a 'portal'. Going through this portal will fundamentally change the readers' perception of the world around them. A little bit further, Mankiw/Taylor underline that this shifting experience may if not must lead to serious conflicts with common beliefs or experiences (ibid.). This conflict is a 'normal' part of the learning experience since students get to know a world that they cannot see 'physically'. It *has to* irritate them. Students here become prepared to open themselves to a new world through the acquaintance of tools of abstract reasoning. Necessarily they need to neglect or even set aside common sense frames for social interaction gained through life experience: "The challenge, therefore, is to set aside that everyday understanding and think of the term or concept as economists do" (ibid.). We find this imperative again in the textbook of Samuelson/Nordhaus (2010, xx) or in the textbook of Gwartney et al. (2006, 5).

Taking seriously these quotes, economic education is successful when the student has learned to think differently, that is, to think with the abstract tools of economists. This also means that, in order to graduate, one needs to overcome thinking like the one who has opted for the economics curriculum in the first place. But how do you actually think as an economist? What kind of abstraction does it imply? And finally, what kind of subjectivity do students have to adopt in order to see 'how the world really works'?

Students are led to see the world through the eyes of an entrepreneurial self, a subject position originating in the archetype of *homo oeconomicus* (Foucault 2010 [1978–9], lecture 9; Bröckling 2016, xiv). Although none of the analyzed textbooks explicitly introduces this economic anthropology, its specific rationale can be described as the omnipresent key tone of the genre, found on almost every single page. As we have seen in section 4, Frank/Bernanke/Johnston create the figure of an 'economic naturalist' in order to illustrate this rationale: "Our ultimate goal is to produce economic naturalists – people who see each

The educational process is here accordingly to governmental techniques introduced by Foucault restated as a production process: a production process of an economic subjectivity through its inner and free adoption by living individuals. *Students themselves* become the primary actors of this production process. What they learn to do as economic subjects is to calculate. In the most distinguished situations of daily life, this subject continuously balances costs and benefits – always searching for an individually optimal outcome of her decisions. Miller points out that the universality of this economic rationale does not only expand to different life situations but also to different feelings and motivations bound to individual decisions, hence, to the most interior and private parts of human existence (Miller 2012, 6; see also Gwartney et al. 2006, 5).

In the given data sample, students of economic introductory courses receive a constant flow of examples, end-of-chapter questions, quizzes and pictorial information. Through these didactical features, students are appealed to conceive their lives as an economic enterprise and their life experiences as governed by economic laws: "Economics touches *every aspect of our lives* and the fundamental concepts which are introduced can be applied across a whole range of life experiences" (Mankiw/Taylor 2014, x; emphasis added). Ranging from questions of love and power to art, health and education, economics textbook knowledge allows for definite and true decisions in daily life. To apply a calculating rationale in a whole range of daily examples therefore becomes a decisive didactical feature of standard economic education. In the end, the educational subject shall have learned to *lead and govern itself* on the basis of given identity and action options. In this sense, subjectivational processes and techniques may unleash a feeling of powerfulness or even superiority.

The paradox and clue of this economic subjectivation is the fact that the subject being produced already exists. In the performative compliance with the identity option offered, the subject realizes and incorporates a truth that before was not tangible, an abstract and conceptual truth (section 3). In this sense, the subjectivational process introduced by economics textbooks produces subjects that had always existed before – but up to this point only as "real fictions" (Bröckling 2016, 10 ff.).

The frame "Become who you are!" offers an identity option that reveals itself as true in the very moment of compliance. Hence, it is a *productive* frame. In a similar sense, Zuidhof speaks of standard economic education in sharp difference to classical liberal education as "market constructivist" education (Zuidhof 2014, 176 f.). According to this last frame, economic education is not just meaningful because one can learn who he is, but actually because one can become the one she ever was. Although this 'who' as well as the production process of this 'who' is strongly social and standardized in character, the subject nevertheless supposes to establish a unique and distinguished identity. Therein lays the ambivalence of a life in modern (economic) subjectivity.

6 Conclusion

Section 5 clearly showed that the frames reconstructed in the course of this chapter do actually bare the possibility to tie them together by means of a synchronizing story line. The arising bigger picture, the "arrangement of interpretation" (Keller 2011a, 243; transl. by the author) of the economics textbook discourse could start with the introduction of a non-tangible space of economic laws governing individual and social action (frame 1). Students then learn that these laws do not only reign outside, but also *within themselves* (frame 3). The content of these laws and thereby of the students themselves is a rational, optimizing pattern of behavior. Due to its acclaimed ontological character, the realization of the pattern becomes imperative, leading to homogenized behavior in the social arena of a competitive market (frames 2 and 3).

Regardless of the question whether this narration or other synthetized narrations promise to be meaningful, here I want to stress upon the fact that *to the addressed audience* the discourse does not offer this possibility to reflect upon the possible meaning of economic education. One of the key features of the frames reconstructed in sections 4 and 5 is the transfer of a specific *content and quality* of an identity option. The process of this transfer and its possible reactions, at least for the readers, remains widely implicit. Students are not being confronted with the fact that any classificatory act is a "process of decision-making", and hence, "every verbal expression can be understood as an 'act of power' because it coins a specific reality, a specific term, thereby excluding other possibilities" (Keller 2011a, 244; transl. by the author). At least the sample considered here does *not* univocally shed light on the fact that students might decide freely to adopt certain frames and correlating identity offerings or not. In the end, one (and only one) decision shall be made: to accept and incorporate the 'brutal truths of economics'. In this specific sense, the subjectivational process described in section 5 and its specific form (section 3) and content (section 4) of knowledge is pervasive in character (see also Graupe/Steffestun 2018). Especially when taking into account the potential public reach of the economics textbook discourse (see section 2), such findings raise serious concerns.

Furthermore, with the ends lying *outside* the educational sphere and subjects as described in sections 4 and 5, its success obviously cannot be evaluated from the perspective of this sphere and subjects. It is certainly this alienation of economic education from educational purposes that opens way for a loss of meaning for students (and teachers). This is to say that the questions, imaginations and expectations of economics students actually do not take part in their study experience – or only the one of a disturbing factor (Pühringer/Bäuerle 2019).

In order to overcome this danger of meaninglessness and alienation, potential reforms of economic education and especially its didactics should once again open up the decision for students how to deal with the subject matter in question and help them to adequately and responsibly deal with it in scientific as well as ordinary ways. It is precisely the gap of control irritating human capital theorists – a space of ultimate freedom – that actually constitutes the

The power of economics textbooks 67

attempt of education in the former sense. This is what *Bildung* originally meant to establish and foster.

Notes

1 In my analysis I also considered Mankiw/Taylor (2014): *Economics*. Both textbooks rarely differ.
2 By 'introductory textbooks' I mean those used in basic modules commonly termed as 'Econ 101'.
3 In 1992 there were 20 active publishers operating in the economics textbooks market (Lopus/Paringer 2012, 297 f.). The four remaining are McGraw-Hill Irvin, Pearson Education, Cengage Learning and Worth.
4 Hence, my specific research interest here is not the genealogical or field-sociological background of the frames and identity offerings given, but merely the identification and typization of these frames and identity offerings themselves. In this sense I did not carry out a sociogenetic typification but a sensegenetic typification.
5 By 'introductory chapters' I mean the preface, chapter 1 and – if thematically relevant – also chapter 2.
6 As remains to be shown, Mankiw here 'in a nutshell' introduces all of the reconstructed frames and identity offerings. See section 6 for possible ways of synthesizing them.
7 When talking about 'economic' or 'rational' thought, decision-making or action in the following, I always mean Beckers's narrow definition: the application of a maximizing calculus on the basis of ever fixed preferences in a competitive market context (Becker 1978 [1976], 4 f.).
8 The term 'human capital' arises in the late 1950s in the newly emerging field of 'economics of education'. It was mainly developed by economists from the University of Chicago (especially by Jacob Mincer, Theodore Schultz and Gary Becker).
9 It is commonly referred to in the chapters concerning growth theory (McConnell/Brue/Flynn 2009, 10; Mankiw 2015, 527 ff.; Frank/Bernanke/Johnston 2013, 509 ff.; Gwartney et al. 2006, 352; Schiller 2008, 339 ff.; Krugman/Wells 2015, chap. 24) and wage determination (McConnell/Brue/Flynn 2009, 283 f.; Samuelson/Nordhaus 2010, 339, 353 f., 361 f.; Mankiw 2015, chap. 19–1b; Frank/Bernanke/Johnston 2013, 339 ff.; Gwartney et al. 2006, 551 ff.; Schiller 2008, chap. 16; Krugman/Wells 2015, 544 ff.). McConnell/Brue/Flynn (2009, 451 f.) additionally use the concept in the context of the economics of migration and development (McConnell/Brue/Flynn 2009, chap. 39; see also Schiller 2008, 742, 749).
10 I am aware of only one attempt to apply Foucauldian power analysis in the context of economics textbooks (Zuidhof 2014).
11 Some authors explicitly reflect their textbooks in a political context: "Let those who will write the nation's laws if I can write its textbooks" (Barnett/Samuelson 2007, 143). See also Mankiw: "In making these decisions [of selecting textbook contents], I am guided by the fact that, in introductory economics, the typical student is not a future economist but is a future voter. I include the topics that I believe are essential to help produce well-informed citizens" (Mankiw 2016, 170).

References

Aslanbeigui, N., Naples, M. I. (eds.) (1996): *Rethinking Economic Principles: Critical Essays on Introductory Textbooks*. Chicago: Irwin.

Barnett, W. A., Samuelson, P. A. (2007): An Interview with Paul A. Samuelson. In: Barnett, W. A., Samuelson, P. A. (eds.): *In Inside the Economist's Mind: Conversations with Eminent Economists*. Malden: Blackwell, 143–164.

68 *Lukas Bäuerle*

Becker, G. (1962) (1978) [1976]: *The Economic Approach to Human Behavior*. Chicago: University of Chicago Press.

Becker, W. E. (2000): Teaching Economics in the 21st Century. *Journal of Economic Perspectives* 14(1): 109–119.

Bröckling, U. (2016): *The Entrepreneurial Self: Fabricating a New Type of Subject*. Los Angeles: Sage.

Christensen, J. (2017): *The Power of Economists Within the State*. Stanford: Stanford University Press.

Colander, D. (1989): The Invisible Hand of Truth. In: Colander, D., Coats, A. (eds.): *The Spread of Economic Ideas*. Cambridge: Cambridge University Press, 31–36.

Elzinga, K. G. (1992): The Eleven Principles of Economics. *Southern Economic Journal* 58(4): 861–879.

Foucault, M. (1983): The Subject and Power. In: Dreyfus, H. L., Rabinow, P. (eds.): *Michel Foucault: Beyond Structuralism and Hermeneutics*. 2nd edition. Chicago: University of Chicago Press, 208–228.

——— (1991) [1978]: Governmentality. In: Burchell, G., Gordon, C., Miller, P. (eds.): *The Foucault Effect: Studies in Governmentality: With Two Lectures by and an Interview with Michel Foucault*. Chicago: University of Chicago Press, 87–104.

——— (1995) [1975]: *Discipline and Punish: The Birth of the Prison*. 2nd edition. New York: Vintage Books.

——— (2010) [1978–79]: *The Birth of Biopolitics: Lectures at the Collège de France, 1978–79*. Edited by Senellart, M., translated by Burchell, G. New York: Palgrave Macmillan.

Frank, R. H., Bernanke, B., Johnston, L. (2013). *Principles of Economics*. 5th edition. New York: McGraw-Hill Irwin.

Fullbrook, E. (2009). The Meltdown and Economics Textbooks. In: Reardon, J. (ed.): *The Handbook of Pluralist Economics Education*. London: Routledge, 17–23.

Giraud, Y. (2014). Negotiating the 'Middle-of-the-Road' Position: Paul Samuelson, MIT, and the Politics of Textbook Writing, 1945–55. *History of Political Economy* 46 (Supplement 1): 134–52.

Gottesman, A., Ramrattan, L., Szenberg, M. (2005). Samuelson's Economics: The Continuing Legacy. *The Quarterly Journal of Austrian Economics* 8(2): 95–104.

Graupe, S. (2019). "Waging the War of Ideas": Economics as a Textbook Science and Its Possible Influence on Human Minds. In: Decker, S., Elsner, W., Flechtner, S. (eds.): *Advancing Pluralism in Teaching Economics: International Perspectives on a Textbook Science*. London and New York: Routledge, 173–190.

Graupe, S., Steffestun, T. (2018). "The Market Deals out Profits and Losses" – How Standard Economic Textbooks Promote Uncritical Thinking in Metaphors. *JSSE – Journal of Social Science Education* 3: 5–18. Pluralist Thinking in Economic and Socioeconomic Education.

Grimes, P. W. (2009). Reflections on Introductory Course Structures. In: Colander, D., McGoldrick, K. (eds.): *Educating Economists*. Cheltenham: Edward Elgar, 95–98.

Gwartney, J. D., Stroup, R., Sobel, R. S., Macpherson, D. A. (2006). *Economics: Private and Public Choice*. 11th edition. Mason: Thomson South-Western.

Keller, R. (2011a). *Wissenssoziologische Diskursanalyse: Grundlegung eines Forschungsprogramms*. 3rd edition. Interdisziplinäre Diskursforschung. Wiesbaden: VS Verlag für Sozialwissenschaften.

——— (2011b). The Sociology of Knowledge Approach to Discourse (SKAD). *Human Studies* 34(1): 43–65.

The power of economics textbooks 69

———— (2013). Zur Praxis der Wissenssoziologischen Diskursanalyse. In: Keller, R., Truschkat, I. (eds.): *Methodologie und Praxis der Wissenssoziologischen Diskursanalyse*. Wiesbaden: VS Verlag für Sozialwissenschaften, 27–68.

Klamer, A. (1990). The Textbook Presentation of Economic Discourse. In: Samuels, W. J. (ed.): *Economics as Discourse. An Analysis of the Language of Economists*. Dordrecht: Springer Netherlands, 129–154.

Krugman, P., Wells, R. (2015). *Economics*. 4th edition. New York: Worth Publishers.

Lopus, J. S., Paringer, L. (2012). The Principles of Economics Textbook: Content Coverage and Usage. In: Hoyt, G., McGoldrick, K. (eds.): *International Handbook on Teaching and Learning Economics*. Cheltenham, UK and Northampton, MA: Edward Elgar, 296–303.

Maesse, J. (2013). Die Dialektik von Ökonomie, Diskurs und Regierung. Zur Einleitung. In: Maesse, J. (ed.): *Ökonomie, Diskurs, Regierung*. Wiesbaden: Springer Fachmedien Wiesbaden, 9–32.

Maesse, J. (2019). The Schoolmaster's Voice: How Professional Identities Are Formed by Textbook Discourses in Mainstream Economics. In: Decker, S., Elsner, W. & Flechtner, S. (eds.): *Advancing Pluralism in Teaching Economics. International Perspectives on a Textbook Science*. London and New York: Routledge, 191–213.

Mankiw, G. (2015). *Principles of Economics*. 7th edition. Stamford, CT: Cengage Learning.

———— 2016. The Tradeoff Between Nuance and Clarity. *Eastern Economic Journal* 42(2): 169–170.

Mankiw, G., Taylor, M. (2014). *Economics*. 3rd edition. Andover: Cengage Learning.

McConnell, C., Brue, S., Flynn, S. (2009). *Economics*. 18th edition. Boston (u.a.): McGraw-Hill Irwin.

Miller, R. (2012). *Economics Today*. 16th edition. Boston: Pearson Addison-Wesley.

Pahl, H. (2011). Textbook Economics: Zur Wissenschaftssoziologie eines wirtschaftswissenschaftlichen Genres. *Prokla* 164(41): 369–387.

Pinto, L. E. (2007). Textbook Publishing, Textbooks, and Democracy: A Case Study. *Journal of Thought* 42(1–2): 99–121.

Pühringer, S., Bäuerle, L. (2019). What Economics Education Is Missing: The Real World. *International Journal of Social Economics* 46(8): 977–991.

Samuelson, P., Nordhaus, W. (2010). *Economics*. 19th edition. Boston: McGraw-Hill Irwin.

Schiller, B. (2008). *The Economy Today*. 11th edition. Boston: McGraw-Hill Irwin.

Schultz, T. W. (1960). Capital Formation by Education. *Journal of Political Economy* 68(6): 571–583.

Skousen, M. (1997). The Perseverance of Paul Samuelson's Economics. *Journal of Economic Perspectives* 11(2): 137–152.

Smith, L. M. (2000). *A Study of Paul A. Samuelson's Economics: Making Economics Accessible to Students*. Dissertation. Palmerston North, NZ: Massey University.

Zuidhof, P.-W. (2014). Thinking Like an Economist: The Neoliberal Politics of the Economics Textbook. *Review of Social Economy* 72(2): 157–185.

Part 2

Economic governmentalities

5 The constitution of neoliberal governmentality from early neoclassical economics to public choice theory

Ceyhun Gürkan

1 Introduction

Michel Foucault, a true polymath within the humanities and social sciences, provides a fertile and unprecedented ground for a new critical understanding of neoliberal governmentality as the present form of global power in its relation to neoclassical economics. Defying the usual academic specializations and disciplinary divides, his work opens up new ways of approaching politics and economics. Foucault demonstrates how economics played a crucial role in the constitution of classical liberal and, in turn, neoliberal governmentality. Foucault's work also helps us understand how economics in the late 19th century became expert knowledge that laid the foundation for neoliberal governmentality, a 'norm imposing' power modality and 'normative political reason' (Brown, 2015; Dardot & Laval, 2013). His analysis of economics as part and parcel of the (neo)liberal governmentality rests on the particular conception of power. Foucault (2007), identifying three forms of power (sovereignty, discipline, security management), shows particularly how economics played a decisive role in the transition from the disciplinary mode of power regulated by police to the security-management modality of power. He also presents a rigorous method and analysis as well as a history of government to analyze this critical role of economics around its three interrelated dimensions: knowledge, power/government, and ethics. In doing so, Foucault presents us with a historical, methodological, and analytical framework to elaborate on the evolution of modern economic analysis in its relation to (neo)liberal power. However, one of the missing points in Foucault's work is the absence of the analysis of public choice theory as part of neoliberal governmentality. Another one is a complete analysis of the relationship between early neoclassical economics and the subsequent neoliberal governmentality, with a focus on the specific power modality of security management.

Neoclassical economics was born out of the so-called marginalist revolution in economics in the late 19th century and public choice theory developed after 1940. Foucault (2008) examines, to a degree, how liberal governmentality based on classical political economy underwent a colossal transformation over

DOI: 10.4324/9780367817084-7

74 Ceyhun Gürkan

the late 19th century, but he is much more focused on the role of 20th-century neoliberal ideas in this revolution crafting a new political reason against Keynesian politics and economics. Nevertheless, he refers very little to early neoclassical economics, and public choice theory is left completely unnoticed in his account. Given that neoclassical economics with its early and late versions (e.g., new consensus in macroeconomics, behavioral economics, new institutional economics, etc.) and public choice theory are the hegemonic knowledge of economic analysis, discourse, and practice that govern and control the teaching of economics on a micro level (Zuidhof, 2014) and the administration of the state at a macro level, an attempt at incorporating early neoclassical economics and public choice theory into Foucault's history of neoliberal governmentality will be helpful for conceiving the governmental actuality of neoliberalism around its current effects and phenomena.

For Foucault, (neo)liberal governmentality is not reducible to economics and, no less, economic policies. And yet, economics as "knowledge-power" (Foucault, 2008: 19) has always been lateral to (neo)liberal power and governmentality. This being so, neoclassical economics and public choice theory are not to be understood simply as scientific knowledge analyzing the functioning of the capitalist market economy at micro and macro levels. Given their overreach to non-economic relations, spheres, and structures through the application of economic knowledge to the social realm, both theoretical bodies build up and disseminate a specific normative social and political rationality. Following Foucault's analytics and historical survey into governmentality, the particular question to be addressed is how the marginalist turn in economics and later public choice theory, which takes its starting point from Knut Wicksell's neoclassical economics (Buchanan, 1987; Wicksell, 1958), have reformulated the governmental reason of classical political economy by modifying especially its moral aspects and its articulation with different forms of power (i.e., sovereignty, discipline, and security management). In studies of Foucault's analytics of power and governmentality, the place of early neoclassical economics and public choice theory are largely left untouched or underevaluated, except for a few studies (Amariglio, 1988, 1990; Birken, 1990; de Lima, 2019; Gürkan, 2016; Olssen, 2018). The present chapter takes a step towards filling this gap and aims at contributing to the studies of Foucault and governmentality. Before going into this deeply, the problem and method concerning the power and influence of economics over the social and political life will be specified referring to James Buchanan, the founding father of public choice theory.

2 Problem and method

With the neoliberal revolution throughout the 1980s, Buchanan and public choice theory became influential on governments as they started reforming their policies, organizations, and administrative and political reason. During the post–World War II period, Keynesian theory and policies played an essential role in guiding the economy and public policies. This also holds true for its

Constitution of neoliberal governmentality 75

guiding power in governing public reason about socio-economic matters. The rise of protest movements in the West during the late 1960s was in some respects directed against the disciplinary formation of society under the auspices of the bureaucratic control system that the Keynesian central planning economic model entailed to achieve the aims of full employment and sustainable mass demand that induces investment. This model based on the bureaucratic welfare state was, as Richard Sennett (2006: 27–37) defines, a Weberian 'social capitalism' that created an 'iron cage' because of its highly functional and hierarchical structure despite its certain democratic and progressive aspects. Alongside the new trends in left politics at that time, public choice and monetarism strove to increase their intellectual power of influence and significance for guiding the struggles of masses for freedom *vis-à-vis* the increasing comprehensive state actions. As Keynesianism was becoming a "common enemy" (Foucault, 2008: 79) at the diverse poles of the political spectrum, public choice scholars took on a political task and action in theory and practice. Public choice theory and its supporters set down the essential principals for guiding the public reason through neoliberal economics and provided an operational framework for economists and politicians as they sought to make new formulations to conduct the social, political, and economic course of movements. Buchanan himself got involved in public debates as part of the public choice school's political mission for promoting normative political economics to guide political and public debates. He occasionally participated in the meetings of the Joint Economic Committee of the US Congress founded in 1946 and expressed his thoughts on public finance and political issues. Buchanan also took a position against the student protests endorsed by left academics and supported tax-protest movements in the 1970s (Brennan & Buchanan, 2000). During the course of social movements in the 1960s and 1970s, Buchanan's approach to politics and economics changed from a libertarian attitude against the state towards embracing strict regulations by means of state authority (Fleury & Marciano, 2018). His aim was to take control of the social unrest against capitalism and reformulate a new way of the security of the market, which explains his support of Reagan's conservatism and neoliberal policies.

Buchanan produced considerable volumes of books and articles on public choice theory and constitutional political economy. His analysis of modern society has economic, political, fiscal, and normative–ethical dimensions. It is economic because his theory is concerned with overcoming the crisis of economics by redirecting it on the theoretical course of subjective choice (Buchanan, 1981, 1999) and the will of individualistic freedom. Buchanan's analysis (1964, 1975, 1987) is normative and political because it aims at sharpening the critique of the state/political market and the economic/fiscal course of affairs that make a case for the *Leviathan* form of state. Buchanan's theory deals mainly with fiscal policies because he believes that public finance as a science and art of government guides the collective and individual choices of public goods in a market environment and as such lies at the center of politics. Buchanan assigns a critical and defining role to political economists in guiding the public reason towards an ideal society he imagines. As such, in Buchanan's setup politics and economics have two dimensions: positive and normative. On the positive side, he sets out to explain *scientifically* the actual course of economic and political events and developments. On the normative side, from a constitutionalist political economy perspective, he aims at guiding the governmental reason of state as well as the behavior of individuals as they inveigh against the state on the way towards making a new social contract. Finally, Buchanan's public choice theory (1978, 1988) has a strong ethical dimension, which has received less attention, because it aims to construct and govern the moral attitudes, behaviors, and subjectivities of individuals in accordance with the rules of the market that emerge out of the rational expectations of individuals and set limits to the state. Buchanan (2008: 472–474) in his recent work turned to Kant's moral philosophy and called for a 'deontological turn' in political economy as a way to govern the conducts and choices of individuals. Buchanan's formulation of internal governmentality of subjects for the constitution of the market society can be best understood within the framework of Foucault's analytics of power and governmentality, which can establish a clear link between the inner logic of the theory and its performative power shaping the reality around their intersectional ties and disparities.

Within liberalism, government through economy can be carried out by making use of economics in two ways: economics as expert knowledge or economics as a means of strengthening individual empowerment. Buchanan sides with the latter and advances an economic and ethical critique of the first model. In doing so, his theory becomes committed to building a certain governmental reason for the state and the acts of individuals. But the vector of governmental relations does not originate from the state, directing itself towards individuals; it is quite the reverse due to its comparatively low costs of government within society. The liberal model of government of the public and individuals has two dimensions. The first includes the interactions between individuals as part of the population under the governmental authority informed by market rules, and the second is the internal governmentality of morality imposing certain restrictions on acts, which means in-depth government through self-government. Buchanan has developed public choice theory to shape this multi-layered governmentality through the economics-based intelligibility of politics and, no less, ethics thereby laying the foundation for the government of the state and individuals without making a break between the two.

Buchanan's public choice theory is highly interdisciplinary and has several aims at micro and macro levels. To bring them together and develop a comprehensive analysis of this theory, a unifying analytical framework and method are needed. Foucault's nominalism, discourse analysis, and analytics of power/government present us with such an analytical and methodological framework. Foucault's overall work sees things and events in their historical course within a triangle, the corners of which consist of knowledge, power/government, and ethics. Knowledge here does not only stem from the scientific production of savants but is something that grows in relation to everyday experiences in micro and macro domains of social life. Knowledge reaches its true meaning when constituting *the truth* and shaping the governmental reason that guides power relations all over society. Then knowledge becomes 'knowledge-power'. To see theories not as scientific knowledge but, through Foucault's prism, as part of 'knowledge-power' that has a performative, constitutive, and concrete practical influence on social reality shows us the relation of knowledge, power, and ethics. Foucault, paying attention to the history of economics around these three dimensions, identifies the constitutive role of economics in shaping the governmental reason of liberalism and neoliberalism. In his words:

> Economics is a type of knowledge (*savoir*), a mode of knowledge (*connaissance*) which those who govern must take into account . . . Economics is a science lateral to the art of governing. One must govern with economics, one must govern alongside economists, one must govern by listening to the economists.
>
> (Foucault, 2008: 286)

Foucault adds, however, that governmental rationality itself is not an entire derivative of economics and cannot be reducible to it. Government, an ensemble of rationalities, is much more than what economists say, but it is impossible to govern without economics in (neo)liberalism. Taking inspiration from this argument, the following sections characterize economics as public science and inextricable part of the art of government, arguing that the governmental attribute of economics is congenital (since its birth back in the ancient times was seen from the concept of *oikonomia* – the management of household). Therefore, the character of economics as public science and its practical influence on social life can be put by focusing on the notion of government. It is Foucault's merit that we can take up the history of economics as part of the history of government, which allows us to turn this historical account into analytics from a socio-economic perspective.

3 Neoclassical economics as the foundation of neoliberal governmentality

In their book *Economics: Marxian versus Neoclassical* (1987), Richard Wolff and Stephen Resnick explain that the criticism of neoclassical economics cannot be a narrow-scope and finalized critique. According to them, neoclassical economics is not simply an economic doctrine about how the capitalist economy works. It is connected to a general power scheme that shapes the market mechanisms, norms, and rationality in the economic realm as well as culture, habits, and patterns of behavior in the non-economic domains. Resnick and Wolff call for a new critique of neoclassical economics in the neoliberal era because, in Foucauldian terms, they consider neoclassical economics as 'knowledge-power' that programs the state, society, and the conducts of the individual through security management technologies. In this respect, it is necessary to open up another way of criticism beyond the traditional disapproval of neoclassical economics based on the critique of its scientific assumptions and method, which tries to elicit that neoclassical economics does not explain reality. Considering that the neoclassical theory, which presumably does not explain reality, has the greatest potential to produce truths to govern and construct reality, a new critique becomes necessary. This critique should first identify the links between neoclassical economics and neoliberal governmentality. As such, a new line of criticism is required for the understanding of the dynamism of symbolic tools, political reason, and self- and social technologies of neoclassical economics that disseminate neoliberal norms and rationality starting from economics education. When the problem is described so, Foucault was the first to approach neoclassical economics from this line of criticism.

The term neoclassical was coined by Thorstein B. Veblen in his 1900 article "The Preconceptions of Economic Science" (Veblen, 1900). Veblen (1898, 1909) argues that neoclassical economics with its reductionist, teleological, non-evolutionary, static, and taxonomic theoretical structure was simply the continuation of classical political economy. Thus, he calls it with the term 'neo-classical', which delineates little and simple modification of classical political economy. What is more, Veblen argues that neoclassical economics relies on the same logic of liberalism, which tries to advance capitalist property relations by promoting the 'absentee ownership' detrimental to the industrial system and material production process which secures the welfare of the society at large. Thus, for Veblen, both classical political economy and neoclassical economics are a kind of 'sabotage' (Veblen, 1994) of the industrial system and welfare of the society. Although aiming in a similar direction by calling them 'knowledge-power', Foucault would not agree in total with Veblen because Foucault recognizes essential differences between the two schools. Foucault discusses these differences in terms of liberal governmentality, not economic theorizing and its ideological biases. However, as already noted, Foucault did not examine and analyze the early neoclassical economics as part of the history of liberal governmentality to the full. "So I will skip two centuries," he writes, "because obviously I do not claim to be able to undertake the overall, general, and continuous history of liberalism from the eighteenth to the twentieth century" (Foucault, 2008: 78). He is mainly concerned with the essentials of the path-breaking shift from classical liberalism of the 18th century to 20th-century neoliberalism. Be that as it may, Foucault's rapid move into the 20th century is a very quick shift that leads to a huge lacuna in his 'history of governmentality' between classical liberal and neoliberal governmentality.

Nevertheless, Foucault is certainly aware that the late 19th century should be distinguished from its early years in terms of the concrete political and economic developments. As the late 19th century witnessed the constitution of welfare capitalism under the increasing fiscal, political, and juridical control of the state, which was all the more fortified during the world wars in the 20th century, the power of *laissez-faire* economics lost its scientific reliability and credence among the public, thereby falling from the grace as an instrument for

Constitution of neoliberal governmentality   79

governmental apparatus and rationality. In effect, the rise of neoclassical economics was a response to the then decaying position of economics. Its critique of classical political economy also aimed to restore the power of economics as expert knowledge against the growing impact of political reason shaped by institutionalist, ethical, and legal views. Against the backdrop of increasing juridification of liberalism, the rise in bureaucratic power and state interventions, neoclassical economics changed the discipline towards highly deductive theorizing through mathematical devices in order to renew the liberal art of governing. Despite its mathematical content and facet stripped of political and social aspects of economic life, early neoclassical economics took its bearing from the search for establishing new liberal governmentality. That is, neoclassical economics started developing a new political reason by slightly mentioning politics and its long-established structural elements and ontological foundations. Towards that aim, it sought to remove the elements in economic theorizing that moved economics away from becoming governmental expert knowledge. As the economics cut off its relationship with the neighboring social science disciplines which once formed the indispensable part of economic thinking, neoclassical economics and rationality developed a new approach to them by either declaring them as representing the non-rational aspect of the social system or inventing new problematizations like the 'Adam Smith problem', which aimed to discard social ethics of sympathy from the liberal art of government (Gürkan, 2016: 135).

Foucault is also well aware of the aforementioned developments that changed the epistemic conditions of the production of knowledge and how they had a bearing on the reshaping of the structure of knowledge. Foucault recognizes that there are differences between the early and late 19th century in terms of the knowledge structure of human sciences. Psychology increased its epistemic power over the social sciences in the wake of Freud's analysis of the unconscious in the last quarter of the century (Foucault, 2011: 27). As a result, psychology became the epistemic mainstay of economics with the marginalist revolution. It should be recalled that Alfred Marshall (1962) at this time regarded biology as having the potential to form a new knowledge system for economics, which was the case for Veblen (1898), who called for a Darwinian evolutionary turn in economics. Like Veblen, Marshall seems to be hesitant about acknowledging the supremacy of psychology over biology when he identifies "economic biology" as "[t]he Mecca of the economist" (Marshall, 1962: xii) to develop a dynamic approach to economics, which refers to the evolutionary thinking in economic theorizing. At the back of the changing structure of the human sciences under the auspices of biology and psychology, Foucault is also conscious of the fact that neoclassical economics made modifications in classical governmental reason in *The Birth of Biopolitics* as well as its epistemic structure in *The Order of Things* and then *The Archeology of Knowledge*. In comparison, the transformation of the governmental reason is clearer than the epistemic modification in Foucault's work. Neoclassical economists radically modified classical liberalism shaped by classical political economy, and what is more, these

80   *Ceyhun Gürkan*

modifications were essential for the development of neoliberal governmentality developed as a 'thought collective' (Mirowski & Plehwe, 2009) after 1930 and a global art of government in practice after 1980.

Therefore, neoclassical economics stands at a very critical position and juncture in the overall history of liberal governmentality as presented by Foucault, and it is crucial to understand the specificity, reality, and attributes of neoliberal governmentality. Given that marginalist economics in the late 19th century carried out very radical modifications of classical liberalism, it is fair to say that there are not two types of liberal governmentality as Foucault argues. Three stages or types can be distinguished in the history of liberal governmentality: classical liberalism, neoclassical liberalism, and neoliberalism. Classical liberalism was the early liberalism that was still in the domain of the reason of the state configured by police and discipline; neoclassical/neoliberal economics and governmentality together formed 'advanced liberalism' (Rose, 1993). However, Foucault, if not totally, seems to be ignorant of the importance of the late 19th century in terms of political/economic events and theories. As noted, he has a reason for this deliberate neglect. Foucault states that he does not want to be engaged in presenting the entire history of liberal governmentality and prefers to center his focus on the shift from classical liberalism of the 18th century (Smith) and the early 19th century (Ricardo) to neoliberal governmentality of the 20th century. By doing so, Foucault specifies the aspects of neoliberal governmentality. Nevertheless, there remains a huge gap in the history of (neo) liberal governmentality. He little mentions about the first half of the 19th century around Ricardo's political economy, but they are very much rare when it comes to the late 19th century.

Foucault's approach to early neoclassical economics was a matter of debate between Lawrence Birken (1990) and Jack Amariglio (1988, 1990) in the late 1980s. In this debate, the question of marginalism is about its *episteme*. The authors were the first to ask the position of marginalist economics in Foucault's work. Although their articles are valuable to develop an understanding of Foucault's thoughts on the marginalist turn in economics, this early debate remained in the scope of the question of episteme. This is so because Foucault's analytics of government he developed in his lectures 1977–8 *Security, Territory, Population* and 1978–9 *The Birth of Biopolitics* came to be known fully after 2000.

Foucault (1989, 2002) used the method of archeology in his early works, and he dealt with long-term epistemic structures of knowledge in unity. He distinguishes the pre-classical period of episteme based on 'resemblance' before the 16th century from the classical age, which was based on 'representation' and lasted until the end of the 18th century/early 19th century. Afterward, the modern period develops. The modern era in which Man as a finite being is invented is 'the age of Man'. Over the modern era, man evolved into 'human species' from 'mankind' with the effect of human sciences shaped particularly by psychology and biology as well as political economy and historical philology (2007: 78). Man becomes a subject having a biological and psychological

Constitution of neoliberal governmentality 81

life (the body, mind, desire), working life, and a historical language. 'Classical political economy' gives weight to the body (physical effort to be disciplined in a panoptical system of control) and (neoclassical) economics to mind and desire. The first sees the body as the physical force; the latter conceives it as a neurological and, to a greater extent, psychological force and being. What is more, Foucault within the scope of the archeological method identifies a critical moment in Ricardo's political economy. Ricardo invented 'finite man' in the modern age of episteme (human sciences) and biopolitics as Kant once did in philosophy by bringing the question of the present into philosophy (Foucault, 1988: 87, 89, 95). In his work Foucault (2011: 27) seems that he does not recognize a critical moment or an immense epistemological break in marginalism, but in an interview with Alain Badiou in 1965 he states that Freud's analysis of the unconscious in late 19th century paved the way for a new turn in human sciences, a kind of "deep archeological transformation". Accordingly, psychology started dominating human sciences. This is the very moment that neoclassical economics emerged as a new science of political economy or economics omitting the political. It is also fair to argue that its rise was the emergence of a new governmental reason. In the light of the archeological method of Foucault, the continuity and discontinuity between classical political economy, particularly Ricardian economics, and neoclassical economics are seen around their epistemic structures and position within the wider episteme of more or less the same modern age in unity. Within the framework of the archeological method, this changing epistemic line between them is less discernible in comparison to their altering governmental logic. The modification of governmental reason is clearer and more severe towards a break.

In terms of the epistemic structure of marginalist economics, it is hard to identify another radical 'epistemic break'. Marginalism was still in continuity with the utilitarian philosophy of classical political economy, but it took a huge step, but not the first, to dismantle the classical governmental and political rationality and modify the general epistemic structure of classical political economy situated in naturalism. The first step was taken by John S. Mill, who still regarded the class structure of society and the labor theory of value as the unit of analysis in economics but brought forward active *homo economicus* (the rational economic man) as governmental technology that ceases to be part of the natural and exchange-based market economy. With Mill, political economy entered into its age of Man. As Margaret Schabas (2005) shows, marginalism followed and completed Mill's effort of 'denaturalization' of economics by shifting the focus of economics from nature and the reason of nature towards the calculative reasoning of man within a strict hedonistic conception of the existence of human being. The oscillation from nature to the human mentality blended with a strong psychological grounding was a great step to modify the epistemic structure of classical political economy, which makes economics a 'mental science'. As *homo economicus* in classical political economy is the natural limits of the state intervention, in neoclassical economics the hedonistic economic man becomes "a lightning calculator of pleasures and pains" as Veblen

(1898: 389) sarcastically criticizes. Shortly after Mill, marginalism developed further this shift towards a complete 'mental science' (Schabas, 2005) in a way to make a break with classical naturalism in terms of more or less active governmental reason based on the human mind, whether in the form of welfare-planning bureaucratic mentality as in the British neoclassical economics, single political leader as in the Italian neoclassical economics, single super-rational *homo economicus* in the market behaving according to alternative costs as in the Austrian neoclassical economics, or rational civil collective action in the political market as in the Swedish neoclassical economics, which is close to Buchanan's neoliberal economics (Kayaalp, 2004). So, we observe three types of *homo economicus* in the history of liberal governmentality: first, 'untouchable' *homo economicus* in classical political economy who specifies the natural border of the state under the rule of an 'invisible hand'; second, the neoclassical *homo economicus* as an absolute mental being who is solely directed by desires and self-interests; third, the neoliberal *homo economicus* as an acting agent who responds to the environment which is to be constructed in an economization process. Under the present condition of authoritarian neoliberalism, Wendy Brown (2015: 213) mentions another type of the neoliberal *homo economicus* to be sacrificed for the market economy, particularly for the sake of the financial industry.

As such, the specificity of marginalism in the late 19th century lies in a modification of the epistemological structure of classical political economy and a radical change close to a break in terms of governmental reason, which laid the foundations for neoliberalism. As classical political economy evolved from Smith, Ricardo, and Mill towards neoclassical economics, the marginalist turn made clearer in-depth modifications of the previous forms and structure of knowledge and political reason. Nature/physics and the working man were replaced by psychology and the desiring man within the same age of Man. At that time, biology was seen by radical and critical evolutionary economists like Veblen as the alternative approach against the neoclassical economics, having the potential to recast the historical aspect of the former in a dynamic way as well as having an alternative governmental reason. However, modern biology based on the Darwinian evolutionary theory, then, could not establish another successful rupture in epistemic structure and governmentality within economics as 'knowledge-power', which, however, is crucial today to envisage the alternative against the epistemic and governmental matrix of neoclassical/neoliberal economics.

When Foucault turns to genealogy, power, and government, he details this great transformation in the late 19th century more but does not specifically make it part of the history of liberal governmentality. And yet, when we look at his mentions about marginalism and early neoclassical economists, we see that Foucault is well aware of how important it is for neoliberal governmentality because marginalism, as noted, carried out radical modifications in the classical liberal governmentality. And this is not about the discarding of the labor theory of value by the utility theory of value. There are other radical modifications by

Constitution of neoliberal governmentality   83

early neoclassical economics. Accordingly, we are moving away from classical naturalism towards the human agency and radical humanism around the question of calculative human reason against the reason of nature and reason of the state in which classical political economy was placed. Thus it can be argued that marginalism and classical political economy were situated in more or less the same episteme but produced different governmentalities. The relationship between episteme (long-term knowledge structure) and governmentality reason (political power) is another issue to be taken up thoroughly, but it is fair to say that the 19th century saw two radically different governmental rationalities.

Foucault (2008: 61–62, 118–121, 219ff) discusses neoclassical modifications that laid the foundations of neoliberal governmentality over the period from 1870 to 1930 in a dispersed manner, but their main context is the shift from classical liberal governmentality to neoliberal governmentality. He accords critical importance to early neoclassical economics in three shifts: the first shift is the reconception of *homo economicus* by neoliberal governmentality as a competitive and consumer subject rather than a subject of equal exchange and material production. The second shift from classical liberal to neoliberal governmentality occurs in the context of the move from the naturalist conception of the market to the constructivist and 'active governmentality' that considers the market as a field of permanent intervention and a field to be constructed around the competition principle, which, in turn, becomes the model and benchmark of all governmental reason and practice. The third shift is from the classical conception of labor around the idea of labor power, which refers to the effort of the physical body, to the neoliberal conception of the worker as a self-enterprise or entrepreneur. So, the meaning of work, worker, and wage changes, and they are not characterized anymore by antagonistic social relations, working time, and material conditions. They acquire their meaning through human mentality, subjective point of view, and individuals' rational choices.

In neoliberal governmentality, a normative political project, we see a constructivist and active government that generalizes the economic rationality and practices across the society at large in which individuals as competitive self-enterprises unfold. This entire story and discourse about the economization of life, constructivist governmentality, and competitive self-entrepreneurial agency began with the marginalist revolution in economics. In this sense, although it is still a debatable issue to argue that it was a radical epistemological break in the widest sense, one thing is certain – there is a radical transformation towards a clear-cut rupture materialized by early marginalist economics in terms of governmentality, which was later perfected by neoliberalism over time up until the present.

To recap, neoclassical economics shifted the field of analysis of economic theory from production to consumption. In doing so, neoclassical economics considers competition, not the equal exchange, as an organizing principle of the economy and society. It has made human behavior an object of economic study. As such, it discovers the entrepreneur as a singular subject. But it does not understand the mechanics of the entrepreneur's movement.

Neoclassical economics mostly understands the entrepreneurial subject as a natural being within the static relations of material conditions of production and consumption. Joseph Schumpeter (1950, 1961) develops this discovery in capitalism from a sociological and historical point of view. And Schumpeter conceptualizes the entrepreneur as an extraordinary subject, almost like a hero. Neoliberalism modifies this conception of hero-entrepreneurship into mass-entrepreneurship in a way to construct everyone as a single entrepreneur and, as such, to form an entrepreneurial society under permanent and active governmentality. Thus, there are continuities and discontinuities between neoclassical economics (early marginalism, the Schumpeterian modification, and established orthodoxy in the 1920s) and neoliberal governmentality (ordoliberalism, American anarcho-capitalist neoliberalism, and Austrian neoliberalism). Public choice theory is another type of neoliberal governmentality that has been carved out within these continuities, discontinuities, and modifications, which Foucault completely left untouched.

4 From neoclassical to neoliberal governmentality: Buchanan and public choice theory

Foucault's study of neoliberalism is centered on German ordoliberalism and the American Chicago School. Foucault was not interested in the theory of public choice, just as he kept early neoclassical economics out of the history of liberal governmentality. There is no reference to public choice theory in his work on neoliberal governmentality. However, if Foucault had seen the economic and political situation of neoliberalism today, and looked at how the behaviors and subjectivities are shaped in the private and social/political sphere within the current neoliberal structure and how the state reason is formed, he would have given to public choice theory a certain place in his work on neoliberal governmentality.

Public choice theory is in the focus of critical theory today. The main reasons are the following: first of all, this theory is dominant in economic theory and politics. It is the essential inspiration for the new public management model and neoliberal governance based on using economics as a business form of expert knowledge for constructing the wide-ranging performative indicators, although Buchanan would not agree with the overlap of his theory with the model *vis-à-vis* the expansion of the bureaucracy under the model (Knafo, 2019: 4–7), which is an interesting case to see the articulation of a theory with the reality it is opposed to. Public choice theory opposes representative democracy, especially the democratic model of the Keynesian welfare state. It sees faulty public policies and democratic mechanisms as the cause of economic crises. Collective politics, being inherently evil, creates the conditions for the political market of rent-seeking behaviors. The idea of public interest is impossible, and this idea should not be enforced. The idea of public interest and democratic collective policy mechanisms should be abandoned. The state should be restructured according to the principles of competition and entrepreneurship.

But this would not mean to weaken the reduction of the state force. The political and economic order should not be left to the idea of spontaneous order as Hayek argued. The state, which should be formed in accordance with neoliberalism, should construct the market and the appropriate human subjectivity and patterns of behavior (Olssen, 2018). In this respect, the political sphere and subjectivity should be constructed according to the economy. In other words, *homo politicus* representing the collective politics around the public interest should be eliminated by *homo economicus* (Brown, 2015). Public choice theory is a branch of 'economic imperialism' whose core assumptions are 'self-interest', 'market exchange', and 'individualism' (Udehn, 1996). As such, it is an application of economics to non-economic fields through these assumptions, in which context it develops normative constructivist policies through which the economy is constructed as a 'game'. It supports both economization and constructivism; in this sense public choice theory should be taken into the analysis of governmentality to reveal its political rationality and governmental technologies of the social and the self.

Based on the elucidations and literature review back in section 2, when it is understood as an economic theory, public choice theory is defined as a branch of political economy in the form of the economics of politics. When it is seen at the level of abstraction around its assumptions, the focus of public choice theory is the question of how the content and volume of public services/goods in the democratic market society are determined collectively and how they are realized simultaneously. But the theory is much more than an economic theory. Public choice theory has certain normative aspirations about human subjectivities and deserves attention from a governmental perspective. The theory connects the existence, functioning, and critique of public authorities and the structure of publicity to radical individualism. What is more, it attributes the constitutional construction of the political sphere to the rational choices and interests of individuals who produce the rules of economy and the institutions. At this point, establishing a legitimate and systematic neoliberal bond between the state/politics and the individual, the transformation of rules and institutions in accordance with neoliberal governmentality becomes a task for public choice theory.

The political task of the theory is to present an explanation of not only the complex political structure that arises from interpersonal interactions but also the neoliberal construction of the structure and subject. Normatively, for Buchanan, the task of the constitutional political economist is to assist individuals as citizens who want to control their social order while continuing to seek the rules of the political game that will best serve their purposes. The transformation of individuals' behaviors and institutions can be accomplished by the existence of a comprehensive new political economy that focuses and works on human action, not social engineering as adopted by the Keynesian planning model. Public choice theory aims to make the fundamental ideas of the market economy operational in practice to maintain the freedom and welfare of autonomous individuals who create the values of the political and social

86 *Ceyhun Gürkan*

complex, which derives from the interrelation of human actions. According to this normative view, it is essential to focus not on single human action but instead on behaviors between one another in the political and social structure, which should be dissociated from representative democracy and collective politics.

Since representative democracy does not prevent the expansion of the state and does not have a mechanism to regulate personal interests, it encourages the reproduction of rent-seeking behaviors in a political structure. Public choice theory has two solutions, one being political and the other ethical. Since politics is not necessarily concerned with the public in Buchanan's setup, it can expand the state in line with the economic interests realized in the realm of politics or the political market. At the constitutional level, it is necessary to formulate rules restricting the state, which future governments must obey. These rules are designed compliant with the rational expectations of individuals about the future. As these rules operate, the mutual play of personal interests can simultaneously ensure equilibrium in the market (invisible hand) and the preservation of stability and protection of individual freedoms in public and collective life. Foucault mentions the rising of "party governmentality" (Foucault, 2008: 191) against the state governmentality in the 20th century. In effect, Buchanan's theory of voting and rules is directed against 'party governmentality' that expands the scope of the state budget in close relation with the mass and public interest. Buchanan tries to build up strict individualistic governmentality to restrict 'party governmentality', which shifts his focus to ethics. This also demonstrates that neoliberal governmentality relies on a highly interdisciplinary economic theory in which discipline acquires its true meaning in the sense of the internal disciplining of individuals and interrelations.

The second solution is at an ethical and normative level, and this precisely defines the internal governmentality of public choice theory that seeks to construct a specific subjectivity. Buchanan's theory is known for its generalization of economics, but its constructivist nature is less emphasized. This is more about its normative character that employs external and internal constructivist forces. The external force is the small but strong state, the other being what Foucault would describe as 'the technology of the self'. The latter tries to establish disciplinary power in the subjectivity as permanent internal governmentality of individuals in a way to set the limits subjects cannot surpass in their civic life. For self-government and internal regulation of individuals according to the market rules, Buchanan (2008) in a recent text considers Kant with an eye to incorporating the Kantian deontological ethics as a self-technology and the way of internal limitations of the self for establishing the disciplinary power and morality into the neoliberal governmentality in defense of the market economy, as the ordoliberals once did to establish the market economy as the sole and true moral way of social and civic life. However, the present mode of liberal self-government includes not only the Kantian morality and imperatives to ensure "conduct of conducts" (Foucault, 2007: 389) from within for the market game to play, but also external imperatives that are seen clearly from

Constitution of neoliberal governmentality 87

the politics of austerity, which turns self-government to self-sacrifice under the sway of the populist and authoritarian neoliberalism.

5 Conclusion

Neoclassical economics and the neoclassical-based theory of public choice have been reconsidered in the light of Foucault's analytics and history of government through Foucault's nominalist, archeological, and genealogical method that understands the structure and constitution of social life based on the power of knowledge and interactions of individuals. By elaborating on early neoclassical economics further in Foucault's work in its relation to neoliberal governmentality and filling a gap in Foucault's history of neoliberal governmentality through the analysis of public choice theory, the chapter has also provided a methodological and analytical framework in a historical context for the question of how economics has become the socially diffuse public science of the art of government in (neo)liberalism. The foregoing discussion in the context of public choice theory with a specific focus on Buchanan has shown that the power of economics on public debates relies on its achievement of governmental power that turns it into a public science by constituting a relation between knowledge, power/government, and ethics. Although Buchanan is opposed to the type of economics as expert knowledge, he aims to make the constitutional political economy the public science that is committed to and geared towards developing a constant and daily critique of the state power in the mindset and attitudes of individuals in a neoliberal way, as Foucault describes. On the other side, Foucault's critical attitude against neoliberal capitalism, which has been and is still supported by public choice, exhibits a contrary and opposed disposition through the ethical critique of the Kantian deontology as contemplated by Buchanan for the purpose of setting the insurmountable limits of the market in theory and practice. Foucault's archeological, political, and ethical analytics is helpful not only to analyze the neoliberal complex in its actuality and entirety but also to invent an alternative governmentality through an active critique of our historical presence, thereby taking action in the form of "counter-conducts" (Foucault, 2007: 389) for the alternative present and future.

References

Amariglio, J. (1988). The body, economic discourse, and power: An economist's introduction to Foucault. *History of Political Economy*, 20(4), 583–613.

Amariglio, J. (1990). Reply to Lawrence Birken. *History of Political Economy*, 22(3), 562–569.

Birken, L. (1990). Foucault, marginalism, and the history of economic thought: A rejoinder to Amariglio. *History of Political Economy*, 22(3), 557–562.

Brennan, G. & Buchanan, J. (2000). *The power to tax: Analytical foundations of a fiscal constitution.* The collected works of James M. Buchanan, vol. 9. Indianapolis: Liberty Fund.

Brown, W. (2015). *Undoing the demos: Neoliberalism's stealth revolution.* New York: Zone Books.

Buchanan, J. (1964). What should economists do? *Southern Economic Journal*, 30(3), 213–222.

88   *Ceyhun Gürkan*

Buchanan, J. (1975). A contractarian paradigm for applying economic theory. *The American Economic Review*, 65(2), 225–230.

Buchanan, J. (1978). Markets, states, and the extent of morals. *The American Economic Review*, 68(2), 364–368.

Buchanan, J. (1981). Introduction: L.S.E. cost theory in retrospect. In J. Buchanan & G. G. Thirlby (eds.), *L.S.E. essays on cost* (pp. 3–16). New York/London: New York University Press.

Buchanan, J. (1987). The constitution of economic policy. *The American Economic Review*, 77(3), 243–250.

Buchanan, J. (1988). Contractarian political economy and constitutional interpretation. *The American Economic Review*, 78(2), 135–139.

Buchanan, J (1999). *Cost and choice: An inquiry in economic theory*. The collected works of James M. Buchanan, vol. 6. Indianapolis: Liberty Fund.

Buchanan, J. (2008). In search of *homonculus politicus*. *Public Choice*, 137, 469–474.

Dardot, P. & Laval, C. (2013). *The new way of the world: On neoliberal society*. London/New York: Verso.

de Lima, I. V. (2019). Foucault on the marginal revolution in economics: Language and the Cartesian Legacy. *Review of Political Economy*, 31(1), 60–74.

Fleury, J.-B. & Marciano, A. (2018). The making of a constitutionalist: James Buchanan on education. *History of Political Economy*, 50(3), 511–548.

Foucault, M. (1988). The art of the telling the truth. In L. D. Kritzman (ed.), *Politics, philosophy, culture: Interviews and other writings 1977–1984* (pp. 86–95). London: Routledge.

Foucault, M. (1989). *The order of things: An archeology of the social sciences*. London/New York: Routledge.

Foucault, M. (2002). *Archaeology of knowledge*. London/New York: Routledge.

Foucault, M. (2007). *Security, territory, population, Lectures at the Collège de France 1977–1978*. New York: Palgrave Macmillan.

Foucault, M. (2008). *The birth of biopolitics, Lectures at the Collège de France 1978–1979*. New York: Palgrave Macmillan.

Foucault, M. (2011). Felsefe ve psikoloji (Philosophy and psychology). In I. Ergüden (ed.), *Felsefe sahnesi (The scene of philosophy)* (pp. 19–30). İstanbul: Ayrıntı.

Gürkan, C. (2016). The politics of neoclassical economics: Insights from Foucault's history of governmentality. *History of Economic Ideas*, 24(3), 117–143.

Kayaalp, O. (2004). *The national element in the development of fiscal theory*. New York: Palgrave-Macmillan.

Knafo, S. (2019). Neoliberalism and the origins of public management. *Review of International Political Economy*. Published online.

Marshall, A. (1962). *Principles of economics*. London: Macmillan.

Mirowski, P. & Plehwe, D. (eds.) (2009). *The road from Mont Pèlerin: The making of the neoliberal thought collective*. Harvard: Harvard University Press.

Olssen, M. (2018). Neoliberalism and democracy: A Foucauldian perspective on public choice theory, ordoliberalism, and the concept of the public good. In D. Cahill, M. Cooper, M. Konings & D. Primrose (eds.), *The SAGE handbook of neoliberalism* (pp. 384–396). London: Sage.

Rose, N. (1993). Government, authority and expertise in advanced liberalism. *Economy and Society*, 22(3), 283–299.

Schabas, M. (2005). *The natural origins of economics*. Chicago/London: The University of Chicago Press.

Schumpeter, J. A. (1950). *Capitalism, socialism and democracy*. New York: Harper & Brothers Publishers.

Schumpeter, J. A. (1961). *The theory of economic development: An inquiry into profits, capital, credit, interest and the business cycle*. Cambridge, MA: Harvard University Press.

Sennett, R. (2006). *The culture of the new capitalism*. New Haven/London: Yale University Press.

Udehn, L. (1996). *The limits of public choice: A sociological critique of the economic theory of politics*. London: Routledge.

Veblen, T. (1898). Why is economics not an evolutionary science? *The Quarterly Journal of Economics*, 12(4), 373–397.

Veblen, T. (1900). The preconceptions of economic science. *The Quarterly Journal of Economics*, 14(2), 240–269.

Veblen, T. (1909). The limitations of marginal utility. *The Journal of Political Economy*, 17(9), 620–636.

Veblen, T. (1994). *The engineers and the price system*. London: Routledge/Thoemmes Press.

Wicksell, K. (1958). A new principle of just taxation. In R. A. Musgrave & A. T. Peacock (eds.), *Classics in the theory of public finance* (pp. 72–118). London: MacMillan.

Wolff, R. D. & Resnick, S. A. (1987). *Economics: Marxian versus neoclassical*. Baltimore/London: The John Hopkins University Press.

Zuidhof, P.-W. (2014). Thinking like an economist: The neoliberal politics of the economics textbook. *Review of Social Economy*, 72(2), 157–185.

6 Competitive power
Elements of Foucauldian economics

Flemming Bjerke

1 Introduction

For Foucault power is practices that deliberately interfere with other subjects' *free* acts and thoughts. This implies that marketing is an exercise of power, and that power is constitutive for competition. As far as economics ignores this role of power, its analyses of markets and the tasks of economists are poor.

Generally mainstream economics conceives power as compulsive (hard power), implying that competition excludes power:

> [C]apitalism is a system of generalized choice in which the extensive opportunities to walk away from any transaction preclude the private use of sanctions in the absence of collusion.
>
> (Bowles & Gintis, 1998: 11)

It is of course generally true that the buyer's opportunity to *exit* an offer (Hirschman, 1970: 21–30) means that the market is not compulsive, but it may well involve *non-compulsive (soft) power*.

Conceiving power as compulsive only implies a *concentration concept of market power* where a monopoly reduces freedom and exercises power maximally:

> [A] firm exercising monopoly power . . . can raise its price above marginal cost without losing all its clients.
>
> (Tirole, 1994: 282)

More generally, market power is an ability associated with few sellers to raise prices and still sell the products:

> When the number of suppliers declines, the possibility of diminished competition (or collusion) . . . increases, and the ability of individual suppliers to raise prices can be increased.
>
> (OECD, 2017: 10)

However, this is a flawed definition of market power because it *is immune to empirical observations of firms' actual exercise of (soft) power in the market*. In marketing,

DOI: 10.4324/9780367817084-8

Competitive power 91

it is trivial that customers may be influenced by the 4 or 5 Ps (parameters): price, product, placement, promotion and PR that each covers a large number of elaborate means of soft power. Galbraith suggests this ignorance of power has poor scientific reasons:

> Nothing is so important in the defense of the modern corporation as the argument that its power does not exist, that all power is surrendered to the impersonal play of the market.
>
> (Galbraith, 1983: 120)

Even heterodox economics has a strong inclination to consider market power as compulsive and an effect of concentration (Moudud, Bina & Mason, 2012).

In section 2, I will outline a power concept that includes non-compulsive power, and this is used in section 3 to show how power constitutes competition. Section 4 will detail how competitive power is practiced, and in section 5 I will show how competition forms competitive systems and dispositives. Section 6 will draw consequences for the market society. I do not treat the works on the power of finance, lobbying, bargaining and contracts.

To clarify the analysis, I will use Moss's work on the junk food market in the US from the 1990s to 2013 to illustrate the role of competitive power.

2 Power presupposes freedom

Foucault defines power as *acts upon acts* (including speech acts) with calculated effects, that is, power is *practices* or *technologies* of acting on other subjects' practices[1] (Foucault, 1982: 786). Due to the subjects' freedom, power also implies resistance. In the market this means that competitors have to take customers' exit and voice (protests) in consideration (Hirschman, 1970).

This power concept is at odds with Lukes's more conventional concept, where power affects the subjects contrary to their interests. I divide Lukes's concepts into hard (compulsive) and soft power (Lukes, 2005: 22, 30, 36):

1 *Hard power.*
    - *Coercion* threatens the subject with punishment or missed reward.
    - *Force* deprives the subject of opportunities. *Manipulation* is force which the subject does not recognize.

2 *Soft power.*
    - *Influence* affects the subject without using force or coercion.
    - *Authority* influences the subject by means of reason.

But, *Lukes does not consider soft power as power.* This discrepancy between Foucault's and Lukes's power concepts is not just a disagreement of terms: First, hard power consists of using the *means* of punishment, deprivation and threat to control the freedom of the subjects.[2] But, the purpose of soft power is control

92 *Flemming Bjerke*

of freedom as well. Therefore it is inappropriate not to consider soft power as power. Exercising soft power is also manipulation if drawbacks are kept secret, for example the use of scientific results to compose junk food so that it creates addictivity. This example also demonstrates how soft and hard power sometimes cannot be distinguished: The consumers are simultaneously free and enforced to choose addictive junk food. Second, Foucault analyses how hard and soft power are combined, e.g. as discipline (Raffnsøe, Gudmand-Høyer & Thaning, 2016: 194–96). Therefore, in the first place, it is analytically appropriate to merge hard and soft power. Third, according to Foucault, power *may or may not* be exercised in the *interests* of (a majority of) the subjects, e.g. customers. Fourth, as Galbraith explains, competitive societies are particularly dependent on soft power. But Galbraith seems to understand soft power as any social forming (social conditioning) (Galbraith, 1983: 34). However, assuming that any social determination is exercise of power empties the power concept of its distinctive meaning (Taylor, 1984: 173). Power must be defined as intentional, e.g. marketing. However, *the very existence of non-intentional determination implies that it merges with the effects of power.*

Using Hirschman's concepts of exit, voice and loyalty, an overview is summarized in Table 6.1. When soft power is used, loyal subjects accept authority, while non-loyal subjects may be influenced, or avoid influence (exit), or protest (voice). In case of no loyalty, hard power coerces and forces the subjects; in the market this is mainly seen as forced exit or fines. Alternatively, hard power may subjugate subjects to loyalty. Except for legal matters, market power is normally soft power: influence, authority and soft manipulation.

Foucault summarizes what should be analyzed in a power analysis (Foucault, 1982: 792):

1 *The system of differentiations* which are both the results of and the conditions that permit actions upon the actions of others: law, status and privilege, economic differences, know-how, etc.
2 *The types of objectives* of exercising power: the maintenance of privileges, authority, trades, functions, the accumulation of profits, etc.
3 *The means of bringing power relations into being*: threats, discourse, economy, surveillance, etc.
4 *Forms of institutionalization*: traditions, apparatuses, systems of apparatuses, etc.
5 *The degrees of rationalization*: the effectiveness and costs of the applied technologies of power.

Table 6.1 Forms of power

	No loyalty	Loyalty
Soft power	Influence/exit/voice	Authority
Hard power	Forced exit/coercion	Subjugation

Competitive power 93

Even though power presupposes freedom, and the power of institutions is acquiesced by the subjects, it offers nevertheless the holders of power opportunities to exploit advantages and to defend *privileges* (differences). Thus, a *circularity* is implied because the exercise of power is enabled by differentiations (e.g. accumulation of capital) which it is usually the objective to maintain or strengthen, and even institutionalize and rationalize. So, power is among the causes in the principle of circular cumulative causation, which to Myrdal explained how inequalities are maintained and re-enforced, implying that *irreversibility and dis-equilibrium* are associated with the exercise of market power (O'Hara, 2009: 94–96). Similarly, Hannah Arendt rejects power as depending on hard power. She founds power on freedom and considers it to be *productive and constitutive of the individuals* (Maze, 2018). Therefore the exercise of power is partly indeterminate. This point is elaborated in Table 6.2, where power may have *expected* as well as *unpredictable effects*. Unintended determinations may be known *conditions* or *uncertainty*.

Latour observes that the exercise of power is not a diffused and passive determination of subjects that just results in expected effect, it is rather transformed and translated by the subjects in performative practices, entailing that rulers have power over the subjects' conditions (Latour, 1984: 275–277) but also face unpredictable reactions and effects. In general, the exercise of power endeavours to reduce non-intended determination and unpredictable effects.

However, Arendt's understanding of power in terms of concerted actions of a group who empowers the ruler to act on behalf of the group (Arendt, 1970: 24) implies that the technologies of power used inside and outside an institution or group differ. To avoid unpredictable and non-intended events, performative translations, within a firm are surveyed, evaluated, sanctioned, etc. much closer inside than outside.

As rulers depend on the subjects' subjugation, institutions may always be overthrown or deteriorate. Exercise of power may turn into a *power struggle* or even open confrontation. But due to fear of consequences, the parties usually settle a power struggle by *negotiations, agreement or co-operation* and end up with a degree of *domination and institutionalization* where one party more or less surrenders. So, power relations are *reciprocal dependency relations*: The rulers depend on the subjects' acquiescence to keep their power and privileges, and the subjects depend on the institutionalized power for their means of everyday life, e.g. the market.

Foucault has analyzed a number of historical configurations of technologies of power (dispositives). Here, I will outline the discipline dispositive, whereas,

Table 6.2 Determination, knowledge and power

Determination	Power	Not-intentional
Knowing	Expected effects	Conditions
Not knowing	Unpredictable effects	Uncertainty

94 Flemming Bjerke

in section 4, I will return to the governmentality dispositive. *Discipline* is a dispositive of power and dominance founded on a range of technologies organized in two dimensions: supervision and self-regulation:

1   *Supervision* allocates individuals in space and time with specified coordinated functions to perform. Their acts are observed, processed and regulated to maximize or refine output, and they are educated to perform their functions.
2   *Self-regulation*[3] Individuals are educated and formed to make them responsible for performing their functions by themselves.

To conclude, power has a hard and a soft aspect that interfere with subjects according to various models (dispositives) and associated technologies of power. In section 3, I will explain how soft power and governmentality are constitutive for competition. In section 4, I will expound that while discipline dominates inside the firm, competitive power is based on governmentality. That is, the soft power of governmentality includes the economists' exercise of professional technologies aimed at (loyal or non-loyal) subjects in the market. This generates circular processes of maintaining and developing social differences, not least as to the commitment of capital. In section 5, I will elaborate the concept of the competitive dispositive and associated competitive systems, and section 6 will expound the aspects of how competition forms society.

3 Analyzing competition as exercise of power

Whereas the traditional concentration concept of power ignores how marketing practices exercise power, a Foucauldian approach implies that firms' relations with their customers *are* exercise of soft power, and that *competition must be defined in terms of power*.[4] The exercise of power within the economy is not a deviation or an imperfection, but a ubiquitous aspect of the economy. As Bellofiore puts it:

> [E]conomic theory has to put at the heart of its discourse not the 'imperfections' of the market, but rather the 'normality' of power and conflict.
> (Bellofiore, 2013: 430)

Power is a constitutive element of the economy: The firms are institutions of disciplinary power that produce, develop and sell commodities. Markets are arenas for exercise of soft marketing power that is first and foremost a productive and ordering power (Foucault, 1990, 1994a, 2013).

Moreover, power "is exercised and does not exist except when it is exercised" (Foucault, 1997: 15) "and put into action" (Foucault, 1982: 788). Power is not just a maintenance or renewal of economic relations but a continual, active constituent of the economic relations. Thus, there is no market if no

Competitive power 95

power is exercised to establish, maintain and develop it *and* its actors through cumulative circular exercise of power (Bourdieu, 2005: 195–196).

3.1 The competitive power principle

Analyzing competition as exercise of soft power facilitates a proper definition of competition and collusion.[5] Here, the *target* is the buyers (or sellers) that are acted upon, and the *market* is an institutional setup enabling buyers and sellers to communicate and exchange decontextualized things or services (Callon, 1998: 16–19). Competition or collusion exist when:

1   Two or more actors use technologies of power to influence *overlapping targets, the field of competition/collusion.* The overlap is delimited and defined by time, place, distribution channels, contact channels, communication media, group of actors,[6] etc.
2   The power exercised over the target provides the actors with *resources* (first and foremost profits) for exercise of power – and the target's members with resources for consumption or exercise of power.
3   The power exercised over the target by each actor may change the *resources of the other actors* to exercise power over the target.
4   Actors are destroyed or forced to *exit* when their *status* concerning their command over resources and means of power are *evaluated* as being too poor.

Altogether, these four points constitute *the competitive power principle*, which means that competitors affect each other's economic status by exercising power over their targets.

Competition and collusion are distinguished by their effect on the other actors: When actors, to improve their own status, exercise power over the mutual target, and thereby harm each other's status, the relation is a *competition* relation. When the actors benefit from each other's power exercise over the mutual target, the relation is a *collusion* relation.

Figure 6.1 illustrates the elementary form of competition/collusion relations. Actor 1 and actor 2 have an overlapping (communal) target which constitutes the field of competition/collusion. Each actor may to some extent influence the other actor's targets and thereby influence the other actor's opportunity to influence the target.

In general, competing actors have both competition and collusion relations to each other, so when competition and competitors are mentioned in the following pages, the collusive aspect is implied.

The competitive power principle was seen in action when the eleven biggest US food companies could not collaborate about a health policy after Sanger, CEO at General Mills, at a meeting in 1999 rejected a proposal from Mudd, vice president at Kraft, for the development of healthier food. Instead, the industry continued to collude and compete about manipulating the consumers'

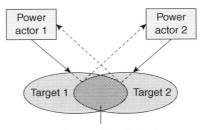

Figure 6.1 The competitive power principle

eating habits by utilizing the bliss point, a combination of salt, sugar and fat that makes food addictive, stimulates hunger and increases obesity, diabetes, etc. Later the companies promoted skipping regular meals to replace them with snacks, which promoted further health problems.

The overlapping of the *targets* varies with the means of power considered and with the horizon of time. The relations between competitors' targets are generally complex; the target of one competitor often overlaps a combination of targets of other competitors and constitutes competitive networks, e.g. the promotion of cola together with salty food boosts both hunger and thirst, thus creating a competitive network *vis-à-vis* other soft drink providers. Moreover, the more the targets overlap, the higher is the risk of intense competition. Therefore, reducing the field of competition by means of differentiation and segmentation neutralizes and reigns competition and its risks (Alderson, 2006a: 122–135; Czepiel & Kerin, 2012). On the other hand, the actors within the target may also compete and thereby strengthen the power of the main competitors.

Exercising power over the target generally affects the competitors whether or not they know it. When indirect effects are considered, competition creates an intentional horizontal power relation: *indirect power* exercised through the mutual target. In order to avoid unpredictable effects, the technologies of competitor analysis are used (Czepiel & Kerin, 2012). But otherwise, competitors are just a condition of exercise of market power or a source of uncertainty (cf. Table 6.2).

Technologies that calculate the *status* and possible *forced exit* of the firm are among the constitutive setups of the market. Kurunmäki and Miller explain how the calculative infrastructure as well as exit conditions are preconditions for the establishment of markets and firms:

> [A] process of co-creation, through which a financial and legal entity has been formed in tandem with the calculative infrastructure through which it is assessed and regulated.
>
> (Kurunmäki & Miller, 2013: 1100–1118)

Competitive power 97

But the market not only presupposes legal, accounting and financial practices. Callon and Muniesa (2005) emphasize also the role of the technologies and procedures (algorithms) that calculate with prices, as well as devices enabling buyers and sellers to be identified, and encounter and negotiate. Moreover, rules regulating trade and competition must be implemented before a market can exist, so that prices may be fixed and amounts of various goods exchanged. This entails that goods, to be sold, should be objectively separable and ready to be embedded into the customer's context (*singularization*). The actors of the market, including the consumers, must be like calculating devices that, through imagining and estimating courses of action, adjust themselves to the singularized goods of the specific market. Thus, assuming an automatic equilibrium will be attained (for instance with Walras's tatonnement) is nothing but a prejudice without foundation in reality if all these calculations, institutions and devices are not sufficiently investigated.

4 Competitive power technologies

It is not only the technologies and devices constituting the market that are crucial for the market and its actors. Additional technologies and calculation methods "make economic actors think, reckon and behave as competitive, profit-seeking actors" (Rose, 1999: 65). Therefore the actors acquire and apply *knowledge* about planning as well as methods of investigating and predicting the reactions of the target and competitors. In order to improve their status, the actors also *rationalize* the technologies of the exercise of power.

4.1 Soft power in marketing management

The role of marketing as exercise of soft power may be elucidated by Foucault's concept of governmentality. *Governmentality* is *conduct of conduct*, a "more or less calculated and rational activity . . . employing a variety of techniques and forms of knowledge, that seeks to shape conduct" (Dean, 2010: 11). Governmentality implies a relation of self to self where free individuals govern their own and others' mentality (Foucault, 1987: 130–131). Governmentality deals with subjects inside and outside institutions, supplementing or substituting the control dimension of discipline (conduct of self-regulation). It operates through practices of liberty which structure and shape people, making free people more predictable (Dean, 2010: 194).

Foucault brings governmentality back to pastoral power, which has four main features which here I apply to marketing:

1   The primary target is the *flock*, i.e. the customers play the major role,
2   *Benevolence*, i.e. serving the target,
3   *Supervision* of the flock, i.e. surveying, knowing and servicing the target, and
4   *Individualisation*, i.e. helping each customer getting her particular needs satisfied and developed (Foucault, 2004: 128–133, 219).

98 *Flemming Bjerke*

Governmentality has spread out into society and been replicated, adapted and refined (Foucault, 1982: 784), not least in the marketing. The governmentality of marketing was developed during the era of marketing management to influence the customs and habits of the population (Skålén, Fellesson & Fougère, 2005), and to this end it analyzes actual and potential customers.[7] Part of these techniques is disseminating knowledge, but also keeping knowledge secret. For instance, junk food is not only developed and promoted to create addiction, but information of its harmful effects on our health is also suppressed.

Inside the firm, management has to dominate employees to render the firm able to act as a collective actor exercising market power over its targets and competitors as well as ensuring development and avoiding deterioration of the firm as a collective actor (Cheong & Miller, 2000; Skålén, 2011). That the power technologies are adjusted to the exercise of market power is reflected in the development of marketing management (Skålén & Fougère, 2007). Skålén, Fellesson and Fougère (2005) observe that from the 1950s onward, a combination of discipline and governmentality became increasingly important in marketing management – as well as in other fields of management (Le Texier, 2012: 13).

Thus, competition has enforced modern management to develop organizations as a refined combination of discipline and governmentality (Fougère & Skålén, 2013). Competition benchmarking has, for instance, entailed a discipline which is based on a segmentation of the production process as well as a self-regulating and responsible workforce (Miller & O'Leary, 1996).

4.2 The construction of competitive rationality

According to Herbert Simon, rationality is not substantial, but procedural. But, instead of assuming like Simon that solving puzzles realizes *the* universal model of human rationality (Newell, Simon & others, 1972), it must be observed that techniques of problem solving are learned and therefore must be "analysed in the multiple and diverse fields in which they are formulated" (Mennicken & Miller, 2014: 18–38). Therefore they are also changing in time, space and social context and are even conflictual. Thus, *technologies being the tools for making rational decisions are not themselves rational, but technologies of rationalization. Thus a business economist is not rational per se, but has acquired a rationalizing capability of choosing and combining alternative technologies that should produce rational choices.*

It is not just marketing and the evaluation of a firm's status and opportunities that are providing rational solutions, other power technologies, such as internal auditing, are rationalizing as well:

> internal auditing can be conceptualized as providing: ex post assurance about the exercise of economic activities within management's preconceived frameworks and ex ante advisory services that enhance the rationality of economic activities and the accompanying controls of organizations.
> (Mihret & Grant, 2017: 699–719)

Competitive power 99

This enhancement of economic rationality is effectuated by means of an *evaluation and regulation aspects* of power technologies. The *evaluation* aspect has four steps that make *truth* and *value* (goals, ends, purposes, etc.) emerge and change:

1 Establishing criteria of merit.
2 Constructing standards.
3 Measuring performance and comparing it to standards.
4 Synthesizing and integrating data into judgments of merits (House & Howe, 1999: 17).

On the basis of the evaluations, the *regulation* aspect of power technologies not only forms and accomplishes rational decisions, but it also produces *rationalization* by means of business plans that combine strategic plans (based on competitor, SWOT, portfolio, etc. analyses), tactical plans (concerning production, marketing, organization, accounting, finance, etc.) and operational plans. Competitive rationality is constructed by combining and developing rationalizing technologies so that evaluations lead to regulations that aim at strengthening predictability of targets, competitors, suppliers, profitability, etc. and avoiding uncertainty.

5 The competition dispositive

The principles for how all these rationalizing technologies are integrated constitute the competition dispositive. *A dispositive integrates different technologies/practices* regarding things, discourses, power and technologies of the self (Deleuze, 1989; Foucault, 1988: 18) according to principles that determine:

1 "a *heterogeneous entity* consisting of discourses, institutions, architecture plans, statutory decisions, laws, administrative measures, scientific enouncements, . . . as well as unsaid matters."
2 "the nature of the *link between these heterogeneous elements*"
3 "*a strategic function*", because the dispositive is "a formation that has as function to respond to an urgency" (Foucault, 1994b: III.299, my translation).

Starting from these three points, I will next elaborate the model in Figure 6.2. The model illustrates how the competition dispositive determines the principles of the links within the market system and the system surrounding each competitor, as well as the competition spurred by strategical interaction between these systems.

The competitive power principle is the impetus for how the competition dispositive incites each competitor to link up with and collaborate with other actors (targets, suppliers, consultants, media, industrial organizations, government offices, universities, etc.) to form a *competitor system*. The competitor is also integrated with financial, industrial, commercial and property rights institutions, or involved in multinational corporations (Miller & Rose, 1990; Jessop, Nielsen & Pedersen, 1991). These actors are related to each competitor

Figure 6.2 The competition dispositive

depending on their importance and on whether they are neutral or helpers or adversaries.

It is to strengthen the firm's competitive power and handle the unpredictability and uncertainty stemming from competitors, targets, etc., that a competitor system is organized. Since all competitors organize a surrounding system afflicted by unpredictability and uncertainty, the competitive power principle integrates a *market system realizing a non-intended market strategy* that link competitor systems together in competitive and collusive relations and actions that produce internal unpredictability and uncertainty, and therefore risk.

The non-intentional market strategies become "great anonymous, almost unspoken strategies which coordinate the loquacious tactics" (Foucault, 1990: 95). The unintended market strategy is a more or less unavoidable collective principle for applying and developing power and knowledge technologies that promise to accumulate advantages and benefits, and which no single competitor or competitive system fully controls or may exit without loss (Foucault, 1980, 1990). A SWOT analysis (which every competitor may perform to profit) is, for instance, a technology to elaborate a *strategy* of a competitor system operating *within* the unintended market strategy.

Since Sanger, CEO of General Mills, in 1999 rejected Mudd's proposal for development of healthier food, the market for junk food has realized an unintended market strategy promoting competitor strategies of still more diversified junk food based on scientific investigation of how to make consumers addicted. Mudd clarified what happened:

> Sanger was trying to say, 'Look, we're not going to screw around with the company jewels here and change the formulations because a bunch of guys in white coats are worried about obesity.'
>
> (Moss, 2013)

Sanger, being concerned with the company's profitability and risks associated with a future health-promoting strategy, probably had to refuse the

Competitive power   101

implementation of a deliberate health-improving market strategy. In this case, the unintended market strategy became to avoid any health policy. In other cases, the state and its various agencies play an important part in setting rules for markets, and firms often struggle for power over relevant parts of the state (Bourdieu, 2005: 204).

A corollary of the discrepancy between competitor and market systems and strategies is that a dispositive implies a discrepancy between individual experiences and social events. What each interacting actor (e.g. in a firm) experience may be eliminated at the social level (e.g. the market) where other traits of interaction may be accentuated as social events entailing patterns of facts beyond aggregated experiences (Raffnsøe, 2002: 1:72). Adam Smith preempted this principle with his concept of the invisible hand that explains how experiences and purposes deviate from social events: Every individual strives to maximize his revenue without considering the public interest.

> [But, the individual] is in this . . . led by an invisible hand to promote an end [, the interest of society,] which was no part of his intention.
> (Smith, 1776: IV.II.331)

However, prejudice about the competition dispositive on the micro-level should not overrule actual investigations of a market as producing social events. The junk food industry, for instance, satisfies consumers' cravings, but regarded as social events, it actually also profits from stimulating and manipulating consumers to aggravate their own health (Moss, 2013). In the next section, I discuss certain social patterns which are generated by the competitive dispositive.

6 The role of competitive power in the market society

Simmel has partially pre-empted the competitive power principle and analyzed the consequences of its growing importance. For Simmel, competition is a substitute for direct conflict. As conflict implies power struggle, and power for Foucault is a substitute for war (Foucault, 1997: 21), Simmel's concept of competition may contribute to detail Foucault's concept of power, that is, how competition contributes to avoid war.

6.1 Competition tends to dominate society

According to Simmel, no society is without conflicts (*Streit*), but the conflicts may take place in the form of competition. Competition is indirect conflict dependent on the appreciation of a third party, that is, unlike direct conflict, the outcome is not in the hands of any of the combatants. Therefore, it is a misunderstanding to conceive competition as warfare (as does Shaikh, 2016: 260).

Competition forms the subjectivity of the competitors: Though it is indirect, the ferocity of competition is comparable with that of a fight. The negative sides of competition are that it contradicts the principle of equality and realizes

102 *Flemming Bjerke*

the brutality of the objective of victory, that is, it is destructive to competitors – and their missions. As Davies puts it, "the task of the competitors themselves is to maximize inequality in ways that benefit themselves" (Davies, 2014: 63). This corresponds with Wroe Alderson's power principle that describes how the market spurs cumulative circular processes of growth and power:[8]

> An individual or an organization, in order to prevail in the struggle for survival, must act in such a way as to promote the power to act. The power principle is especially important in relation to the expansion of a growing system. As a system grows, it is increasing its power or capacity to carry on its regular processes on a greater scale. . . . The difficulty is that there is no escape from risk because the risks associated with inaction are often more severe than the risks of action.
>
> (Alderson, 2006b: 107–108)

Thus, not only do competitors exercise power over their customers, they have to do so as efficiently as possible (cf. Hicks's lazy monopolist) and therefore strive to intensify and expand the exercise of power over customers. Competitive markets are vigorously self-promoting and imperialistic and tend to occupy and subdue other systems (e.g. the welfare state) and unregulated spheres (e.g. the ocean bottom in search of minerals) to itself.

A market system "which makes isolated markets into a market economy, regulated markets into a self-regulating market" is the principle of the modern market economy (Polanyi, 1944: 60). That is, *the competitive dispositive has become a dominant dispositive* that tends to subordinate and absorb other forms or power: the legal, disciplinary and governmentality dispositives.

6.2 Growth and differentiation

A consequence of the imperialism of the market system is that competition creates a perpetually developing and differentiating society, rather than a single firm's victory. Referring to Chamberlin, Alderson observes that market heterogeneity is fundamental. That is, *for a firm not to exit the market, it must have monopolistic advantages* to exercise market power.[9]

Thus, the circular growth processes not only imply quantitative growth, but also increase differentiation and segmentation. The firms utilize that as "economic activity expands, opportunity proliferates" (Alderson, 2006a: 128). The search for monopolistic advantage then spurs an "unending search for differential advantage" because the profit incentive "is directed toward differential advantage" (Alderson, 2006a: 116). Therefore, besides bankruptcies, mergers, take-overs, etc., growth and differentiation are the main way of avoiding failure in the competitive power struggle (which is exactly what Moss's investigation of the junk food market exemplifies).

As differentiation is pervasive, it is *generally* a misunderstanding that competition equalizes prices within an industry (Shaikh, 2016: 262). Porter elaborates the differentiation process when he outlines the three main generic strategies of an industry: cost leadership, differentiation of products and focus on specific customer segments (Porter, 2008: 12–17). The differentiation process also contradicts the self-fulfilling non-realism of microeconomics' equilibrium analyses of competition of homogeneous products: Since competitors fight for victory, competition in homogeneous markets should dissolve itself by creating monopolies. Since most markets are not monopolies, equilibrium analysis – instead of reserving homogeneous markets to special cases – invents (empirically unverified) conditions of equilibrium that should neutralize competition. The reality is that growth and differentiation are immanent in the market society; it is *generally* an exception that prices are equalized.

6.3 Generalized competition and risk

Simmel also observes how competition affects society in a more general way: Competitors have to do their utmost to subject themselves to the masses, but also to lead them. In a competitive society, *not only do all fight against all, but at the same time all fight for (the appreciation of) all*. The market society realizes a *general competition* about attention, legitimacy, prestige, money, time, resources, etc. – or of the human soul, as Simmel writes (Werron, 2014: 63). All firms tend to compete with each other, and everything tends to compete with everything.

But the target is basically not known by the competitors and tends to be a fiction (Werron, 2009), implying that the competitive society is always risky. However, understanding competition in the light of governmentality clarifies that the technologies of *market analysis* partially compensate for these risks by making the target more predictable.[10] But analyzing competition for predictive and risk-avoiding purposes requires a balance between identifying too few and too many competitors (Lehmann & Winer, 2007: 30). That is, the analyses of markets and competitors tend to be restricted so that general competition and its effects tend to be ignored.

The general competitive environment entails a general risk that also spurs the exercise of power for the purpose of growth and differentiation. But, this and the cumulative effects hereof tend to be ignored even though they involve increasing exercise of power and may effectuate harmful effects. A market society is a risk society. As Beck explains:

> Therein lies its internal dynamic – not malevolence, but the market, competition, division of labor, all of it just a bit more global today.
>
> (Beck, 1992: 51)

The growing importance of the competitive dispositive implies growing risks, which big data seems perfectly suited to remedy so that, in the aftermath of the digital revolution, the natural outcome of the market society seems to be surveillance capitalism.

104 *Flemming Bjerke*

6.4 *The rationalizing economist has to exercise power*

Business economists apply the power technologies discussed earlier, but they have to comply with the power exercised inside the firm: They evaluate and regulate, but they are also themselves evaluated and regulated. As Alderson explains, competition induces the firm – and hence forms its employees accordingly – to exercise power in order to profit from growth and differentiation. Economists have the primary information of and access to the objects of the target, competitors, suppliers, internal matters, etc. and are expected to evaluate these according to the competition principle. A rationalizing business economist is a subject that by means of acquired calculative and performative technologies and skills contributes to the strategic rationalization and proliferation of the firm so that its competitive status as to profitability, evaluated by the accounting technologies, is satisfactory or even improving. To enable the economists to perform all this, firms establish regimes of truth, and engage both in networks of knowledge creation (Heizmann & Olsson, 2015: 756–769) and in practicing and developing disciplines of business economics.

Thus, due to the competitive power principle, the business economist must engage in the firm's use of the power technologies to effectuate an on-going rationalization of both internal and external power technologies (Callon, 1998: 24) as well as continual growth and differentiation. That is, assemblages of machines and humans, where humans are more or less enslaved into being a functional part (Lazzarato, 2014), tend to be continually developed in order to enhance competitiveness. The multiplicity of managerial rationalization technologies is handled by a multiplicity of rationalization experts that realize the productivity of power and are co-ordinated according to the competitive dispositive so their power skills rationalize the integration of individuals and things into a market that exploits the targets and unfolds the competitor system.

The dominance of the competitive dispositive incites business economists to adopt a nearly inescapable cynicism or naivism because they must commit themselves and their creativity to support and exercise competitive market power over the targets in order to ensure growth, differentiation and profit. The economist is not paid for figuring out whether this effectuates harmful social events. For instance, chief operating officer Dunn at Coca-Cola was fired for having stopped marketing cola in public schools (Moss, 2013).

7 Conclusion

Economics generally excludes empirical analyses of how the soft market power of marketing is exercised. Using Foucault's concepts of power offers a fruitful way of analyzing marketing as an exercise of power, which implies that competition must be defined in terms of power. The competitive power principle consists of describing how competition and tacit collusion are indirect forces that stem from competitors using power technologies to interfere with a mutual target of customers.

Competitive power 105

By relating to institutions, each competitor builds a system that develops strategies and tactics of power in order to profit from its targets. However, a market also constitutes a market system which realizes non-intended and self-establishing strategies. The competitive power principle is the driving force that constitutes the competitive dispositive as the integration principle of competitive systems, market systems and strategies that is the dominant ordering of the modern market society.

Because marketing is the exercise of power, there is no guarantee that the market develops for the best for its customers. Business economists are rationalizing in that they acquire and develop technologies of power and have to exercise their rationalizing power skills to promote profitable developments, be they sustainable or not.

In markets, power is particularly dynamic and productive, inducing a continual development of rationalization, differentiation and growth to open new profitable opportunities, thus spreading to and taking over more and more parts of society, nature and personal experience. Moreover, in the market society everyone tends to compete with everyone for power, time, attention, money, etc. And all this promotes surveillance capitalism.

Notes

1 This includes acts upon feelings and thoughts as far as the ways of thinking and feeling are founded on the social rules and schemes of language and behavior (Merleau-Ponty, 2016).
2 Even the extreme and total terror and torture within the Nazi concentration camps had, besides sheer killing and suffering, the purpose of controlling the prisoners' tiny freedom by creating a state of absolute terror, apathy and obedience (Sofsky, 1997: 35, 248).
3 Concerning self-regulation of firms see (Miller & O'Leary, 1996; Skålén, Fellesson & Fougère, 2005; Fougère & Skålén, 2013).
4 Thus, the concept "vertical competition" is a confused term for the exercise of power constitutive of (horizontal) competition.
5 Here collusion is used mainly in the sense of *tacit collusion*, not in the sense of agreed or arranged collusion.
6 By 'actor' is meant either an individual or a collective actor or a composite assemblage of humans, symbols and things, e.g. a firm.
7 However, there are elements of disciplinary power in marketing as well (Kasabov, 2004).
8 Cf. (Bourdieu, 2005: 202).
9 Decreasing returns to scale throughout an industry may perhaps constitute a possible, rare exception to the competitive drift towards increasing heterogeneity or concentration.
10 This is changing with the use of big data and artificial intelligence. The target becomes still more known in detail and marketing still more tailored towards single individuals.

References

Alderson, W. (2006a). Competition for differential advantage. In: Wooliscroft, B., Tamilia, R. D. & Shapiro, S. J. (Eds.), *A twenty-first century guide to Aldersonian marketing thought*. New York: Springer.

106 *Flemming Bjerke*

Alderson, W. (2006b). The power principle. In: Wooliscroft, B., Tamilia, R. D. & Shapiro, S. J. (Eds.), *A twenty-first century guide to Aldersonian marketing thought*. New York: Springer.

Arendt, H. (1970). *On violence*. New York: Houghton Mifflin Harcourt.

Beck, U. (1992). *Risk society: Towards a new modernity*. London: Sage.

Bellofiore, R. (2013). A heterodox structural Keynesian: Honouring Augusto Graziani. *Review of Keynesian Economics*, *1*(4), 425–430.

Bourdieu, P. (2005). *The social structures of the economy*. Cambridge and Malden: Polity.

Bowles, S. & Gintis, H. (1998). Power in competitive exchange. In: Samuel Bowles, M. F. & Pagano, U. (Eds.), *The politics and economics of power*. London and New York: Routledge.

Callon, M. (1998). *The laws of the markets*. Sociological review monograph. Oxford: Blackwell Publishers.

Callon, M. & Muniesa, F. (2005). Peripheral vision: Economic markets as calculative collective devices. *Organization Studies*, *26*(8), 1229–1250.

Cheong, S. -M. & Miller, M. L. (2000). Power and tourism: A Foucauldian observation. *Annals of Tourism Research*, *27*(2), 371–390.

Czepiel, J. A. & Kerin, R. A. (2012). Competitor analysis. In: *Handbook of marketing*. Cheltenham: Edward Elgar.

Davies, W. (2014). *The limits of neoliberalism: Authority, sovereignty and the logic of competition*. London: Sage.

Dean, M. (2010). *Governmentality: Power and rule in modern society*. London: Sage.

Deleuze, G. (1989). Qu'est-ce qu'un dispositif? In: Foucault, M. (Ed.), *Michel Foucault philosophe*. Paris: Seuil.

Foucault, M. (1980). La poussière et le nuage. In: Foucault, M. (Ed.), *Dits et écrits I–IV*. Paris: Gallimard.

Foucault, M. (1982). The subject and power. *Critical Inquiry*, *8*(4), 777–795.

Foucault, M. (1987). The ethic of care for the self as a practice of freedom: An interview with Michel Foucault on January 20, 1984. *Philosophy & Social Criticism*, *12*(2–3), 112–131.

Foucault, M. (1988). Technologies of the self. In: Martin, L. H., Gutman, H. & Hutton, P. H. (Ed.), *Technologies of the self: A seminar with Michel Foucault*. London: Tavistock.

Foucault, M. (1990). *The history of sexuality: An introduction, volume I*. New York: Vintage.

Foucault, M. (1994a). Les mailles du pouvoir. In: Foucault, M. (Ed.), *Dits et écrits I-IV*. Paris: Gallimard.

Foucault, M. (1994b). *Dits et écrits I-IV*. Paris: Gallimard.

Foucault, M. (1997). *"Il faut défendre la société": Cours au Collège de France, 1976*. Paris: Gallimard.

Foucault, M. (2004). *Sécurité, territoire, population: Cours au Collège de France, 1977–1978*. Paris: Gallimard.

Foucault, M. (2013). *La societé punitive: Cours au Collège de France, 1973–1974*. Paris: Gallimard.

Fougère, M. & Skålén, P. (2013). Extension in the subjectifying power of marketing ideology in organizations: A Foucauldian analysis of academic marketing. *Journal of Macromarketing*, *33*(1), 13–28.

Galbraith, J. K. (1983). *The anatomy of power*. New York: Houghton Mifflin.

Heizmann, H. & Olsson, M. R. (2015). Power matters: The importance of Foucault's power/knowledge as a conceptual lens in KM research and practice. *Journal of Knowledge Management*, *19*(4), 756–769.

Hirschman, A. O. (1970). *Exit, voice, and loyalty: Responses to decline in firms, organizations, and states*. Cambridge: Harvard university press.

House, E. & Howe, K. R. (1999). *Values in evaluation and social research*. London: Sage.

Jessop, B., Nielsen, K. & Pedersen, O. K. (1991). Structural competitiveness and strategic capacities: Rethinking the state and international capital. In: Nielsen, K., Jessop, B. & Hausner, J. (Eds.), *The transition to post-socialism: Scandinavian and Polish perspectives*. Krakow: Krakow Academy of Economics Press.

Kasabov, E. (2004). Power and disciplining: Bringing Foucault to marketing. *Irish Marketing Review*, *17*(1–2), 3.

Kurunmäki, L. & Miller, P. (2013). Calculating failure: The making of a calculative infrastructure for forgiving and forecasting failure. *Business History*, *55*(7), 1100–1118.

Latour, B. (1984). The powers of association. *The Sociological Review*, *32*(1_suppl), 264–280.

Lazzarato, M. (2014). *Signs and machines: Capitalism and the production of subjectivity*. Los Angeles: Semiotex(t).

Lehmann, D. R. & Winer, R. S. (2007). *Analysis for marketing planning*. New York: McGraw-Hill, Irwin.

Le Texier, L. (2012). The uses and misuses of Foucault for thinking management: A case for a theory of managerial governmentality. Paper, Gredeg-Cnrs, Law, economics and management research group, Nice University.

Lukes, S. (2005). *Power: A radical view*. Hampshire: Palgrave Macmillan.

Maze, J. (2018). Towards an analytic of violence: Foucault, Arendt & Power. *Foucault Studies*, *25*(2), 120–145.

Mennicken, A. & Miller, P. (2014). *Michel Foucault and the administering of lives*. Oxford: Oxford University Press.

Merleau-Ponty, M. (2016). *Signes*. Paris: Gallimard.

Mihret, D. G. & Grant, B. (2017). The role of internal auditing in corporate governance: A Foucauldian analysis. *Accounting, Auditing & Accountability Journal*, *30*(3), 699–719.

Miller, P. & O'Leary, T. (1996). The factory as laboratory. *Science in Context*, *7*(3), 469–496.

Miller, P. & Rose, N. (1990). Governing economic life. *Economy and* Society, *19*(1), 1–31.

Moss, M. (2013). The extraordinary science of addictive junk food. *New York Times Magazine*. www.nytimes.com/2013/02/24/magazine/the-extraordinary-science-of-junk-food.html.

Moudud, J. K., Bina, C. & Mason, P. L. (2012). *Alternative theories of competition: Challenges to the orthodoxy*. New York: Routledge.

Newell, A., Simon, H. A. & Others. (1972). *Human problem solving*. Englewood Cliffs, NJ: Prentice-Hall.

OECD. (2017). *Competition assessment toolkit: Volume 1. Principles*. Paris: OECD.

O'Hara, P. A. (2009). The principle of circular and cumulative causation: Myrdal, Kaldor and contemporary heterodox political economy. In: *The foundations of non-equilibrium economics*. New York: Routledge.

Polanyi, K. (1944). *The great transformation*. Boston: Beacon Press.

Porter, M. E. (2008). *Competitive strategy: Techniques for analyzing industries and competitors*. New York: Simon and Schuster.

Raffnsøe, S. (2002). *Sameksistens uden common sense, volume 1–3*. Copenhagen: Akademisk forlag.

Raffnsøe, S., Gudmand-Høyer, M. & Thaning, M. S. (2016). *Michel Foucault: A research companion. Philosophy as diagnosis of the present*. Basingstoke and New York: Palgrave Macmillan.

Rose, N. (1999). *Powers of freedom: Reframing political thought*. Cambridge: Cambridge University Press.

Shaikh, A. (2016). *Capitalism: Competition, conflict, crises*. Oxford: Oxford University Press.

108 *Flemming Bjerke*

Skålén, P. (2011). Service marketing control as practice: A case study. *Qualitative Market Research: An International Journal, 14*(4), 374–390.

Skålén, P., Fellesson, M. & Fougère, M. (2005). *Marketing, government and governmentality.* Proceedings of the CMS Conference 2005.

Skålén, P. & Fougère, M. (2007). Be(com)ing normal – not excellent: Service management, the gap-model and disciplinary power. *Journal of Organizational Change Management, 20*(1), 109–125.

Smith, A. (1776). *An inquiry into the nature and causes of the wealth of nations: Volume one.* London: Strahan and Cadell.

Sofsky, W. (1997). *Die Ordnung des Terrors: Das Konzentrationslager.* Frankfurt: Fischer.

Taylor, C. (1984). Foucault on freedom and truth. *Political Theory, 12*(2), 152–183.

Tirole, J. (1994). *The theory of industrial organization.* Cambridge: MIT Press.

Werron, T. (2009). *Zur sozialen Konstruktion moderner Konkurrenzen: das Publikum in der "Soziologie der Konkurrenz"*, May. Luzern: Workingpaper des Soziologischen Seminars, Universität Luzern.

Werron, T. (2014). On public forms of competition. *Cultural Studies: Critical Methodologies, 14*(1), 62–76.

7 Feelings in crisis

The emotional and affective dimension of neoliberal economics in Greek crisis prone society

Elena Psyllakou

1 Introduction: when in crisis

While the outbreak of the long-lasting Greek economic crisis paved the way to political projects and techniques of governance inspired by neoliberal doctrine, economic experts advocating the primacy of the economy were gaining more and more ground in public debate and policy-making, as well as in governmental positions. In the meantime, like-minded politicians, journalists, public intellectuals and academics drew more and more on economic discourse to ground their arguments in favour of rapidly imposed policies of austerity. This orchestrated argumentation constituted a certain type of neoliberal governmentality that has been accurately described as a regime of post-political biopower (Kioupkiolis, 2013) and extensively analysed as relying, among others, on mediatised practices of emergency, exception, and (re-)inventing identities (e.g. Athanasiou, 2012; Butler & Athanasiou, 2013; Mylonas, 2014, 2017; Stavrakakis, 2014). In this turmoil, and as several counter-discourses started to emerge, emotional and affective failings operated as a key to the imposition of the new political project. In their insightful research on the emotional responses of the Greek citizens to the financial crisis, Davou and Demertzis (2013) observe that media interpretations and representations of crisis have been consistently using "negative emotional discourse" that "includes conditions of anger, rage, wrath, anxiety, fear, threat, distrust and depression", linking the crisis to "trauma" and "shock"and leading to a sense of "numbness" and "inaction" (2013, pp. 93–105). On his part, commenting on discursive repertoires and strategies in the Greek crisis, Stavrakakis notices a process "of creating and sustaining shame and guilt" that is then used to legitimise austerity as a means of "punishment" (2014, p. 35).

However, the encounter of neoliberal economics and mainstream media at the time has been triggering more kinds of emotional articulations. Far from a structural distress, these discursive encounters have been systematically building on a new, productive and emotionally fulfilling "normality". Moving from "crisis" to "life goes on", the turn to entrepreneurship, market and individual action, that are the "taken for granted" socio-political and cultural implications of the neoliberal doctrine (e.g. Dardot & Naval, 2014; Dean, 2009), is portrayed

DOI: 10.4324/9780367817084-9

110   *Elena Psyllakou*

in familiar emotional and affective practices which, as argued here, are transferred to the economic field. By bringing such stories to the foreground, this chapter is intended to map the emotional and affective articulations of this new "normality" in discursive encounters between economics and the media. Greek bank advertising is taken as an exemplary source in this respect. The analysis takes a comparative conceptual framework that explores the question of "emotion" both in the early philosophical background of neoliberalism(s), as elaborated mainly by Hayek, and in recent critical work on the emotional and affective implications of neoliberal governance. In doing so, it stresses the specificities of the emotional and affective normality of neoliberal economic discourse as constructed against the background of "exception". It further argues that between the philosophical understanding of neoliberal rationality as non-emotional and the critical dualistic perception of emotional governmentality as positive/negative lies a sphere of engaging emotional fluidity that is constitutive of "actually existing neoliberalism(s)".

2 Any room for emotions? On the philosophical background of neoliberalism(s)

In the aftermath of the Great Depression and World War II and in the wake of the Cold War, a group of "individual" scholars defining themselves as "liberals" were breaking new ground in an open-ended battle of ideas. After a decade at least of publications, meetings, correspondence and discussions, the initiative to meet at Mont Pelerine signified the establishment of a liberal thought collective that was as much academic as it was political (Bjerre-Poulsen, 2014; Burgin, 2012; Mirowski & Plehwe, 2009; Peck, 2008; Plehwe & Walpen, 2006). The meeting took place in April 1947 and led to the formation of the Mont Pelerine Society (MPS), which up until today signifies the ideological core of neoliberal policies.

Hayek's opening address set the frame of the discussion (Hayek, 1947/1967). Even though most of the attendees were economists, the aim was to involve as widely as possible historians, lawyers, political philosophers and more who would share their "individual" knowledge for one purpose: to rediscover the basic principles of liberalism, to reconstruct liberal philosophy and lastly to formulate a "complete programme of liberal economic policy" that would be "generally accepted" (Hayek, 1947/1967, pp. 149–153). Their work would be both transnational and interdisciplinary, and their nascent society would be both open and closed, made of people who share "certain common convictions" (Hayek, 1947/1967, p. 158). A few days later their Statement of Aims marked the beginning of an "ideological movement" which would defend a free society relying on private property and competitive market (Bjerre-Poulsen, 2014, pp. 205–209; Statement of Aims as cited in Montpelerin.org). Vague as it may have been, Hayek's opening address together with the Statement of Aims are revealing of an initial effort − yet not necessarily shared by all MPS members (e.g. Burgin, 2012, p. 9; Bjerre-Poulsen, 2014, p. 202; Peck, 2008, p. 25) − to

Feelings in crisis 111

contextualise in political and cultural terms a series of economic policies that were to be planned and introduced in different political and cultural contexts.

In the following years, "neoliberal" economic theory increasingly shifted beyond "technical economics" towards questions of politics and everyday life. What is of interest for this analysis is how this brought forward re-conceptualisations of freedom, knowledge, human action as selfish or altruistic, and "unconscious habits". Therefore, drawing mostly on the work of Hayek, Friedman and Becker, "neoliberal" thought suggested an understanding of economic freedom as a means to political freedom (Friedman, 1962/2002, pp. 7–8; Hayek, 1960/1978, pp. 1–21); decentralised utilisations of knowledge "which is not given to anyone in its totality" and the significance of a "man on the spot" who is aware of the particular circumstances of time and place (Hayek, 1945; Hayek 1960/1978, pp. 22–31); individual responsibility for the full use of knowledge to the achievement of certain ends (Hayek, 1960/1978, pp. 85–87); practices of selfishness and altruism in families organised around a leading figure and their reflection in the market place (Becker, 1974, 1981); disengagement of a person's sex from labour and household activities (Becker, 1985); allocation of non-working time to the benefit of economic welfare (Becker, 1965); the importance of "firmly established habits and traditions" in "gradual and experimental change" (Hayek 1960/1978, pp. 62–64); a "common sense" on progress (Friedman, 1962/2002; Hayek, 1960/1978); and a clear distinction between the "irrational" and the "non-rational", suggesting that the latter describes more appropriately the "unconscious features" such as "mere habits" or "meaningless institutions" which penetrate the individual's action towards the achievement of his/hers goals (Hayek, 1960/1978, p. 34).

Putting together these "neoliberal" frames of socio-political and cultural practices, what is striking – yet not surprising – is the absence of "emotions", "feelings", "sentiments" or "affects". It is striking if we consider on the one hand that certain perceptions of emotional and/or affective states have been granted a significant position in classical liberal ideas (e.g. Mill,1909/2009; Smith, 1759/1984) and on the other that in the post-World War II period psychological and psychoanalytical discourses proliferated and gradually penetrated different spheres of economic production and labour activities (e.g. Hardt, 1999; Illouz, 2007). In the aforementioned theoretical frames, emotions are incidentally mentioned by Hayek when he admits the insufficiency of a strictly intellectual approach, claiming that the cause of liberty may not prevail "unless emotions are aroused". However, he immediately confines them to an "indispensable aid" which is "neither a safe guide nor a certain protection against error" (Hayek, 1960/1978, p. 6). He then takes it a step further equating emotions with "moral or intellectual weakness", and most importantly placing emotions at the exact opposite of "inner-freedom" (Hayek, 1960/1978, p. 21). This more or less brings his discussion to an end. It seems that whatever lies in the sphere of the "unconscious", the "habit", the "meaningless" or the "non-rational" could be of some use for the "rational" realisation of the "neoliberal" project so long as they stay "non-emotional".

112 *Elena Psyllakou*

If we take Hayek's perception of emotions as typical of a "neoliberal" approach, then the exclusion and negation of emotions as well as the identification of feeling with being "unfree", combined with the persistence on the primacy of rationality, safety and certainty and a dualistic "right or wrong", become crucial for understanding neoliberalism as a regime of emotional governance. On the other hand, critical academic work on neoliberalism(s) observes that there is a growing interest in a so-called emotional and affective performance as a prerequisite for neoliberal policies (Coleman, 2016; Hanley, 2015; Richard & Rudnyckyj, 2009). Adding to this, Slobodian debunks many common myths about "neoliberal" thought, such as perceiving self-regulating markets as autonomous entities, understanding democracy as synonymous to capitalism, pursuing the disappearance of the state, supporting the primacy of the individual and economic rationality, and even the idea of *homo economicus* since neoliberal imaginaries seemed more interested in a *homo regularis* that aims not at maximizing profit but the chances of survival (2018, pp. 2, 224–235). Having stressed a significant shift in the perception of 'neoliberalism(s), this chapter will now focus on how emotions become after all a constitutive part of neoliberal governmentality.

3 Feeling e(a)ffectively

In recent decades, critical work on localised manifestations of the neoliberal doctrine has been growing fast, adding pieces to a theory of neoliberal governmentality which is to a large extent inspired by the Foucauldian work on power and biopolitics (e.g. Foucault, 1978, 1978–1979/2008). In this frame, neoliberal economics cannot be seen independently from re-inventing a certain type of subjectivity based on entrepreneurship, free trade and individual action. Of course, the story is a bit more complicated. While aiming at the primacy of market economy, power apparatuses of neoliberal governmentality are affected not only by local conditions but also by individuality itself. Dean's argument is crucial in this respect. In her work on neoliberal fantasies she explores how neoliberal ideology does not rely on "symbolically anchored identities" such as "worker", "student" or "housewife", but on "converged imaginary identities" that in multiple and variable ways build on personal creative potential and individuality (Dean, 2009, pp. 49–73). In this sense, any aspect of human life could be engaged in the neoliberal purpose and any individual state works, even when emotional or affective (cf. Binkley, 2011; D'Aoust, 2014).

That said, the question of how different emotional and affective strategies can become means of neoliberal power should first deal with their modes of operation, which are the focus of this section. Even though this chapter does not explore the conceptual resources of emotions, feelings and the recent "affective turn" in social sciences (e.g. Hoggett & Thompson, 2012; Oatley, Keltner, & Jenkins, 2006; Leys, 2011; Wetherell, 2014; Willis & Cromby, 2019), it does recognise that they reflect separate social, material and bodily conditions and therefore they should be seen as separate categories of analysis, yet not irrelevant to each other. Drawing on Massumi's perception of affect as

Feelings in crisis 113

"pre-personal intensity" (1987/2005), Shouse in his account suggests a helpful theorisation according to which "feelings are personal and biographical, emotions are social, and affects are prepersonal" (2005). Moreover, while emotions and feelings are considered as important factors for decision-making by triggering certain ideas, modes of cognition as well as perceptions and memories of what our bodies do or have done during "emoting" (Damasio, 2010; Menon, 2014; Payne, Levine, & Crane-Godreau, 2015), affect is "something indefinable, something that escapes discourse and conceptualisation" (Avramopoulou, 2018).

Interestingly enough, recent approaches, that differentiate between emotions and affects and emphasise the latter's autonomy, intensity, embodiment, and ability to produce meanings, make some room for a perception of affect as producing economic effects. In his popular paper "The Autonomy of Affect" (1995) Massumi mentions how "faith", certain "mindsets" and "feelings about the future" are considered by economists (in specific by Robert L. Heilbroner and Lester Thurow) as capable of changing "real" economic conditions as well as economy itself does (1995, p. 106). In this context, he suggests three prominent traits that this chapter takes into consideration when exploring affective strategies: they are "transversal", "meta-factorial" and "ubiquitous" (Massumi, 1995, pp. 106–107). One more trait could be added here, probably implied in Massumi's approach (see also Massumi, 2010) but clearly articulated in Ahmed's work: affects operate by their effect of circulation "as a form of capital", as "the accumulation of affective value over time" that is attributed to certain signs, objects and subjects, while affects are produced by circulating among them (2004a, pp. 120–121). Hence feelings appear in objects as they are shaped through processes of production, circulation, exchange and so on. Bridging the gap between emotions and affects, Ahmed coins also the notion of "affective economies" to describe how emotions "do things . . . through the very intensity of their attachments", establishing alignments between individuals and communities or bodies and social spaces (2004a, p. 119). Despite their differences both Massumi and Ahmed seem to recognise that when it comes to affective states, there is always something that escapes, something that cannot be articulated, and that places affects on the edge of meaning. This makes the question of emotional and affective neoliberal strategies even more intriguing.

Elaborating on the emergence of affective cultural politics, Anderson raises the clear-cut question of how affects, in their current perception, can become objects of neoliberal power. Attunement and spatiality receive here a prominent analytical function. Dealing with this question, Anderson speaks of a "transitive excess of affect" that is "targeted", "intensified" and finally "attuned" by accordingly excessive power apparatuses, constituting a so-called "logistics of affect" (2010). These processes develop in an "affective present" that is "multiple", "differentially related to and lived" as well as shared through "structures of feeling" and "affective atmospheres" (Anderson, 2014, 2015). The former implies the existence of collective moods, while the latter comes to unsettle the distinction between "emotions" and "affects" by suggesting an attunement

114 *Elena Psyllakou*

of the "pre-prepersonal" to the "transpersonal" and vice versa that operates in moments of neoliberal emergence (Anderson, 2009, 2014, 2015).

While dealing with "neoliberal" emotional and affective strategies as highly complex, geographically, historically and culturally contextualised and to a certain extent escaping, we should not ignore approaches that detect a generic "emotional logic" of neoliberalism. Binkley's work makes a contribution in this direction, suggesting that this emotional logic relies on reflexivity, instrumentality and the government of intimacy. Drawing on subject constructions of late modernity, he examines how encouraging people to talk about their emotions resulted in "re-inventing" the self as an "emotionally enterprising subject" (2018, p. 581). He argues that while governing intimate life has increasingly been turning "interiority" into a project of self-interested action (Binkley, 2012, 2018), the organisation of production in neoliberal contexts relies on emotionality "through the rendering of emotional life as a medium of self-reflection and instrumental action" (2018, p. 581). While the former encourages the interpretation of emotional experience, the latter interferes to orientate this interpretation towards the "affective assets" of "optimism", "resolve" and "emotional resilience" – especially in contexts of risk and uncertainty (2018, p. 585). Paraphrasing Ahmed's comment on how former hierarchy between reason and emotions tends to be displaced by a hierarchy between emotions (Ahmed, 2004b, pp. 3–4), we could argue that this pursuit of specific affective assets, while others are excluded or thought of as non-instrumental, implies a certain kind of "neoliberal cultivation" towards a state of being emotionally performative and effective (see also Ahmed, 2010a, 2010b, on the promise of happiness and how it offers a "hopeful performative"; Hardt & Negri, 2009, pp. 376–383 on the state of happiness).

Contrary to an exclusion or negation of emotions implied in early "neoliberal" philosophical thought, these approaches show how neoliberal techniques of governance are actually interrelated with emotional and affective strategies. What is further argued in this chapter is that these strategies are articulated so much on representations of emotional responses as on narrative affective fluidity (see also Keen, 2003). Taking bank advertising as economic discourse in media apparatus, the next section illustrates such strategies in advertising storytelling, and explores how they comprise the affective present of a neoliberal fantasy in the making. The emphasis will be on the narrative use of structures of feeling and affective atmospheres, emotional and affective assets, emotional and affective charges, as well as self-reflexivity, instrumentality and intimacy as they penetrate aspects of economics of everyday life through processes of attunement and transference.

4 Structuring feeling: the case of bank advertising

In a media ecosystem that interprets and reconstructs aspects of the economic crisis using "negative" emotional discourse, bank advertising, considered as a distinct discursive genre of mass communication, is a bright exception. Of course, this is partly explained by the obvious purpose of reaching consumers and selling bank services. However, the interesting part for this discussion lies in their storytelling and how it specifically rearticulates popular interpretations of the economic and social effects of the Greek crisis using emotional and affective strategies. This case is mostly evident in the advertising campaigns launched by Piraeus Bank, which comprise the material of this analysis. Piraeus Bank was not only a leading financial company in the restructuring of the Greek banking system during the crisis (e.g. Kyriazopoulos & Logotheti, 2019) but also a significant source of advertising income for the majority of the mainstream media (press, TV, and Internet) (Piraeus Bank Group, 2015, 2016). Advertising videos that were shown between 2009 and 2016 for TV and Internet promotion of the bank's services and products were analysed using a methodological framework of Foucauldian approaches to discourse analysis (Foucault, 1969/1982; Keller, 2013) combined with critical discourse analysis (CDA) (Fairclough, 2003; Forchtner & Wodak, 2017; Kress & van Leuween, 2001; Wodak, 1989) and the Essex School (see for example, Howarth, Norval, & Stavrakakis, 2000). This section provides a critical illustration and analysis of the main findings against the backdrop of the aforementioned conceptual framework on the emotional and affective strategies of neoliberal power.

I can!

At a time when Greek society was facing a steep reduction in total income per capita of up to 25% and while unemployment and poverty were rising at equivalent rates (e.g. Mavridis, 2018), seeking to promote a savings account surely sounds out of place and it probably is. But when presented as a self-reflexive "I can do it" challenge, it acquires an instrumental affective charge that is expected to engage and motivate the audience to carry out a certain action: check any place possible for forgotten loose coins and use them for a savings account. This strategy is employed in an advertisement published in around 2011 for the promotion of the bank's savings account "Boro [I can]" (Piraeus Bank, 2011a). Besides the inventive use of the first-person singular that identifies the bank's service with a possible client, the most interesting part is how it replaces "affordability" with "consciousness" and "potential". The storytelling consists in successive images of everyday life with hints of forgotten or misplaced loose coins: in the lining of a bag, between sofa pillows, under the car seats, in a jean's pocket, in a pencil box and so on. At the same time, the voice-over performer describes how one, two or five euros "may not make a difference for everyday life" – although they did at the time – but they could make a difference for a savings account. Calling for an adjustment of economic thinking to small amounts of money, this story fosters the confidence of economic potential when it was consistently disputed in several other rearticulations of the economic crisis.

116 *Elena Psyllakou*

Together with the "I can" challenge, the same advertisement relates a "savings" activity with a reward – in this case a special interest rate. This motivating notion becomes central in two following advertisements, but with intensified emotional and affective charges. The first appears at around the same period of time, again for the promotion of a savings account that was called "Aksizei [It is worth it]" (Piraeus Bank, 2011b). Reward is perceived as the motive to act but also as a response to certain actions. The critical part is how this storytelling places the raising of deposits by one euro per month for special interest rate in the intimate space of home and the affective atmospheres of companionship, motherhood and caring: a young man anxiously makes a surprise cake for his girlfriend; an excited child shows his mother a plant in a handmade pot; a dog fetches the newspaper for his/her owner. The common ground of these intimate moments is that they portray efforts which, irrespective of the outcome, deserve some kind of reward. The rewarding response is also performed with affectively charged expressions – a smile, a kiss, a hug, a head pat and so on. Moreover, the practical value given again to euro coins and the slogan "start with what you can" seems to rebuild a sense of "economic potential", this time attributing to the effort the affective charges that flow from intimate moments to bank services consumption. It could be argued that if taken together these two advertisements can also be thought of as re-conceptualising the value of money and therefore naturalising the effects of austerity politics. At the same time, the emphasis on "effort" and "reward" builds interdiscursive connections with relatively frequently encountered metaphors in media discourse where the acceptance of austerity was articulated as "sacrifice" (Davou & Demertzis, 2013, pp. 114–120; Kountouri & Nikolaidou, 2019), raising expectations for a return to economic stability as a kind of "reward".

The second storytelling that revolves around the notion of "reward" is not so much encouraging action but rather self-reflexivity and individuality. It was 2015, and Piraeus Bank had already launched the slogan "Bank in your own sense", initiating the strategy of individual meaning. In this context, the advertisement of a term deposit service builds on individual understandings of "reward". Men and women, most of them between 35 and 45 years old in an office dress code, are supposedly asked to explain what "reward" means for them, while their smiling, thinking and nostalgic faces succeed one another on screen (Piraeus Bank, 2015a). It is observed that all given meanings are signified by bodily expressions, positive and encouraging words of others as well as a feeling of fulfilment in occasions related to companionship, marriage, family, work and so on. Then this primacy of individual meaning with all its emotional and affective impacts is transferred to the bank as the voice-over performer explains that "in Piraeus Bank" reward "takes the form you give to it" (Piraeus Bank, 2015a). A similar strategy employs individual understandings of "will" and "freedom" but this time aiming less at instrumental action and more at the re-invention of individuality in common structures of feeling.

Your measures, your life

It was in around 2012 that Piraeus Bank's advertisements started to discursively relate economic activities with images of being free. First appears a story of a soldier who in a humorous way is acting against all rules and norms when he asks for permission to go in and out of the camp at his own will: to do some personal chores, then have a coffee and maybe meet a partner later in the evening. Of course, he gets a negative answer from the obviously irritated commander (Piraeus Bank, 2012). Since the military service is mandatory for men in Greece, the place and context of the story reflect very common and popular storytellings, many of which indeed share elements of bittersweet humour. Yet the immediate impact of a mandatory military service is of course confinement and lack of free movement. Taking this confinement as undisputable, the advertisement transfers this rule-breaking wish to act "at one's own will" in the economic field and more specifically in one of the bank's services, using the slogan "in some cases you cannot do what you wish to do. In Piraeus Bank's term deposit +Plus −Minus you can" (Piraeus Bank, 2012). Adding to this, while the military is a place of collective training that minimises individuality, the bank appears as the exact opposite: a place of limitless individuality that is united with others by the common wish to act freely.

A similar slightly different storyline of "acting at one's own will" appears in a following advertisement, in 2014, which promoted the term deposit "Tailored to you" (Piraeus Bank, 2014a). In this case, restrictions imposed on "one's will" are not institutional as in the military camp case but contingent and they are basically everywhere. Using retro-vintage effects, the advertisement tells the story of a young man from his childhood until his joining the navy, capturing moments when something – a wall, a girl, a bicycle, a sun umbrella, a bedcover, a uniform – is well over his size. This size issue seems to be causing different kinds of emotional reactions such as frustration, embarrassment or happiness. These emotional fragments together with the visual effects and the linearity of the narration form a nostalgic biography. Then comes the ascertainment that "in life not everything is tailored to you" and therefore the bank emerges again as a place of exception where all services can be "tailored" to each individual customer.

In the meantime, around 2013, this wish to "act at one's own will" or measurements is complemented by a wish to be "free". Promoting the term deposit "Return and Freedom" two consecutive advertisements build on the affective charge of facial expressions and body movements that reflect happiness and carelessness: waking up out in nature, stretching bodies somewhere in the mountains, doing yoga, hanging from trees, dancing in the house, playing games in open spaces, moving playfully, biking in the city, watching the sunrise, traveling by car, being by the sea and so on (Piraeus Bank, 2013a, 2013b). It may be of some importance to mention that in each of these images there is mainly one character/body. The voice-over performer defines these visual moments as individual meanings of freedom. However, in this case the bank

118   *Elena Psyllakou*

does not rearticulate itself as a place of exception that secures the customer's freedom but rather, using the voice-over, it presents its service as if it is the outcome of the bank's own perception of freedom – namely, the customers' freedom to use their capital and receive high returns (Piraeus Bank, 2013a, 2013b). Claiming for the bank a certain individual meaning of freedom, which is, however, profitable for the customer, the advertisement aligns the bank with the characters shown, and it establishes common structures of feeling free, and affective atmospheres related to senses of freedom as the latter are transferred from any aspect of life to the economic field.

Even though these advertisements do not relate explicitly with the economic crisis context, they do refer to one of its major effects, namely lack of economic freedom both in policy-making and everyday life or in other words lack of possibility to freely determine it (e.g. Kioupkiolis, 2013). If the former advertisements deal with the issue of having an economic potential, the latter deal with the ability to use this potential in the first place, and more accurately to use it freely. While establishing itself as space of economic motivation, reward and freedom of action for others, the bank uses advertising to rearticulate its part in the Greek economic crisis, claiming for itself practices of contribution, support, community and even a driving force to the future. These advertising storytellings could be seen as an effort on behalf of the company to regain people's trust (Davou & Demertzis, 2013). What is of interest for this discussion is how it also moves from emotional and affective strategies of re-inventing individuality to structures of feeling that foster collective moods, mostly related to production and consumption.

Living indicators/indicated life

Since 2010, still the early days of economic crisis, at least four advertising videos present the bank as a key agent of a socially, culturally and environmentally informed economic practice, or the other way around. The advertisements build on the slogan "we give life to economic indicators" and use the symbol of a paper bird made out of a business paper which flies around Greece, showing various aspects of everyday life. In one of these videos, the voice-over performer relates "giving life to indicators" with development and progress and most of all with the people, since indicators are thus brought "closer" to them. Indeed, they seemingly "support start-ups and protect on a daily basis thousands of jobs", they help people consider their "ideas" and "knowledge", and they take initiatives for culture, heritage and the environment (Piraeus Bank, 2010a). As the paper bird flies around parks with children playing, construction sites, offices, university sites, museums, wind parks, the sea and so on, everything seems to be working or, as argued here, seems to be in a state – both physical and emotional – of "functional normality". However, the paper bird is not there only to observe but also to act "supportively" and "helpfully" in people's lives, implying that they are in need. A following advertisement using the same symbol and the same narrative resources portrays a society that needs "protection of jobs", "family aid" for "income" and the "future of the

Feelings in crisis 119

children", as well as "services in isolated areas" (Piraeus Bank, 2010b). Against a strong sense of abandonment that emerged at the time (e.g. Frangos et al., 2012), people should not feel alone.

Bearing this self-imposed, emotionally charged duty of preserving "normality" and orchestrating life (see also Piraeus Bank, 2015b), health, jobs and production become the main sectors of the bank's salutary intervention – if not intrusion. Around 2009, it launches the deposit account "Health and Family", relating this initiative with a monthly compensation "in case of job loss" (Piraeus Bank, 2009a). The advertisement begins with an emotionally ambiguous body position of a married man around 40, closing his eyes with his hands, while the voice-over performer, speaking on behalf of the bank, appeals to men like him, saying, "In Piraeus Bank we know that when you have a family, you may have a lot on your mind. You are more worried. Or maybe not?" (Piraeus Bank, 2009a). And then the tones of expressiveness change and it is revealed that he is just playing a game with his daughter and wife which becomes increasingly fun. More than relating this emotional outcome with "buying" this bank service, this storytelling minimises the effects of a job loss by placing one's health in the safe hands of the banking system, which then takes all the worries away.

In the same vein, but using unusually dramatic tones, the bank advertises "aid and financing programs" for small and medium-sized enterprises, aiming at "the protection of 50,000 jobs" (Piraeus Bank, 2009b). When the real effect on employment was just starting to show, this specific storytelling consists in signs of a possible loss: empty chair in an office, in a restaurant, in a shoe shop and finally an empty sunbed. Unemployment was of course a major social problem at the time, and it was articulated in narrations of anxiety and suffering. But the story tells us more than a practice of corporeal responsibility. Besides relating a job position with a certain lifestyle, this narrative sequence transfers the feeling of a job loss in different aspects of life, making the bank's presence vital for preserving the state of things. With the leading slogan "So as no position is left empty" (Piraeus Bank, 2009b), the bank services are articulated not only as a guarantee of job positions but of a life without losses.

The strategy of "living indicators" as a condition for preserving a worry-less and loss-less functional normality would be of less interest if it did not strengthen people's attachment to production and consumption. While launching special services for agriculture and stock-farming as well as business investment, more storytellings were giving life to the land (Piraeus Bank, 2014b), a childhood to production (Piraeus Bank, 2014c), and a voice to business (Piraeus Bank, 2016a). The affective and emotional charges of a relationship of care, even the intimacies developed between parents and children, are transferred to a relationship between the producer and the process of production, while a company acquires all the traits attributed to its owner: "ideas, vision, knowledge and talents, strains and sleepless nights, his/her people that give their best, his/her partners and clients, a part of the economy that tries to get

120 *Elena Psyllakou*

back to the forefront, jobs, productivity, innovation, the basis for development" (Piraeus Bank, 2016a).

To these engaging stories of how to feel secure, act normally and attach to objects of production, stories of consuming come to be added. In 2016, a humorous campaign named "budget stories" promoted pre-paid cards for "budget control and freedom of movement". These stories have one thing in common: they aim at restoring popular practices of "spending" which were affected by the economic crisis – Christmas presents, marriage ceremony, clothes, hobbies, summer vacation, student life, an unexpected second baby and so on (Piraeus Bank, 2016b). In teaser videos they are characterised in a cinematic mode as "based on true stories . . . life stories . . . dramatically real" (Piraeus Bank, 2016b). And in fact they are, but the point lies again in the bank's intervention. Besides taking for granted that the wish to spend exceeds one's economic potential, these stories naturalise a limitless wish to consume, where the object of spending is irrelevant and the feelings range between anxiety, shame and acceptance of the fact that some dreams of spending may be hard to fulfil. In this interdiscursive framework shared by these stories, the bank that promotes the wish to spend also raises the possible risks and appears once again as a saviour.

Move on

If the emotional and affective strategies that emerged so far appeal to self-reflexive instrumental actions, the primacy of individuality, energies that are transferred from different aspects of everyday life to economy and also structures of "in need/protection" and "precarity/security" that are resolved through trust to a leading entity, a sole advertisement that was released in 2013 sets in motion the affective economic effect of the expectation of the future. Launching the main slogan "stable because it moves", the discursive environment of the advertisement brings both the bank and the people into a self-reflexive position that considers the past and leads to an unavoidable "moving on". Using exceptionally two voice-over performers, the first part raises a self-reflection on time and experience, and how "the future becomes the past", and how "the new becomes old" and "something new takes its place" and how in this, if you stop moving, you will miss the future, what comes next which is "always more important than what preceded" (Piraeus Bank, 2013c). Leaving no room for the present, this narration encourages the audience to follow the example of the bank, forget the past and move on to the future. The second narrative voice presents how the bank has "taken safe steps forward" in favour of business, agricultural economy and so on and therefore how it became a leader in the new banking reality. It is "stable" because it "moves", or to be precise it reclaims for itself one of the most intense and influential structural lacks caused by any crisis: the lack of stability. Against the background of Greek cities and Greek nature, a runner, old couples, babies, shopkeepers, athletes, cleaners, farmers and working women become the moving bodies of what is stable. It is worth mentioning that this future is not described as better, but only as other and more importantly other than the past. Moving is the only thing that takes place in the present.

5 Conclusion: feeling works

While mediatised rearticulations of the economic crisis were aiming at people's numb resilience and acceptance of neoliberal policy-making, these advertisements were aiming at the re-attachment of people to the established economic institutions and to economic practices. And to a certain extent they, indeed, evoked fragments of early "neoliberal" philosophical thought. The reconfiguration of economic potential, the creation of a space of economic freedom, the establishment of instrumental links between the bank and society as well as between the individual and his/her means and resources of production, the presentation of the bank as a driving force to the future proved to be key strategies of a localised neoliberal economic discourse; one that aims at maximising economic activity even when the resources are hardly available; one that advocates the primacy of economy in culture, society and everyday life in a time of floating meanings and identities; one that highlights freedom.

However, in these structural contradictions, the use of emotions and affective strategies proved to be a meaningful bridge, lying in the emotional engagement of affective fluidity and in the attunement of the individual to the collective and vice versa. Personal challenge and reward, a strong sense of individuality developed in collective spaces of work and everyday life, a common need for security and protection, and the common expectation of something other comprise the emotional strategies of a functional normality in the making. At the same time, the narrative resources relied to a large extent on the effect of circulation of affects and intimacies, together with their intensities and embodiments, from different spheres of everyday life to economic activity, multiplying the meanings of the latter. Of course, the exploration of the effects of these strategies on the perceptions of everyday people would add significantly to this discussion. Even though this lies beyond the range of this approach, it could still be assumed that what flows creates space not only for power but also for resistance.

References

Ahmed, S. (2004a). Affective economies. *Social Text*, *22*(2 (79)), 117–139, doi:10.1215/01642472–22–2_79–117.

Ahmed, S. (2004b). *The cultural politics of emotion*. Edinburgh: Edinburgh University Press.

Ahmed, S. (2010a). *The promise of happiness*. Durham and London: Duke University Press.

Ahmed, S. (2010b). Happy objects. In M. Gregg & G. J. Seigworth (Eds.), *The affect theory reader* (pp. 29–51). Durham and London: Duke University Press.

Anderson, B. (2009). Affective atmospheres. *Emotion, Space and Society*, *2*(2), 77–81, doi:10.1016/j.emospa.2009.08.005.

122 Elena Psyllakou

Anderson, B. (2010). Modulating the excess of affect: Morale in a state of "total war". In M. Gregg & G. J. Seigworth (Eds.), *The affect theory reader* (pp. 161–185). Durham and London: Duke University Press.

Anderson, B. (2014). *Encountering affect: Capacities, apparatuses, conditions.* Surrey and Burlington: Ashgate.

Anderson, B. (2015). Neoliberal affects. *Progress in Human Geography, 40*(6), 734–753, doi:10.1177/0309132515613167.

Athanasiou, A. (2012). *I krisi os katastasi "ektaktis anagkis": Kritikes kai antistaseis [Crisis as a state of "emergency": Critiques and resistances].* Athens: Savvalas.

Avramopoulou, E. (Ed.). (2018). Introduction. In E. Avramopoulou (Ed.), *To syn-aisthima sto politiko: Ypokeimenikotites, eksousies kai anisotites ston sychrono kosmo [Affect in the political: Subjectivities, power and inequalities in the modern world]* (pp. 11–67). Athens: Nissos.

Becker, G. (1965). A theory of allocation of time. *The Economic Journal, 75*(299), 493–517, doi:10.2307/2228949.

Becker, G. (1974). A theory of social interactions. *Journal of Political Economy, 82*(6), 1063–1093, doi:10.2307/1830662.

Becker, G. (1981). Altruism in the family and selfishness in the market place. *Economica, 48*(189), 1–15, doi:10.2307/2552939.

Becker, G. (1985). Human capital, effort, and the sexual division of labor. *Journal of Labor Economics, 3*(1 (2)), S33–S58, doi:10.1086/298075.

Binkley, S. (2011). Happiness, positive psychology and the program of neoliberal governmentality. *Subjectivity, 4*(4), 371–394, doi:10.1057/sub.2011.16.

Binkley, S. (2012). The government of intimacy: Satiation, intensification, and the space of emotional reciprocity. *Rethinking Marxism, 24*(4), 556–573, doi:10.1080/08935696.2012.711062.

Binkley, S. (2018). The emotional logic of neoliberalism: Reflexivity and instrumentality in three theoretical traditions. In D. Cahill, M. Cooper, M. Konings, & D. Primrose (Eds.), *The Sage handbook of neoliberalism* (pp. 580–595). London: Sage.

Bjerre-Poulsen, N. (2014). The Mont Pèlerin society and the rise of a postwar classical liberal counter-establishment. In L. Van Dongen, S. Roulin, & G. Scott-Smith, G. (Eds.), *Transnational anti-communism and the cold war: Agents, activities and networks* (pp. 201–217). Hampshire: Palgrave Macmillan.

Burgin, A. (2012). *The great persuasion: Reinventing free markets since the depression.* Cambridge, MA: Harvard University Press.

Butler, J., & Athanasiou, A. (2013). *Dispossession: The performative in the political.* Cambridge and Malden: Polity.

Coleman, R. (2016). Neoliberal capitalism, emotion and morality. *States, Power, Emotion.* Retrieved from <https://emotionalstates.wordpress.com/2016/07/07/neoliberal-capitalism-emotion-and-morality/>.

Damasio, A. (2010). *Self comes to mind: Constructing the conscious brain.* New York: Pantheon Books.

D'Aoust, A.-M. (2014). Ties that bind? Engaging emotions, governmentality and neoliberalism: Introduction to the special issue. *Global Society, 28*(3), 267–276, doi:10.1080/13600826.2014.900743.

Dardot, P., & Naval, C. (2014). *The new way of the world: On neoliberal society.* London and New York: Verso.

Davou, B., & Demertzis, N. (2013). Feeling the Greek financial crisis. In N. Demertzis (Ed.), *Emotions in politics. The affect dimension in political tension* (pp. 93–123). Hampshire and New York: Palgrave Macmillan.

Dean, J. (2009). *Democracy and other neoliberal fantasies: Communicative capitalism and left politics*. Durham and London: Duke University Press.

Fairclough, N. (2003). *Analyzing discourse: Textual analysis for social research*. London and New York: Routledge.

Forchtner, B., & Wodak, R. (2017). Critical discourse studies: A critical approach to the study of language and communication. In B. Forchtner & R. Wodak (Eds.), *The Routledge handbook of language and politics* (pp. 135–149). London and New York: Routledge.

Foucault, M. (1978). *The history of sexuality, vol. 1: An introduction* (R. Hurley, Trans.). New York: Pantheon Books.

Foucault, M. (1982). *The archaeology of knowledge* (A. M. Sheridan-Smith, Trans.). New York: Pantheon Books (Original work published 1969).

Foucault, M. (2008). *The birth of biopolitics: Lectures at the Collège de France, 1978–79* (G. Burchell, Trans.). Hampshire and New York: Palgrave Macmillan (Original work published 1978–1979).

Frangos, Chr. C., Frangos, Con. C., Sotiropoulos, I., Orfanos, V., Toudas, K., & Gkika, E. (2012). The effects of the Greek economic crisis on eating habits and psychological attitudes of young people: A sample survey among Greek university students. In S. I. Ao, L. Gelman, D. Hukins, A. Hunter, & A. M. Korsunsky (Eds.), *Proceedings of the world congress on engineering 2012, vol. 1* (pp. 485–489). London: Newswood Limited.

Friedman, M. (2002). *Capitalism and freedom*. Chicago and London: The University of Chicago Press (Original work published 1962).

Hanley, C. (2015). Neoliberalism, emotional experience in education and Adam Smith: Reading the theory of moral sentiments alongside The wealth of nations. *Journal of Educational Administration and History*, 47(2), 105–116, doi:10.1080/00220620.2015.996868.

Hardt, M. (1999). Affective labor. *Boundary 2*, 26(2), 89–100, doi:10.2307/303793.

Hardt, M., & Negri, A. (2009). *Commonwealth*. Cambridge, MA: The Belknap Press of Harvard University Press.

Hayek, F. (1945). The use of knowledge in society. *American Economic Review*, 35(4), 519–530, doi:10.2307/1809376.

Hayek, F. (1978). *Constitution of liberty*. Chicago and London: The University of Chicago Press (Original work published 1960).

Hayek, F. (1967). Opening address to a conference at Mont Pelerin. In F. Hayek (Ed.), *Studies in philosophy, politics and economics* (pp. 148–159). Chicago: University of Chicago Press (Original work published 1947).

Hoggett, P., & Thompson, S. (Eds.). (2012). *Politics and the emotions: The affective turn in contemporary political studies*. New York and London: Continuum.

Howarth, D., Norval, A. J., & Stavrakakis, Y. (Eds.). (2000). *Discourse theory and political analysis*. Manchester: Manchester University Press.

Illouz, E. (2007). *Cold intimacies: The making of emotional capitalism*. Cambridge and Malden: Polity.

Keller, R. (2013). Doing *discourse research: An Introduction for social scientists* (B. Jenner, Trans.). London: Sage.

Keen, S. (2003). *Narrative form*. Hampshire and New York: Palgrave Macmillan.

Kioupkiolis, A. (2013). Towards a regime of post-political biopower? Dispatches from Greece, 2010–2012. *Theory, Culture & Society*, 31(1), 143–158, doi:10.1177/0263276413501705.

Kountouri, F., & Nikolaidou, A. (2019). Bridging dominant and critical frames of the Greek debt crisis: mainstream media, independent journalism and the rise of a political cleavage. *Journal of Contemporary European Studies*, 27(1), 96–108. doi:10.1080/14782804.2019.1581600.

124   *Elena Psyllakou*

Kress, G., & van Leuween, Th. (2001). *Multimodal discourse: The modes and Media of multimodal communication.* London: Arnold.

Kyriazopoulos, G., & Logotheti, M. R. (2019). How mergers and acquisitions affected the basic accounting elements of Greek Banks during the Euro years 2002–2018. *Journal of Accounting, Business and Finance Research, 7*(2), 24–39, doi:10.20448/2002.72.24.39.

Leys, R. (2011). The turn to affect: A critique. *Critical Inquiry, 37*(3), 434–472, doi:10.1086/659353.

Massumi, B. (1995). The autonomy of affect. *Cultural Critique, 31* (The Politics of Systems and Environments, Part II), 83–109, doi:10.2307/1354446.

Massumi, B. (2005). Notes on the translation and acknowledgements. In G. Deleuze & F. Guattari (Eds.), *A thousand plateaus* (pp. xvi–xviii). Minneapolis: University of Minnesota (Original work published 1987).

Massumi, B. (2010). The future birth of the affective fact: The political ontology of threat. In M. Gregg & G. J. Seigworth (Eds.), *The affect theory reader* (pp. 52–70). Durham and London: Duke University Press.

Mavridis, S. (2018). Greece's economic and social transformation, 2008–2017. *Social Sciences, 7*(1), 1–14, doi:10.3390/socsci7010009.

Menon, S. (2014). *Brain, self and consciousness explaining the conspiracy of experience.* Bangalore: Springer.

Mill, J. S. (2009). *On liberty.* n.p.: The Floating Press (Original work published 1909).

Mirowski, Ph., & Plehwe, D. (Eds.). (2009). *The road from Mont Pèlerin: The making of the neoliberal thought collective.* Cambridge, MA: Harvard University Press.

The Mont Pelerin Society. (1947). *Statement of aims.* Retrieved from <www.montpelerin.org/statement-of-aims/>.

Mylonas, Y. (2014). Crisis, austerity and opposition in mainstream media discourses of Greece. *Critical Discourse Studies, 11*(3), 305–321, doi:10.1080/17405904.2014.915862.

Mylonas, Y. (2017). Liberal articulations of the "enlightenment" in the Greek public sphere. *Journal of Language and Politics, 16*(2), 195–218, doi:10.1075/jlp.15022.myl.

Oatley, K., Keltner, D., & Jenkins, J.M. (2006). *Understanding emotions.* Cambridge, MA, Oxford and Victoria: Blackwell Publishing.

Payne, P., Levine, P. A., & Crane-Godreau, M. A. (2015). Somatic experiencing: Using interoception and proprioception as core elements of trauma therapy. *Frontiers in Psychology, 6*, 1–18, doi:10.3389/fpsyg.2015.00093.

Peck, J. (2008). Remaking laissez-faire. *Progress in Human Geography, 32*(1), 3–43, doi:10.1177/0309132507084816.

Piraeus Bank. (2009a). *Katathetikos logariasmos "Ygeia kai oikogeneia" – Diafimisi* [*Deposit account "health and family" – advertisement*]. Retrieved from <www.youtube.com/watch?v=bhVt4A-cJoU>.

Piraeus Bank. (2009b). *Enischysi kai chrimatodotisi epicheiriseon – Kefalaio kinisis – Diafimisi* [*Business aid and funding – working capital – Advertisement*]. Retrieved from <www.youtube.com/watch?v=iaxsql-bKaY>.

Piraeus Bank. (2010a). *Etairiki ypefthinotita – Koinonia kai politismos – Diafimisi* [*Corporate responsibility – society and culture – advertisement*]. Retrieved from <www.youtube.com/watch?v=kHEMOaq2itk>.

Piraeus Bank. (2010b). *Koinonia – Etairiki Ypefthinotita – Diafimisi* [*Society – corporate responsibility – advertisement*]. Retrieved from <www.youtube.com/watch?v=8LuZhN_DKFY>.

Piraeus Bank. (2011a). *Apotamieftikos logariasmos "Boro" – Diafimisi* [*Savings account "I can" – advertisment*]. Retrieved from <www.youtube.com/watch?v=2MRKnNO7h4k>.

Piraeus Bank. (2011b). *Apotamieftikos logariasmos "Aksizei" – Diafimisi* [*Savings account "It is worth it" – advertisment*]. Retrieved from <www.youtube.com/watch?v=pI-7qijLeFY>.

Piraeus Bank. (2012). *Prothesmiaki katathesi +Syn -Plin* [*Term deposit +plus −minus*]. Retrieved from <www.youtube.com/watch?v=0oII18WR2FY>.

Piraeus Bank. (2013a). *Prothesmiaki katathesi "Apodosi kai eleftheria" – Diafimisi* [*Term deposit "return and freedom" – advertisement*]. Retrieved from <www.youtube.com/watch?v=J5hN6lb0T6I>.

Piraeus Bank. (2013b). *Prothesmiaki katathesi "Apodosi kai eleftheria" – Diafimisi, 2* [*Term deposit "return and freedom" – advertisement, 2*]. Retrieved from <www.youtube.com/watch?v=Q44w-SlZN18>.

Piraeus Bank. (2013c). *Nea etairiki kampania – Diafimisi* [*New corporate campaign – advertisement*]. Retrieved from <www.youtube.com/watch?v=Mv85zaXViyw>.

Piraeus Bank. (2014a). *Prothesmiaki katathesi "Sta metra sou"* [*Term deposit "tailored to you"*]. Retrieved from <www.youtube.com/watch?v=hwUDkQh71_0>.

Piraeus Bank. (2014b). *Symvolaiaki georgia kai ktinotrofia* [*Contract livestock farming program*]. Retrieved from <www.youtube.com/watch?v=edbMHYb4pCg>.

Piraeus Bank. (2014c). *Enas crhonos symvolaiaki trapeziki* [*A year of contract banking*]. Retrieved from <www.youtube.com/watch?v=Qe5fsA2ZfCU>.

Piraeus Bank. (2015a). *Prothesmiaki katathesi "Sta metra sou" me epivravefsi* [*Reward term deposit "tailored to you"*]. Retrieved from <www.youtube.com/watch?v=mpJBh7uegYU>.

Piraeus Bank. (2015b). *Stirizoume tin elliniki oikonomia kai koinonia* [*We support Greek economy and society*]. Retrieved from <www.youtube.com/watch?v=IVU7vOOrThM>.

Piraeus Bank. (2016a). *Anaptyxiaki trapeziki "Eimai"* [*Development banking "I am"*]. Retrieved from <www.youtube.com/watch?v=Es_F8wIFCIU>.

Piraeus Bank. (2016b). *Budget stories apo tin Trapeza Pireos* [*Piraeus bank budget stories*]. Retrieved from <www.youtube.com/watch?v=MBJ-GqbwSVo&list=PL7lVGKxTi2sB2JtScvC51KsfgPLAVPUVR>.

Piraeus Bank Group. (2015–2016). *Oikonomikes katastaseis kai loipes plirofories* [*Financial statements and other information*]. Retrieved from <www.piraeusbankgroup.com/el/Investors/Financials/Financial-Statements?category=4374-2016-law>.

Plehwe, D., & Walpen, B. (2006). Between network and complex organization: The making of neoliberal knowledge and hegemony. In D. Plehwe, B. Walpen, & G. Neunhöffer (Eds.), *Neoliberal hegemony: A global critique* (pp. 27–50). London and New York: Routledge.

Richard, A., & Rudnyckyj, D. (2009). Economies of affect. *Journal of the Royal Anthropological Institute, 15*(1), 57–77, doi:10.1111/j.1467-9655.2008.01530.x.

Shouse, E. (2005). Feeling, emotion, Affect. *M/C Journal, 8*(6). Retrieved from <http://journal.media-culture.org.au/0512/03-shouse.php>.

Slobodian, Q. (2018). *Globalists: The end of empire and the birth of neoliberalism.* Cambridge, MA: Harvard University Press.

Smith, A. (1984). *The theory of moral sentiments.* Indianapolis: Liberty Fund (Original work published 1759).

Stavrakakis, Y. (2014). Debt society: Psychosocial aspects of the (Greek) crisis. In K. Kenny & M. Fotaki (Eds). *The psychosocial and organization studies: Affect at work* (pp. 33–59). Hampshire and New York: Palgrave Macmillan.

Wetherell, M. (2014). Trends in the turn to affect. *Body & Society, 21*(2), 139–166, doi:10.1177/1357034x14539020.

Willis, M., & Cromby, J. (2019). Bodies, representations, situations, practices: Qualitative research on affect, emotion and feeling. *Qualitative Research in Psychology*, 1–12, doi:10.1080/14780887.2019.1656361.

Wodak, R. (Ed.). (1989). *Language, power and ideology: Studies in political discourse.* Amsterdam and Philadelphia: John Benjamins Publishing Company.

8 Laboratories for economic expertise

Lay perspectives on Italian disciplinary economics

Gerardo Costabile Nicoletta

1 Introduction

Economic expertise appears to be one of the most important organizational assets in global governance. This idea spreads from wider social public discussions to the deepest world of academia. While normative and prescriptive theoretical productions of global governance have reified forms and content of expertise and hypothesized subjects in a set of descriptive and procedural rules (Cayarannis et al., 2001), social studies of economics are currently offering several fundamental analytical starting points to understand the power and influence of economics in global political economy (see Maesse's contribution in this volume). This new scientific effort aims to overcome critical political economy representations of economic expertise as the mere linguistic appearance of dominant material class interests and hegemonic concepts (Van Apeldoorn, 2002; Bieler & Morton, 2001). At the same time, newer insights in social studies of economics critically reframe visions of politics of expertise which implicitly assume economic expertise as a self-referential and autopoietic product of professional experts (Radaelli, 1999).

This chapter draws upon various strands of critical studies to offer a contribution to social studies of economics beyond the subjectivist-objectivist divide. The analysis proposes a transnational historical sociology of economics in the Italian national-linguistic context centred on a conceptualization of economic expertise as a power device. The chapter aims to highlight the contingent, contextual and relational dimensions of forms of power of economics, questioning the expert-lay relation in economics. I refer to laypeople as all those molecular and heterogeneous agencies which contingently and contextually resist, refuse, sabotage and threaten dominant socio-technical divisions of labour and relation of propriety. Accordingly, economist discursive practices are interpreted as producers of specialized epistemic fields able to establish the apparent neutrality of technologies of government. The argument is sustained by a theoretically informed narrative of three particular historical experiences from contemporary Italy understood as laboratories for economic expertise. The socio-historical narrative documents how transnational networks of economics, institutions, discourses and practices created discursive mechanisms able to

DOI: 10.4324/9780367817084-10

separate socio-political subjectivities from material and organizational issues to get them in line within the socio-technical divisions of labour and relations of propriety.

The chapter is organized as follows. Section 2 introduces the ideas of laboratories of economic knowledge, jurisdictions and programmes to underline the strengths and limits of social studies on the analysis of the power of economics. It is argued that, amongst multiple dimensions of expertise, the power of economics should be analyzed from the discursive construction of the object of its intervention, i.e. laypeople. Section 3 further elaborates these conceptual tools in a theoretical discussion focusing on the relationship between economic experts and laypeople. The perspective that is presented informs the historical narrative of section 4, which is separated into three sub-sections. Section 4.1 reconstructs how economist interventions in Italy have produced spaces of affirmation for accumulation processes, experimenting with monetarism and developmental programmes. In this laboratory, it is argued, economic discursive practices aimed to separate socio-technical issues from social management and to get populations and territories in line with the Atlantic division of labour. Section 4.2 shows how economists have innovated technologies of thought to deal with the unmanageable reactions of socio-political subjectivities. The section highlights how transnational dialogues, systems of inscription, discourses and policy practices link together to rearticulate political society and state-cadre claims over national regulatory space. Finally, section 4.3 illustrates how economists have promoted the European Union (EU) as a new institutional socio-spatial configuration to foster industrial restructuring and financial innovations able to sterilize workplace tensions and to separate at the highest level of decision-making in economic policy. The section will show how economic expertise aimed to transform the Italian context aligning population and territories 'according to transnational preferences. Such attempts clashed with silent resistances and explosive insubordinations of its object of intervention: laypeople.

2 The power of economics and the laboratory for economic expertise

The idea of a laboratory associated with economic discipline is not new. The most common example of laboratory for economic expertise is the 'Chicago Boys', a group of neo-monetarist post-doc students, who experimented with neoliberal economic reforms in authoritarian Chile (Foxley, 1983; Klein, 2007; Dezalay & Garth, 2011). The case of the Chicago Boys can easily be taken as a clear example of how ideas from global economic knowledge and policy practices intervene to shape national and local contexts. This idea of a national system used as a laboratory for specific policy programmes refers to the more general question about how global, domestic and local dimensions interact through globally produced knowledge working in specific socio-spatial contexts. Liberal constructivist approaches of epistemic community and advocacy coalitions have assumed that institutional learning and knowledge transfer by experts occurs due to growing complexity of global governance tools and mechanisms (Haas, 1992; Cayarannis et al., 2001). Indeed, if it is true that professional formations linked by and for global governance exist, we cannot simply assume the socio-political foundation of institutional forms within which groups of economic experts emerged in a position of power.

Moving beyond the opaque and ambiguous category of experts, inhabiting global governance, Fourcade (2006) suggests studying economists as part of transnational networks that are constantly redefining their (national) professional jurisdictions in order to empower their positions, in both global and domestic social stratification. Fourcade reminds us how, through the universalism of economic thought, its formal-modelling and abstract method, economics as a professional jurisdiction is easily applicable everywhere as a technology of bureaucratic power, shaping states and societies. The creation of economic jurisdiction is made "through its participation in the ongoing economic reconstruction of societies" (Fourcade, 2006:183), in a way that has allowed economists to creatively construct nation-state apparatuses in which the profession of economics has found its privileged place of professional and social institutionalization. The international and national diffusion of capital investments is the Trojan horse through which professional economists influence societies both materially and discursively. Therefore, each corner of the globe can be seen as the potential playground in which professional economists apply abstract knowledge to control the general conditions of labour activity. This construction and reconstruction of domains of intervention by economists as agents of globalization seem to have an auto-generative principle since it is "largely an endogenous process, rather than a result of *external forces*" (Fourcade, 2006:183; emphasis added). In this vision, economists follow the capital expansion and support it through the production of knowledge, while local agents, state technical elites and political society at large are somehow forced to get more and more 'economical'. Even though the subjective creativity of professional economists would be able to set up laboratories to shape society at large, we have to consider that there exist creative and resistive practices adopted by agencies on the playground of economic governance. These creative resistances, I will argue, force economists to continually redefine their interventions.

Overcoming this subjectivist starting point, Dezalay and Garth (2011) have placed economist agencies within a macrostructural sociology enriched by a Bourdieusian reflexive and middle-range theory of the field. In their analysis, the internationalization of state apparatuses represents a field of power in which core countries' professionals experiment with governmental practices. More specifically, the international market of governing expertise, which is mainly constituted by complex professional hierarchies of economics and law experts, represents a field where different socio-political forces engage to survive within imperialistic geopolitical tensions. The internationalization of state apparatuses has set a series of specific competitive dynamics in place between national technical elites and new professional subjectivities, in a global confrontation for gaining more power on domestic and international levels. In this intra-expert dynamic, peripheral countries are used as laboratories for core countries' juridical and economic experiments to impact future policy agendas. The exchange of theoretical knowledge, operative tools and institutional trust finds its experimental field in places where locals are caged in underdeveloped and subalternate positions. Eventually, the reflexive and structural sociology of expertise focuses on structural determinants shaping economists' power within the limits of their semantic and professional universe to improve their capacity to colonize state command hierarchies. The concept of the field, as the crystallization of power relations, appears unable to take into account the relational dimension that exists outside of pyramidal intra-elite conflicts. State technical elites and professionals belong to broader institutional and symbolic fields from which political society at large, subaltern groups and social formations are excluded.

Enlarging the analysis to what exists outside of different professional fields, Eyal and Bockman (2002) have stressed the role of local receivers of globally crafted programmes in the reproduction of economic discursive practices. Drawing upon Foucauldian framework and its sociological translation operated by Latour, they show how Eastern European real socialism was transformed in a laboratory for economic knowledge through which transnational networks were able to reorient economic debates and policies. According to this analysis, changes in economic policy take shape from constant transnational dialogues in which the role of translation is crucial, since it means "the ability of network builders to devise an interpretation that aligns their interests with the network's new recruits whose support and resources are crucial for its survival" (Eyal & Bockman, 2002:314). The reproduction of economic discursive practices is thus managed by complex networks of agents, tools, texts, inscriptions and discourses, which are strategically mobilized to shape economic knowledge and debates in particular contexts. Indeed, economic experts are merely a component of these complex chains of significant inscriptions, contextually translating socio-political programmes and inventing new methods and devices for economic transactions (Eyal & Bockman, 2002). For this reason, experts and expertise must be analyzed as two distinct dimensions, and the recognition of the role of audiences, receivers and laypeople, who are all involved in the formation of expertise (Eyal & Buchholz, 2010), must also be considered. The next section proposes a theoretical discussion that focuses on the role of this broader field of analysis in the social formation and political intervention of economic expertise.

3 The biopolitics of economic expertise

Professional activities, intra-elites' conflicts over knowledge and symbols, organizational dynamics and audience construction are all shaping local and national contexts. This section discusses how this 'outside' dimension can be thought of and integrated into social studies of economics. If, sociologically speaking, there is not an expert without its counterpart, the layperson, the

130 Gerardo Costabile Nicoletta

expert-lay relationship is anything but given. Instead, it is the result of a complex social-historical construction process in which mechanisms of inclusion and exclusion, acts of denomination and technologies of classification mesh with material conditions, technical language, gestures and practices giving shape to social and political projects. This processuality rests on particular social, political and epistemic orders in which representations and calculations are terrains through which forms of power operate. Considering these relational dynamics can show how globally produced abstract knowledge, institutions, state apparatuses and professional agencies link. For this reason, this section goes back to how economics emerged as a disciplinary field and how it structured its epistemic field. It will be argued that the discursive formations of economics create perceptive and linguistic patterns that shape experiences, practices, gestures and discourses of those who are outside its narrow semantic and professional field.

The disciplinary separation of the economic domain from the rest of social and political affairs emerged during the 19th century as an intellectual reaction against the First Workers International lay appropriation of the quasi-transcendental category of labour-value produced by Scottish political economy (Foucault, 2013; Van der Pijl, 2011). Starting from a subjectivist reinterpretation of value by the marginalist revolution and its onto-epistemic corollary, economics was academically institutionalized at the beginning of the 20th century (Van der Pijl, 2011). To this disciplinary enterprise, Anglo-Saxon liberalism and its geopolitics offered the transnational network necessary to spread through Europe, where pure economics had to confront older philosophical traditions of thinking around material organizations and relations of propriety. Despite the fact that economics emerged because of state-phobia (Foucault, 2004), its epistemic field has played a fundamental role in the construction of national regulatory spaces, upon which the same idea of economy emerged. Due to the engagement of academic and professional organizations in national public institutions and international governance, this form of disciplinary economics has discursively reproduced the idea of economy as a given central category for framing any kind of political and institutional project: a force that political society can only affirm to be independent from social management (Mitchell, 2002:245). In confronting different particular normative interpretations of management, economics has developed its universal language, systems of explanation and modes of intervention in the public sphere. Mobilizing this apparatus, the economic expert (re)produces its discursive position in the socio-technical division of labour. This discursive position is grounded in specific representations of material and organizational life that deny validity to other forms of organizational projects. Separating the capitalist relation of propriety and socio-technical division of labour from social knowledge, economics' discursive practice produces its lay counterpart.

The expert-lay distinction operated by disciplinary economics is embedded in broader institutionalized discursive practices that establish social measurements, acts of denomination and classification, and exclusion as relations of power. Discourses and mundane practices make possible the economy as a

Laboratories for economic expertise 131

socio-technical organization in which several devices of calculation are able to organize socio-technical settings (Mitchell, 2002:2). In this sense, the discursive practices of economics operate through sophisticated technologies of thought made by specific procedures of inscription, notation, data collection and counting (Miller & Rose, 1990) and are sustained by the production of meta-historical narratives as organizing myths (Wallerstein, 2001:51). These meta-historical representations are meant to reinterpret retrospectively and normatively unknown processualism from the past with economic conceptual apparatuses. Both the synchronic and diachronic operativity of economics' epistemic field allow objects of discourse to be rendered in particular conceptual forms in order to be amenable to intervention and regulation. This interplay results in discursive mechanisms that define subjects and domains as intelligible and manageable, whereby positive knowledge and institutionalized practices create new technologies of governmentality to normalize actual or potential threats. People who are not participating in the linguistic formalization of this process and who are not (yet) consecrated to economics become, in this way, the object of economic discursive practices. In this sense, because of the separation of individuals, groups and organizations from the management of their autonomous (re)production, discursive practices of economists create their lay counterparts as subaltern so as to be in line with the dominant socio-technical division of labour and relations of propriety.

From this point of view, the power of economics is not merely the formal linguistic reflection of material structures; neither can it be uniquely defined as a set of elite strategies or professional jurisdictions. The power of economics is rooted in the dissemination of knowledge devices that are operating locally, connecting transnational networks, epistemic apparatuses and technologies of bureaucratic power to deal with contingent and contextual situations. In Foucauldian terms, economic expertise is a device that creates and shapes knowledge, connecting heterogeneous elements to generate tactical and strategic goals (Foucault, 2013). It is not identifiable with a specific social formation, professional field, institution or ideology, but it denotes the contingent and strategic relation between groups, ideas and procedures. In this sense, transnational networks of economic experts are an immanent subjectivity of the device of economic expertise, mobilizing discourses, resources, media influences and academic production to deal with contingent and immediate situations. The biopolitics of economic expertise is a social microphysics constructed over a collective entity of populations and territories, separating and re-aligning individuals and organizations within socio-technical divisions of labour.

In the prescriptive definition of fundamental aspects of (re)productive life, the device of economic expertise has to repeatedly face different obstacles, resistances and hostilities. Economic governmentality is a "politically contested terrain" (Sanyal, 2008:255) where those who are governed confront, contest, sabotage and negotiate with the agents of governmentality and their neutrally presented political practices. In turn, such unpredictable and creative resistances by laypeople force economics to permanently restructure the forms and

132 *Gerardo Costabile Nicoletta*

procedures of its intervention and sterilize potential and/or actual insubordinations against the socio-technical settings and relation of propriety. In this sense, reactions and insubordinations profane what economics separates in a sacred zone. In Agamben's (2009) theological interpretation of economy, profanation is a set of de-subjectivization practices of giving back to common use what the device of *oikonomia* (management) has separated into a sacred zone. Drawing from this suggestion, we consider our perspective to be a lay perspective that critically re-appropriates the subalternate position that economic discourses produce over people not consecrated to its socio-epistemic order, which questions and investigates what the disciplinary separation of social sciences sacralizes: the socio-technical division of labour and relations of propriety.

From this lay perspective, laboratories for economic expertise are not simply the product of symbolic exchanges within professional fields for the conquest of commanding state hierarchies, nor are they simply a form of legal jurisdiction through which abstract knowledge defines the general condition of people's forms of life. Rather, laboratories for economic expertise are transnational spaces of affirmation socio-historically crafted by and for economists and their discursive practices that aim at getting populations and territories in line with specific socio-political programmes. Since the 'living matter' of these laboratories is not so pliable and often profanes what economics sacralizes, transnational networks, institutions, system of inscriptions and modes of intervention all connect to innovate technologies of government. These strategic connections aim to separate from social management fundamental aspects of (re)productive life in specific socio-technical settings. Therefore, the lay perspective will highlight how economic expertise has separated from social and political subjectivities the design of their (re)productive life while inserting them in the needs of accumulation processes. Reactions and insubordination of subjectivities emerge from economic discursive formations and, in turn, innovate the economists' intervention.

4 Lay perspective on Italian disciplinary economics

Throughout the last thirty years, economists' discourses have held a privileged position in Italian structural reforms, in both the centre-left and centre-right government coalitions. The 2010 technical government lead by the ordoliberal economist Mario Monti, which surfaced in the midst of the debt sovereignty crisis in Europe, is just the latest example of economists' role in aligning national governmental agendas with transnational economic imperatives. This powerful position produced and was produced by representations of the economy as a zone that is neutral and separate from social claims, to be managed by technical measures that are guided by economic experts.

Through our lay perspective, this section proposes a transnational historical sociology of the forms of power of economics within the narrative of three experiences in contemporary Italy. The research is based on a qualitative bibliographical selection of both primary and secondary sources, which recompose key discursive events within the Italian national-linguistic field. Firstly, the narrative analyzes the economic experiment of monetarism and developmental policy. Economists' discursive interventions are interpreted as an attempt to separate the definition of economic order from social pressures to shape rural social settings in accordance with the new socio-technical division of labour crafted in the US hegemonic ascendancy. Then, it is shown how economists' discursive practices intervened to curb and rearticulate trade unions' claims, practices of insubordination and state-cadre pervasiveness. Finally, it is shown economists on the front lines of the construction of the EU as an institutional field to constitutionally separate monetary policy from socio-political pressure and to experiment with new socio-spatial sites of affirmation.

4.1 The making of the Italian model of development (1922–1950)

A degree of continuity with liberal governmental programmes characterized the first years of the fascist regime (Mattei, 2017). Initially, with its strong affirmation of the scientific division of labour in factories and its discipline enforced on the countryside, the fascist regime represented an armed form of liberalism, able to satisfy industrial and agrarian interests, with the compliance of the Atlantic powers (Gallo, 2009). However, in the aftermath of the 1929 crisis, liberal hegemony in the definition of the economic order began to be challenged. New economic public institutions intervening in the financial and industrial crisis, forged by state-cadres such as the Istituto per la Riscostruzione Industriale (Institute for Industrial Reconstruction) and Instituto Nazionale di Economia Agraria (National Institute of Agrarian Economics), entirely overcame traditional liberal practices for governing economic life while fascist corporative economics profaned pure economic dogmas. Within these ideological and organizational dynamics, a new generation of state economic technicians engaged in measuring activities and mapping the composition of the Italian population. Throughout the 1930s, statistical and demographic studies increased so much that in 1936 Istitutio Nazionale di Statistica (National Institute of Statistics) produced its first survey while national development became the core of a scientific enterprise within the institutional apparatuses (Patriarca, 2012).

The research department of the Italian central bank, the *Servizio Studi*, was at the centre of this institutional empowerment process. It represented, at the same time, the new-born brain of state financial monopolism and the leading domestic hub of international intellectual exchanges for young economists through fellowship programmes and experiences abroad (Scatamacchia, 2005). The link offered by the central bank research department gave institutional form to consolidated transatlantic networks and dialogues, enforced by the activity of private organizations such as the Rockefeller Foundation (Gemelli, 2005; Attal, 2012). In fact, against the coercive discipline of corporative economics imposed by the fascist regime, the intellectual resistance developed in transnational spaces of exchanges of ideas, theories, discourses and scientific

134   *Gerardo Costabile Nicoletta*

practices. Due to these exchanges, Italian economics remained well connected to the Anglo-Saxon world thanks to the role of the *Servizio Studi* as the headquarters in the production of economic data, inscription, documents and analysis (Scatamacchia, 2005).

In 1943, when it was becoming clear that the fascist regime was collapsing, a group of Catholic economists intervened with a programmatic manifesto entitled the *Codice Camaldoli*. Reverberating ordoliberal principles of social market economy and constitutional order, this manifesto expressed the Catholics' biopolitical project founded on social hierarchies, professional authority, family and productivity. It was the product of the economization of Catholic public discourse, and it saw the integral intervention of state economic institutions as a virtuous experience for the construction of a proper Christian socio-economic order (Persico, 2014). According to Catholic economists working in emerging state institutions, public holdings and state apparatuses could act positively on the formation and accumulation of capital (Baietti & Farese, 2010).

In the ideological framework outlined by Catholic economists, the state could question the relations of propriety when these appeared to be unwilling to create collective wealth (Magliulo, 1999). Moreover, in order to guarantee social justice and overcome class conflict, Catholic economists saw it necessary to transform proletarians into proprietors through state interventions in the agrarian relations of propriety. For different reasons, the Communist Party (PCI) at the time also shared the same productivist appeal, interpreting the factory system as the natural socio-technical organization (Righi, 2011), on which to construct a robust democratic state projected towards a socialist society. Both Catholics and Communists worried about the social unrest in the countryside. In fact, the end of fascism's ruralist discipline led to the outbreak of peasant jacqueries and revolts. Peasants' insubordinations questioned the socio-technical division of labour and relations of propriety. At the same time, they proposed alternative socio-political management of (re)productive life through common propriety of private estates (Ammendolia, 1990; Renda, 1980).

In 1946, during the discussion about the ratification of the expert statement of Bretton Woods that took place in the constituent assembly of the new-born Republic, the consensus over state interventionism of the anti-fascist alliance was immediately rearticulated. Translating Hayek's and Robbins's ideas on market federalism, the liberal economist and Rockefeller fellow Luigi Einaudi discursively insulated any possible alternative to the integration of state apparatuses into higher international political organisms, which was hoped would be better than the golden standard that the interwar years had destroyed (Masini, 2012; Cafaro, 2008). With the discourse of a binding engagement with the international community, the years of the constituent assembly became years of active austerity measures used as a therapy for guaranteeing monetary stability as the fundamental condition for economic development.

From 1945 to 1948, this discourse informed the so-called *linea Einaudi*. As the governor of the central bank and minister of budget, Einaudi applied the quantitative monetary theory and liberal governmental practices on the national economy, experimenting with the first set of monetarist policies of the postwar era. The tax increase, the abolition of political prices over food and the stop on bank credit to new industries intended to discipline any extra-economic attempts at managing purchasing power. Meanwhile, the reports of the Treasury structured a new national economic balance, which was built on the accounting of resources of internal production, public expenditures, investments and family consumption. Since the linking of commercial balance to any possible economic-political programmes, innovations in accounting started to offer powerful cognitive infrastructure for the discourse on external constraints.

In 1947, US government interventions enforced the new state's binding engagement. The Marshall Plan suspended the activities of the Bretton Woods institutions and intervened to financially and scientifically sustain industrial and technological development, importing new procedures, inscriptions and reports. In order to contain any possible political threats to US geopolitical aspirations, American experts pushed for the integration of the country into divisions of labour oriented to and guided by the US. The austerity therapy of liberal economists created the need for extraordinary interventions to foster capital formation and socio-technical developments, even shortly after the end of the Marshall Plan aid. It is in this context that the territories of southern Italy become the privileged object of economist discursive practices. Already since 1946, the Association for the Industry in the South (SVIMEZ), founded by Catholic economists, translated the southern question from a socio-political issue into a technical and economic object, to be studied, treated and guided by economic experts. With the *Servizio Studi*, the SVIMEZ became the new gravitational centre for Anglo-Saxon economists who found Italy an interesting case study for economics (D'Antone, 1995). Overpopulation became the common object of intervention for Catholic economists and international economic experts. At the centre of its scientific production and in order to curb the excess of workforce and limited resources, the economist Rosenstein-Rodan (1943, 1944) presented the project of integration of underdeveloped areas within the global division of labour. In 1948, as the head of International Bank for Reconstruction and Development, Rosenstein-Rodan invented the impact loan, a plan investment based on an organic programme of long-term development. Invited by the *Servizio Studi*, the economist Vera Lutz (1963) later formalized her vision on the export of manpower as the privileged solution for resolving territorial imbalance. The idea that emerged out of this was the total restructuring of agrarian settings to liberate manpower that could fulfil export-led industries' needs.

These discursive formations that emerged in transnational networks of economics were practically sedimented in the institution of the *Cassa per le opere straordinarie per il Mezzogiorno* (Fund for the south) founded in 1950. Based on a meta-historical representation of economic development, the *Cassa*'s extraordinary intervention intended to foster the conditions for capital formation and accumulation in southern areas through the mobilization of unused manpower and the creation of a sound basis for industrialization. It aimed at intervening

136 *Gerardo Costabile Nicoletta*

directly, through an expert-technical and independent guide, in the transformation of land settlements and in the mechanization of agricultural sectors as well as in the construction of communication infrastructures and tourist facilities. Connecting the Catholic biopolitical projects, US geopolitical aspiration and the liberal discourse, the economic expertise separated rural social formations from their own management of (re)productive life and got the population and territories in line with the production of the export-oriented industrialization of the new Atlantic division of labour.

4.2 The crisis as governing expertise (1960–1977)

At the beginning of the 1960s, the geopolitical conditions that guaranteed the functioning of industrial development disappeared. New productivity system calculations imposed by the General Agreement on Tarif and Trade and European Economic Community international agreements increased the rhythm of techno-organizational restructuring. Moreover, the restored convertibility and the Eurodollar markets offered investors strategies for escaping from state-cadre economic programmes. In this section, I illustrate how economic expertise linked new systems of inscription, new modes of intervention and financial innovations to curb and reframe rising claims over the definition of economic policy agenda, disciplining both trade unions and state-cadres.

The discursive mechanism crafted over the Italian southern territories and populations transformed socio-technical settings and, at the same time, increasingly enforced state-cadre public holding interventions. Throughout the 1950s, state-cadres had in fact expanded their influences over central sector industrial and service production, controlling 80% of the GDP through a capillary system of agencies for the management of public holdings performance and supply-side policies. In the 1960s a new phase of the *Cassa per il Mezzogiorno* engaged in direct public industrial investments in the southern regions as well as in the functional control of the mobility of the southern population in order to feed northern industrial accumulation needs (Ferrari-Bravo & Serafini, 1973). Crafted as subjectivity in the exodus from the countryside to the industrial triangle (Milan, Turin, Genoa), the populations started to radicalize. In 1962, a general strike of metalworkers, the manpower on which the export-led industry depended, enormously empowered the bargaining power of trade unions and obtained a substantial increase in wages. Since then, trade unions began to ask to sit at the table of economic programming opened by centre-left coalitions, aiming to change the direction of the model of development beyond low wages and low consumption (Lama, 1976).

This reformist appeal was immediately curbed by the management of the currency crisis, which was characterized by a new deflationary therapy. With the help of a new US loan, the central bank could face monetary instability through restrictions and avoid devaluation. This anti-inflationary policy imposed a violent restructuring of industrial sectors, provoking a crisis in full employment policies and political party machinery pervasiveness. With the

Laboratories for economic expertise 137

return of deflationary therapy following the financial instability in 1963, the *Servizio Studi* engaged in knowledge production aimed at forecasting the economic behaviour of families, firms and public agencies. The interests of the economists of the *Servizio Studi* start to focus on the impact that central bank monetary policies had over people's expectations and activities. The renovation of the *Servizio* was promoted by the neo-governor Guido Carli, a highly reputable economist, who emerged out of corporativist economics and later affirmed himself in international economic institutions. Carli framed the central bank discourse around the idea of profit as the engine of development and credit as a fundamental element in investments. To guarantee the profits, it was necessary to link wage and productivity and enhance financial markets. In this discourse, the instrumental (i.e. political) use of the credit system by state-cadre elites and their political parties represented the main obstacle for an efficient economic system.

In 1962, financed by the Ford Foundation, the American economist Ackley (1962) published an econometric representation of the model of development for SVIMEZ. In the same years, an econometric model started to be experimented by the *Servizio Studi*, accompanied by short-term and long- to middle-term macroeconomic analyses. Its chief consultant was the US-based economist Franco Modigliani, who remained particularly active in public interventions on national media, as well as in the economic-academic production in specialized journals (Asso, 2010). Transposed by the *Servizio Studi*, the econometric model posed the balance of payment as the only independent variable in the economic system, namely a mathematical model which provided codified accounting practices to forecast the national economy as integrated into a highly competitive and unstable context. With the increasing social pressures and political conflicts over monetary management, the central bank economists adopted the econometric model to insulate calculations from the national government and political pressures (Peluffo, 2000).

Economists' innovations perform linguistic asymmetry in the knowledge of the economy in order to experiment with spaces of independence from sociopolitical pressures of the central bank. This system of inscription (re)produced by economic expertise caged trade unions and centre-left reformism in a lay position. New calculation technologies offered the discursive terrain where the wage increases of 1962 began to be depicted by economists as an internal shock. The innovation that emerged in the transnational symbolic exchange of economists did not stop the increasing pressure over financial management and industrial productivity. Public sectors continued to grow, especially in southern regions as indirect and politically mediated income redistribution. More importantly, the uprising of the political society of the 1970s forced the implementation of organic social legislations such as the *Statuto dei lavoratori* (1970). Workplaces became the terrain upon which radical fractions of trade union movement theorized the autonomy of the working class as the engine of technological development (Tronti, 2006). From 1969 the increasing tensions for the diffusion of extra-economic practices in workplaces and industrial cities

138 *Gerardo Costabile Nicoletta*

became a serious problem for the economic governmentality. Sabotage and insubordination created an unmanageable incognito for economic programmes (Wright, 2002; Negri, 2012).

In 1974, the oil shock, capital outflows and increasing inflation led to a crisis of balance of payments. The central bank imposed a new austerity therapy to curb imports and consumption. In this context, experts of the International Monetary Fund experimented with massive loans conditioned to policy measures to stop the financial crisis. The econometric model of the *Servizio Studi* inspected the IMF 'letter of intention' and accepted the conditional loan. This emergency offered the terrain to rearticulate the increasing power of trade unions with the new context. Already in 1972, the economist Sylos Labini (1972) called for a new role of responsibility for trade unions in the context of growing global competition. In the same years, public interventions concerning the insertion of consumption in wage index, known as the 'Modigliani Controversy', opened a new discursive field which was successful in getting trade unions to accept low wages as a condition for rescuing productivity and avoid inflation (Masini, 2004). In 1976, Modigliani was invited by the PCI political and economic research centre to share his idea that inflation and balance of payments were the main interests of workers (Cattabrini, 2012). Simultaneously, the PCI then supported the cut of salaries and a new deflationary therapy. Hoping to obtain a seat in government, the PCI adhered to the austerity programme interpreted as anti-consumeristic policy. According to the general secretary of PCI, austerity could have been an occasion to transform the country (Berlinguer, 1977). In 1977, the EUR congress of Confederazione Generale Italiana del Lavoro (Italian General Confederation of Labour) marked up the end of wage growth as an independent variable. After being separated from claims over monetary policy, trade unions entered in the economic discursive field, accepting productivity and international competition as neutral domains.

4.3 Economic experts as an EU constitutional force (1979–1993)

The reactions, resistances and insubordinations by socio-political subjectivities forced economists to innovate technologies of government experimented with during industrial development. In this section, I conclude by narrating the active role taken by economists in accommodating industrial restructuring and financial innovations as technologies of government in order to sterilize conflicts in workplaces and in the management of public finance by political parties. Since the *Piano Pandolfi* (1979), the European monetary coordination became the new terrain on which to construct knowledge hierarchies to discursively separate socio-political pressure from economic agenda.

In 1981, the economic expert of the different governments of the late 1970s, Beniamino Andreatta, together with the neo-governor of the central bank Ciampi, organized an open conspiracy to end the central bank's coverage of unsold state bonds. Conceived in the professional exchange between the

Servizio Studi and the Massachusetts Institute of Technology (MIT), the London School of Economics (LSE) and Chicago University (Quaglia, 2005), the 'divorce' became the metaphor expressing the separation of decisional centres of state expenditure and the institute issuing money. With this decision, the Ministry of Treasury policies were judged by the markets (Andreatta, 1991), thus linking the financial resources of economic policy to investor preferences. The privatization of public debt was ratified without parliamentary discussion, and the undemocratic nature of this fundamental decision over state financing brought an end to the executive in 1982.

In 1983, the vice president of the European Commission, Étienne Davignon, pushed for the creation of an expert group that would be able to represent European industries and construct a permanent dialogue with them (Van Apeldoorn, 2002:85). The European Round Table of Industrialists was constituted as the organic intellectual group of European industry for the setting up of policy agendas and the relaunching of continental profitability. The discourses of euro-pessimism and euro-sclerosis pointed to a new social and political composition of valorization processes, which were forged on the absolute impossibility of returning to wage-driven policies. Labour-market rigidity became the leitmotif describing the source of stagflation. In the same year, a consultative scientific committee composed of economic experts was founded to study public debt management. The group of experts intended to guide the Ministry of Treasury towards the liberalization of financial sectors. For economic experts, 1992 represented a unique occasion to transform Europe as an economic and juridical space. According to the Italian economist Mario Monti, Europe offered a further step towards opening the door to the financial innovation that was needed to impose a competitive regime to credit institutes and force public administrations to engage in international competition (Castiglioni, 2013).

In its survey of Italy 1984–85, the Organisation for Economic Co-operation and Development (OECD) suggested that national government strongly implement reforms for overcoming political obstacles (Fouskas, 1998:83), such as the unwillingness of the political party machine to privatize public holdings and renounce their income (political) redistribution. In 1986, the macroeconomic policy group issued a report focusing on the role of capital in unemployment reduction. The report, presented by Modigliani, sustained that, in order to solve unemployment, a new wave of economic growth could be achieved through a series of fiscal and monetarily adequate policies (Castiglioni, 2013:35). Rescuing productivity and profitability became urgent for improving internationally linked financial services, for liberalizing financial sectors and for fostering industrial restructuring. Socialist neo-reformism resisted representing the national economy as a new economic growth locomotive supported by a modification of GDP calculation rules (Graziano, 2007:279) while workplace conflicts were sterilized by industrial restructuring.

In 1986, the European Single Act constrained monetary policy and liberalization directives and finally integrated them within the international financial

140　*Gerardo Costabile Nicoletta*

system. With the institutional automatism launched by ESA, negative integration and deregulation were implemented in the midst of highly unstable political consensus. The construction of a scaffolding for European economic governance became the centre of economist discursive practices devising new economic methods able to confine economic reforms to technical and neutral domains. In 1992, during the intra-governmental arrangement of the Maastricht treaty, the juridical inquisition against extra-market practices of the governing class, known as *Tangentopoli*, offered the political vacuum for extra-parliamentary guidance by the *Servizio Studi* economists. In the definition of Maastricht parameters, the technocratic management of public finance through economist practices enforced economist positions and achieved what was not possible to achieve through parliamentary channels (Carli, 1993; Dyson & Featherston 1996). The privatization of public holdings, the abolition of wage indexation and the liberalization of financial sectors began in 1993 with the technical government guided by the former governor of the central bank Ciampi.

The Italian neoliberal experiment has been forged by economists in order to discipline the political class and get workers' institutions in line with the restructuring era of the 80s. The dismissal and definitive end of the *Cassa per il Mezzogiorno* in 1992 reframed the socio-spatial configuration objectivating territories as collective economic actors facing off in international competition (Salento, 2014) and thus re-territorialized sites of affirmation for economic expertise to more local contexts. While decision-making is moved to a higher level of governance designated to lessening "short-run political pressures on the formulation of economic policy" (Gill, 1998), a new developmental framework, with its highly technical language, redefines territories through forms of bureaucratic power, economic discourses and policy practices, crafting subjectivities in line with the new European socio-technical division of labour.

5 Conclusion

This chapter has investigated forms of power of economics, focusing on contextual reactions and contingent resistances of the object of economic intervention: laypeople. From this lay perspective, economic expertise is not a neutral organizational asset. It does not represent an autopoietic force producing self-referential knowledge in order to let particular fractions survive in social stratification; neither is it a mere battlefield for national and international professional vocation. Instead, economic expertise is the relationship between professionals, theories, data, operative epistemologies, institutions, public interventions, and social and geopolitical tensions. This concatenation of heterogeneous elements is produced within the tension between transnational networks and institutions facing contingent situations. As the historical narrative has shown, the connection of Catholic biopolitical project, US geopolitical aspirations and (neo)liberal programmes created new strategical fields of knowledge to reframe potential threats over postwar order. The discursive mechanisms produced by economic interventions objectivized southern territories and population, representing

Laboratories for economic expertise 141

the economy as an independent and separated domain from social conflicts and political management. In doing so, economic expertise subjectivized southern peasantry as exportable manpower got in line within the Atlantic division of labour. Through knowledge devices operating locally, economic expertise shaped socio-political subjectivities consecrated to economic epistemic fields. In this way, lay subjectivities were caged in a subaltern position, misrecognizing the arbitrariness and the socio-political foundation of economics.

The economists' discursive position in defining way of life enjoyed power and authority as long as those subjectivities did not reclaim the power of definition of government agenda. As I have shown, during the 1970s unforeseen and unmanageable reactions of lay subjectivities overthrew the effectiveness of economic discursive practices. Due to these reactions, transnational networks of economists had to contextually innovate representations, calculations and interventions. The European neo-constitutional initiative represents an institutionalized site of affirmation for economic expertise to foster accumulation processes and innovate technologies of government. In this way, economic expertise has forged its lay population integrated within the permanent restructuring of socio-technical divisions of labour but immanently ready to explode to lay bare the arbitrariness of the epistemic field of economics.

References

Ackley G. (1962). *An econometric model of Italian post war growth*. SVIMEZ, Rome.

Agamben G. (2009). *What is an apparatus?* Stanford University Press, Stanford.

Ammendolia I. (1990). *L'occupazione delle terre in Calabria 1946–1949 (Proletari senza Rivoluzione)*. Gangemi Editore, Rome.

Andreatta B. (1991). *Il divorzio tra Tesoro e Bankitalia e la lite delle comari: uno scritto per il Sole-24ore*. Available at www.ilsole24ore.com/fccmd=art&artId=891110&chId=30.

Asso P. (2010). *Franco Modigliani: L'impegno civile di un economista*. Protagon editori, Toscani.

Attal F. (2012). *The Rockefeller foundation fellows and grants in the humanities and social sciences, 1924–1970: Renewing social sciences, reshaping academic disciplines, and the making of a transnational network in Italy*. Rockefeller Archive Center, New York.

Baietti S. & Farese G. (2010). Sergio Paronetto and the Italian economy between industrial reconstruction of the 1930s and the reconstruction of the country in the 1940s. *The Journal of European Economic History*, vol. 39, no. 3, pp. 411–425.

Berlinguer E. (1977). *Austerità occasione per trasformare l'Italia*, Editori Riuniti, Rome.

Bieler A. & Morton A.D. (2001). *Social forces in the making of the new Europe: The restructuring of European social relations in the global political economy*. Palgrave Macmillan, London.

Carli G. (1993). *Cinquant'anni di vita italiana*, collaboration with Paolo Peluffo. Economica Laterza, Bari.

Castiglioni C. (2013). *Il tecnocrate. I trascorsi del prof. Mario Monti, economista e fiduciario dei poteri*. Kaos edizioni, Milano.

Cayarannis E.G., Pirzadeh A. & Popescu D. (2001). *Institutional learning and knowledge transfer across epistemic communities*. Routledge, London.

Cafaro P. (2008). La lira italiana e l'integrazione monetaria internazionale: il dibattito in sede di Costituente. In *Il dilemma dell'integrazione. L'inserimento dell'economia Italiana nel sistema occidentale (1945–1957)*, edited by A. Cova. Franco Angeli, Milano.

142   *Gerardo Costabile Nicoletta*

Cattabrini F. (2012). Franco Modigliani and the Italian left-wing: The debate over labor cost (1975–1978). *History of Economic Thought and Policy*, vol. 1, pp. 75–95.

D'Antone L. (1995). L' 'interesse straordinario' per il Mezzogiorno (1943–60). *Meridiana*, no. 24.

Dezalay Y. & Garth B.G. (2011). Hegemonic battles, professional rivalries and the international division of labour in the market for the import and export of state-governing expertise. *International Political Sociology*, vol. 5, pp. 276–293.

Dyson K. & Featherstone K. (1996). Italy and EMU as a Vincolo Esterno': Empowering the technocrats, transforming the state. *South European Society and Politics*, vol. 1, no. 2, pp. 272–299.

Eyal G. & Bockman J. (2002). Eastern Europe as laboratory for economic knowledge: The transnational roots of neoliberalism. *American Journal of Sociology*, vol. 108, pp. 310–352.

Eyal G. & Buchholz E. (2010). From the Sociology of intellectuals to the sociology of intervention. *Annual Review of Sociology*, vol. 36, pp. 117–137.

Ferrari-Bravo L. & Serafini A. (1973), *Stato e Sottosviluppo. Il caso del Mezzogiorno Italiano*. Feltrinelli editore, Milano.

Fourcade M. (2006). The construction of global profession: The transnationalization of economics. *American Journal of Sociology*, vol. 112, no. 1 (July), pp. 145–194.

Foucault M. (2013). *Le parole e le cose. Un'archeologia delle scienze umane*, Bur, Milano.

Foucault M (2004). *Nascita della biopolitica. Corso al Collége de France (1978–1979)*. Feltrinelli editore, Milano.

Foxley A. (1983). *Experimentos neoliberals en América Latina*. Colecciòn Estudios CIEPLAN, Santiago Chile

Fouskas V. (1998). *Italy, Europe, the left: The transformation of Italian communism and the European Imperative*. Ashgate, London.

Gallo E. (2009). Italy and Spain: Different patterns of state/society complexes in the contemporary era. *Journal of Contemporary European Studies*, vol. 17, no. 2, pp. 255–270.

Gemelli G. (2005). Un imprenditore scientifico e le sue reti internazionali: Luigi Einaudi e la fondazione Rockefeller. *Le Carte e la Storia*, vol. 1, pp. 189–202.

Gill S. (1998). European governance and new constitutionalism: Economic and monetary union and alternatives to disciplinary neoliberalism in Europe. *New Political Economy*, vol. 3, no. 1, pp. 5–26.

Graziano M. (2007). *Italia senza Nazione? Geopolitica di una identità difficile*. Donzelli editore, Roma.

Haas P. (1992). Introduction: Epistemic communities and international policy coordination. *International Organization*, no. 46.

Klein N. (2007). *The shock doctrine: the rise of disaster capitalism*. PM Press, New York.

Lama L. (1976). *Intervista sul sindacato*, edited by Massimo Riva. Laterza, Roma and Bari.

Lutz V. (1963). *Italy: A study in economic development*. Oxford University Press, Oxford.

Magliulo A. (1999). La Costituzione economica dell'Italia nella nuova Europa. Un' interpretazione storica. *Miscellanea Studi e note di economia*, vol. 3, p. 99.

Masini F. (2004). *SMEmorie della lira. Gli economisti italiani e l'adesione al sistema monetario europeo*. Franco Angeli, Milano.

Masini F. (2012). Luigi Einaudi and the making of the neoliberal project. *History of Economic Thought and Policy*, pp. 39–59.

Mattei C. E. (2017). Austerity and repressive politics: Italian economists in the early years of the fascist government. *The European Journal of the History of Economic Thought*, vol. 24, no. 5.

Miller P. & Rose N. (1990). Governing economic life. *Economic and Society Journal*, vol. 19, no. 1.

Laboratories for economic expertise 143

Mitchell T. (2002). *Rule of experts: Egypt, technopolitics, modernity.* University of California Press, Stanford.

Negri A. (2012) [1977]. *La forma Stato: Per la critica dell'economia politica della Costituzione.* Baldinig Castoldi Dalai editore, Milano.

Patriarca S (2012). A total science: statistics in liberal and fascist Italy. *Journal of Modern Italian Studies*, vol. 17, no. 4.

Peluffo P. (2000). "Il cavallo non beve": Dibatti degli anni Sessanta su politica monetaria e programmazione economica. In *Guido Carli, Scritti scelti, a cura di Paolo Peluffo Federico Carli.* Laterza, Roma and Bari.

Persico A.A. (2014). *Il codice Camaldoli. La DC e la ricerca della 'terza via' tra Stato e mercato (1943–1993).* Guerini editore, Milano.

Quaglia L. (2005). Civil servants, economic ideas and economic policies: Lessons from Italy. *governance. International Journal of Policy, Administration and Institutions*, vol. 18, no. 4, pp. 545–566.

Radaelli C.M. (1999). The public policy of the European Union: Whither politics of expertise? *Journal of European Public Policy*, vol. 6, no. 5, pp. 757–774.

Renda F. (1980). *Contadini e democrazia in Italia 1943–1947.* Guida Editori, Napoli.

Righi A. (2011). *Biopolitics and social change in Italy: From Gramsci to Pasolini to Negri.* New York: Palgrave Macmillan.

Rosenstein-Rodan P. (1943). Problems of industrialization of Eastern and South-Eastern Europe. *The Economic Journal*, vol. 53, no. 210–211, pp. 202–211.

Rosenstein-Rodan P. (1944). The international development of economically backward areas. *International Affairs (Royal Institute of International Affairs 1944)*, vol. 20, no. 2 (April), pp. 157–165.

Sanyal K. (2008). *Rethinking capitalist development: Primitive accumulation, governmentality and post-colonial capitalism.* Routledge, London.

Salento, A. (2014). *The neo-liberal experiment in Italy: False promises and social disappointments.* CRESC Working paper series. University of Manchester.

Scatamacchia R. (2005). Un laboratorio per la Ricostruzione: Il Servizio Studi della Banca d'Italia. In *Politiche scientifiche e strategie di impresa: le culture olivettiane e i loro contesti*, edited by G. Gemelli. Adriano Olivetti Foundation, Rome.

Sylos Labini P. (1972). *Sindacati, inflazione e produttività.* Laterza, Roma and Bari.

Tronti M. (2006) [1966]. *Operai e capitale.* Derive e Approdi, Roma.

Van Apeldoorn B. (2002). *Transnational capitalism and the struggle over European integration.* Routledge, London and New York.

Van der Pijl K. (2011). The wage of discipline: Rethinking international relations as vehicle of Western hegemony, spectrum. *Journal of Global Studies*, vol. 4, no. 1, pp. 5–26.

Wallerstein I. (2001). *Unthinking social-sciences: The limits of nineteenth-century paradigms.* Temple University Press, Philadelphia.

Wright O. (2002). *Storming heaven: Class composition and struggle in Italian autonomist Marxism.* Pluto Press, London.

Part 3

Economists in networks

9 Who are the economists Germany listens to?[1]

The social structure of influential German economists

Stephan Pühringer and Karl M. Beyer

1 Introduction: power and economics

During the last decades there was a long-lasting debate among economists and other social scientists on the question to what extent economic thought has an impact on the course of (economic) policy-making as well as on the society in general (Christensen, 2017; Fourcade, 2009; Hall, 1989; Hirschman & Berman, 2014). Hence, particularly economists active in policy advice and public discourses stress the (long-term) influence of economic thought and thus partly even develop strategies to maximize their impact. As early as in 1936, Keynes in the "General Theory" famously stressed the importance of economic ideas, at least in the long run: "The ideas of economists and political philosophers . . . are more powerful than is commonly understood. Indeed the world is ruled by little else" (Keynes, 1936, p. 383). And yet in the beginning of the 21st century Larry Summers (2000, p. 1), due to his roles as U.S. Secretary of Treasury under Clinton and later as director of the National Economic Council under Obama, arguably one of the politically most influential economists during the last decades, stresses, "(W)hat economists think, say, and do has profound implications for the lives of literally billions of their fellow citizens".

In contrast to these considerations, within the German economic debate, around the year 2000 several economists bemoaned a decline of political and societal influence of academic economics, partly due to ignorant politicians and public authorities, partly also due to an alleged problematic development of the economics discipline, that is, a sole focus on methodological rigor to the disadvantage of political relevance (Franz, 2000; Frey, 2000b). One possible solution to overcome the perceived impotence of economic advisors was brought forward by the then president of the German Institute for Economic Research (DIW Berlin) Klaus Zimmermann. Zimmermann (2004, p. 401) remarked, "Given that European and German policy-makers are hesitant to proactively seek advice, the media channel is of central importance. In my view it is the silver bullet of policy advice". He further argued that he requests the DIW department heads to participate actively in public debates and the media.

The question whether and to what extent economics as a scientific discipline as well as distinct economists have a political and societal impact is still

DOI: 10.4324/9780367817084-12

148 *Stephan Pühringer and Karl M. Beyer*

a highly contested issue among economists. However, during the last decades and particularly after the recent global financial crisis, there was a lively debate on the relationship between economics and politics. Some empirical evidence indicates that in spite of the critique on the state of economics in the aftermath of the crisis, economists and economic experts continue to be fairly present in public debates. Haucap, Thomas, and Wagner (2014) for instance examined the media presence of German (social) scientists from summer 2013 to summer 2014 and found that economists are by far the most cited scientists in public debates. In fact, eight out of the ten scientists with the highest number of media appearances and overall about two thirds of the scientists quoted in opinion-forming German newspapers are economists. Haucap et al. (2014) conclude that no other science receives by far the same amount of attention of German policy-makers and the German media. Hence, economists seem to have a specific access to power over the channel of public debate.

Against this backdrop, there is growing interest in the scientific discipline of economics in other social sciences as well (see e.g. Fourcade, 2009; Lebaron, 2001; Maesse, 2015, 2018; Rossier et al., 2017, or Rossier & Benz in this volume). In this context, economics is not only analyzed as the dominant discipline within the social sciences but also often understood as a "discipline of power" in modern societies, which produces political and economic elites and thus has a considerable societal impact. In this vein Hirschman and Berman (2014) stress the heterogeneous devices by which economists influence the political process and thus policy-making. The authors differentiate between the professional authority of economics, the institutional positions of economists and the establishment of a specific economic style of reasoning in political discourse. For them, the latter aspect especially points to the increased importance of economic knowledge in the governance of capitalist economic systems after World War II. In this respect Fourcade (2006, p. 162) concludes, "economics has become more central to the nation . . . because the nation itself has become more economic".

In the literature on the role of economists in public debates, several authors stress the specific role of highly visible "public economists" in the sense of "public intellectuals", who are capable to "make a public intervention" (Eyal & Buchholz, 2010, p. 210), because they are very active and influential in political and public debates. Lebaron (2006) as well as Maesse (2015) thus introduce a Bourdieusian approach, which stresses the compound role of economic experts within a trans-epistemic field of academia, media, politics and business. Thus, the insignia of symbolic capital for being an economist, for instance the designation "Professor of Economics", confers power on academic economists and therefore increases their potential impact in political and public debates. The authors thus conclude that "economists are the producers of economic beliefs" (Lebaron, 2001, p. 91) and that "economic knowledge . . . has a special status as a cultural resource for discursive interventions into the political and the economic world" (Maesse, 2015, p. 286).

Who are the economists Germany listens to? 149

Against the backdrop of recent work on the political and societal impact of economics and distinct economists, respectively, this chapter aims to examine individual, research and institutional characteristics as well as established professional networks of what are considered to be "influential economists" in Germany. In providing an actor-based empirical analysis, we contribute to the current debate on the political and societal influence of economists by elaborating on the significance of biographical features and professional networks as conditions for becoming an influential economist. In doing so, we further elaborate on channels of influence or potential power devices, which structure the trans-epistemic field of economic expertise in Germany.

The remainder of the chapter is structured as follows: In section 2 we relate our work to current debates on the state of and recent trends within German economics, and on existing power devices concerning economic policy-making. Section 3 introduces our methodological approach, which is based on biographical and bibliometric research as well as social network analysis. In section 4 we provide our main empirical results. At first, we describe common individual, research and institutional patterns of influential economists in Germany. After that we then dive deeper into their institutional and co-authorship networks in order to examine the significance of existing power structures within German economics. In the final section we sum up our main contribution and offer some concluding remarks.

2 On the current state of economics in Germany

2.1 The special role of ordoliberalism in German economic policy-making

In the European and particularly German context, which is of interest in this chapter, there is a long tradition of politically influential and thus powerful economists and professional networks dating back to the immediate postwar period. In the German Federal Republic in the first decades after World War II, economists played crucial roles in policy-making at several levels. First, professors of economics held powerful political positions; for instance, Ludwig Erhard as chancellor and Alfred Müller-Armack and also Karl Schiller as influential ministers.[2] Second, economic advisors, mainly from the ordoliberal or German neoliberal school of economic thought,[3] were directly involved in the foundation of the German Federal Republic (e.g. the currency reform of 1949). Third, a network of ordoliberal economists in close collaboration with employers' associations served as promoter of the formative vision of "Soziale Marktwirtschaft" (social market economy) in the years of the "German economic miracle" (Ötsch, Pühringer, & Hirte, 2017; Ptak, 2004). Against this backdrop, many scholars stress the formative impact of ordoliberalism on German and partly also European economic policy-making (Biebricher, 2018; Campbell & Pedersen, 2014; Lechevalier, 2015). Other scholars show the strong dominance

150   *Stephan Pühringer and Karl M. Beyer*

of German neoliberal networks among economists with significant influence on media and policy advice in postwar Germany and highlight trajectories of their persistence up to today (Ptak, 2009; Pühringer, 2018).

Particularly in the aftermath of the global financial crisis and during the debates on European crisis policies ordoliberalism re-entered public as well as academic debates, when the German economics discipline was heavily criticized for its alleged conservatism and its support for austerity policies. Stiglitz, for instance, stressed the extraordinary position of German economics as follows:

> What is very clearly true . . . is that German economics is different from economics everywhere else in the world. They still believe in austerity even though the IMF, which is not a left-wing organization, has said austerity doesn't work.
>
> (Joseph E. Stiglitz, cited in: Phillips, 2016)

In a similar vein, several scholars stressed idiosyncrasies of "German economics" such as (i) a traditional conservative approach concerning economic policy-making (Münchau, 2014; Phillips, 2016), (ii) the central role of institutionalized economic policy advice (Campbell & Pedersen, 2014; Pühringer & Griesser, 2020) as well as (iii) the existence of an ordoliberal power structure organized around think tanks supported by German employer associations (Flickenschild & Afonso, 2018; Ötsch et al., 2017). In the course of the debate on German economics induced by criticism mainly from U.S. and U.K. economists, for instance Burda, then president of the *Verein für Socialpolitik* (German Economic Association), defended German economists and in particular the members of the German Council of Economic Experts, the main economic policy advice body in Germany, publicly also referred to as "economic wise men". In doing so, Burda explicitly stressed the international orientation of this important policy advisers and even "vouch(es) for their mainstream academic views" (Burda, 2015). Indeed, recent surveys among German economists report a rising trend of internationalization and Americanization of German economics (Fricke, 2015) similar to other countries and disciplines (Fourcade, 2006; Rossier & Bühlmann, 2018).

Hence, in regard to the European debt crisis the majority of German economists were against stark austerity measures imposed on Southern European countries and thus were opposing the position of the German government as well as of leading (and publicly influential) orthodox economists (Fricke, 2015). In general, however, there seems to be a remarkable difference between the majority of comparably younger, internationally oriented economists and older, politically and publicly influential ordoliberals (see also Grimm et al., 2018, on this issue).

A similar example of such a tension among German economists also became obvious during what was later called the Cologne dispute over method (*Kölner Methodenstreit*) in 2009 (Caspari & Schefold, 2011). The conflict emerged after the University of Cologne decided to change the denomination of professorial chairs from "economic policy" to "modern macroeconomics", which also marked a shift from traditional ordoliberal policy-orientation to quantitative formal mathematical methods. Therefore, the dispute was again between older economists supporting a petition entitled "Save economic policy at the universities" and younger, internationally oriented supporters of a petition named "Rebuild economics according to international standards".

2.2 Top-level research vs. policy advice?

A further debate among economists revolves around the question whether there is a cleavage within the German economics profession between top-level research and policy advice. Haucap and Mödl (2013) argue that there exists a pronounced division of labor between economists focusing on top-level research on the one hand and economists engaging in policy advice on the other hand. Furthermore, they suggest that the nature of this division of labor is rather substitutive than complementary as economists normally do not engage in both activities during the same period of time. Furthermore, the authors indicate that the view of a temporal division of labor by individual economists, which means focusing at first on top-level research and afterwards on policy advice, is also misleading. There is not sufficient evidence in support of this hypothesis. Schmidt (2013), president of the Leibniz Institute for Economic Research and chairman of the German Council of Economic Experts, in contrast, opposes this cleavage view. He indicates that leading public economists in Germany usually are not only excellently qualified, but a majority also publishes in top-tier economic journals. Hence, it is somehow misleading to focus solely on research rankings to evaluate economists' research skills.

3 Data and methodological approach

On a methodological level, we combine biographical and bibliometric research with social network analysis. We make use of the impact ranking of the German newspaper *Frankfurter Allgemeine Zeitung* (FAZ) published yearly since 2013, which consists of an integrated overall ranking and three sub-rankings, each of which represents one essential pillar of economists' "influence": (i) a research ranking reflecting the impact of economists on the scientific community, (ii) a media ranking capturing the presence of distinct economists in newspapers, magazines and television, and (iii) a political impact ranking, which represents the direct channel of influence of economists on policy-makers.[4] The ranking is very popular in Germany and thus symbolically reflects the state of economics as a powerful academic discipline. Hence, the FAZ entitles its ranking with the statement, "The economists, the country listens to" ("Auf diese Ökonomen hört das Land"). Against this backdrop, we first compiled a dataset, which includes the 50 most influential economists for each category of the FAZ ranking from the years 2015–2018.[5] In doing so, in a first step

152 *Stephan Pühringer and Karl M. Beyer*

Table 9.1 Variables

Individual	Research	Institutional
Gender	Research field	Research institutes & academic think tanks
Current primary affiliation	Ordoliberal reference	
Place of primary affiliation		Ideological & advocatory institutions
Nationality		
Year of birth		Public governance bodies
Place of PhD		German public policy petitions

Note: The first three institutional variables contain both current and former connections.

we calculated the relative share of citations (academic ranking), quotes (public ranking) and mentions (politics ranking) for each year. In a second step, we computed an average weighted impact over the years 2015–2018, which then served as our indicator for an economist's impact in the respective categories (see appendix for a list of the 20 most influential economists in each category). As a result, because a number of economists appear in more than one sub-ranking, our overall dataset comprises 122 economists.

In a further step between March and July 2019, we then collected a broad spectrum of biographical information for each economist. Our dataset contains a broad range of individual, research and institutional data, which we extracted from CVs and biographical notes, publication records and bibliographic databases as well as websites of institutions and governmental authorities.[6] Table 9.1 presents the variables collected.

In a third step, we collected bibliometric information on the co-authors for each economist[7] between August and September 2019. Since there is no single source which meets all our requirements, we combined the data extracted from the following different sources: co-authors from Web of Science (two and more joined publications), Google Scholar profiles (all co-authors mentioned), ResearchGate (four and more) and EconLit (two and more).[8] As a result, we did collect at least one co-author for 96 economists of our dataset.

In a final step, we employed a social network analysis using the standard software Pajek (Mrvar & Batagelj, 2016; Nooy et al., 2018) to unveil the professional networks amongst influential economists. In doing so, we made use of both our data on personal-institutional relations to compute a two-mode network of economists and their connections to institutions, and further exploited our bibliometric information on co-authorships to show networks of co-authorships among influential economists in Germany.

4 The profile of economists Germany listens to

We started our evaluation with checking for overlaps between the different rankings. First of all, rather surprising, there is no overlap between the top 50 economists who are part of the research and the media ranking. Consequently, the economists, who are influential in research, differ without exception from those who are influential in the media. On the other hand, there is a rather strong overlap between the politics ranking and the media ranking (21 economists, including the top three of both rankings), and a rather minor overlap between the research ranking and politics ranking (seven economists, only two in the top 20 of the research ranking and all of them beyond the top 30 of the politics ranking). Thus, the research ranking unsurprisingly differs fundamentally from the other two "public rankings", which in turn provides some evidence for the argument that there seems to be a division of labor between top-level research economists and those economists more strongly involved in the public and political arena. By contrast, the strong overlap between the politics and media ranking suggests that these channels of political and societal influence are somehow connected. We assume that especially strong media presence fosters the diffusion of one's individual economic expertise to policy-makers. From this perspective, the media strategy of Zimmermann mentioned in the introduction seems to be quite successful.

4.1 Personal details

An evaluation of our group of economists by gender exhibits that there exists a massive gender bias. The overwhelming share of the economists is male with only a few female exceptions (Table 9.2). Compared to the already substantial overall gender bias within German economics with only 26% of all researchers at German institutions being female (Friebel & Wilhelm, 2019), the male bias within the FAZ ranking is still extraordinarily distinct.

Analyzing the primary affiliations (Table 9.3)[9] indicates that almost all research economists (48 out of 50 or 96%) have a primary university affiliation, 34% of them also having a primary affiliation with an − mostly economic − research institute. Media economists and policy advice economists, on the contrary, have fewer primary affiliations with a university (61.2% and 79.2%), but slightly higher affiliations with an (economic) research institutes (38.8% and 50%). A unique feature of the media ranking is that financial sector economists (18.4%, four of them among the top 11 economists of the ranking) and to a lesser degree think tank economists (8.2%, two of them among the top ten economists) play a substantial role within the German public economic discourse. But think tank economists also have some influence on the political level (8.3%).

Most economists, who publicly declare their nationality, are German citizens (Table 9.4; 70.3%, 73.2% and 90.9%). The reasons for the lower shares

Table 9.2 Gender ratio

Gender	Research	Media	Politics	All
Female	2%	6%	10%	4.9%
Male	98%	94%	90%	95.1%

154   *Stephan Pühringer and Karl M. Beyer*

Table 9.3 Primary affiliations

Category of primary affiliation[a]	Research	Media	Politics	All
University	96%	61.2%	79.2%	79%
(Economic) research institute	34%	38.8%	50%	37%
Financial sector	–	18.4%	–	7.6%
Think tank	–	8.2%	8.3%	4.2%
Central bank	2%	2.1%	–	1.7%
International organization	–	2.1%	–	0.8%
Other	4%	2.1%	4.1%	3.4%

Note: [a] multiple primary affiliations are possible.

Table 9.4 Nationality

Nationality	Research[a]	Media[b]	Politics[c]	All[d]
German	70.3%	73.2%	90.9%	76.6%
Austrian	10.8%	2.4%	2.3%	5.3%
Swiss	13.5%	2.4%	2.3%	6.4%
British	2.7%	2.4%	–	2.1%
U.S.-American	–	19.5%	6.8%	9.6%
Italian	2.7%	–	–	1.1%
Belgian	2.7%	2.4%	–	2.1%
French	2.7%	2.4%	2.3%	2.1%
Greek	2.7%	–	–	1.1%

Notes: [a] 37 economists declared their citizenship, three of them with a dual citizenship; [b] 41 economists, two with a dual citizenship; [c] 44 economists, two with a dual citizenship; [d] 94 economists, six with a dual citizenship.

of German research and media economists relative to policy economists are different. In case of the research ranking, economists with Austrian or Swiss citizenship are also quite important. This is partly due to the methodology behind the ranking, as economists located not only at German institutions were considered, but also at Austrian and Swiss institutions. In case of the media ranking, a fifth of the economists has a U.S. citizenship (19.5%). That is because "star economists" from the U.S. (e.g. Joseph Stiglitz, Paul Krugman or Maurice Obstfeld) have a remarkable impact on the public economic discourse in Germany.

Inspecting the average age of the economists per ranking indicates that research economists (57.1 years) are significantly younger than media (60.4 years) and, to a lesser degree, policy advice economists (59.3 years). This outcome is driven again by the methodology behind the research ranking which is focusing only on the research impact of the last five years. Therefore, it is easier for younger economists to become part of the research ranking.

Examining the place of PhD (Table 9.5) reveals a remarkable variety especially within the leading research economists, as 33 different universities conferred a PhD to 47 economists, who declared their place of PhD, with the

Table 9.5 Place of PhD

Research[a]		Media[b]		Politics[c]		All[d]	
U. of Vienna	4	MIT	6	MIT	4	MIT	8
TU Berlin	3	U. of Cologne	5	U. of Cologne	4	U. of Cologne	7
U. of Bonn	3	Princeton U.	3	Princeton U.	3	U. of Kiel	7
U. of Kiel	3	U. of Kiel	3	U. of Mannheim	3	U. of Mannheim	5
U. of Zurich	3	U. of Mannheim	3				

Notes: [a] 47 economists; [b] 43 economists; [c] 44 economists; [d] 109 economists.

University of Vienna at the top with four PhDs. This indicates that, in contrast to Britain and the U.S., the research landscape is far less hierarchical (Aistleitner et al., 2018; Fourcade, 2009) and thus a PhD from a rather small group of top-tier universities is not mandatory to become a successful researcher. Even more remarkable is that only one research economist got his PhD from a U.S. or British elite university. Contrary to research economists, the media and politics rankings exhibit a slightly lesser variety with 43 PhDs respective to 44 PhDs obtained from 25 respective to 28 different universities. A particularly striking feature in contrast to the research ranking is that 13 media economists and 12 policy advice economists received their PhD from an U.S. or British elite university. The fact that some foreign star economists appear in these rankings can only partly explain this result, as after neglecting them nevertheless five or ten economists are graduates of U.S. or British elite universities.

4.2 Research profile

A deeper look into the research profiles of the ranked economists (Table 9.6) reveals remarkable differences regarding the academic field of work. In case of research economists less than half (48%) are located in the narrower field of economics, followed by business (34%), environmental science (8%), and mathematics and statistics (6%). In contrast to this distribution the overwhelming majority of media economists and, to a lesser extent, policy advice economists are located in the field of economics (94.9% respective to 74.1%). Regarding the former, the fields of finance (7.7%) and business (5.1%) are of some importance, and regarding the latter besides business and finance (both 6.1%), agricultural science (8.2%) also becomes relevant.

The reasons for this varying distribution within the research ranking as well as for its differences to the media and politics rankings can be found in the construction of the original dataset by the FAZ. In case of the research ranking, the Web of Science database was used and obviously a rather generous definition of economist was deployed. In contrast to that the media ranking is based on a quite narrow definition, as the FAZ only looked for the catch phrases economist (Ökonom★) and economic researcher (Wirtschaftsforscher★) within the media discourse. As a consequence, e.g. business economists (Betriebswirt★) were ignored by definition.

156   *Stephan Pühringer and Karl M. Beyer*

Table 9.6 Field of research

Research field[a]	Research	Media	Politics	All
Economics	48%	92.3%	81.6%	68.2%
Business	34%	5.1%	6.1%	18.2%
Finance	4%	7.7%	6.1%	5.5%
Agricultural science	2%	–	8.2%	4.5%
Environmental science	8%	2.6%	4.1%	4.5%
Mathematics and statistics	6%	–	–	2.7%
Health science	4%	–	4.1%	2.7%
Others	6%	–	4.1%	3.6%

Notes: [a] multiple fields of research are possible. "Others" include gerontology, psychology, social policy and physics.

Furthermore, we also dived deeper into the publication records of the ranked economists to look for possible ordoliberal references in the form of at least three publications in ordoliberal journals.[10] We find that 8% of the research economists have an ordoliberal reference in their publication record, whereas 20.8% of the media economists and 24.5% of the policy advice economists show an ordoliberal reference. Neglecting financial sector and foreign star economists within the media ranking, even 32.3% of media economists have a connection to the ordoliberal research program.

4.3 Non-university activities

In a third field of analysis we ask for the non-university activities of our ranked economists, including potential ideological orientations and political involvements. Looking at their broad non-university spectrum of activity we differentiate between current and former linkages to politico-economic and public governance institutions. In doing so, we report connections to (economic) research institutes, think tanks and foundations on the one hand, and policy advice and other governmental bodies, central banks and international organizations on the other hand. Finally, we also screen the economists for petition-signing activities.

Table 9.7 illustrates the connections to (economic) research institutes and academic think tanks. Our data exhibits that a great majority of the economists within all rankings have or had an affiliation with economic research institutes from the German-speaking countries. Especially the CESifo network (34), followed by the IZA (25), and the DIW (23) are to be highlighted. In addition, also the British CEPR with 24 current or past connections is relevant for economists across the rankings. Other foreign research institutes and academic think tanks of some relevance, by contrast, are mainly linked to media and policy advice economists. From this, we conclude that especially the leading German economic research institutes and their networks[11] are essential biographical pillars for becoming an influential economist. Our data shows that

Who are the economists Germany listens to? 157

Table 9.7 Research institutes and academic think tanks[a]

	Research	Media	Politics	All
German (economic) research institutes				
CESifo	16	12	20	34
IZA	14	7	12	25
DIW	9	9	13	23
IfW	4	8	5	13
ZEW	3	4	10	11
CFS Frankfurt	2	8	2	10
MPI for research on collective goods	6	2	3	8
ARGE-Institute[b]	–	7	7	7
RWI	3	4	6	7
IAB	2	2	2	6
MPI of economics	5	–	1	5
Reinhard Selten Institute	3	1	2	4
WZB	3	–	2	4
Foreign institutes and academic think tanks				
CEPR	11	10	13	24
NBER	1	8	5	12
INET	2	5	6	8
PIIE	–	5	2	5
CREMA	3	1	1	4
WIFO	2	2	2	4
Brookings Institution	–	4	1	4
Hoover Institution	2	2	–	4

Notes: [a] at least four connections. [b] ARGE-Institute is not an economic research institute but serves as a networking platform of German economic research institutes.

52% of all research economists, 60.4% of all media economists and 77.6% of all policy advice economists have or had an affiliation with them. Considering also important foreign economic research institutes[12] the share rises to 56%, 72.9% and 81.6%.

The data on the linkages to ideological or advocatory think tanks, foundations and institutions (Table 9.8) reveals a somewhat different picture. While research economists are hardly connected to these kinds of entities, media and policy advice economists are considerably linked to ideologically driven institutions. A closer look exhibits that institutions of the conservative, ordo- and neoliberal spectrum are much more popular than progressive and union-linked institutions. While on the individual level one research economist, three media economists and 11 policy advice economists have a connection to the progressive, union-linked camp, four research economists, 13 media economists and 14 policy advice economists have linkages to the conservative, neo- and ordoliberal camp. Hence, it is striking that especially in the media there exists an enormous ordo- and neoliberal bias.

Our dataset exhibits that there also exist substantial connections to public governance bodies on the (inter)national level, although unequally distributed

158   *Stephan Pühringer and Karl M. Beyer*

Table 9.8 Ideological or advocatory think tanks, foundations and institutions[a]

	Research	Media	Politics	All
Conservative, ordo- and neoliberal				
IW Köln	–	6	4	7
INSM	–	4	5	6
Erhard Foundation	–	5	4	5
Hayek Society	–	5	3	5
Herzog Institute	1	3	4	5
Kronberger Kreis	–	5	4	5
Economic Council CDU	–	4	5	5
Eucken Institute	–	3	2	3
Naumann Foundation	1	2	2	3
NOUS	–	3	2	3
Prometheus	–	3	2	3
Progressive, union-linked				
Böckler Foundation	–	3	6	6
Ebert Foundation	1	2	5	5
Keynes Society	1	2	5	5
Non-partisan				
Plenum of Economists	6	8	10	17
Denkraum Für Soziale Marktwirtschaft	–	3	3	3
INET Council on the Euro Zone Crisis	–	3	3	3
Group of Thirty	–	3	1	3

Note: [a] at least three connections.

between the rankings, as illustrated in Table 9.9. An institutional breakdown exhibits, first, that regarding German governmental bodies the German Bundestag has with 47 by far the most individual connections, followed by the Federal Ministry for Economic Affairs and Energy with 21 connections. The reason for this remarkable number of connections to the Bundestag is that committees of the Bundestag regularly invite economists to hearings as experts. What our data also reveals is that in addition advisory councils play an important role as mediating institutions or interfaces between the German governmental system and the economics profession. On the international level, second, the ranked economists are often linked to the European Commission (19) as well as to the World Bank (18) and the International Monetary Fund (IMF) (17). Finally, also central banks play a noteworthy but minor role. A breakdown by ranking reveals that with 48 out of 49 or 98% of almost all policy advice economists have linkages to (inter)national public governance bodies, followed by media economists with 85.4%. Considering only German governmental bodies (without Austria and Switzerland), a nevertheless impressive 89.8% of all policy advice economists are connected to them. In contrast to that, due to numerous international star economists being part of the ranking, with 41.7% much fewer media economists are linked to the latter. Research economists, in turn, have with 42% or 26% considerably less connections. These results, again,

Who are the economists Germany listens to? 159

Table 9.9 Governmental bodies, international organizations and central banks[a]

	Research	Media	Politics	All
German governmental bodies				
German Bundestag	6	25	37	47
Federal Ministry for Economic Affairs and Energy	6	16	16	21
of which: Board of Economic Advisors[b]	5	6	9	12
German Federal Government	2	5	12	13
German Council of Economic Experts[b]	–	9	9	12
Federal Ministry of Finance	–	4	9	10
of which: Board of Economic Advisors[b]	–	2	4	4
Federal Ministry of Education and Research	2	2	7	8
German Data Forum (RatSWD)[b]	2	1	3	4
Federal Ministry of Labour and Social Affairs	1	1	4	4
of which: Rürup Commission[b]	1	1	4	4
Federal Ministry of Food and Agriculture	1	–	3	4
Foreign and supranational governmental bodies				
European Commission	6	8	13	19
European Parliament	–	2	4	5
French Government	–	3	3	5
Council of Economic Advisers (United States)[b]	–	4	1	4
International organizations				
World Bank	5	10	10	18
IMF	3	12	8	17
OECD	6	4	8	13
United Nations	1	4	5	7
IPCC	3	2	3	5
WEF	–	3	4	5
Central banks				
German Bundesbank	4	3	6	10
European Central Bank	2	5	5	9
Federal Reserve Bank of New York	–	3	2	4

Notes: [a] at least four connections; [b] advisory council. Note: Only the current ministries are listed, and individual connections to former ministries with different titles are assigned accordingly.

are in line with the view of a division of labor between top-level research and policy advice within the economics profession, although indicating that the division of labor is somewhat limited.

Finally, we review a further channel of active public policy involvement with respect to our ranked economists. For this, we evaluate a collection of 15 German public policy petitions by economists from 1992 to 2018. Our results show that research economists are comparatively cautious when signing economist petitions. Twelve or 24% of them have signed at least one out of eight public policy petitions, resulting in 20 signatures in total. In contrast to that, media economists are more active as 17 or 35.4% have signed at least one out of 14 petitions, 39 signatures in total. Most active by far are policy advice economists: 27 or 55.1% have at least signed one out of 15 economist petitions, 66 signatures in total.

160 *Stephan Pühringer and Karl M. Beyer*

4.4 *Professional networks among influential economists*

In the previous three sections we have described existing patterns and frequently occurring features for our ranked economists regarding personal details, research profiles and connections to non-university institutions and (inter)national public governance bodies. In a subsequent step we explicitly intend to examine the professional networks among these economists. In a first step, we analyze the networks on the institutional level by focusing on connections to politico-economic think tanks, foundations and other similar institutions as well as on signed public policy petitions. In doing so, we do not differentiate between the rankings. In a second step, we investigate professional linkages by means of co-authorship data.

The whole network consists of 177 nodes, among them 78 economists and 99 institutions/petitions. The average degree is 5.3 and the overall density of the network is 0.06. For our analysis of social structures of the institutional networks among influential economists in Germany we applied the community detecting algorithm Louvain Method to highlight distinct communities in this two-mode institutional-personal network. Overall, the clustering algorithm yields six clusters. Among them, as Figure 9.1 illustrates, there are four partly intertwined main clusters with a degree centrality of 57 (the "ordo-/neoliberal cluster" A, light gray on the bottom right), 59 (the "mainstream cluster" B, black, at the center), 22 (the "transnational economics cluster" C, gray at the bottom left) and 25 (the "progressive cluster" D, dark gray, at the top) connected nodes, respectively. The "progressive cluster" D is organized around the Böckler Foundation, the Ebert Foundation and two petitions in favor of a European Banking Union and against the German debt-brake and thus reflects a rather progressive, Keynesian-oriented positioning. Cluster C is organized around international institutions, encompassing international economists such as Joseph Stiglitz, Paul Krugman or Thomas Piketty, well-known for their rather critical stance on German economic crisis policies (see e.g. Rieder & Theine, 2019 for further details). The second largest cluster B represents the German economic mainstream and is mainly organized around the leading German economic research institutes such as the CESifo or the IZA. The largest cluster A, in turn, represents a rather conservative, ordo- and neoliberal economic policy orientation. This cluster is organized around the INSM, the Erhard Foundation and the neoliberal public policy petition "Hamburger Appell" (Funke et al., 2005), and is quite tightly connected to the German economic mainstream (cluster B). In contrast to that, the international cluster C and the progressive cluster D are connected to other clusters to a much lesser extent. Hence, the network graph in Figure 9.1 indicates, in line with recent studies on German economics (see section 2.1), that ordoliberal power structures are still relevant today. First, many influential economists, who successfully engage in public and political debates, are connected to ordo- and neoliberal networks. Second, these economists are also tightly connected to the German economic mainstream.

Who are the economists Germany listens to? 161

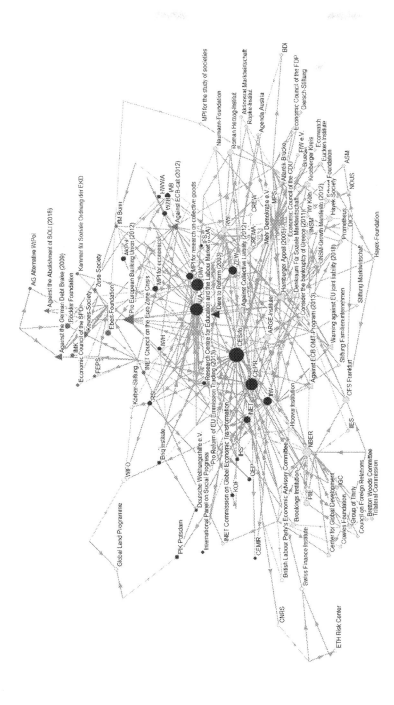

Figure 9.1 Personal-institutional network of influential economists in Germany. Nodes with only one connection are excluded. Dots represent individuals, circles represent institutions and triangles petitions, bold/thin lines indicate actual/former connections.

For analyzing the professional linkages among our sample by means of co-authorships we compiled a one-mode network of personal relations. Applying the same clustering methodology as for the institutional network analysis we found two quite different results. Whereas the extent of professional networks among media and policy advice economists are comparably low, the analysis of co-authorship networks among research economists yields some interesting results.

The overall co-authorship network of our sample of influential economists consists of 299 economists, among them 64 listed in the FAZ ranking. Overall, our analysis reports eight clusters with at least one common co-authorship. As already indicated, the clustering structure of the overall co-authorship network among our sample of influential German economists is strongly driven by leading research economists. For instance, the black cluster A at the center in Figure 9.2 connects 12 of the 64 influential economists with at least one common co-authorship, among them ten of the top 50 research economists, while the sum of co-authors connected in this cluster is 49. This cluster is organized around the ETH Zurich and furthermore comprises the two economists (Ernst Fehr and Urs Fischbacher) leading the research ranking. Another densely connected cluster is the agrarian economists cluster B at the top left and institutionally based at the Thünen Institute and the University of Göttingen. Although this cluster only comprises four influential economists (of which only one is part of the research ranking, the other three of the politics ranking), it connects 29 co-authors, which points to a very close collaboration inside the cluster. In a similar vein, the dark gray cluster C at the top right also represents a densely connected research network at the Viennese University of Natural Resources and Life Sciences with even 39 co-authors. The light gray cluster D at the bottom represents another research cluster in the field of business studies. In contrast to the densely connected research groups in the aforementioned clusters, influential economists in the categories media and politics are mostly rather loosely connected. However, as the clustering shows particularly, politically influential economists are either connected by their cooperation through economic research institutes or by joint expert opinions and policy briefs, such as the annual report of the GCEE. To sum up, our co-authorship network provides some empirical evidence that there exist close professional collaborations in form of research clusters among our sample of influential economists in Germany, especially among research economists. Of course, these clusters are often organized around institutions in German-speaking countries. Other ranked economists, however, are only loosely or not at all connected to these "German" research clusters. Therefore, we cautiously conclude that on the one hand professional collaborations represented by common co-authorships are probably quite helpful for becoming an influential research economist in Germany. On the other hand, this factor seems to be of rather limited importance for economists with public and political influence.

Who are the economists Germany listens to? 163

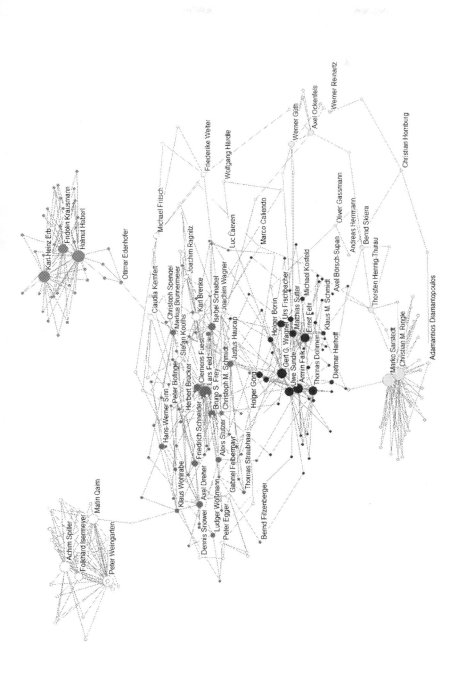

Figure 9.2 Overall co-authorship network among influential economists. Size of the nodes indicates the number of co-authorships. At least one common co-authorship.

5 Concluding remarks

In this contribution, we employed social network analytical methods on a unique dataset comprising biographical and bibliometric information of the most influential economists in Germany with the aim to explore common biographic, institutional and research patterns as well as professional networks and thus to unveil power structures within the German economics profession. In doing so, we made use of the FAZ ranking of economists, where influence is separated in the fields of research, media and politics and therefore is designed to highlight the elite segment of the economics profession in Germany.

Against this backdrop, we can draw the following main conclusions: First of all, the segment of influential economists in Germany is almost exclusively male and thus even more gender biased than the overall German economics profession. Second, a breakdown by ranking reveals some interesting differences: (i) while research economists cover a broad range of research fields, media and policy advice economists are predominantly located in the (narrower) field of economics; (ii) the media ranking exclusively contains a substantial number of financial sector economists as well as international "star economists". Third, the division of labor between top-tier research and policy advice within the German economics profession is to some extend also reflected within the group of influential economists. There are (i) hardly or no individual overlaps between the research ranking and the other two rankings and (ii) while a striking majority of media and policy advice economists have connections to (inter) national public governance bodies, only a minority of research economists are linked to them. Fourth, although our biographical analysis is limited in scope,[13] we find also some indications for internationalization within our sample. On a personal level, 28.4% of the economists in our sample received their PhD from a university outside the German-speaking area. Furthermore, the international orientation is also reflected in the rather high number of connections (66 out of 119 economists or 55.5%) to research institutes, think tanks and public governance bodies located at the international (non-German-speaking) level. Fifth, the ordoliberal bias within the German economics profession also appears in our group of influential economists. This bias, however, is restricted to media and policy advice economists. A considerable number of them are connected to the ordoliberal research program and/or have connections to the German conservative, ordo- and neoliberal institutional network, which, in turn, is closely connected to the German economic mainstream. In contrast to that, progressive economists are far less represented in our sample, and their linkages to the German economic mainstream are limited.

Overall, for becoming an influential economist in Germany it seems to be helpful to be professionally associated with the leading German economic research institutes and their networks. Furthermore, our analysis reveals that due to the obviously less hierarchical nature of the German-speaking economics profession when compared to the U.S., a successful research economist does not need to have a PhD from or work at a small range of top-tier universities.

Who are the economists Germany listens to? 165

Rather it seems much more effective to collaborate with other influential research economists from the German-speaking countries. For becoming an influential media and policy advice economist, in turn, research collaborations seem to be less crucial. For these economists it is probably just as important to be connected to politico-economic networks in Germany, whether they are partisan or not. Of course, having visible linkages to governmental institutions, especially institutionalized policy advice bodies, will in turn increase an economist's impact on politics and the media.

To sum up, our analysis provides some evidence of common patterns and similarities among the population of influential German economists. While we made use of social network analysis to detect communities among our sample, our analyses could open up a venue for further research employing quantitative approaches such as multi-correspondence analyses (MCA) from a field theoretical background (see for instance Rossier & Benz in this volume).

Notes

1 Stephan Pühringer gratefully acknowledges funding by the Austrian Science Fund FWF (grant number ZK60-G27).
2 For a detailed list of economic professors in political positions in Germany see Frey (2000a).
3 To put it short, ordoliberal scholars distinguish between the ordo principle, also referred to as an "economic constitution", and the field of economic policy. Whereas the government is responsible for the overall economic order, it should at the same time avoid intervening in the economic process itself, thereby historically opposing Keynesian-oriented economic planning. Hence ordoliberal policies range from anti-trust legislation to austerity-oriented fiscal policies.
4 The overall ranking contains the top 100 economists, whereas each sub-ranking roughly comprises the top 50 economists.
5 Due to a change in its ranking methodology before 2014 and as the following ranking for 2014 is not fully publicly accessible, we start with the ranking for 2015.
6 We did not collect biographical information for three historical economists (Milton Friedman, Friedrich A. Hayek and John M. Keynes) out of the 122 economists since we are mainly interested in contemporary economists.
7 In doing so, we furthermore did not consider nine bank economists (Stefan Bielmeier, Carsten Brzeski, David Folkerts-Landau, Michael Heise, Ulrich Kater, Jörg Krämer, Holger Schmieding, Gertrud Traud and Jörg Zeuner), as they mostly have not authored scientific publications. Furthermore, we excluded eight foreign economists mostly from U.S. institutions (Angus Deaton, Paul Krugman, Maurice Obstfeld, Thomas Piketty, Kenneth Rogoff, Robert Shiller, Joseph Stiglitz and Lawrence Summers), as we are mainly interested in the co-authorship networks of the economists of the German-speaking countries.
8 Although Web of Science does contain all academic fields, it is restricted to a range of mostly international academic journals. As a consequence, various economists especially of the media and politics ranking are only covered insufficiently due to a low number of publications in these journals. Hence, we have supplemented the Web of Science data on co-authors with data from other databases.
9 In all following tables and figures, the three historical economists are not considered.
10 These journals are *ORDO – Jahrbuch für die Ordnung von Wirtschaft und Gesellschaft* and *Zeitschrift für Wirtschaftspolitik* as well as *Perspektiven der Wirtschaftspolitik*. Whereas the

166 *Stephan Pühringer and Karl M. Beyer*

first two are traditional ordoliberal journals, the latter is a prominent platform for the promotion of ordoliberal ideas to policy-makers.

11 Our sample includes CESifo, DIW, HWWI, IAB, IfW, IMK, IWH, IZA, RWI, MPI, SAFE, WZB and ZEW.

12 Our sample includes Brookings Institution, Bruegel, CEPII, CEPR, CNRS, Hoover Institution, IFS, IIES, INET, IHS, KOF, NBER, PIIE, WIFO and WIIW.

13 We did not gather data on their whole academic career paths. Therefore, our analysis of internationalization is quite limited.

References

Aistleitner, M., Kapeller, J., & Steinerberger, S. (2018). The Power of Scientometrics and the Development of Economics. *Journal of Economic Issues*, 52(3), 816–834.

Biebricher, T. (2018). Ordoliberalism as a Variety of Neoliberalism. In J. Hien & C. Joerges (Eds.), *Ordoliberalism: Law and the Rule of Economics* (pp. 103–113). Oxford and Portland, OR: Hart Publishing.

Burda, M. (2015). Dispelling Three Myths on Economics in Germany. *VOX, CEPR's Policy Portal*. Retrieved from http://voxeu.org/article/dispelling-three-myths-economics-germany

Campbell, J. L., & Pedersen, O. K. (2014). *The National Origins of Policy Ideas: Knowledge Regimes in the United States, France, Germany, and Denmark*. Princeton: Princeton University Press.

Caspari, V., & Schefold, B. (Eds.) (2011). *Wohin steuert die ökonomische Wissenschaft?: Methodenstreit in der Volkswirtschaftslehre*. Frankfurt: Campus Verlag.

Christensen, J. (2017). *The Power of Economists Within the state*. Stanford: Stanford University Press.

Eyal, G., & Buchholz, L. (2010). From the Sociology of Intellectuals to the Sociology of Interventions. *Annual Review of Sociology*, 36(1), 117–137.

Flickenschild, M., & Afonso, A. (2018). Networks of Economic Policy Expertise in Germany and the United States in the Wake of the Great Recession. *Journal of European Public Policy*, 49(4), 1–20.

Fourcade, M. (2006). The Construction of a Global Profession: The Transnationalization of Economics. *American Journal of Sociology*, 112(1), 145–194.

Fourcade, M. (2009). *Economists and societies: discipline and profession in the United States, Britain, and France, 1890s to 1990s*. Princeton: Princeton University Press.

Franz, W. (2000). Wirtschaftspolitische Beratung: Reminiszenzen und Reflexionen. *Perspektiven Der Wirtschaftspolitik*, 1(1), 53–71.

Frey, B. S. (2000a). Does Economics have an Effect? Towards an Economics of Economics. Working Paper. Institute for Empirical Research in Economics University of Zurich. (36). Retrieved from http://e-collection.library.ethz.ch/eserv/eth:25540/eth-25540-01.pdf

Frey, B. S. (2000b). Was Bewirkt die Volkswirtschaftslehre? *Perspektiven Der Wirtschaftspolitik*, 1(1), 5–33.

Fricke, T. (2015). How German Economists Really Think. Retrieved from www.ineteconomics.org/perspectives/blog/how-german-economists-really-think

Friebel, G., & Wilhelm, S. (2019). Women in European Economics. Retrieved from www.women-economics.com/index.html

Funke, M., Lucke, B., & Straubhaar, T. (2005). Hamburger Appell. Retrieved from www.deutschlandreform.com/uploads/6/6/0/9/6609430/hamburger_appell.pdf

Who are the economists Germany listens to? 167

Grimm, C., Kapeller, J., & Pühringer, S. (2018). Paradigms and Policies: The Current State of Economics in the German-Speaking Countries. ICAE Working Paper Series, 77.

Hall, P. A. (Ed.) (1989). *The Political Power of Economic Ideas: Keynesianism Across Nations.* Princeton, NJ: Princeton University Press.

Haucap, J., & Mödl, M. (2013). Zum Verhältnis von Spitzenforschung und Politikberatung: Eine empirische Analyse vor dem Hintergrund des Ökonomenstreits. *Perspektiven Der Wirtschaftspolitik,* 14(3–4), 346–378.

Haucap, J., Thomas, T., & Wagner, G. G. (2014). Zu wenig Einfluss des ökonomischen Sachverstands? Empirische Befunde zum Einfluss von Ökonomen und anderen Wissenschaftlern auf die Wirtschaftspolitik. List Forum Für Wirtschafts- Und Finanzpolitik, 40(4), 422–436.

Hirschman, D., & Berman, E. P. (2014). Do economists make policies? On the political effects of economics. *Socio-Economic Review,* 12(4), 779–811.

Keynes, J. M. (1936). *The General Theory of Employment, Interest And Money.* London: Palgrave Macmillan.

Lebaron, F. (2001). Economists and the Economic Order.: The field of economists and the field of power in France. *European Societies,* 3(1), 91–110.

Lebaron, F. (2006). "Nobel" economists as public intellectuals: the circulation of symbolic capital. *International Journal of Contemporary Sociology,* 43(1), 88–101.

Lechevalier, A. (2015). Eucken under the Pillow: The Ordoliberal Imprint on Social Europe. In A. Lechevalier (Ed.), Social Europe – a dead end: What the Eurozone crisis is doing to Europe's social dimension (pp. 49–102). Copenhagen: DJØF-Publishing.

Maesse, J. (2015). Economic experts: A discursive political economy of economics. *Journal of Multicultural Discourses,* 10(3), 279–305.

Maesse, J. (2018). Austerity discourses in Europe: how economic experts create identity projects. Innovation: *The European Journal of Social Science Research,* 31(1), 8–24.

Mrvar, A., & Batagelj, V. (2016). Analysis and visualization of large networks with program package Pajek. *Complex Adaptive Systems Modeling,* 4(1), 47. https://doi.org/10.1186/s40294-016-0017-8

Münchau, W. (2014, November 16). The Wacky Economics of Germany's Parallel Universe i. Retrieved from www.ft.com/intl/cms/s/0/e257ed96-6b2c-11e4-be68-00144feabdc0.html#axzz3zftCZwc2

Nooy, W. de, Mrvar, A., & Batagelj, V. (2018). *Exploratory Social Network Analysis with Pajek.* Cambridge, MA: Cambridge University Press.

Ötsch, W., Pühringer, S., & Hirte, K. (2017). *Netzwerke des Marktes: Ordoliberalismus als Politische Ökonomie.* Wiesbaden: Springer VS.

Phillips, M. (2016, August 16). Joseph Stiglitz on Brexit, Europe's long cycle of crisis, and why German economics is different. *Quartz.* Retrieved from https://qz.com/1161496/which-republicans-voted-against-the-tax-bill/

Ptak, R. (2004). *Vom Ordoliberalismus zur sozialen Marktwirtschaft: Stationen des Neoliberalismus in Deutschland.* Opladen: Leske und Budrich.

Ptak, R. (2009). Neoliberalism in Germany: Revisiting the Ordoliberal Foundations of the Social Market Economy. In P. Mirowski & D. Plehwe (Eds.), *The Road from Mont Pèlerin: The Making of the Neoliberal Thought Collective* (pp. 98–138). Cambridge, MA: Harvard University Press.

Pühringer, S. (2018). The Success Story of Ordoliberalism as Guiding Principle of German economic policy. In J. Hien & C. Joerges (Eds.), *Ordoliberalism: Law and the Rule of Economics* (pp. 134–158). Oxford and Portland, OR: Hart Publishing.

Pühringer, S., & Griesser, M. (2020). From the 'Planning Euphoria' to the 'Bitter Economic Truth': The Transmission of Economic Ideas into German Labour Market Policies in the 1960s and 2000s. *Critical Discourse Studies*, online first. Retrieved from https://doi.org/10.1080/17405904.2019.1681283.

Rieder, M., & Theine, H. (2019). 'Piketty is a Genius, but. . . ': an Analysis of Journalistic Delegitimation of Thomas Piketty's Economic Policy Proposals. *Critical Discourse Studies*, 11(23), 1–16.

Rossier, T., & Bühlmann, F. (2018). The Internationalisation of Economics and Business Studies: Import of Excellence, Cosmopolitan Capital, or American Dominance? *Historical Social Research*, 43(3), 189–215.

Rossier, T., Bühlmann, F., & Mach, A. (2017). The Rise of Professors of Economics and Business Studies in Switzerland. *European Journal of Sociology*, 58(02), 295–326.

Schmidt, C. M. (2013). Research with Impact. Forschung und Politikberatung am RWI. RWI Position. (54), 1–26.

Summers, L. H. (2000). International Financial Crises: Causes, Prevention, and Cures. *American Economic Review*, 90(2), 1–16.

Zimmermann, K. F. (2004). Advising Policymakers Through the Media. *The Journal of Economic Education*, 35(4), 395–406.

Appendix

Table 9.10A Average weighted impact over the years 2015–2018

FAZ media impact 2015-18			FAZ political impact 2015-18			FAZ research impact 2015-18		
Rank	Name	Quotes*	Rank	Name	Mentions*	Rank	Name	Citations*
1	Hans–Werner Sinn	6.46%	1	Hans–Werner Sinn	12.00%	1	Ernst Fehr	10.77%
2	Clemens Fuest	6.27%	2	Clemens Fuest	10.12%	2	Urs Fischbacher	5.38%
3	Marcel Fratzscher	6.25%	3	Peter Bofinger	5.63%	3	Didier Sornette	3.74%
4	Jörg Krämer	4.50%	4	Marcel Fratzscher	5.22%	4	Bruno S. Frey	3.74%
5	Michael Hüther	3.60%	5	Lars Feld	4.32%	5	Michael Frese	3.56%
6	Carsten Brzeski	2.22%	6	Gustav Horn	4.14%	6	Christian Ringle	3.15%
7	Thomas Mayer	2.11%	7	Michael Hüther	3.58%	7	Adamantios Diamantopoulos	2.98%
8	Thomas Piketty	1.95%	8	Rudolf Hickel	2.01%	8	Christian Homburg	2.78%
9	Holger Schmieding	1.90%	9	Folkhard Isermeyer	1.99%	9	Armin Falk	2.58%
10	Jörg Zeuner	1.82%	10	Justus Haucap	1.95%	10	Helmut Haberl	2.09%
11	Lars Feld	1.70%	11	Christoph Schmidt	1.88%	11	Marko Sarstedt	2.05%
12	Peter Bofinger	1.69%	12	Thomas Straubhaar	1.59%	12	Fridolin Krausmann	2.03%
13	Christoph Schmidt	1.61%	13	Claudia Kemfert	1.57%	13	Thorsten Hennig-Thurau	2.01%
14	Paul Krugman	1.52%	14	Paul Krugman	1.47%	14	Oliver Gassmann	1.89%
15	Ferdinand Dudenhöffer	1.42%	15	Bert Rürup	1.35%	15	Reinhard Busse	1.88%
16	Joseph Stiglitz	1.34%	16	Martin Hellwig	1.34%	16	Klaus M. Schmidt	1.85%
17	Stefan Bielmeier	1.32%	17	Achim Wambach	1.16%	17	Karl Heinz Erb	1.79%
18	Ulrich Kater	1.23%	18	Thomas Mayer	1.14%	18	Axel Dreher	1.66%
19	Gustav Horn	1.21%	19	Axel Börsch-Supan	1.14%	19	Werner Reinartz	1.62%
20	Bert Rürup	1.12%	20	Heiner Flassbeck	1.06%	20	Alois Stutzer	1.59%

Source: FAZ-impact rankings and own calculations

* The percentages indicate the annually weighted averages from the FAZ-rakings from 2015-2018

10 Global production and circulation of dominant ideologies

Mexico from the default debt crisis to the Brady Plan (1982–1989)

Johanna Gautier Morin

1 Introduction

Since the 1990s with the Argentinian collapse, the Russian fiasco, and the Greek scandal, the legitimacy of the International Monetary Fund (IMF) and the World Bank seems prejudiced in the eyes of world public opinion. Long subject to criticism from left-wing activists and "Third World" advocates during the 1980s–1990s, these organizations became the target of authorized voices (Williamson, 1998; *The Economist*, 2000; Stiglitz, 2002). The Latin American stagnation exacerbated this negative image in the 1980s (Easterly, 2000). It went wrong in 1982 when Mexico was on the verge of bankruptcy and declared a moratorium on its debt to negotiate an emergency rescue plan with the IMF, the U.S. Federal Reserve, the U.S. Treasury, and multiple international investment banks. This episode marked a turning point in the history of the IMF (McKinnon, 1993; Boughton, 2000), as well as in transnational banking business and regulation. For the following decade, the Fund repeatedly imposed structural adjustments that did not achieve the expected outcomes and inaugurated a ten-year external debt crisis that spread to Argentina, Brazil, Chile, Uruguay, and the Philippines (Heyde, 1987; Masson, 2007). Bradlow (2000) and Marangos (2004) accused the Fund of imposing a top-down view of economic policies, which set aside the social dimension of these reforms and neglected human rights issues. From Lindholm (1977) to Klein (2007), many authors and official reports have blamed the Fund for its ill-adapted experimental methods and considered the terms of conditionality of its loans to be responsible for the macroeconomic catastrophe (UNDP, 2003; SAPRIN, 2004). The resulting recession aggravated the "legitimation crisis" of these "money doctors" (Habermas, 1973; Drake, 1994; Woods, 2006: 84–103). Since then, the IMF itself has contributed to understanding the causes and culprits of the crisis by engaging in self-criticism (Rogoff, 2003; Sgard, 2005; Martinez-Vazquez *et al.*, 2001; Dreher *et al.*, 2015).

However, this vision has overshadowed the role and agency of the Mexican government in the negotiations leading to liberalization reforms and the crucial role played by the international investment banks and banking associations that cooperated as soon as the risk of default became an imminent threat. Indeed,

DOI: 10.4324/9780367817084-13

Global production of dominant ideologies   171

inflows of foreign capital had increased in Mexico after the oil shocks (López Herrera *et al.*, 2015). In this context, the Mexican crisis marked a turning point in the history of global financialization.

The massive bailout orchestrated by the IMF to avoid a systemic and global banking crisis was a success. A common language shared by institutions and individuals from distinct socio-political contexts emerged at the heart of the negotiations. The long process of circulation and institutionalization of the dominant "general inventory" of economic ideas favored the presence of economists in the Mexican government (Colander & Coats, 1989). The renewal of political elites in a country where neoliberalism had a specific national development turned Mexico into a key actor in the game played by international organizations, foreign investment banks, and the U.S. Treasury, despite the revolutionary tradition of the single-party system (Babb, 2001; Romero Sotelo, 2016).[1] This chapter aims at understanding how negotiations have been conducted in a context of financial dependence and proposes a renewed interpretation of international financial cooperation and the role of economists in the ideological convergence that went along with the circulation of capital flows.

The section 2 presents the data, methods, and theoretical framework adopted in this chapter. The section 3 explores the links between the renewal of the elites and the production of the dominant ideology in the 1980s. The section 4 exposes the terms of the crisis and analyzes it as a proxy to understand the structural mechanisms of Mexican economic policies. The section 5 examines the global convergence in economic rationale at the heart of the negotiations between the Mexican government, the IMF, the U.S. Treasury, and investment banks involved in the defaulted loans. The section 6 highlights the failures of the reforms and adjustment programs.

2 Data and method

We consider that the application of economic thoughts and doctrines in Latin America has shaped multilateral institutions and financial practices globally, contrary to the dominant view of the history of liberal imperialism, which saw the sub-continent as an under-integrated periphery (Rostow, 1960). Following the subaltern studies' approach (Appadurai, 1986), we examine how liberal thoughts and theories have been integrated into Mexican political culture to inform the circulation of economic beliefs and practices on a global scale (Hauswedell *et al.*, 2019).

Theoretically, we investigate the programmatic work of Pierre Bourdieu and Luc Boltanski on the "production of the dominant ideology" (Boltanski & Bourdieu, 1976). The literature has not yet fully exploited the theoretical potential of this text. It has never been translated and still seems confusing for many readers, since it adopted the form of its topic and commingled stereotypes, commonplaces, inconsistencies, and discrepancies. Imitating Flaubert's *Dictionary of Received Ideas* (Flaubert, 1881), the authors compiled a broad series of sources illustrating the dominant ideology shared by economic elites and the

172   *Johanna Gautier Morin*

media, through published texts, public statements, filmed debates, bibliographies, graphs, figures, definitions, and images. Heir to a long tradition in the sociology of knowledge (Durkheim, 1912; Parsons, 1951) and perpetuating the legacy of Marx and Engels's critical analysis of the dominant ideology (Marx & Engels, 1932), this unique work was embedded in French political life. However, we can carefully transpose this theoretical approach to the transnational network of investment bankers, financial experts, and government officials who helped resolve the Mexican default debt crisis.

In order to do so, we use quantitative and qualitative data from IMF confidential documents, staff reports, and secretariat's circulars (Washington); U.S. Treasury and Federal Reserve documents (Washington and New York); OECD economic surveys (Paris); Bank of International Settlements' documents (Basel); press articles from Mexico, the United States, the United Kingdom, and France; investment banks' private archives (Midland Bank, Société Générale, Crédit Lyonnais); decrees and declarations by the Mexican President and members of government; and correspondence between all the parties held in the U.K. National Archives in Kew. Paul A. Volcker's papers held at the Seeley G. Mudd Manuscript Library in Princeton, NJ, contributed to the understanding of the bailout negotiations. We also interviewed former IMF President Jacques de Larosière, who was supervising the negotiations, and exploited Larosière's and his successor Camdessus's memoirs (Camdessus, 1995; Larosière, 2016). This data allows us to evaluate the spillover effect of the Mexican episode on international governance and private capital distribution.

3 Production of the dominant ideology: from political strategy to cultural change

During the 1970s and 1980s, the transnational neoliberal shift has rooted international expertise in a social philosophy that transcended economic policies (Brint, 1996). The energy crisis, the financialization of the global economy, and the information technology revolution have disrupted the power game by providing opportunities for emerging fractions and challenged the position of old-established social groups. National elites were neither homogeneous nor static, and the dominant emerging economic ideologies served the interests of a "nebula" of dominant groups, sharing converging interests despite the diversity of their social and cultural origins (Khan, 2012).[2]

Bourdieu and Boltanski showed how rhetoric and symbolic discourses supported similar transformations through an "optimistic evolutionism" and popularized a new classification system. They referred to this evolution as "converted conservatism" aimed at excluding both the conservative rear-guard and the progressive vanguard doomed to remain confined to the margins. Political and economic advisers, business leaders, mainstream media, and institutional experts promoted this "converted conservatism" as inevitable. This rhetoric undermined any political culture that would contradict it and embraced the theory of historical evolutionism by positioning the elite beyond political conflicts. The ideology of the death of ideologies imposed the idea of the finiteness

Global production of dominant ideologies   173

of all political options, confirmed by the "lessons of history," which showed the shortcomings of past political regimes. In that respect, the famous Mexican artist Cantinflas mocked President Echeverría Alvarez: "We are neither of the left, nor of the right, but entirely the opposite" (Calomiris & Haber, 2015: 366). The "converted conservatism" imposed a new vision and division of social values based on the opposition of two polarized registries:

Table 10.1 The affirmation of neoliberal values and new socio-cultural perspectives[1]

Old-fashioned conservatism and utopianism	Optimistic evolutionism
Past	Future
Tradition	Modernity
Archaism	Innovation
Inertia	Flexibility
Trade unionism	Entrepreneurship
Fixity	Pragmatism
Socialism	Technology
Fascism	Leadership
Political ideology	Science
Interventionism	Freedom

Note: [1] This table synthesizes the keywords' polarizing discourses, as Bourdieu and Boltanski identified them in a scattered way throughout their analysis (Boltanski & Bourdieu, 1976: 45–65).

The "optimistic evolutionism" was authorized and reinforced by the intellectual and scientific support of institutions "at the intersection of the academic field and the field of power" (Boltanski & Bourdieu, 1976: 67).[3] In this regard, professional economists were particularly exposed to this ambiguity between the fields, at the crossroads of academia, political expertise, consulting, business and media (Abbott, 1988; Maesse, 2015; Schmidt-Wellenburg & Lebaron, 2018). Their growing importance inspired Markoff and Montecinos to talk about the "ubiquitous rise of economists" in all sectors, even beyond their initial training (Markoff & Montecinos, 1993).

The redefinition of social positions was not limited to the elite of developed and democratic countries, contrary to the impression most Western literature might give. In some "developing" countries, according to the tripartition of the time, non-democratic political regimes and planned economies experienced the same social changes during the 1980s (San Miguel, 2004; Kothari, 2005). Rising fractions influenced by monetarist and public choice theories aimed their criticisms at the Keynesian interventionism of former regimes (Centeno & Silva, 1998; Heredia, 2018).[4] Among the groups jockeying for power in the Mexican regime, the supporters of this new *doxa* used their expertise as leverage to influence decision-makers and the public (Fourcade, 2009).

The Mexican crisis revealed the ideological struggles between experts within the single party. Economists inspired by developmentalism and dependency theory, and trained at Cambridge University,[5] fought against the growing

174 *Johanna Gautier Morin*

influence of orthodox economists educated at Yale, such as Jesús Silva Herzog Flores and Miguel Mancera, who finally came to power when President Miguel de la Madrid was elected in 1982 (Babb, 2001: 171–198). Elite groups thus opposed each other within an institutional frame that circumscribed the field of power between those governing the state and those representing private power. The 1980s witnessed the rise, within the government, of economic experts who would have remained outsiders a few decades earlier (Dezalay & Garth, 2002).

The transnational dimension of their trajectory reinforced their position (Seabrooke & Henriksen, 2017). The renewal of the political elite corresponded to the liberalization of the state-controlled economy initiated to cope with the external pressure of international competition and the internal social and economic crisis (Rodríguez & Ward, 1994). Their legitimacy was anchored in their proclaimed scientific neutrality (Fourcade, 2006). In that sense, Mexico was not an isolated case.[6] There was a structural function in the expansion of the dominant ideology. The discourse of power is not strictly meant to convince:

> Its primary function is to direct action or to maintain the cohesion among executives by reinforcing, through ritual reassertion, the group's belief in the necessity and the legitimacy of his action. Converts preaching converts, those believers educated in the same dogma and endowed with the same thinking and action patterns, the same ethical and political dispositions, can forgo the proof, the wholeness and the logical control, agreeing only to explain the few elements about which their action is criticized or rejected. Their disjoint discourse occults the essential points, which are exactly everything that goes without saying, everything that is self-evident as long as it is tacitly understood between the self, anything that cannot be revealed without betraying the official intention of the discourse.
>
> (Boltanski & Bourdieu, 1976: 6)

The Mexican crisis presented an excellent opportunity for industrialized countries to reinvent their hegemony "by transitioning from the post-war 'embedded liberal' world order to the Reagan-Thatcher model of neoliberalism and global capitalism." Multilateral institutions transformed "their mandates to accommodate these ideological changes" (Chorev & Babb, 2009: 461). The circulation of ideas unfolded in a multidimensional configuration. In a regime born of a revolution and led by an authoritarian ruling elite (Garrido, 2005; Langston, 2017), the logic of self-preservation of the dominant group compelled the Mexican *apparatchiki* to appoint a new political staff with a profile consistent with the standards of multilateral institutions. The evolution of the standards of governance in the 1980s–1990s led to the emergence of the infamous "Washington consensus." The end of the Bretton Woods system in 1971–73 left its institutions in desperate need of defining a new legitimate *raison d'être* (George, 1992; Chorev & Babb, 2009). They seized the fight against inflation and over-indebtedness as a new battle horse (Wolf, 1965; Bradlow, 2000).

Global production of dominant ideologies   175

Contrary to the experiences of the Chilean Chicago Boys under the Pinochet regime (Silva, 2009; Gautier Morin & Rossier, 2021). Mexico's bailout plans of the 1980s were systematically mediated by the international financial community and justified by developmentalist rhetoric and free-market experiments (Gunder Frank, 1984; Jorge & Salazar-Carrillo, 1988; Woods, 2006). Indeed, according to the IMF's original articles, its responsibility to "promote" liberalization was limited to "current account transaction (i.e., goods and services) but not capital account (i.e., debt, portfolio equity and direct and real estate investment)" (Moschella, 2009: 858). Theoretically, member countries had the right to control capital movements until the 1995 amendment of IMF statutes, which gave the Fund full authority over transnational capital flows. The case of Mexico shows that such a modification of the institutional design was already embedded in the 1980s programs (Goldman, 1982).

4 The crisis: a proxy to unveil information mechanisms

In February 1982, the constant decline in Mexican international reserves compelled the government to devaluate the peso.[7] From 1954 to 1976, Mexico had a fixed exchange rate regime, and its external debt was denominated in U.S. dollars. In 1980–81, the U.S. Federal Reserve raised its interest rates.[8] As a result, Mexican debt increased sharply, while devaluation did not seem to stop the outflow of international reserves. The problem was not new to the government: since independence, Mexico had to deal with an external debt that made the country structurally vulnerable (Marichal, 1989; Costeloe, 2003). Similarly, in a remarkable transnational comparative study on the stability of banking systems, Charles Calomiris and Stephen Haber demonstrated how banking crises and credit scarcity were embedded in the political history of Mexico, where authoritarian political leaders, bank insiders, and minority shareholders formed coalitions of interest groups that determined access and distribution of capital. The expropriations perpetrated by the Institutional Revolutionary Party (PRI) worried most bankers who rarely engaged in investments (Calomiris & Haber, 2015: 331–389).

Between 1824 and 2001, Mexico spent more than 45% of the time in a state of default or restructuring (Oosterlinck, 2013: 700). After the first oil crisis, the country faced drastic currency devaluations. The oil manna allowed an unprecedented rise in world oil prices until 1979–80 and urged Mexico to invest heavily to meet international demand. The country became the sixth-largest producer in the world in 1980. The government accumulated external debts with international private banks to make such investments, and the IMF acted as a guarantor on behalf of Mexico, which gave the organization authority over the country's economic policies (Salas-Porras, 2014). However, when international oil prices fell abidingly, Mexico faced the worst liquidity crisis since the revolution. Severe devaluations were not sufficient to solve the problem (Gracida, 2007; Ángel Mobarak, 2010; Bruner & Simms, 1987).

On August 12, 1982, Jesús Silva Herzog, Mexican Secretary of Finance and Public Credit, informed U.S. Federal Reserve Chairman Paul Volcker, U.S. Treasury Secretary Donald Regan, and IMF Managing Director Jacques de

176 *Johanna Gautier Morin*

Larosière "that Mexico would be unable to meet its August 16 obligation to service an $80 billion debt" (Federal Deposit Insurance Corporation, 1997: 192). According to American journalist Joseph Kraft, Herzog landed in Washington on August 13 to negotiate a moratorium on commercial bank debt. "In retrospect, after similar moves by many other countries, Silva Herzog's action hardly seems singular. At the time, in fact, it was a bombshell that shook an entire universe" (Kraft, 1984: 2–4).

What was fundamentally new, according to José Ángel Gurría, current secretary-general of the OECD and former director of the Public Credit Department of Mexico under Herzog, was that they did not

> crawl to the international financial community as debtors seeking relief through some minor adjustment that could be made backstage. We walked in through the front door. We said we had a major problem with a capital P. We did not say the problem was a particular debt. We said the problem was the whole international financial structure. We said it was everybody's problem.
>
> (quoted in Kraft, 1984: 3)

Indeed, the Mexican crisis posed a threat to the international banking system. Among the U.S. banks exposed to the Mexican default risk, the ratio of credit outstood to more than 30% of their capital funds for 54 establishments and up to 48% for Bank of America, 73% for Manufacturers Hanover, 81% for the European American Bank, and 115% for the Allied Bank International.[9] David Knox, World Bank Vice President for Latin America, urged commercial banks to increase their lending and encourage the recovery of growth in the region, or, at least, to establish provisions for the potential losses since international creditors were so deeply involved in the Mexican debt.[10] Creditor banks finally agreed, at a meeting held at the Federal Reserve Bank of New York on August 19–20, to extend the loan to Mexico to $1.5 billion through the Bank of International Settlements (BIS). The U.S. government committed to lending $2 billion. The IMF designed these "bridging" loans to gain time to develop its support program, which would reach $4 billion over the next three years (BIS, 1984). This episode can thus be understood as the bailout of international banks, more than the rescue of Mexico.

5 Global convergence in economic rationale

When granted, the extension of the loan guaranteed by the IMF and the BIS was conditional on a set of "arrangements," according to IMF terminology (Eckaus, 1986; Khan & Sharma, 2003; Babb & Carruthers, 2008). The borrowing country ought to

> adopt comprehensive programs worked out in close consultation with the Fund and calculated to restore satisfactory payments positions over a

Global production of dominant ideologies 177

period of time. These arrangements are intended to provide assurance . . . of sufficient inflows of credit to permit orderly and gradual adjustment.

(IMF, 1983: 19)

Close cooperation was needed between international bodies, private financial institutions, and the national government to "attain the goals of sustainable debt-servicing and viable balance of payments positions" (IMF, 1983: 79).

The press referred to the Mexican tragedy as a *deus ex machina*, but the IMF adjustment program had been discussed for two years before the liquidity crisis hit the country. According to the IMF staff report for the 1982 consultation with Mexico, the Fund had been discussing with representatives of the Mexican government since November 1981 (IMF, 1982c). However, coordination failed at finding a solution. On September 1, 1982, the Mexican government nationalized the private banking system, imposed comprehensive exchange controls, and suspended all private sector debt payments and most public sector principal debt payments. The Bank of Mexico devalued the peso several times before the end of the year. Inflation rates reached 100% in December and brought the country into a severe recession. Per capita GDP declined by 11% over the next five years. During the same period, wages fell by about 30%, unemployment increased, and investment and consumption contractions slowed down economic growth (Buffie & Krause, 1989: 153–154).

The IMF and the Mexican government finally reached an agreement after the election of President Miguel de la Madrid in 1982. Former negotiators Jésus Silva Herzog became Secretary of Finance and Public Credit, Miguel Mancera Aguayo, Director General of the Bank of Mexico, and Héctor Hernández Cervantes, Secretary of Commerce. IMF staff representatives began working with Ariel Buira, Executive Director for Mexico. These men represented a new guarantee for the IMF, and the organization warmly welcomed their appointments. De la Madrid had voiced support for the stabilization program during his campaign, which was considered a "break in tradition" that made the Fund staff optimistic about future outcomes (Maroni, 1982). Relationships between the IMF and Mexican officials had been tense until then. The Fund reproached the Mexican to keep the organization "in the dark": the Mexicans declined to respond to the questionnaire the IMF had sent them and indicated that they did not want another visit from a Fund team (Truman, 1982). After the elections, it was thus in the Mexican government's interest to send "a team of English-fluent, foreign-trained technocrats whose close personal connections within international financial circles were an important asset" to negotiate the fate of the country with international banks, the IMF, and the U.S. government (Babb, 2001: 177).

Changes in political and administrative staff led to a shift in public policy towards development and liberalization. Nearly 25% of the officials had studied in U.S. universities (Centeno, 1994: 117). Herzog, Aguayo, Cervantes, and Buira were all economists, graduating from Yale, Melbourne, and Manchester, respectively. These institutions were not the temple of neoliberalism, as were

178 *Johanna Gautier Morin*

the University of Chicago and Columbia in the 1960s.[11] Nevertheless, they were a place of design and standardization of economic expertise and political advice. Moreover, the political legitimacy of these new ministers and secretaries was based mainly on Western expertise. Mancera and Silva had studied with Federal Reserve Chairman Paul Volcker when he taught at Yale.

Beyond transnational circulation, a dissenting Mexican intellectual current, supported since the interwar period by a class of entrepreneurs and businessmen, had developed a strong lineage in the Austrian tradition of Hayek and Mises. The banker and intellectual Luis Montes de Oca, founder of the Banco Internacional and member of the Mises's Society for the Renewal of Liberalism, had introduced the Mont Pelerin Society to Mexico (Merchant, 2002; Denord, 2002; Mirowski & Plehwe, 2009; Romero Sotelo, 2016). The more the single-party regime fell into crisis, the more influential this trend became in the Mexican upper class (Romero Sotelo *et al.*, 2014). Although the new generation of policymakers was not associated with neoliberal think tanks, their training, and knowledge of English, facilitated their communication and understanding with international experts.

A new generation of "technopols" combined economic-oriented technical expertise taught abroad (mainly in the U.S.) with local political involvement. "Cosmopolitan ideas, understood, applied, and developed according to universalistic professional standards, became part of their selves" (Dominguez, 1997: 16). This set of intellectual tools was all the more critical for the success of negotiations with multilateral organizations and foreign administrations since IMF-supported programs were not preconceived. They were to be considered as a process that evolved along with a "multiplicity of potential pathways, driven by exogenous economic events, by policy actions of the national authorities" (Mussa & Savastano, 1999: 84–85).

As a result, the more national staff shared the economic principles and worldviews of IMF staff, the more quickly the program could be implemented. Finally, the March agreement was adopted

> at the behest of the new financial authorities, aimed at re-establishing a better balance between aggregate demand and supply as a means of curbing inflation and strengthening the balance of payment. The key element of this program [was] a reduction in the overall financial deficit of the public sector by the equivalent of 3% of GDP.
>
> (IMF, 1982d: 3)

The program also encouraged "the depreciation of the peso and substantial increases in prices and tariffs of basic goods and services" (IMF, 1982d: 7).

6 Failures and experimentations

In December 1982, the IMF Extended Arrangement finally approved a three-year loan of $3.8 billion to the Mexican government. The government

Global production of dominant ideologies 179

committed to engaging free-market reforms regarding fiscal austerity, reduction of public expenditures, privatization of state-owned enterprises, lowering of trade barriers, deregulation of the national industry, and liberalization of foreign investment. The contract stipulated,

> during the period of the extended arrangement, Mexico shall remain in close consultation with the Fund. These consultations may include correspondence and visits of officials of the Fund to Mexico or of representatives of Mexico to the Fund. Mexico shall provide the Fund, through reports at intervals or dates requested by the Fund, with such information as the Fund requests in connection with the progress of Mexico in achieving the objectives and policies set forth.
>
> (IMF, 1982a)

In other words, Mexico remained under the IMF trusteeship for almost a decade. Other programs were adopted in 1986 and 1989, lasting until 1993, before the peso crisis in 1994–95 (Barkbu *et al.*, 2012).

IMF's conditionalities imposed the restructuration of every aspect of the national economy. The semantic field used in the reports is enlightening: restructuring was associated with ideas of "satisfactory maturity," "progress," or "relevance" (IMF, 1982b: 12–13). During this decade of continuous restructuring, no IMF report assessed the efficiency and accuracy of the programs implemented. The report on the renegotiation of Mexico's External Debt of October 2, 1986, praised the attachment of the representatives of the governments of Mexico and the 14 creditor countries "to the successful implementation of the program, in particular, the revitalization of the productive sector of the economy, the liberalization of the trade system, and the improvement of public finances" (IMF, 1986).

The absence of evaluation and self-criticism revealed a lack of practical analysis. Michel Camdessus, managing director of the Fund from 1987 to 2000, was convinced that the problems Mexico was facing came from the government's inability or unwillingness to implement IMF requirements properly (Camdessus, 1995). He supported the idea shared by most orthodox economists that "government policy is the primary cause of economic depressions" (Bergoeing *et al.*, 2002: 16). Camdessus welcomed the "outstanding results" of stabilization program during his first mandate: the deficit aggregate balance in public finances (more than 15% of the GDP in 1987) moved into surplus during the 1990s, and inflation eased from 160% to 8% (Camdessus, 1995: 36). However, these parameters were not neutral since economic indicators did not take into account sustainable development, living standards, and development indices (Berthélemy & Lensink, 1995).

The Mexican crisis marked a turning point in the history of sovereign debt. International creditors' financing and adjustment strategies of the 1970s showed its limits. The first solutions adopted focused on short-term "damage-containment" policies (Griffith-Jones, 1989: 3). However, the Mexican crisis

180   *Johanna Gautier Morin*

affected the majority of emerging markets and Latin American economies. In the 1980s, bank loans and foreign private capital declined sharply. Until the 1982 crisis, Mexico depended on governmental loans from commercial banks, multilateral financial institutions (IMF, World Bank, and Inter-American Development Bank), and foreign governments (mainly the United States) to finance its external deficit (Jorge & Salazar-Carrillo, 1988). By the end of the decade, Mexico had radically changed the way it attracted foreign capital (see Table 10.2). The domestic economy was opening up to international capital flows, lowered its barriers for foreign investment, privatized state corporations, and extended stock exchange operations to private companies in the Bolsa de Valores de México, as well as in foreign exchanges, especially New York.[12]

In September 1983, the Organization of American States (OAS) held a conference in Caracas, Venezuela, on the problem of external debt in Latin American and Caribbean States. The idea emerged that countries should collaborate to exert collective pressure on the international financial community to establish different operating conditions: payment moratoriums would become habits rather than exceptions. Many observers have interpreted the Caracas consensus as an attempt to form a debtor cartel, and collectively suspend debt service payments, which would have threatened the entire global financial market (Anguiano Roch, 2000: 235).[13] It became clear that the global financial community could no longer negotiate loan conditionality without debtor countries. Since international creditors were so involved in Latin American external debts, David Knox, World Bank Vice President for Latin America, evoked earlier, advised commercial banks to establish provisions for their potential losses. However, nothing came out of the Caracas meeting because each government preferred to negotiate individually with the IMF and private banks.[14]

In 1989, the new president, Carlos Salinas de Gortari, the "first economist to achieve the presidency, and the first with a Ph.D. (from Harvard)" (Ai Camp, 2017: 3–4), launched a new phase in the external debt restructuring, with the implementation of the Brady Plan (after Nicholas Brady, U.S. Treasury secretary). The debt relief plan implicitly recognized the evidence at the end of the

Table 10.2 The financing of the Brady Agreement (US$ million)

	Total	IMF	IBRD	Other	Own	Ratio[1]
Costa Rica	216	51	35	102	28	0.87
Mexico	7000	1697	2010	2050	1243	0.82
Philippines	670	170	150	107	243	0.64
Uruguay	463	34	65	38	326	0.30
Venezuela	2380	880	500	600	400	0.83

Source: (OECD, 1992: 16; World Bank, 1990, 1991; IMF, 1991: 77). [1] The ratio refers to the foreign contribution to the financing of the Brady deal.

Global production of dominant ideologies 181

"lost decade" that many countries would not be able to repay their debts even if payment deadlines were further stretched (Sachs, 1989). The Plan called on commercial banks to step up lending to developing countries. This multilateral consensus induced a financial innovation with the creation of a secondary market that allowed debtors to trade their debt.[15] The IMF and the World Bank played a key role in facilitating the lending and liquidity for Latin American governments. The area of application of their prescriptions soon exceeded Latin American or Western countries to reach Pakistan (Butt & Jamal, 1988), India (Sau, 1983), Nigeria (Alawode, 1992), and Namibia (Morrell, 1983).

7 Conclusion

The implementation of the economic policy reforms resulting from the negotiations between the transnational networks of foreign banks, multilateral organizations, and sovereign governments must be understood at the heart of the production and circulation of the dominant ideologies that flourished in the 1970s–80s. The agency of the Mexican government, although limited by financial dependency, was not null, and the appointment of economists who graduated in U.S. and U.K. top universities as ministers and secretaries highlighted the country's degree of integration into financial globalization. Long considered a periphery of economic modernity, Mexico was, in fact, a central actor in the culture of the new capitalism. On the one hand, Mexican entrepreneurs and thinkers had contributed since the 1930s to the global development of neoliberal thinking. On the other hand, the IMF and commercial investment banks did not strictly design their arrangements during the debt crisis to save Mexico from bankruptcy but to avoid a systemic and global banking crisis.

The *ad hoc* structural adjustment plans and experimental reforms transformed Mexico and many other Latin American countries into the laboratory of economic policy experimentations that found their institutional legitimacy in the affirmation of the "Washington consensus" during the 1990s. Mexico contributed to the emergence of transnational technocratic expertise, both as a field for financial innovation and a proactive agent for economic integration. In that respect, the global tripartition of the 20th century between advanced, developing, and underdeveloped countries, according to the classic scheme of historical evolution, was the fruit of the dominant vision and division of the world whose legacy must be challenged and questioned by contemporary literature.

Notes

1 From the National Revolutionary Party (PNR) created in the aftermath of the revolution to the Institutional Revolutionary Party (PRI) in power until 2000, Mexico had no experience of a democratic regime all along the 20th century.
2 The term "nebula" captures the potential divergence between the economic interests of designated social groups but highlights how their beliefs and value system converged towards the same political agenda (Topalov, 1999).

182 *Johanna Gautier Morin*

3 The identification of these institutions has been a work in progress worldwide for more than a decade, and the coverage of the international database is not yet complete (this includes data collection by the EurElite Project, the EASE-Project, the Swiss Elite Observatory, PELA-USAL in Latin America, etc.).

4 Economics as an academic field went through an existential crisis in the 1970s, especially in the United Kingdom and the United States. For the first time in economic history, with the global recession of 1973–75, inflation and unemployment rates exploded at the same time, while the Keynesian *doxa* had naturalized the idea that they were inversely proportional. Public sector borrowing increased and became an obsession in public debates. Since Keynesian theories proved incapable of addressing stagflation, the monetarist school and its quantity theory of money appeared as the only answer capable of solving the mystery of inflation (Jones, 2012; Mirowski & Plehwe, 2009; Burgin, 2012).

5 Namely, socialist-oriented economists like Carlos Tello Macías, former Secretary of Budget and Planning, and José Andrés de Oteyza, Minister of Commerce and Industrial Development, in the cabinet of José López Portillo.

6 We can draw a parallel with Algeria, which has experienced a similar transition within its single-party system. This oil-producing country also had to borrow from the IMF and implemented its structural adjustment plan in the 1980s (Yefsah, 1992; Entelis, 2016).

7 Seeley G. Mudd Manuscript Library, Princeton, NJ, Paul Volcker's Papers (MC279), Box 24. Board of Governors of the Federal Reserve System. Incoming telegram from Mexico (02508) on February 3, 1982.

8 See Federal Funds Rate Historical Charts online: www.macrotrends.net/2015/fed-funds-rate-historical-chart.

9 Paul Volcker's Papers (MC279), Box 24, Restricted-controlled documents.

10 Crédit Lyonnais Archives, M. A. David Knox to the *Agence France Presse* (AFP), February 25, 1986, SEF0305 4 F 0247 FRA/AFP-AP23, Int.-Eco.-Dette flt1, AFP 252116 FEV 86.

11 See the influence of Chicagoan theories in Latin America (Guillén Romo, 1994; Biglaiser, 2002).

12 Especially banks that had been nationalized in 1982, and the company Teléfonos de México.

13 Crédit Lyonnais Archives, Latin American Debt Folder (1985–1988), Box 91AH115.

14 M. A. David Knox to the *Agence France Presse* (AFP), February 25, 1986.

15 Banks could swap their loan portfolios against shares and better-quality obligations.

References

Abbott, A. (1988). *The System of Professions: An Essay on the Division of Expert Labor*. Chicago: The University of Chicago Press.

Ai Camp, R. (2017). Democratizing Mexican Politics, 1982–2012. *Oxford Research Encyclopedia of Latin American History*. Oxford: Oxford University Press, 1–23.

Alawode, A. A. (1992). Financial Deregulation and the Effectiveness of Bank Supervision in Nigeria. *Savings and Development*, *16*(1), 101–113.

Ángel Mobarak, G. A. (del). (2010). La Paradoja del desarrollo financiero *in* Kuntz Ficker, S. (ed.). *Historia económica general de Mexico de la colonia a nuestros días*. Mexico: Colegio de Mexico, Secretaría de Economía, 635–666.

Anguiano Roch, E. (2000). México y la globalización financiera. *Foro Internacional*, *40*(2), 213–254.

Appadurai, A. (1986). Theory in Anthropology: Center and Periphery. *Comparative Studies in Society and History*, *28*(2), 356–361.

Global production of dominant ideologies   183

Babb, S. (2001). *Managing Mexico. Economists from Nationalism to Neoliberalism*. Princeton, NJ: Princeton University Press.

Babb, S. & Carruthers, B. (2008). Conditionality: Forms, Function, and History. *Annual Review of Law and Social Science*, 4, 13–29.

BIS. (1984). CH-000583–8A.BISA.7.18.12.DEA.16.43, BIS-World Bank data-sharing, 1984–04/1988–11–24: Statistics on external indebtedness: bank and trade-related non-bank external claims on individual borrowing countries and territories at end-December 1982 and end-June 1983. OECD and BIS. April 1984.

Barkbu, B., Eichengreen, B., & Mody, A. (2012). Financial crises and the multilateral response: What the historical record show. *Journal of International Economics*, INEC-02584, 1–14.

Bergoeing, R., Kehoe, P. J., Kehoe, T. J., & Soto, R. (2002). Policy-Driven Productivity in Chile and Mexico in the 1980s and 1990s. *The American Economic Review*, 92(2), 16–21.

Berthélemy, J.-C., & Lensink, R. (1995). The Impact of the Brady Plans on Debt Reduction and Short-Term Growth. *Savings and Development*, 19(2), 175–190.

Biglaiser, G. (2002). The Internationalization of Chicago's Economics. *Economic Development and Cultural Change*, 50(2), 269–286.

Boltanski, L., & Bourdieu, P. (1976). La production de l'idéologie dominante. *Actes de la recherche en sciences sociales*, 2(2–3), 3–73.

Boughton, J. M. (2000). *The IMF and the Silent Revolution: Global Finance and Development in the 1980s*. Washington, DC: IMF.

Bradlow, D. D. (2000). Rapidly Changing Functions and Slowly Evolving Structures: The Troubling Case of the IMF. *Proceedings of the Annual Meeting (American Society of International Law)*, 94, 152–159.

Brint, S. (1996). *In an Age of Experts: The Changing Role of Professionals in Politics and Public Life*. Princeton, NJ: Princeton University Press.

Bruner, R. F., & Simms, J. M. Jr. (1987). The International Debt Crisis and Bank Security Returns in 1982. *Journal of Money, Credit and Banking*, 19(1), 46–55.

Buffie, E., & Krause, A. S. (1989) Mexico 1985–86: From Stabilizing Development to the Debt Crisis. *in* Sachs, J. D. (ed.), *Developing Country Debt and the World Economy*. Chicago: University of Chicago Press, 141–168.

Burgin, A. (2012). *The Great Persuasion. Reinventing Free Markets since the Depression*. Cambridge, MA: Harvard University Press.

Butt, M. S., & Jamal, H. (1988). A Monetarist Approach to Inflation for Pakistan. *Pakistan Economic and Social Review*, 26(2), 69–88.

Calomiris, C., & Haber, S. (2015). *Fragile by Design: The Political Origins of Banking Crises and Scarce Credit*. Princeton, NJ: Princeton University Press.

Camdessus, M. (1995). La crise financière mexicaine, ses origines, la réponse du FMI et les enseignements à en tirer. *Revue d'économie financière*, 33, 35–45.

Centeno, M. A. (1994). *Democracy within Reason: Technocratic Revolution in Mexico*. Philadelphia: Pennsylvania State University Press.

Centeno, M. A., & Silva, P. (Eds.). (1998). *The Politics of Expertise in Latin America*. New York: St Martins.

Chorev, N., & Babb, S. (2009). The Crisis of Neoliberalism and the Future of International Institutions: A Comparison of the IMF and the WTO. *Theory and Society*, 38(5), 459–484.

Colander, D. C., & Coats, A. W. (1989). *The Spread of Economic Ideas*. Cambridge: Cambridge University Press.

184 *Johanna Gautier Morin*

Costeloe, M. P. (2003), *Bonds and Bondholders, British Investors and Mexico's Foreign Debt, 1824–1888*. Westport: Praeger.

Denord, F. (2002). Le prophète, le pèlerin et le missionnaire. La circulation internationale du néo-libéralisme et ses acteurs. *Actes de la recherche en sciences sociales, 145*, 9–20.

Dezalay, Y. & Garth, B. G. (2002). *The Internationalization of Palace Wars: Lawyers, economists and the contest to transform Latin American states*. Chicago: The University of Chicago Press.

Dominguez, J. (Ed.). (1997). *Technolopols: Freeing Politics and Markets in Latin America in the 1990s*. University Park: Pennsylvania State University Press.

Drake, P. W. (1994). *Money Doctors, Foreign Debts, and Economic Reforms in Latin America from the 1890s to the Present*. Lanham: SR Books.

Dreher, A., Sturm, J.-E., & Vreeland, J. R. (2015). Politics and IMF Conditionality. *The Journal of Conflict Resolution, 59*(1), 120–148.

Durkheim, E. (1912). *Les formes élémentaires de la vie religieuse*. Paris: PUF.

Easterly, W. (2000). The Lost Decades: Developing Countries Stagnation in Spite of Policy Reform, 1980–1998. Washington DC: Development Research Group. World Bank.

Eckaus, R. S. (1986). How the IMF Lives with Its Conditionality. *Policy Sciences, 19*(3), 237–253.

The Economist. (2000). The Washington Dissensus. *The Economist*. 23 June.

Entelis, J. P. (2016). *Algeria: The Revolution Institutionalized*. London: Routledge.

Federal Deposit Insurance Corporation (1997). *History of the Eighties: Lessons for the Future: An Examination of the Banking Crises of the 1980s and early 1990s*. Washington: FDIC Division of Research and Statistics.

Flaubert, G. (1881). *Bouvard et Pécuchet*, Paris: Alphonse Lemerre.

Fourcade, M. (2006). The construction of a global profession: the transnationalization of economics. *American Journal of Sociology, 112*(1), 145–194.

Fourcade, M. (2009). *Economists and Societies: Discipline and Profession in the United States, Britain, and France, 1890s to 1990s*. Princeton: Princeton University Press.

Gautier Morin, J. & Rossier, T. (2021). The interaction of elite networks in the Pinochet regime's macro-economic policies. *Global Networks*, online first. DOI: 10.1111/glob.12300.

Garrido, L. J. (2005). *El Partido de la revolución institucionalizada (medio siglo de poder político en México). La formación del nuevo estado (1928–1945)*. Mexico: Siglo Ventiuno Editores.

George, S. (1992). Vieilles institutions et nouveaux désordres: la Banque mondiale et le Fonds monétaire international à la fin du XXe siècle. *L'homme et la société, 105–106*, 25–33.

Guillén Romo, H. (1994). El Neoliberalismo en América Latina. *Investigación Económica, 54*(209), 107–144.

Goldman, D. (1982). The Mexico Debt Crisis and the International Monetary Fund. *EIR Economics, 9*(33), 4–6.

Gracida, E. M. (2007). Reflexiones sobre el pensamiento económico en México, 1970–1986. *Iberoamericana, 7*(26), 67–87.

Griffith-Jones, S. (1989). The International Debt Problem: Prospects and Solutions *in* Singer, H. W., & Sharma, S. (eds.). *Economic Development and World Debt*. New York: St. Martin's.

Gunder Frank, A. (1984). World Economic Crisis and Third World in the Mid-1980s. *Economic and Political Weekly, 19*(19), 799–804.

Habermas, J. (1973). *Legitimationsprobleme im Spätkapitalismus*. Frankfurt: Suhrkamp.

Hauswedell, T., Körner, A. & Tiedau, U. (2019). *Re-Mapping Center and Periphery. Asymmetrical Encounters in European and Global Contexts*. London: UCL Press.

Heredia, M. (2018). The International Division of Labor in Economists' Field: Academic Subordination in Exchange for Political Prerogatives in Argentina. *Historical Social Research/Historische Sozialforschung, 43*(3), 303–328.

Heyde, J. M. (1987). The Baker Plan Struggles for Results. *Harvard International Review, 9*(4), 36–38.

IMF (1982a). Mexico Extended Arrangement Agreed at Executive Board Meeting 82/168. December 23, 1982. EBS/82/208, Supplement 4.

IMF (1982b). Mexico Extended Arrangement agreed at Executive Board Meeting 82/168. Attachment II: Technical Memorandum of Understanding. December 23, 1982.

IMF (1982c). Mexico – Staff Report for the 1982 Article IV Consultation. SM/82/121. June 25, 1982.

IMF (1982d). Statement by Mr. Buira on Mexico. Executive Board Meeting 82/99. July 16, 1982.

IMF (1983). Annual Report of the Executive Board for the Financial Year Ended April 30, 1983. Washington, DC.

IMF (1986). Report on Renegotiation of Mexico's External Debt, prepared by the Western Hemisphere Department (WHD) and the Exchange and Trade Relations Department (ETR), October 2, 1986. EBS/86/225.

IMF (1991). International Capital Markets: Developments, Prospects, and Key Policy Issues. *World Economic and Financial Surveys*. Washington, DC: IMF Publications.

Jones, D. S. (2012). *Masters of the Universe: Hayek, Friedman, and the Birth of Neoliberal Politics*. Princeton, NJ: Princeton University Press.

Jorge, A., & Salazar-Carrillo, J. (1988). *Foreign Investment, Debt, and Economic Growth in Latin America*. New York: Springer.

Khan, M. S., & Sharma, S. (2003). IMF Conditionality and Country Ownership of Adjustment Programs. *The World Bank Research Observer, 18*(2), 227–248.

Khan, S. R. (2012). The Sociology of Elites. *Annual Review of Sociology, 38*, 361–377.

Klein, N. (2007). *The Shock Doctrine: The Rise of Disaster Capitalism*. New York: Metropolitan Books.

Kothari, U. (Ed.). (2005). *A Radical History of Development Studies: Individuals, Institutions, and Ideologies*. Chicago: University of Chicago Press.

Kraft, J. (1984). *The Mexican Rescue*. New York: The Group of Thirty.

Langston, J. (2017). *Democratization and Authoritarian Party Survival: Mexico's PRI*. New York: Oxford University Press.

Larosière (de), J. (2016). *Cinquante ans de crises financières*. Paris: Odile Jacob.

Lindholm, R. W. (1977). A Tested Program for Third World Economic Development. *The American Journal of Economics and Sociology, 36*(2), 165–169.

López Herrera, F., Santillán Salgado R. J., & Cruz Ake S. (2015). Volatility Dependence Structure between the Mexican Stock Exchange and the World Capital Market. *Investigación Económica, 74*(293), 69–97.

Maesse, J. (2015). Economic Experts: A Discursive Political Economy of Economics. *Journal of Multicultural Discourses, 10*(3), 279–305.

Marangos, J. (2004). Was Shock Therapy Consistent With Democracy? *Review of Social Economy, 62*(2), 221–243.

Marichal, C. (1989). *A Century of Debt Crises in Latin America: From Independence to the Great Depression, 1820–1930*. Princeton, NJ: Princeton University Press.

Markoff, J., & Montecinos, V. (1993). The Ubiquitous Rise of Economists. *Journal of Public Policy, 13*(1), 37–68.

186 Johanna Gautier Morin

Maroni, Y. (1982). Mexico: Implementation of April 21 Stabilization Program, Restricted. Paul Volcker's Papers (MC279), Box 24, Folder *Mexico 1982–1984*, Seeley G. Mudd Manuscript Library, Princeton, NJ.

Martinez-Vazquez, J., Rioja, F., Skogstad, S., & Valev, N. (2001). IMF Conditionality and Objections: The Russian Case. *The American Journal of Economics and Sociology, 60*(2), 501–517.

Marx, K., & Engels, F. (1932). *Die deutsche Ideologie* [1846]. Moscow: Marx-Engels Institute.

Masson, P. R. (2007). The IMF: Victim of Its Own Success or Institutional Failure? *International Journal, 62*(4), 889–914.

McKinnon, R. I. (1993). The Rules of the Game: International Money in Historical Perspective. *Journal of Economic Literature, 31*(1), 1–44.

Merchant, L. A. (2002). *Colapso y reforma. La integración del sistema bancario en el México revolucionario, 1913–1932*. Mexico: Miguel Ángel Porrúa-Universidad Autónoma de Zacatecas.

Mirowski, P., & Plehwe, D. (Eds.). (2009). *The Road From Mont Pelerin: The Making of the Neoliberal Thought Collective*. Cambridge, MA: Harvard University Press.

Morrell, J. (1983). The International Monetary Fund and Namibia. *Africa Today, 30*(1–2), 17–22.

Moschella, M. (2009). When Ideas Fail to Influence Policy Outcomes: Orderly Liberalization and the International Monetary Fund. *Review of International Political Economy, 16*(5), 854–882.

Mussa, M., & Savastano, M. (1999). The IMF Approach to Economic Stabilization. *NBER Macroeconomics Annual, 14*, 79–122.

OECD Development Center. (1992). An Assessment of the Brady Plan Agreements. *Working Paper, 67*, 1–46.

Oosterlinck, K. (2013). Sovereign debt default: Insights from history. *Oxford Review of Economic Policy, 29*(4), 697–714.

Parsons, T. (1951). *The Social System*. New York: The Free Press.

Rodríguez, V. E., & Ward, P. M. (1994). Disentangling the PRI from the Government in Mexico. *Mexican Studies/Estudios Mexicanos, 10*(1), 163–186.

Rogoff, K. (2003). The IMF Strikes Back. *Foreign Policy, 134*, 38–46.

Romero Sotelo, M. E., Ludlow, L., & Arroyo, J. P. (Eds.). (2014). *El Legado intellectual de los economistas mexicanos*. Mexico: UNAM,

Romero Sotelo, M. E. (2016). *Los orígenes del neoliberalismo en México. La Escuela Austriaca*. Mexico: Fondo de Cultura Económica/UNAM.

Rostow, W. W. (1960). *The Stages of Economic Growth: A Non-Communist Manifesto*. London: Cambridge University Press.

Sachs, J. (1989). Making the Brady Plan Work. *Foreign Affairs, 68*(3), 87–104.

Salas-Porras, A. (2014).. Las élites neoliberales en México: ¿cómo se construye un campo de poder que transforma las prácticas sociales de las élites políticas? *Revista Mexicana de Ciencias Políticas y Sociales, LIX*(22), 279–312.

San Miguel, P. L. (2004). La representación del atraso: México en la historiografía estadounidense. *Historia Mexicana, 53*(3), 745–796.

SAPRIN. (2004). *Structural Adjustment: The SAPRIN Report: The Policy Roots of Economic Crisis, Poverty and Inequality*, London: Zed Books.

Sau, R. (1983). Structural Adjustment in the Indian Economy: IMF Model of Import-Pushed Growth. *Economic and Political Weekly, 18*(19/21), 779–788.

Schmidt-Wellenburg, C., & Lebaron, F. (2018). There is No Such Thing as 'the Economy': Economic Phenomena Analysed from a Field-Theoretical Perspective. *Historical Social Research, 43*(3), 7–38.

Seabrooke, L. & Henriksen, L. F. (Eds.) 2017. *Professional Networks in Transnational Governance*. Cambridge: Cambridge University Press.

Sgard, J. (2005). Le principal, l'agent et l'évaluateur: comment expliquer l'échec du FMI en Argentine? *Critique internationale, 27*, 31–41.

Silva, P. (2009). *In the Name of Reason: Technocrats and Politics in Chile*, Philadelphia: Penn State University Press.

Stiglitz, J. (2002). *Globalization and Its Discontents*. New York: W. W. Norton & Co.

Topalov, C. (1999). *Laboratoires du nouveau siècle. La nébuleuse réformatrice et ses réseaux en France (1880–1914)*. Paris: Editions de l'EHESS.

Truman, T. (1982). Restricted document addressed to Paul Volcker. Board of Governors of the Federal Reserve System. April 20, 1982. Seeley G. Mudd Manuscript Library, Princeton, NJ.

UNDP. (2003). *Human Development Report 2003*. New York: Oxford University Press.

Williamson, J. (1998). The Washington Consensus Revisited. In Emmerij, L. & Nuniiez del Arco, J. (eds.). *El desarrollo economico y social en los umbrales del siglo XXI*. Washington, DC: IDB.

Wolf, C. Jr. (1965). The Political Effects of Economic Programs: some indications from Latin America. *Economic Development and Cultural Change, 14*(1), 1–20.

Woods, N. (2006). *The Globalizers: The IMF, the World Bank, and Their Borrowers*. Ithaca: Cornell University Press.

World Bank. (1990). *World Debt Tables, 1990–91, Country Tables*. Washington, DC: World Bank Publications.

World Bank. (1991). Financial Flows to Developing Countries. *Quarterly Review*. Paper #21968. Washington, DC: The World Bank Debt and International Finance Division.

Yefsah, A. (1992). L'armée et le pouvoir en Algérie de 1962 à 1992. *Revue des mondes musulmans et de la Méditerranée, 65*, 77–95.

11 Economists in public discourses

The case of wealth and inheritance taxation in the German press

Hendrik Theine

1 Introduction

In this chapter, I investigate the role of economists in public discourses on wealth and inheritance taxation in the German press. I do so by drawing on the recent "cultural turns" in regulation theory and post-Marxist thinking, in discussing economists as organic intellectuals – a term coined by Antonio Gramsci to describe the class-related nature of thinkers – and their role in society. In particular, economists are perceived to either shape the political and economic agendas in favour of the capitalist classes ("hegemonic organic intellectuals") or call into question current policy regimes that favour dominant accumulation regimes ("counter-hegemonic organic intellectuals").

To that end, text-mining methods are used to identify economists in the newspaper articles on wealth and inheritance taxation in seven German print outlets between 2000 and 2018. Media economists – the subset of economists that is present in media debates – are investigated regarding their quantitative appearance in the different newspapers and over time, their paradigmatic orientation as well as their political affinities.

This chapter shows that well-known economists frequently occur in the newspaper coverage, which is no surprise given their position as directors of influential research institutes or experts in this particular field of economic research. Over time, varying levels of occurrences are identified which can be partly explained by the publication of books on wealth taxation and the broader issue of economic inequality. Considering paradigmatic orientations, this chapter indicates a stark dominance of economists associated with mainstream economics and ordoliberalism, who are closely associated to market-liberal organisations. Much less frequently occurring are post-Keynesian economists and other heterodox economists with ties to social–democratic and left-winged organisations. This pattern is reinforced by the political orientation of the newspapers. Given the role of economists as organic intellectuals in the political economy, such results point to a continuing legitimation and normalisation of the structural power of the capital class to assert their interests regarding low wealth and inheritance taxation.

As said, the role of economists in public discourses is investigated drawing on the example of wealth and inheritance taxation in Germany. The German

DOI: 10.4324/9780367817084-14

Economists in public discourses 189

case is an illustrative example, because wealth inequality is particularly striking in Germany, which is one of the most unequal countries in the Eurozone area in terms of the wealth distribution (Bach et al., 2018; Leitner, 2016). One major reason for the persistence of wealth inequality is the transfer of wealth over generations in the form of gifts and inheritances, which leads to about 25 to 40 per cent of overall wealth in Germany being inherited (Fessler & Schürz, 2018; Leitner, 2016). Simulations indicate that the overall value of bequests and gifts has increased sharply in recent years, reaching annual amounts of around 200 to 300 billion euros per year, which is equivalent to about 10 per cent of national income (Bach & Thiemann, 2016).

Yet, the different forms of wealth taxation (net wealth taxes, taxation of income generated from wealth such as capital income or rents, or the taxation of inheritance) play a very limited role in the German tax system. In sum, the different forms of wealth taxation result in approximately 1 per cent of GDP since the mid-1990s (Bach, 2018, 2014).[1] A major reason is the expiration of the wealth tax in 1997 and rather low levels of revenue generated from the inheritance taxation due to extensive tax exemptions on business assets and on transfers to family members (Theine, 2019; Scheve & Stasavage, 2012; Houben & Maiterth, 2011).[2]

From a (post-)Marxist perspective, specific state policies such as the design of the tax system are the terrain of political struggles and historical contestations between different classes, class fractions and groups in society.[3] Taxes can tell much about the dominance of certain classes and class fractions as well as the influence of other social forces (Jessop, 2016). In this account, the minor role of wealth taxation vis-à-vis other forms of taxation (taxes on consumption and labour income) can be regarded as the result of structural power of the capital class that is able to assert their interests. And indeed, detailed investigations of interest group influence on wealth and inheritance taxation signify the intensive lobbying by business and wealthy interest groups for continuing low level of inheritance and wealth taxation or even the abolishment thereof (Theine, 2020; Butterwegge, 2018; Hartmann, 2018).

This contribution is structured in the following way: section 2 discusses the "cultural turns" in regulation theory and post-Marxist thinking with a particular focus on the role of economists as organic intellectuals, section 3 introduces the methodological considerations of the empirical investigation, section 4 presents the main results and section 5 concludes.

2 The regulation approach, its cultural turns and economists as organic intellectuals

This chapter is situated in the recent 'cultural turns' in regulation theory and post-Marxist thinking that highlight the role of linguistic and semiotic elements, discourses and language in capitalist trajectories at large and the regulation of specific accumulation regimes more specifically (e.g. Angermuller, 2018; Jessop & Sum, 2018; Maesse, 2018; Sum & Jessop, 2013). A prime

190   Hendrik Theine

example of taking cultural turns seriously is the post-disciplinary approach "cultural political economy" (CPE) mainly developed by Sum and Jessop (2013). They emphasise the foundational nature of semiosis (any process of sense- and meaning-making) in social relations. Semiotic features play a fundamental role in interpreting and understanding actual events and processes as well as in reducing their complexity. At the same time, CPE remains rooted in the regulation approach as it emphasises the embeddedness of semiotic features in the broader sets of capitalist social relations.

Moving from rather general remarks to more specific investigations of economic practices, and in particular, of economic policies, Jessop (2010) highlights the role of discursively selective economic "imaginaries" that, vis-à-vis structurally selective institutions, frame individual subjects' lived experience of the inordinately complex world. In stabilising and prioritising some economic activities, they justify certain social positions over others, and, by and by, normalise the legitimacy of some economic activities from a broad set of possible activities while at the same time disqualifying other (alternative) activities (Jessop, 2010). Economic imaginaries are selectively defined due to the discursive and material biases of specific economic paradigms.

Among the main forces involved in the (re)definition and articulation of specific economic imaginaries at the micro-, meso- or macro-level are various actors in the civil society such as think tanks, intellectuals, international bodies, organised interests and social movements. Furthermore, the mass media are also crucial intermediaries in mobilising elite and/or popular support behind competing imaginaries (Jessop, 2010).

In this chapter, I focus on the role of economists who, due to their expert status, play a key role in defining, articulating and normalising specific economic imaginaries. It is Antonio Gramsci (1971/2003) who was among the first concerned with the role of intellectuals from a Marxist perspective. For him, intellectuals play a decisive role in the political economy as they have the time, material resources and outstanding public standing which enable them to shape and influence public debates on contested issues and to define the validity of diverse knowledge claims.[4] In particular, he coined the term "organic intellectual" to stress that even though intellectuals typically perceive themselves as neutral and autonomous from class-based interests, they actually are not. In contrast, for Gramsci organic intellectuals are closely connected to different social classes as they promote and consolidate a specific conception of the world that provides awareness and (internal) coherence of classes in their economic, political and social fields. Thus, by promoting and consolidating specific conceptions of the world, they play an active part in privileging certain class positions and their interests over others.

O'Neill and Wayne (2018) go on to subdivide organic intellectuals into hegemonic organic intellectuals and counter-hegemonic organic intellectuals. Hegemonic organic intellectuals work on behalf of the capitalist class to help shape the broader political moral, social and cultural agenda and, thus, act as "the dominant group's 'deputies' exercising the subaltern functions of social hegemony and political government" (Gramsci, 1971/2003, p. 118). In contrast, counter-hegemonic organic intellectuals call into question the dominant frames of reference, assumptions and policy trends that favour specific accumulation regimes and capitalism more generally (O'Neill & Wayne, 2018).

Specifying the different roles of economists, Maesse (2015, 2017) suggests that they often act as authoritative and legitimising actors in societal discourse due to the prestige inscribed in their academic positions and their educational credentials. Economists and knowledge from economics has a distinct status as a cultural resource for discursive interventions in the political and economic realm and in public debates.[5]

In the context of media debates, the so-called media economists (the subset of economists that is present in such debates) typically use a specific set of discursive strategies, but are at the same time required to "convert" their specialised knowledge into more accessible language. Media statements need to be grounded in scientific expertise, otherwise media economists risk their reputation within the academic community, on which their prestige actually depends. It is crucial to note that media statements from economists trigger debate and dissent by fellow scientists, for instance, by calling into question the specific argument or invoking alternative empirical studies. Yet, the scientific standing of fellow economists with a similar paradigmatic orientation (see later) is typically not questioned, which leads Maesse (2017) to argue that, in such a case, media statements by economists unfold their actual efficacy.[6]

Finally, economists tend to hide or even deny their political affinity and ideological convictions in public discourse and portray themselves as "the voice of science," i.e. they only convey subject-related facts and no personal positions (Maesse, 2015; Dow, 2015). Yet, all social science (thus, economic) theorising inevitably incorporates values and ideologies at various stages of research: be it on the level of theory selection and ontological assumptions, the empirical case selection or the specific methods used (Heise, 2019; Dow, 2015; Harvey, 2015; Stretton, 1969). Above that, research has been documenting the affiliation of many economists to political parties, think tanks and organisations, which actively pursue political projects of various kinds (e.g. Salas-Porras, 2018; Schmidt-Wellenburg, 2018; Pühringer, 2017; Plehwe & Walpen, 2006). For instance, Ötsch et al. (2018) show for the case of Germany that there is a long-standing practice of economists being active in the socio-political realm in various ways: as members of political parties, think tanks and foundations or by offering economic advice in expert committees, councils and regulatory bodies.

In summary, it can be drawn from this literature that media economists play an important role as organic intellectuals in media debates to justify and normalise the legitimacy of some economic activities from a broad set of possible activities and, thereby, to defend certain social positions over others. This chapter considers media economists in the debate over wealth and inheritance taxation with a specific focus on their role as (counter) hegemonic organic intellectuals. It does so by making the ideological convictions and political

192 *Hendrik Theine*

affiliations of economists explicit, thereby dismantling the myth of value- and position-free economics.

3 Methodology

In order to analyse the role of (media) economists in the media debates on wealth and inheritance taxation, this study employs text-mining methods in the framework of critical discourse studies (Subtirelu & Baker, 2017; Mautner, 1995). This section explains and discusses the data collected for and used in this study and the text-mining methods.

The corpus of print media articles between 2000 and 2018 contains seven daily and weekly newspapers (see Table 11.1 for details). The newspapers were selected because they are considered to be the most influential and most read quality newspapers in Germany; several of them being listed as *Leitmedium* ("newspaper of record"), which fuel and influence social, political and economic debates on current affairs (Röper, 2018, 2014, 2008, 2004, 2000; Presserelations, 2017; Pfanner, 2011; Weischenberg et al., 2005).[7]

Concerning ownership, several newspapers belong to the ten largest media corporations in Germany. Among them are well-known multi-generational family businesses (Gruner+Jahr, Verlagsgruppe von Holtzbrinck and Axel Springer SE), where not only the ownership of the corporation but also considerable wealth is passed on from one generation to another (see Ferschli et al., 2019, for details). This ownership might imply that the aforementioned corporations have a vested interest in hostile media coverage of wealth and inheritance taxation. Two newspapers have a distinctly different legal structure: *taz*

Table 11.1 Number of articles per newspaper

Newspaper	Type of newspaper	Ownership	No. of articles	Share of total articles (in %)
Welt am Sonntag	Weekly	Axel Springer SE	703	7
Die Zeit	Weekly, Leitmedium	Verlagsgruppe von Holtzbrinck	644	7
Der Spiegel	Weekly,	Gruner+Jahr, Spiegel-Mitarbeiter KG, Rudolf Augstein heirs	431	4
Die Welt	Daily	Axel Springer SE	2332	24
Frankfurter Allg. Zeitung	Daily, Leitmedium	Fazit-foundation	1077	11
Süddeutsche Zeitung	Daily, Leitmedium	Südwestdeutsche Medien Holding	2944	30
taz	Daily	tageszeitung Verlagsgenossenschaft eG	1580	16
Total			**9711**	**100**

Sources: Newspaper ownership is based on Ferschli et al. (2019), kek (2019), Bergmann and Novy (2012), and Groll (2012).

and *Frankfurter Allgemeine Zeitung* belong to a cooperative and a non-profit foundation (Bergmann & Novy, 2012; Groll, 2012).

The editorial stance of the seven newspapers is for sure not clear cut and might have also evolved over time, yet past literature has identified certain tendencies. *Welt am Sonntag* and *Die Welt* are rather bourgeois-conservative outlets with a distinctively market liberal stance towards economic policy issues (Sasse, 2012; Pointner, 2010). *Die Zeit* enjoys a high reputation as a weekly newspaper with high-quality journalism. Its political and economic orientation falls mainly between the centre and left-liberal positions. *Der Spiegel* used to be an outspokenly liberal newspaper, yet gradually leaned towards more conservative positions, which was largely influenced by Stefan Aust, the editor-in-chief from 1994 to 2008 (Wolter, 2016; Burkhardt, 2012). Founded by a group of influential German industrials, the *Frankfurter Allgemeine Zeitung*'s tone since its early years oscillates between liberal and conservative positions (Burkhardt, 2012). Current research endorses this long-standing impression that *FAZ* is rather neoliberal in framing as particularly staff journalists are advocating minimal state intervention and market liberalism (Wolter, 2016; Pointner, 2010; Volkmann, 2006). *Süddeutsche Zeitung* is leaning towards a left-liberal orientation, although media scholars like Wolter (2016) show for the topic of current economic affairs in 1982 and 2003 that most articles were following neoliberal arguments and assessments. *taz*, founded as a self-organised, direct democratic newspaper, takes a rather left-wing, green-alternative stance (Groll, 2012).

The newspaper articles for the final corpus were obtained from several databases (Lexis Nexis, factiva, and WISO) using appropriate keywords[8] and with kind support from Alexander Leipold (forthcoming). After deleting unsuitable articles from the sample,[9] the final corpus consisted of 9711 articles (see Table 11.1). Apart from the articles' headlines, lead paragraphs and main content, the corpus entails information on the authors, publication date and length of the articles.

In order to analyse media economists as organic intellectuals, a comprehensive list was compiled. The initial data was provided by Stephan Pühringer and consisted of all economists holding a professorship at a university in Germany in the 21st century (see Grimm et al., 2018 for details). In order to obtain a larger sample of economists beyond economic professors, this data was updated and extended from various sources: member lists of various academic associations in Germany (such as Keynes Gesellschaft and Verein für Socialpolitik), economists who are listed in rankings by *Frankfurter Allgemeine Zeitung* (2018, 2015, 2013) and *Handelsblatt* (2010), as well as a comprehensive list of German economists active on Twitter compiled by Makronom (Odendahl & Stachelsky, 2019). Finally, well-known international economists were added to the sample based on their own previous research. In total, this resulted in a list of 1422 economists.

As noted earlier, economists tend to make no reference to their ideological convictions, yet, at the same time, they are building their arguments on moral beliefs and political opinions – in particular when it comes to public debates on

194 *Hendrik Theine*

socio-political matters (Dow, 2015; Harvey, 2015). To capture this aspect, this chapter builds on from previous research which regards economics being comprised of different schools of thought or paradigms (for details see Dobusch & Kapeller, 2012; Lee, 2012; Dequech, 2007). More specifically, economics can be differentiated between schools of thought being part of the mainstream, which is made up of the "neoclassical economics" as the dominant core theory with its central assumptions of rationality, ergodicity and equilibrium states as well as characterised by the exclusive acceptance of mathematical-deductive models and positivism as scientific rationales (Heise & Thieme, 2016; Lawson, 2013; Dobusch & Kapeller, 2012; Dequech, 2007). At the same time, several economic schools of thought deviate partly from some of the core neoclassical assumptions but tend to remain in the scientific rationales of mainstream economics (mathematical-deductive models and positivism) – what Colander et al. (2004) call the "edge of the mainstream" (see also Heise & Thieme, 2016; Dequech, 2007). Furthermore, "ordoliberalism" is a specifically German school of thought based around the central tenet of a competitive, market-based society which is ensured by the policy of order ("Ordnungspolitik") of the state (Frey et al., 2010; Ptak, 2009).

Heterodox economic approaches, on the other hand, reject the central axioms of neoclassical economics and are characterised by a methodological openness to less formally mathematical methods of scientific inquiry (Heise & Thieme, 2016). Furthermore, heterodox economic approaches aim at explaining economics as a social provisioning process, which, according to Lee (2012, p. 340), directs the attention of economic analysis towards "human agency embedded in a cultural context and social processes in historical time affecting resources, consumption patterns, production and reproduction, and the meaning (or ideology) of market, state and non-market/state activities engaged in social provisioning." In Germany, heterodox economic approaches play a fairly small role. Given this, post-Keynesian economics is the most frequent heterodox school of thought in Germany (Heise & Thieme, 2016; Frey et al., 2010).

Reflecting this state of affairs in economics, economists are classified as the following according to the paradigmatic orientations: ordoliberal economists, plural mainstream economists and other mainstream economists as the three variations of mainstream economics, as well as post-Keynesians and other heterodox economists as the two variations of heterodox economics. This categorisation was derived from previous research and is based on professional websites and publicly available CVs of the economists in question (Grimm et al., 2018; Ötsch et al., 2018; Heise et al., 2016; Heise & Thieme, 2016).

The conjunction between paradigmatic orientations and stance towards wealth and inheritance taxation is quite straightforward for the most part. Ordoliberal and other mainstream economists tend to be rather hostile towards the reintroduction of wealth taxation and/or a more progressive approach towards inheritance taxation. In terms of political affinities, recent research (Botzem & Hesselmann, 2018; Ötsch et al., 2018; Pühringer, 2017) is able trace close connections of both group of economists to the network of German neoliberalism

Economists in public discourses   195

(e.g. the Kronberger Kreis, Stiftung Neue Soziale Marktwirtschaft or the Hayek Gesellschaft) – all of them being highly critical of higher taxation of inheritance and wealth (Lobbypedia, 2019a, 2019b; Ptak, 2007). Based on the aforementioned terminology, ordoliberal and other mainstream economists can be regarded as hegemonic organic intellectuals shaping the political and economic agenda in favour of the capitalist class.

In contrast, many of the post-Keynesian and other heterodox economists tend to be in favour of higher inheritance taxation and/or a reintroduction of wealth taxation. In terms of political affinities, post-Keynesian economists are closely linked to the Böckler Stiftung or the Keynes Gesellschaft, both part of the "Keynesian-alternative thought collective" (Pühringer, 2017, p. 19). Hence, post-Keynesian and other heterodox economists can be considered counter-hegemonic organic intellectuals as they call into question current policy regimes that favour dominant accumulation regimes.

The plural mainstream economists are a rather heterogeneous group when it comes to their stance towards wealth and inheritance taxation. To be sure, economists such as Thomas Piketty or Paul Krugman have been arguing for a higher taxation of wealth, yet, for others in this group, the position is rather unclear.

4 Results

This section discusses the role of economists in newspaper coverage on wealth and inheritance taxation. It does so by assessing the quantitative appearance of economists in the different newspapers and over time. Then, it focuses on the paradigmatic orientations and political affinities of the economists in order to discuss their role as organic intellectuals in the political economy.

Regarding the quantitative appearance of economists, Table 11.2 displays the 30 most frequently mentioned economists in the newspaper coverage – all male. At first glance, it shows that Thomas Piketty is the most cited economist over the whole period. Likewise, several other international experts are among the 20 most mentioned economists, such as Joseph E. Stiglitz, Paul Krugman and Kenneth Rogoff. Moreover, several well-known German economists show up in the list. Among them are, for instance, Clemens Fuest – president of the Ifo Institute for Economic Research since 2016, as well as his long-standing predecessor Hans-Werner Sinn. Several current and former members of the German Council of Economic Experts (Sachverständigenrat zur Begutachtung der gesamtwirtschaftlichen Entwicklung) are on the list, such as Peter Bofinger, Lars Feld, Wolfgang Franz and Christoph M. Schmidt. In total, the list of economists cited in the newspaper coverage on wealth and inheritance taxation comprises 226 names, most of them mentioned only once or twice.

This result is well in line with previous research that also identified many of the economists listed here as important sources in media debates on economic issues; thus, as media economists. For instance, Clemens Fuest, Hans-Werner Sinn, Michael Hüther and Marcel Fratzscher who are high up on the

196   Hendrik Theine

Table 11.2 30 most frequently mentioned economists

Name	Welt am Sonntag	Die Welt	Frankfurter Allg. Zeitung	Die Zeit	DER SPIEGEL	Süddeutsche Zeitung	taz	sum
Thomas Piketty	6	5	16	14	7	21	14	83
Bert Rürup	4	10	6	6	10	12	1	49
Clemens Fuest	5	8	11	8	3	7	1	43
Hans–Werner Sinn	3	8	8	4	5	11	3	42
Stefan Bach	1	4	5	2	0	16	13	41
Peter Bofinger	2	4	3	4	4	9	8	34
Rudolf Hickel	1	0	4	0	2	7	15	29
Michael Hüther	6	11	5	1	0	4	0	27
Marcel Fratzscher	2	4	4	4	1	4	5	24
Joseph E. Stiglitz	1	2	2	3	2	6	6	22
Markus Grabka	1	3	2	2	3	5	6	22
Paul Krugman	1	0	2	6	3	7	3	22
Lars Feld	2	3	5	2	1	4	1	18
Thomas Straubhaar	5	4	0	2	1	3	1	16
Gert Wagner	1	3	3	1	0	5	2	15
Christoph Schmidt	2	1	2	2	0	3	4	14
Friedrich Heinemann	1	2	2	2	0	7	0	14
Gustav Horn	1	2	1	5	0	3	2	14
Klaus Zimmermann	3	3	2	2	0	1	3	14
Bernd Lucke	2	1	2	5	1	1	1	13
Dierk Hirschel	0	0	0	3	0	4	6	13
Kenneth Rogoff	0	3	2	1	3	3	1	13
Wolfgang Franz	1	4	1	0	0	5	2	13
Stefan Homburg	2	2	4	0	1	2	0	11
Wolfgang Wiegard	0	3	0	2	1	3	1	10
Achim Truger	0	0	3	2	0	1	3	9
Lawrence Summers	0	0	1	5	2	0	1	9
Giacomo Corneo	1	0	3	0	3	1	0	8
Ben Bernanke	1	3	0	1	0	2	0	7
other	28	56	77	55	36	100	47	399
SUM	83	149	176	144	89	280	150	1071

list (Table 11.2) also play a dominant role in the media debates on the financial crisis and are in a leading position in the FAZ ranking of the most influential economists (Frankfurter Allgemeine Zeitung, 2018, 2015; Pühringer & Hirte, 2015). Yet there are also striking differences. Most notably, Stefan Bach, economist at the DIW, is the fifth most cited economist in the coverage on wealth and inheritance taxation, but not listed in the FAZ rankings. In a similar vein, Andreas Hoffmann and Markus Grabka are typically also not that high up on the lists.

Table 11.2 also signifies important differences among the newspapers. Note that the quantitative occurrences of the economists in the different newspaper outlets need to be considered against the background of the number of articles in such newspapers (see Table 11.1). Taking the varying number of newspaper articles into account, a striking pattern emerges that corresponds to political orientation of the newspapers. For instance, *Die Welt* and *Welt am Sonntag*, which are typically regarded as conservative and market-liberal newspapers (see section 3), refer frequently to Clemens Fuest, Hans-Werner Sinn and Michael Hüther, all of them rather market-liberal, conservative economists. In contrast, more progressive or even explicitly left-wing economists are less likely to be referred to: *Die Welt* is not citing Paul Krugman or Rudolf Hickel at all. Likewise, *Welt am Sonntag* rather infrequently refers to those economists. *taz* – a rather progressive newspaper outlet, on the other hand, refers to economists such as Dierk Hirschel, Christoph Butterwegge and Rudolf Hickel (all rather progressive) relatively more than to market-liberal ones, such as Michael Hüther, Clemens Fuest and Stefan Homburg.

Finally, Table 11.2 (last row) indicates that the reference to economic experts is not equally distributed among the seven newspapers (here again, one needs to take the varying number of articles per newspaper into account; see Table 11.1). Doing so, *Die Zeit*, *Der Spiegel* and *Frankfurter Allgemeine Zeitung* refer to economists more frequently, in comparison to *Die Welt*, *Süddeutsche Zeitung* and *taz*.

Considering the appearance of economists over time, Figure 11.1 shows varying levels of occurrences over the years. At the beginning of the 21st century, but also at the end of the period of investigation, there is a scarce appearance of economists in the different newspapers. In contrast, a few years stand out: 2005, 2012–2014 and 2016. A possible explanation for the peak in the latter two years (2014 and 2016) is the publication of the books *Capital in the Twenty-First Century* (2014) by Thomas Piketty and *Verteilungskampf* (2016) by Marcel Fratzscher, which initiated media debates, among others, around the

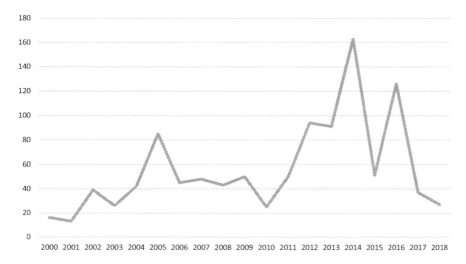

Figure 11.1 Occurrence of economists over time

198   *Hendrik Theine*

issue of wealth and inheritance taxation (see Grisold & Theine, forthcoming; Theine & Rieder, 2019a, 2019b for in-depth analysis of the newspaper debate after the publication of Piketty's book).

I now turn to the paradigmatic orientation of the economists (see section 3 for details on the methodology). Table 11.3 shows that economists associated with mainstream economics are by far the largest group in the newspaper coverage, followed by pluralist mainstream economists and ordoliberalists. Much less frequently occurring are post-Keynesian economists and other heterodox economists. A closer look into the categories reveals that many of the most-cited pluralist mainstream economists are in fact Thomas Piketty and his colleagues and co-authors (for instance Emanuel Saez and Gabriel Zucman). When only German and German-based economists are considered, ordoliberalists make up a large majority of economists in the media coverage.

Here again, Table 11.3 indicates varying extents to which economists are mentioned in the seven newspapers. *Die Zeit, Der Spiegel, Frankfurter Allgemeine Zeitung* and *Welt am Sonntag* mention mainstream and ordoliberal economists the most. In contrast, both groups of economists are least picked up by *taz* and *Süddeutsche Zeitung*. Plural mainstream economists are mentioned most frequently in *Die Zeit, Der Spiegel* and *Frankfurter Allgemeine Zeitung*. In contrast, *Die Welt* and *Welt am Sonntag* almost make no reference at all to plural mainstream economists. Turning to post-Keynesian economists, they are most frequently mentioned in *Die Zeit* and *taz*. The other newspaper outlets only seldom refer to post-Keynesian economists; in particular, *Die Welt* and *Welt am Sonntag* make almost no reference at all. Heterodox economists, finally, are – if at all – mentioned by *Der Spiegel* and *taz*.

In order to consider political affinities, I now draw on several examples of conjunctions between media economists active in the debate on wealth and inheritance taxation and political organisations. Regarding ordoliberal and mainstream economists, several of the frequently occurring media economists are well connected to market-liberal organisations. For instance, Clemens

Table 11.3 Number of economists occurring in newspaper articles according to paradigmatic orientation

Paradigmatic orientation	Welt am Sonntag	Die Welt	Frankfurter Allg. Zeitung	Die Zeit	DER SPIEGEL	Süddeutsche Zeitung	taz	sum
Mainstream Economists	34	59	53	48	35	78	30	337
Plural Mainstream Econ.	12	16	42	38	22	99	47	276
Ordoliberal Economists	23	48	60	31	15	42	7	226
Postkeynesian Economists	3	8	11	16	4	20	32	94
Heterodox Economists	2	3	6	2	7	12	24	56
NA	9	15	4	9	6	29	10	82

Fuest and Lars Feld, both strong advocates of low wealth taxation, are part of the Kronberger Kreis, the academic advisory council of the Market Economy Foundation (Stiftung Marktwirtschaft). The foundation strives for a "renaissance of market oriented policies" which is led by the conviction that "the market offers more freedom and prosperity to society than can statism and government intervention" (Market Economy Foundation 2019). Regarding wealth and inheritance taxation, the foundation opposes a reintroduction of wealth taxation and is rather sceptical when comes to a progressive reform of the inheritance taxation (Lobbypedia, 2019c; Kronberger Kreis, 2015; Bültmann, 2013).

In a similar vein, Michael Hüther, just like Clemens Fuest and Lars Feld, are academic advisors to the Economic Council of the Christian Democratic Union (Wirtschaftsrat der CDU e.V.) (Lobbypedia, 2019d; Wirtschaftsrat der CDU, 2019). The council advocates for economic policies that "best reflect the principles of a social market economy" and represents the interests of small and medium-sized firms as well as multinational companies in Germany (Wirtschaftsrat der CDU, 2019). The council is highly critical of wealth and inheritance taxation as both supposedly jeopardise the innovation capacity and equity basis of German companies (Wirtschaftsrat der CDU, 2018).

As said, post-Keynesian and heterodox economists are less frequently occurring in comparison to ordoliberal and other mainstream economists. For three post-Keynesian and heterodox media economists, Rudolf Hickel, Gustav Horn and Peter Bofinger, political affinities to social-democratic and left-wing organisations can be found. For instance, all three have signed an open letter against the German debt brake and tax cuts in 2009 which were issued by the Macroeconomic Policy Institute (IMK) linked to the German Confederation of Trade Unions (DGB) (Bofinger & Horn, 2009; for details on the debate of the German debt brake see Pühringer, 2014).

Likewise, Rudolf Hickel and Gustav Horn are academic advisors to the Arbeitskreis Steuermythen – a working group with close ties to the Social Democratic Party (SPD) that aims to dismantle "misperceptions and myths" in the German debate over taxation and public finances (Arbeitskreis Steuermythen, 2019). Gustav Horn, finally, was the academic director of the IMK from 2005 until 2019 and has been recently elected as a member of the board of the SPD (Horn, 2019; Social Democratic Party, 2019).

Recalling the aforementioned discussion of economists as organic intellectuals, the imbalance between ordoliberal and other mainstream economists (hegemonic organic intellectuals) on the one hand, and post-Keynesian and other heterodox economists (counter-hegemonic organic intellectuals) on the other hand, signifies a dominance of market liberal positions over interventionist agendas.

5 Conclusion

This chapter investigates the role of economists as organic intellectuals in public discourses drawing on the example of wealth and inheritance taxation in the

200 Hendrik Theine

German press. In particular, economists are conceptualised to either shape the political and economic agendas in favour of the capitalist classes ("hegemonic organic intellectuals") or call into question current policy regimes that favour dominant accumulation regimes ("counter-hegemonic organic intellectuals").

Regarding their quantitative appearance, this chapter shows that well-known economists frequently occur in newspaper coverage, which is no surprise given their position as directors of influential research institutes or experts in this particular field of economic research. Over time, varying levels of occurrences are detected which can be partly explained by the publication of books on wealth taxation and the broader issue of economic inequality.

Considering paradigmatic orientations and political affinities of economists, this chapter indicates a stark dominance of economists associated with mainstream economics and ordoliberalism who are closely connected to market-liberal organisations. Much less frequently occurring are post-Keynesian economists and other heterodox economists linked to social-democratic and left-wing organisations. Given the role of economists as organic intellectuals in the political economy, the imbalance between hegemonic organic intellectuals (ordoliberal and other mainstream economists) and counter-hegemonic organic intellectuals (post-Keynesian and other heterodox economists) points to a continuing legitimation and normalisation of the structural power of the capital classes to assert their interests regarding low wealth and inheritance taxation.

Notes

1 Note that wealth taxation used to play a more substantial role in the overall state revenue. Just after the Second World War, taxes on the different forms of wealth taxation have been much higher with around 3 per cent of GDP. Even further in the past, taxes on wealth have been above 5 per cent of GDP in the Weimarer Republic (Bach, 2018). Seelkopf et al. (2019) suggest that inheritance taxation is one of the early forms of taxation in Germany established on the national level in 1906, but with antecedents on the regional level in various parts of Germany dating back to the 17th century in the city of Hamburg and the principality of Brunswick-Lüneburg. Yet, since the 1990s, taxation of wealth has been reduced substantially.

2 The inheritance taxation could have been strengthened quite "easily" in the 21st century, as it was subject to two constitutional court rulings in 2006 and 2014 which required a reform of the existing tax law. In both incidents, the legislature was given around two years to reform the tax act (see Theine, 2019, table A.1, for details). The subsequent tax reforms showed little to no progress regarding a higher taxation of inheritances. In contrast, several scholars have suggested new exemptions were being introduced into the law, decreasing the taxation of inheritance even further (see for instance Butterwegge, 2018; Horn et al., 2017; Bach, 2016).

3 Poulantzas (1978), for instance, argues that the state is a complex "relationship of forces, or more precisely the material condensation of such a relationship among classes and class fractions" (cited in Jessop, 2019, p. 5); hence, it is an explanandum, not an explanatory principle (Jessop, 2016).

4 To be more precise, for Gramsci everyone engages in intellectual reasoning to certain degrees, as people usually have a specific conception of the world – a "worldview" – which they have forged out of their experience, circumstance and through (mediated)

communication. But, "not all men have in society the function of intellectuals" (Gramsci, 1971/2003, p. 9). This function of being an intellectual is reserved only for a specific group.

5 Maesse (2015) actually suggests that economists not only talk about "economic issues" but that their public interventions stretch far into general political and societal questions. In this sense, they present themselves as "universal intellectuals" in a society that is affected more and more by economic globalisation and the structuring of social and political issues along economic rationales.

6 The appointment of Achim Truger as a member of the German Council of Economic Experts may serve as an illustrative example of critique against economists with diverging paradigmatic orientations. The appointment of Truger, a post-Keynesian economist, by the German trade unions has been heavily criticised in the German media and, among others, by economists with a mainstream economic background. In particular, he was criticised for his perceived lack of scientific standing; his expert status as an economist was called into question (see for an overview: Oxi Redaktion, 2018; D'Ippoliti & Flechner, 2018).

7 Due to database restrictions, *Bild Zeitung* is unfortunately not part of the sample.

8 The keywords used to identify the relevant newspaper articles for this study were wealth taxation and inheritance taxation (and variations thereof in order to capture different ways to refer to such forms of taxation in the German language).

9 A combination of automatic and manual text cleaning methods were used to remove duplicate, corrected and very short articles. Further, internal memos ("Hausmitteilungen"), letters from readers, tables of content, advertisement, book suggestions and event recommendations were excluded from the corpus.

References

Angermuller, J. (2018). Accumulating discursive capital, valuating subject positions. From Marx to Foucault. *Critical Discourse Studies*, *15*(4), 414–425.

Arbeitskreis Steuermythen (2019). *Steuermythen – Fakten gegen Irrtümer, Fehlannahmen und falsche Schlußfolgerungen in der Debatte über Steuerpolitik*. Retrieved from: https://steuer-mythen.de/

Bach, S. (2014). Debate on wealth taxation in Germany. *ECFIN Taxation Workshop 'Taxing Wealth: Past, Present, Future'*. Brussels.

Bach, S. (2016). Erbschaftsteuer, Vermögensteuer oder Kapitaleinkommensteuer: Wie sollen hohe Vermögen stärker besteuert werden? (Inheritance tax, wealth tax or capital income tax). *DIW Berlin Discussion Paper*, *1619*. Retrieved on 17 July 2019 from: https://ssrn.com/abstract=2871833 or http://dx.doi.org/10.2139/ssrn.2871833.

Bach, S. (2018). 100 Jahre deutsches Steuersystem: Revolution und Evolution. *DIW Discussion Papers No. 1767*. Berlin: Deutsches Institut für Wirtschaftsforschung (DIW).

Bach, S., & Thiemann, A. (2016). Reviving Germany's wealth tax creates high revenue potential. *DIW Economic Bulletin*, *6*(4/5), 50–59.

Bach, S., Thiemann, A., & Zucco, A. (2018). Looking for the missing rich: Tracing the top tail of the wealth distribution. *DIW Berlin Discussion Paper*, *1717*. Retrieved on 17 July 2019 from: https://ssrn.com/abstract=3113153 or http://dx.doi.org/10.2139/ssrn.3113153.

Bergmann, K., & Novy, L. (2012). Chancen und Grenzen philanthropischer Finanzierungsmodelle. *Aus Politik und Zeitgeschichte*, *62*(29–31), 33–39.

Bofinger, P., & Horn, G. (2009). Die Schuldenbremse gefährdet die gesamtwirtschaftliche Stabilität und die Zukunft unserer Kinder. *IMK Appell Schuldenbremse*. Retrieved from: www.boeckler.de/pdf/imk_appell_schuldenbremse.pdf

202 *Hendrik Theine*

Botzem, S., & Hesselmann, J. (2018). Gralshüter des Ordoliberalismus? Der Sachverständigenrat zur Begutachtung der gesamtwirtschaftlichen Entwicklung als ordnungspolitischer Fluchtpunkt bundesrepublikanischer Politikberatung. *Leviathan*, *46*(3), 402–431.

Bültmann, B. (2013). Braucht Deutschland eine Vermögensteuer? Argumente zu Marktwirtschaft und Politik No. 122. *Stiftung Marktwirtschaft*. Retrieved from: www.stiftung-marktwirtschaft.de/fileadmin/user_upload/Argumente/Argument_122_Vermoegensteuer_2013_09.pdf.

Burkhardt, K. (2012). *Frankfurter Allgemeine Zeitung*. Retrieved on 20 May 2017 from: www.mediadb.eu/forum/zeitungsportraets/faz.html

Butterwegge, C. (2018). *Krise und Zukunft des Sozialstaates*. Wiesbaden: Springer.

Colander, D., Holt, R., & Rosser Jr, B. (2004). The changing face of mainstream economics. *Review of Political Economy*, *16*(4), 485–499.

Dequech, D. (2007). Neoclassical, mainstream, orthodox, and heterodox economics. *Journal of Post Keynesian Economics*, *30*(2), 279–302.

D'Ippoliti, C., & Flechner, S. (2018). Die Truger-Debatte ist Sinnbild eines tiefergehenden Problems. *Makronom*. Retrieved on 12 December 2019 from: https://makronom.de/sachverstaendigenrat-die-truger-debatte-ist-sinnbild-eines-tiefergehenden-problems-28731.

Dobusch, L., & Kapeller, J. (2012). Heterodox united vs. mainstream city? Sketching a framework for interested pluralism in economics. *Journal of Economic Issues*, *46*(4), 1035–1058.

Dow, S. C. (2015). The role of belief in the case for austerity policies. *The Economic and Labour Relations Review*, *26*(1), 29–42.

Ferschli, B, Grabner, D., & Theine, H. (2019). *Zur Politischen Ökonomie der Medien in Deutschland: Eine Analyse der Konzentrationstendenzen und Besitzverhältnisse*. Institut sozial-ökologische Wirtschaftsforschung report 118, München.

Fessler, P., & Schürz, M. (2018). Private wealth across European countries: the role of income, inheritance and the welfare state. *Journal of Human Development and Capabilities*, *19*(4), 521–549.

Frankfurter Allgemeine Zeitung (2013). Die einflussreichsten Ökonomen in den Medien. *Frankfurter Allgemeine Zeitung*. Retrieved on 28 October 2019 from: www.faz.net/aktuell/wirtschaft/wirtschaftswissen/f-a-z-oekonomenranking-die-einflussreichsten-oekonomen-in-den-medien-12560431.html

Frankfurter Allgemeine Zeitung (2015). F.A.Z.-Ökonomenranking: Deutschlands einflussreichste Ökonomen. *Frankfurter Allgemeine Zeitung*. Retrieved on 28 October 2019 from: www.faz.net/aktuell/wirtschaft/wirtschaftswissen/f-a-z-oekonomenranking-2015-die-tabelle-13786151.html

Frankfurter Allgemeine Zeitung (2018). F.A.Z.-Ökonomenranking: Deutschlands einflussreichste Ökonomen. *Frankfurter Allgemeine Zeitung*. Retrieved on 28 October 2019 from: www.faz.net/aktuell/wirtschaft/wirtschaftswissen/f-a-z-oekonomenranking-2018-die-tabellen-15761727.html.

Fratzscher, M. (2016). *Verteilungskampf*. München: Hanser.

Frey, B. S., Humbert, S., & Schneider, F. (2010). What is economics? Attitudes and views of German economists. *Journal of Economic Methodology*, *17*(3), 317–332.

Gramsci, A. (1971/2003). *Selections from the prison notebooks of Antonio Gramsci (1929–35)*. New York: International Publishers.

Grimm, C., Pühringer, S., & Kapeller, J. (2018). *Paradigms and policies: The state of economics in the German-speaking countries* (No. 77). ICAE Working Paper Series.

Grisold, A., & Theine, H. (forthcoming). "Now, what exactly is the problem?" On the media coverage of economic inequalities and redistribution policies – the Piketty case. *Journal of Economic Issues*.

Groll, T. (2012). *die tageszeitung (taz)*. Retrieved from: www.mediadb.eu/forum/zeitung sportraets/die-tageszeitung-taz.html.

Handelsblatt (2010). *Handelsblatt-Ranking Volkswirtschaftslehre 2010*. Retrieved on 28 October 2019 from: https://tool.handelsblatt.com/tabelle/?id=24&so=1a&pc=900&po=1800

Hartmann, M. (2018). *Die Abgehobenen. Wie die Eilten die Demokratie gefährden*. Frankfurt/M: campus.

Harvey, J. T. (2015). Economics as a scientific discipline. In *Contending perspectives in economics: A guide to contemporary schools of thought*, pp. 6–37. Northampton, MA: Edward Elgar Publishing. Chapter 2.

Heise, A. (2019). Ideology and pluralism: A German view. *Discussion Papers Zentrum für Ökonomische und Soziologische Studien, No. 75*. Zentrum für Ökonomische und Soziologische Studien (ZÖSS), Hamburg.

Heise, A., Sander, H., & Thieme, S. (2016). *Das Ende der Heterodoxie? Die Entwicklung der Wirtschaftswissenschaften in Deutschland*. Wiesbanden: Springer-Verlag.

Heise, A., & Thieme, S. (2016). The short rise and long fall of heterodox economics in Germany after the 1970s: Explorations in a scientific field of power and struggle. *Journal of Economic Issues, 50*(4), 1105–1130.

Horn, G. (2019). *Über mich*. Retrieved from: https://gustav-horn.de/ueber-mich/

Horn, G. A., Behringer, J., Gechert, S., Rietzler, K., & Stein, U. (2017). Was tun gegen die Ungleichheit? Wirtschaftspolitische Vorschläge für eine reduzierte Ungleichheit, *IMK Report, No. 129*, Hans-Böckler-Stiftung, Institut für Makroökonomie und Konjunkturforschung (IMK), Düsseldorf.

Houben, H., & Maiterth, R. (2011). Endangering of businesses by the German inheritance tax?-An empirical analysis. *Business Research, 4*(1), 32–46.

Jessop, B. (2010). Cultural political economy and critical policy studies. *Critical Policy Studies, 3*(3–4), 336–356.

Jessop, B. (2016). *The state: Past, present, future*. Cambridge, UK: Polity Press.

Jessop, B. (2019). The capitalist state and state power. In *The Oxford handbook of Karl Marx*, pp. 298–320. New York: Oxford University Press.

Jessop, B., & Sum, N. L. (2018). Language and critique: Some anticipations of critical discourse studies in Marx. *Critical Discourse Studies, 15*(4), 325–337.

Kek – Kommission zur Ermittlung der Konzentration im Medienbereich (2019). *Medienkonzentration – Mediendatenbank – Der Spiegel*. Retrieved on 23 July 2019 from: www.kek-online.de/medienkonzentration/mediendatenbank/#/profile/media/dl-zs-165.

Kronberger Kreis (2015). Erbschaftsteuer: Neu ordnen statt nachbessern. *Kronberger Kreis No. 60*. Retrieved from: www.stiftung-marktwirtschaft.de/uploads/tx_ttproducts/data sheet/KK_60_Erbschaftsteuer_2015.pdf.

Lawson, T. (2013). What is this 'school' called neoclassical economics? *Cambridge Journal of Economics, 37*(5), 947–983.

Lee, F. S. (2012). Heterodox economics and its critics. *Review of Political Economy, 24*(2), 337–351,

Leipold, A. (forthcoming). Political power and wealth taxation in Germany. A network analysis of press reports on two tax debates. *Journal of Political Power*.

Leitner, S. (2016). Drivers of wealth inequality in Euro area countries. *The Vienna Institute for International Economic Studies (wiiw) Working Paper, 122*. Retrieved on 17 July 2019 from: https://wiiw.ac.at/drivers-of-wealth-inequality-in-euro-area-countries-dlp-3787.pdf.

Lobbypedia (2019a). *Friedrich A. von Hayek Initiative Neue Soziale Marktwirtschaft*. Retrieved on 4 November 2019 from: https://lobbypedia.de/wiki/Initiative_Neue_Soziale_Marktwirtschaft.

204 *Hendrik Theine*

Lobbypedia (2019b). *Friedrich A. von Hayek Gesellschaft*. Retrieved on 28 October 2019 from: https://lobbypedia.de/wiki/Friedrich_A._von_Hayek_-_Gesellschaft.

Lobbypedia (2019c). *Stiftung Marktwirtschaft*. Retrieved from: https://lobbypedia.de/wiki/ Stiftung_Marktwirtschaft

Lobbypedia (2019d). *Wirtschaftsrat der CDU*. Retrieved from: https://lobbypedia.de/wiki/ Wirtschaftsrat_der_CDU

Maesse, J. (2015). Economic experts: A discursive political economy of economics. *Journal of Multicultural Discourses*, *10*(3), 279–305.

Maesse, J. (2017). Deutungshoheit. In *Macht in Wissenschaft und Gesellschaft*, pp. 291–318. Wiesbaden: Springer VS.

Maesse, J. (2018). Discursive Marxism: How Marx treats the economy and what discourse studies contribute to it. *Critical Discourse Studies*, *15*(4), 364–376.

Market Economy Foundation (2019). *Vision*. Retrieved from: www.stiftung-mark twirtschaft.de/en/inhalte/the-foundation/vision/.

Mautner, G. (1995). *"Only Connect": Critical discourse analysis and corpus linguistics*. Lancaster: UCREL. Retrieved on 17 July 2019 from: http://stig.lancs.ac.uk/papers/techpaper/ vol6.pdf.

Odendahl, C., & Stachelsky, P. (2019). Twitter-ranking. *Makronom*. Retrieved on 4 July 2019 from: https://makronom.de/twitter-ranking-econ-einzelwertung-2.

O'Neill, D., & Wayne, M. (2018). On intellectuals. In *Considering class: Theory, culture and the media in the 21st century*, pp. 166–184. Boston: Brill.

Ötsch, W. O., Pühringer, S., & Hirte, K. (2018). *Netzwerke des Marktes: Ordoliberalismus als Politische Ökonomie*. Wiesbaden: Springer-Verlag.

Oxi Redaktion (2018, October 11). Reputations-Firewalls, ideologische Gräben, Politikberatung: Achim Truger und der Sachverständigenrat. *Oxi blog*. Retrieved on 12 December 2019 from: https://oxiblog.de/reputations-firewalls-ideologische-graeben-grundfragen-der-politikberatung-achim-truger-und-der-sachverstaendigenrat/.

Pfanner, E. (2011). Gloves off in German media scramble. *International Herald Tribune*. Retrieved on 18 July 2019 from: www.nytimes.com/2011/03/14/business/global/14bild. html?pagewanted=all.

Piketty, T. (2014). *Capital in the Twenty-First Century*. Cambridge, MA: Harvard University Press.

Plehwe, D., & Walpen, B. (2006). Between network and complex organization: The making of neoliberal knowledge and hegemony. In B. Walpen, D. Plehwe, & G. Neunhöffer (eds.), *Neoliberal hegemony: A global critique*, pp. 27–70. London: Routledge.

Pointner, N. (2010). *In den Fängen der Ökonomie? Ein kritischer Blick auf die Berichterstattung über Medienunternehmen in der deutschen Tagespresse*. Metropolis: VS Verlag für Sozialwissenschaften.

Poulantzas, N. (1978). *Staatstheorie. Politischer Überbau, Ideologie, sozialistische Demokratie*. Hamburg: VSA.

Presserelations (2017). *Jahresbericht 2016*. Retrieved on 4 September 2017 from: www.press relations.de/fileadmin/user_upload/Unternehmen/PDF/170112_Infografik-Zitaterank ing_2016.pdf.

Ptak, R. (2007). Grundlagen des Neoliberalismus. In C. Butterwege, B. Lösch, & R. Ptak (eds.), *Kritik des Neoliberalismus*, pp. 13–86. Wiesbaden: VS Verlag für Sozialwissenschaften.

Ptak, R. (2009). Neoliberalism in Germany: Revisiting the ordoliberal foundations of the social market economy. In P. Mirowski & D. Plehwe (eds.), *The road from Mont Pèlerin: The making of the neoliberal thought collective*, pp. 98–138. Cambridge: Harvard University Press.

Economists in public discourses   205

Pühringer, S. (2014). Kontinuitäten neoliberaler Wirtschaftspolitik in der Krise: Die Austeritätsdebatte als Spiegelbild diskursiver Machtverwerfungen innerhalb der *Ökonomik, ICAE Working Paper Series, No. 30*. Linz: Institute for Comprehensive Analysis of the Economy (ICAE).

Pühringer, S. (2017). *Think tank networks of German neoliberalism power structures in economics and economic policies in post-war Germany* (No. Ök-24). Working Paper Series.

Pühringer, S., & Hirte, K. (2015). The financial crisis as a heart attack: Discourse profiles of economists in the financial crisis. *Journal of Language and Politics, 14*(4), 599–625.

Röper, H. (2000). Zeitungsmarkt 2000: Konsolidierungsphase beendet. *Media Perspektiven, 7*(2000), 297–309.

Röper, H. (2004). Bewegung im Zeitungsmarkt 2004. *Media Perspektiven, 6*(2004), 268–283.

Röper, H. (2008). Konzentrationssprung im Markt der Tageszeitungen. *Media Perspektiven, 8*(2008), 420–437.

Röper, H. (2014). Zeitungsmarkt 2014: Erneut Höchstwert bei Pressekonzentration. *Media Perspektiven, 5*(2014), 254–270.

Röper, H. (2018). Zeitungsmarkt 2018: Pressekonzentration steigt rasant. *Media Perspektiven, 5*(2018), 216–234.

Salas-Porras, A. (2018). American think tank networks and expert debates around the Global Financial Crisis: Keynesian insurgents against austerity defenders. *Policy and Society, 37*(2), 243–259.

Sasse, S. (2012). *Die Welt*. Retrieved from: www.mediadb.eu/forum/zeitungsportraets/die-welt.html

Scheve, K., & Stasavage, D. (2012). Democracy, war, and wealth: Lessons from two centuries of inheritance taxation. *American Political Science Review, 106*(1), 81–102.

Schmidt-Wellenburg, C. (2018). Struggling over crisis: Discursive positionings and academic positions in the field of German-speaking economists. *Historical Social Research, 43*(3), 147–188.

Seelkopf, L., Bubek, M., Eihmanis, E., Ganderson, J., Limberg, J., Mnaili, Y., . . . & Genschel, P. (2019). The rise of modern taxation: A new comprehensive dataset of tax introductions worldwide. *The Review of International Organizations*, 1–25.

Social Democratic Party (2019). *Parteivorstand*. Retrieved from: www.spd.de/partei/personen/parteivorstand/

Stretton, P (1969). *The political sciences: General principles of selection in social science and history*. London: Routledge & Kegan Paul.

Subtirelu, N. C., & Baker, P. (2017). Corpus-based approaches. In J. Flowerdew & J. Richardson (eds.), *The Routledge handbook of critical discourse studies*, pp. 106–119. London: Routledge.

Sum, N. L., & Jessop, B. (2013). *Towards a cultural political economy: Putting culture in its place in political economy*. Cheltenham: Edward Elgar.

Theine, H. (2019). Media coverage of wealth and inheritance taxation in Germany. *Department of Economics Working Paper No. 290*. Vienna: WU Vienna University of Economics and Business.

Theine, H. (2020). Reichtum und Macht. Eine politökonomische Perspektive auf die Erbschaftsbesteuerung in Deutschland. In G. Grözinger, H. Peukert & A. Heise (eds.), *Ökonomie und Gesellschaft (Jahrbuch 31). Ökonomie in der Krise: Analyse – Kritik – Umgestaltung*, pp. 79–96. Marburg: Metropolis.

Theine, H., & Rieder, M. (2019a). 'Piketty is a genius, but. . . ': An analysis of journalistic delegitimation of Thomas Piketty's economic policy proposals. *Critical Discourse Studies, 16*(3), 248–263.

206 *Hendrik Theine*

Theine, H., & Rieder, M. (2019b). 'The billionaires' boot boys start screaming' – a critical analysis of economic policy discourses in reaction to Piketty's 'Capital in the 21st Century'. In J. Mulderrig, M. Farrelly, & N. Montessori (eds.), *Discourse, hegemony and policy in the era of neoliberalism*. Edward Elgar, in press.

Volkmann, U. (2006). *Legitime Ungleichheiten. Journalistische Deutungen vom "sozialdemokratischen Konsensus" zum "Neoliberalismus"*. Wiesbaden: VS Verlag für Sozialwissenschaften.

Weischenberg, S., Malik, M., & Scholl, A. (2005). Journalismus in Deutschland 2005. *Media Perspektiven*, 7(2006), 346–361.

Wirtschaftsrat der CDU (2018). *Jahresbericht 2017. Die Stimme der Sozialen Marktwirtschaft*. Retrieved from: www.wirtschaftsrat.de/wirtschaftsrat.nsf/id/jahresbericht-2017-de/$file/1800252_WR_JB17_150dpi.pdf.

Wirtschaftsrat der CDU (2019). *The economic council*. Retrieved from: www.wirtschaftsrat.de/wirtschaftsrat.nsf/id/english-de.

Wolter, P. (2016). *Neoliberale Denkfiguren in der Presse. Wie ein Wirtschaftskonzept die Meinungshoheit erobert*. Metropolis: Marburg

Part 4

Economics as a scientific field

12 Are there institutionalized pathways to the Nobel Prize in economics?[1]

Philipp Korom

1 Academic excellence and "power through ideas"

Throughout most of the 19th century, the academy had been a parochial world subordinated to the will of locally established churches and politicians. Professors did not aim to produce new knowledge but rather to bring forth men who were sociable and cultivated (McClelland, 1980). What Jencks and Riesman (1968) termed an "academic revolution" – by which they meant the triumph of professors and their norms of meritocracy over boards of trustees composed of non-academics and special interest groups – is essentially a recent development. Publications and recognition from those who are qualified to judge slowly emerged as the prime indicator of scholarly achievement in a growing type of academic institution, the "research university" (Menand et al., 2017), in which the professionalization of scholars takes place.[2]

Today all academic disciplines, including economics, have an elaborate system of awards to recognize academic excellence, mostly with a single *ne plus ultra* award. The best-known awards are the Field Medal in mathematics and the Nobel Prize. Because the Nobel Prize is regarded by laypeople and scientists alike as the acme of scientific achievement, the award gives economists the authority to speak on behalf of science (Lebaron, 2006). However, Laureates themselves have criticized the special standing of the Nobel Prize. Friedrich Hayek, the 1974 Nobel Laureate in economics, feared that the prize could create an aura of hard science certainty around the decidedly social science of economics.[3] Milton Friedman, the 1976 Nobel Laureate, was skeptical about the assumed universality of Laureates' elite expertise: "I myself have been asked my opinion on everything from a cure for the common cold to the market value of a letter signed by John F. Kennedy."[4]

Outside the field of economics, fervent critiques of the prize have charged that the Nobel Prize system does not recognize the unity of the social sciences in theory and in application (Horowitz, 1983). Given research that consistently demonstrates that economists are less likely to contribute to the public good, others argue that the prize stands in direct contradiction to the founder's will, which stipulated that awards should be given to those who have "conferred the greatest benefit on mankind" (Rothstein, 2015).

DOI: 10.4324/9780367817084-16

210   *Philipp Korom*

However, despite all these reservations, the Nobel Prize in economics has lost neither its extraordinary visibility nor its prestige. The prize continuously gives *discursive power* to Nobel Laureates to effectively advance ideas in academics, politics, economics and the media (Maesse, 2015). To give just a few illustrations of the Laureates' impact on the circulation of powerful ideas: Gary S. Becker popularized the notion of "human capital"; Chile implemented an economic recovery plan based on Milton Friedman's policy recommendations in the 1970s; Daniel Kahneman (along with Amos Tversky) changed the way the world thinks about economics, upending the notion that human beings are rational decision-makers; Paul Krugman has become one of the most influential public intellectuals in the social sciences, reaching a wide audience through his columns in the *New York Times*.

The Nobel Prize does not guarantee lasting esteem by fellow scientists, as "the scientific community is acutely sensitive to signs of its members being 'over the hill'" (Zuckerman, 1977, pp. 238–239). With the emphasis on moving ahead, the prestige of Laureates may turn out to be short-lived as their research is superseded by newer contributions. Yet there seems to be little ebb and flow regarding the scientific legitimacy of Nobel Laureates as public intellectuals. This might also be one of many reasons why key ideas of Laureates easily turn into "public ideas" (Hallett, Stapleton, & Sauder, 2019) circulating in the news and being used by different mediators (e.g. journalists) for making sense of current events. Examples of such "public ideas" are nudging (R. Thaler), the prize of inequality (J. Stiglitz), the human development index (A. Sen), economic freedom (M. Friedman), and the tragedy of the commons (E. Ostrom).

Given this power of Nobel Laureates in economics to influence the public ("power through ideas," c.f. Carstensen & Schmidt, 2016), it appears worthwhile to investigate in depth who these scholars actually are. Previous research has categorized Laureates according to their theoretical approaches (Boettke, Fink, & Smith, 2012; Offer & Söderberg, 2016, p. 150f.), identified predictors of the Nobel Prize winners in economics (Chan & Torgler, 2012), analyzed citation trajectories (Bjork, Offer, & Söderberg, 2014), reconstructed intellectual trajectories through oral history interviews (e.g. Samuelson & Barnett, 2007), or analyzed the life cycle of scholarly creativity (Weinberg & Galenson, 2019). What makes this chapter's contribution distinct is its focus on the nexus between academic institutions[5] and (individual) pathways to achieving the highest level of eminence.

My main argument is that publications in the most prestigious journals, socialization in the top departments of the discipline, and receiving the Nobel Prize produce a circle of interdependencies: Publications in top journals such as the *American Economic Review* are a precondition for tenure at top departments such as Harvard University (Heckman & Moktan, 2018). Tenure at prestigious departments then set economists on a trajectory to reach the apex of eminence represented by the Nobel Prize. Finally, Laureates may succeed in further publishing in leading journals, partly because of their reputation. The postulated

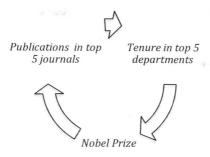

Figure 12.1 Circle of interdependencies

nexus, I will argue, holds true for most but not all cases. The general conclusion is that pathways to eminence in economics are institutionalized and limited.

2 The prize in economic sciences in memory of Alfred Nobel – a celebration of the power of mind and a political enterprise

The Nobel Prize is the prize of prizes; no other award carries comparable prestige. The "Sveriges Riksbank Prize in Economic Sciences in Memory of Alfred Nobel" was not mentioned in Alfred Nobel's original testament of 1895 (Nobelstiften, 1972), as were all other Nobel Prizes, but is based on a donation received by the Nobel Foundation in 1968 from Sweden's Central Bank. Its selection procedures were described by Assar Lindbeck, who dominated the prize committee until recently, as follows:

> Every October a form, to be filled in which suggested candidates, is sent to professors at about 75 departments of economics all over the world [as well as to previous Laureates] . . . About 150 to 200 proposals are regularly received for the economics prize, usually covering some 75 to 125 nominees . . . After receiving the various proposals, the prize committee commissions expert studies of the most prominent candidates, sometimes by Swedish experts but usually by foreigners . . . The "stock" of candidates that is considered annually hovers around 20–30 persons, though usually only a handful of these are regarded as "hot" names each year . . . The prize is finally decided by simple majority in a secret ballot in this plenary session, where all Swedish members of the [Royal Swedish] Academy [of Sciences] (260 persons) have the right to vote if they participate in the meeting.
>
> (Lindbeck, 1985, pp. 46–47)

Regarding the question of what is considered a prize-worthy contribution, "it is probably correct to say that the selection committee has looked, in particular,

212 *Philipp Korom*

at the originality of the contribution, its scientific and practical importance, and its impact on scientific work" (Lindbeck, 2001, p. 212). With hindsight, it also becomes apparent that the prize has been awarded for one or several specific contributions (such as the prize for R. C. Merton or M. Friedman) as well as for lifetime contributions (such as the prize for P. Samuelson or S. Kuznets). Between 1969 and 2018, the prize has been awarded 50 times to 81 Laureates.

Despite the rigorous selection procedures and strong links between the award and other indicators of excellence such as citations (Bjork et al., 2014), there is a political undertone to the prize. Offer and Söderberg (2016) argue, based on extensive archival research, that the prize has never escaped the tenuousness of its founding moment. The conflict over "sound money" and government intervention had reached its pinnacle in Sweden. The Central Bank of Sweden attempted to establish its autonomy from politics, which was dominated by Social Democrats, by seizing control over the interest rate ("Åsbrink's interest coup"). The government responded by limiting the degrees of freedom of the bank's governor, Per Åsbrink. To regain credibility, Åsbrink in turn decided to launch a Nobel Prize in economics that could potentially function as a PR campaign for a "market turn" and a change in fundamental attitudes, in which buying and selling between individuals replace social democratic obligations to different social groups.

Empirically, however, Offer and Söderberg find that the award is split roughly evenly between market liberals and economists whose ideas support the principles of social democracy, suggesting that the prize committee is consistently engaged in a delicate balancing act in order to avoid excessive controversy (Offer & Söderberg, 2016, p. 107f.).

3 Academic institutions and elite formation

The prosopographical approach (Charle, 2015) that I adopt here is interested in what people have in common, rather than in how they stand out as individuals. The method allows to gain insight into a group of individuals as a collective by bringing together relevant biographical data. The portrait of the individual is the intermediate aim of prosopographical research while the ultimate purpose is to collect and analyze data on phenomena, such as career line trajectories, that transcend individual lives. In our case study, the descriptive analysis of the sum of biographical data aims at bringing forth communalities between the professional lives of elite economists, which allows insights into how this group of individuals typically navigates professional careers in institutional contexts.

In this chapter, I will specifically investigate whether Nobel Laureates in economics unfold their careers in similar ways by focusing on two types of academic institutions: departments and journals.

Elite departments: Higher education institutions differ in various structural characteristics (e.g. faculty size, admissions selectivity, level of external support) but also regarding the key criteria by which faculty are selected (Musselin, 2010, p. 94f.). Hermanowicz (2005) argues that what sets apart top-tier from middle- or low-tier departments is that they place the highest premium on research and recruit only colleagues that aspire to be among the best. Given the widespread obsession in economics with hierarchies of excellence (Fourcade, Ollion, & Algan, 2015), economists regularly publish rankings of departments. In a recent worldwide ranking of economics departments, Ph.D. education emerges as a highly concentrated activity with the top few departments scoring substantially higher than all others (Amir & Knauff, 2008). It turns out that the top five (T5) departments are all located in the United States: Harvard University, MIT, Stanford University, Princeton University, and University of Chicago.

Elite journals: Publications in journals are a powerful determinant of eminence in economics (Card & DellaVigna, 2013). In general, there seems to be a consensus about the so-called top five (T5) journals that can be traced back to an early contribution by Pieters and Baumgartner (2002). If finance journals are set aside, then the T5 economics journals that publish articles receiving the bulk of attention by the profession are *American Economic Review* (*AER*), *Econometrica*, *Journal of Political Economy* (*JPE*), *Quarterly Journal of Economics* (*QJE*), and *Review of Economic Studies*.[6] Recent research has begun to study the relationship between publications in T5 journals and tenure prospects. Using econometric models, James Heckman and Sidharth Moktan calculated "incest coefficients" indicating the relationship strength between publications in the T5 journals and (tenure-track) employment in the T5 departments of the discipline. Their main finding is that

> the JPE has a high incest coefficient − 14.3% for Chicago affiliates; the non-house-affiliated AER has a relatively high incest coefficient for Harvard faculty who account for 11.9% of its publication. Most conspicuous is the QJE with a 24.7% incest coefficient for Harvard affiliates and a 13.9% coefficient for MIT affiliates.
>
> (Heckman & Moktan, 2018, pp. 49–50)

Given this cohesive intellectual macrostructure of the discipline, which is clearly dominated by few departments, few journals, and their various interlinkages, it is likely that there are only few elite channels to reach eminence. To probe whether there are few institutionalized pathways[7] for Nobel Laureates, the following sections will systematically analyze information on the careers and publication behavior of 81 Laureates.

4 A prosopographical database

This study is based on a comprehensive biographical database created by the author. Biographical data on 81 Laureates who received the Nobel Prize in economics between 1969 and 2018 were gathered from diverse sources, including official biographies from www.nobelprize.org. However, these biographies rarely contain detailed information on the scholars' time spent in different

214   *Philipp Korom*

employment positions (or visiting professorships). I have thus relied on the economists' official CVs that are mostly available from their personal webpages. Various editions of the *Who's Who in Economics* and biographical dictionaries have proved invaluable as well (Blaug, 1999; Breit & Hirsch, 2009; Vane & Mulhearn, 2005).

To analyze major career pathways, I use sequence analysis (SA). SA refers to a group of approaches to process longitudinal data representing series of states or events in the life trajectories of individuals. SA includes tools to format sequences, to cluster them, or to represent them in graphical forms (Gauthier, Bühlmann, & Blanchard, 2014). The SA data file of this case study uses the so-called vertical "time-stamped-event" (TSE) representation that lists the "events" experienced by each scholar along with the time at which the events occurred. Sequences of events can easily be constructed from this representation. As can be seen in Table 12.1, the "events" of interest are full professorships and the "time" is the age at appointment. Additionally, the table lists the name of the department and its prestige rank. Prestige ranks for economics department are taken from Amir and Knauff (2008). The central methodological idea of this ranking is that the "value" of a department is the sum of the "values" of its Ph.D. graduates, as reflected in the "values" of their current employing departments. As departmental prestige may fluctuate over decades, we would ideally like to draw on longitudinal data, which is not available. I will therefore resort to prestige groups (i.e. rank 1–5), thereby treating department ranks simply as orders of magnitude.

An analysis of extended career pathways takes as well into consideration that scholars might leave their home institution temporarily for appointments as a "visiting fellow," or "visiting professor" at another research institution, such as a university or an Institute of Advanced Study (e.g. the CASBS at Stanford University). I decided to consider only stays that lasted at least one full academic semester (4–5 months).[8] Registering all documented stays for each scholar allows me to construct a dataset with the format outlined in Table 12.2.

Finally, to reconstruct the publication behavior, I used the JSTOR not-for-profit digital library not only to search for publications in journals of a given author, but also to systematically export meta-data of all articles identified. JSTOR assigns research articles to different subjects such as sociology, economics, finance and computer science. I limited the search to the subject category "economics," which includes 181 different journals.

Table 12.1 Snapshot from the sequence data set

Timestamp	Prestige rank	Event	Age	ID	Scholar
1978	rank 11–20	LSE	38	1	Akerlof
1980	rank 6–10	UC-Berkeley	40	1	Akerlof
2014	rank 21 or lower	U of Georgetown	74	1	Akerlof
. . .	. . .	. . .	. . .	. . .	. . .

Table 12.2 Snapshot from the social network dataset

Home institution	Host institution	Year	ID	Scholar
UC-Berkeley	IAS	1967	1	Akerlof
UC-Berkeley	Indian Statistical Institute	1983	1	Akerlof
. . .	. . .	. . .	. . .	. . .

5 Career pathways: Ph.D.-granting departments, professorships, and visiting professorships

To study the career trajectories of all Nobel Laureates, I build partly on a three-strand model as introduced by Light, Marsden, and Corl (1973, p. 9). These strands are the disciplinary, the institutional, and the external career of faculty, with activities in one strand having implications and consequences for all the other strands.

Disciplinary strand: The first career decision is made within the discipline. Students select their field of study before they choose teaching as a career. It is reasonable to assume that students with a strong research orientation opt for a distinguished Ph.D. program. Besides the doctoral degree, further advancement in the disciplinary strand such memberships in academies are mostly dependent on publication success.

Institutional strand: The primary link between the disciplinary and institutional aspects of faculty careers is the prestige of the Ph.D.-granting department, which is found to be more relevant for obtaining a top position than is the level of productivity during the Ph.D. training (Han, 2003; Long, 1978). I will consider only full professorships, thereby neglecting other stages of a typical institutional career such as chairmanship or early career steps (e.g. associate prof.).

External strand: Finally, academic careers involve many activities outside the major appointment. I will focus on visiting fellowships and professorships of a minimum length of one semester after the Ph.D.

5.1 Shifts in the geography of obtaining a Ph.D.

When we look at the Ph.D. institutions of the Nobel Laureates in economics, MIT, Harvard, and U Chicago have clear leading positions ("disciplinary strand"). Altogether, 36 of the 81 Nobel Laureates (44.4%) obtained a doctorate from a T5 department. If we focus on scholars born in the USA only, then the percentage rises from 44.4% to 76.6%. This high proportion of American-born Laureates with doctorates from T5 universities suggests that scholars such as Richard H. Thaler, an American Nobel Prize winner who received his Ph.D. from the University of Rochester, are the strict exception.

A network perspective that considers professor-student connections offers a more revealing picture. Tol (2018) reconstructs the (global) professor-student

216 *Philipp Korom*

network in economics using mostly (but not only) the *Academic Family Tree* (David & Hayden, 2012), a collaborative online tool for building an academic genealogy for different disciplines. In the network, which spans five generations with 350 men and 4 women, 72 Nobel Prize winners belong to one single family tree. Instead of studying the entire network, I will focus only on the largest network subcomponent identified by Tol (2018), which starts with one of the leading German economists of the historical school of economics, Karl Gustav A. Knies (1821–1898).

Figure 12.2 shows a directed acyclic graph because in most cases students learn more from their professors than the other way around. The figure reveals, among other things, that George Stigler, James M. Buchanan, and Ronald Coase were students of Frank Knight, and that Robert Lucas was a great-great-grandstudent of Richard T. Ely. "Master-apprentice relationships" (Heinze, Jappe, & Pithan, 2019) between two Laureates appear as well frequently in this network (Samuelson-Merton junior, Modigliani-Shiller, Tobin-Phelps). In some cases, the relations identified in Figure 12.2 hint to "schools of thought", which developed around at least one key scholar associated with a paradigm and regarded as a model by several pupils. There exists, for example, a network closeness between the various representatives of the first (e.g. F. Knight) and the second generation (e.g. G. Stigler) of the "Chicago School" (Booth, 1982).

The main insight that can be gained from the subgraph (as from the whole network) is that a Ph.D. from one of the T5 departments was rare in the not-so-distant past. Karl Gustav A. Knies and Eugen Böhm von Bawerk (1851–1914) studied in Germany and Austria. Many of their students (e.g. Joseph Schumpeter, Richard T. Elly), grandstudents (e.g. Allyn A. Young) and great-grandstudents (e.g. Frank Knight) were academically socialized in the USA but did not receive their Ph.D. from any of the T5 departments. The network perspective thus reveals that while the key place of training for leading economists today are concentrated in T5 departments, they have been far more variable over time than commonly assumed.

5.2 Main career pathways

To depict the diversity of career trajectories ("institutional strand") and track each individual pattern, I will use a decorated parallel coordinate plot as introduced by Bürgin and Ritschard (2014). Such a plot enables us to identify the most typical career patterns while also revealing the diversity within the entire set of observed career trajectories at the same time. Such a visualization further helps us to understand how professorships throughout a scholar's career relate to the prestige ranks of departments.

In Figure 12.3, each line represents a unique, observed order pattern, and the line width reflects the frequency of the pattern. The lines are jittered to avoid overlapping and to help identify typical patterns; only patterns which make up *at least* 3% of all 80 considered cases are highlighted in dark grey.[9] To facilitate the tracking of distinct patterns, there are gray arrangement zones at the

Pathways to the Nobel Prize in economics?   217

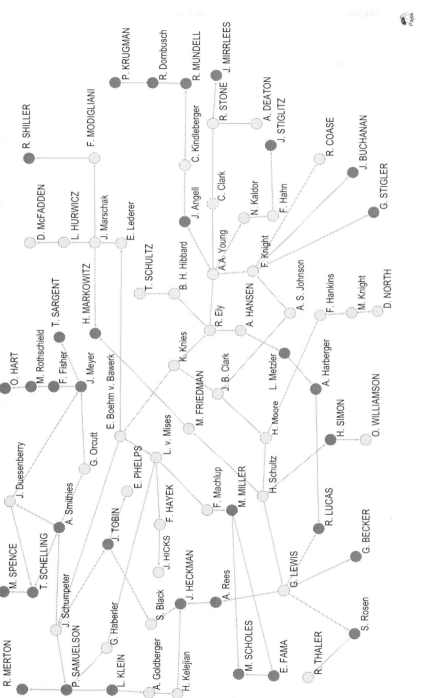

Figure 12.2 Largest subgraph in the professor-student network in economics

Source: Tol, 2018

Note: The names of Nobel Laureates are written in capital letters. Nodes in dark gray indicate a Ph.D. from a T5 department. Directed arcs represent professor-student relationships.

218 *Philipp Korom*

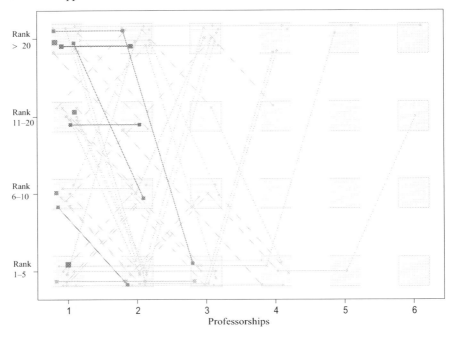

Figure 12.3 Career trajectories clustered by departmental prestige rank groups (Amir & Knauff, 2008)

intersection of the *x* coordinate (stage in a scholar's career) and the *y* coordinate (rank of the department).

Looking at the colored lines in Figure 12.3, we learn that three of the six most frequent patterns lead to T5 departments. We can, for example, derive that a more commonly experienced pattern is to hold at the career beginning two consecutive professorships at departments with ranks below 20 and then be appointed professor at a department with the highest prestige (rank 1–5). The careers of Ronald H. Coase, Arthur W. Lewis, William F. Sharpe, and Alvin E. Roth are marked by such a specific career trajectory, which is highlighted in orange in Figure 12.3. In-house careers are quite widespread as well. Peter A. Diamond, Eugene F. Fama, Milton Friedman, Lars P. Hansen, Merton H. Miller, Paul Samuelson, and Robert M. Solow were all appointed as full professors at one of the T5 departments and did not switch departments. Another striking feature of the most common career paths is that there are very few moves to lower-ranked departments, which are in general rare and only characteristic of the final career steps in the trajectories (professorships 4–6).

Out of the 186 different full professorships considered in the biographical database, 33.9% were held at T5 departments. Out of the 81 Nobel Laureates considered, 42 held at least one full professorship at one of the T5 departments.

Pathways to the Nobel Prize in economics? 219

Many of those who never made it into these elite departments pursued most of their careers outside the USA (e.g. James A. Mirrless, Bertil G. Ohlin, and Reinhard Selten). Combining this aggregate information with the sequential patterns presented in Figure 12.3 allows me to conclude that most Nobel Laureates follow a standardized career path that leads them to the very top in the departmental hierarchy.

5.3 Visiting networks

Elite careers are shaped by two distinct forces: hierarchies and networks. Universities are hierarchical structures in which elites quickly move through lower positions (assistant prof., associate prof.) to reach the final career plateau, from which there is nowhere to go professionally within the very same institution. Elites, however, can also entertain multiple affiliations by visiting other research institutions ("external strand"). By doing so, they establish networks between the home institution and other visiting institutions. To obtain a global view of the relatively large visiting network, I decided to shrink all vertices (i.e. home/ visiting institutions) belonging to a certain (prestige) class to one single vertex. For example, I shrank all US departments belonging to the top five ranked departments to a new vertex labeled "USA {rank 1–5}." The arcs in Figure 12.4 are unidirectional, indicating the number of scholars moving temporarily from a home institution of a certain class to another class of host institutions.[10]

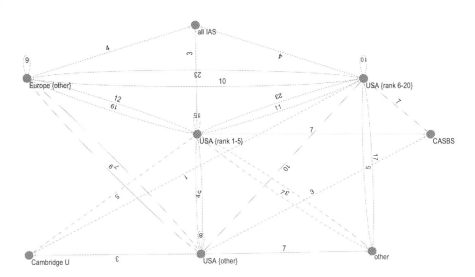

Figure 12.4 Visiting relationships between different types of institutions (*N* = 130)

Note: Arcs indicate the direction of the relationship. Considered are only multiple relationships equal to or greater than three. IAS stands for all Institutes of Advanced Studies (except for the Center for Advanced Study in the Behavioral Sciences, CASBS).

220   *Philipp Korom*

In the "shrunken network," most scholars leave second-tier US departments (rank 6–20) to either visit US top-tier departments (rank 1–5) or to conduct studies at European departments. Moreover, there is a significant inflow from Europe to the top US departments as well as a high circulation between departments belonging to the top five. The overall network structure also suggests that the "big five" are the main magnet in the visiting network, which is confirmed by the "indegree distribution." Although the category "USA (rank 1–5)" encompasses only five institutions, it has an indegree of 65, while a category such as "USA (rank 6–20)" with 11 departments is marked by a comparatively low indegree of 48.[11]

6 Publication in top five journals

In the last step of the analysis, I will investigate whether Nobel Laureates strive not only to work at top departments but also to publish in top journals. There are at least two reasons why we should expect to find Nobel Laureates' publications concentrated in the five leading journals: First, publications in top-notch journals are not only an important measure of visibility but also, at least partly, a rough proxy of the (recognized) excellence of a scholar. Second, and more specifically, there is evidence that publishing in T5 journals has an inbred nature: Editors are likely to select papers of those they know mostly through joint departmental affiliations (Colussi, 2018; Heckman & Moktan, 2018). That editors of the T5 journals and Nobel Laureates are both likely to be associated with a T5 department should therefore positively affect the chances of publication in T5 journals. Moreover, Heckman and Moktan have found evidence that publications in T5 journals are in general a strong predictor of tenure in T5 departments. It is very likely that this institutional link is also important to understand the careers of Nobel Laureates.

In what follows, I aim to establish empirically whether there is indeed a strong connection between publications in top journals and winning the Nobel Prize. Further, I want to know whether the link grew stronger as the discipline matured. To these ends, Figure 12.5 depicts the number of publications in elite and non-elite journals separately for Laureates belonging to four different age groups.

The major insight gained from Figure 12.5 is that Laureates publish on average every second paper in a T5 journal. In general, T5 publications figure high if one considers that JSTOR allows one to search 181(!) economics journals. Scholars such as Herbert Simon, Kenneth Arrow, and Robert J. Aumann have published nearly exclusively in T5 journals. There are only a few scholars with no publications at all in T5 journals. These scholars have in common that they mostly work in research areas that do not represent mainstream economics.[12]

Further, it becomes apparent that the general pattern does not vary much across age groups, which suggests that the link between publishing in T5 journals and receiving the Nobel Prize is not a recent phenomenon at all.

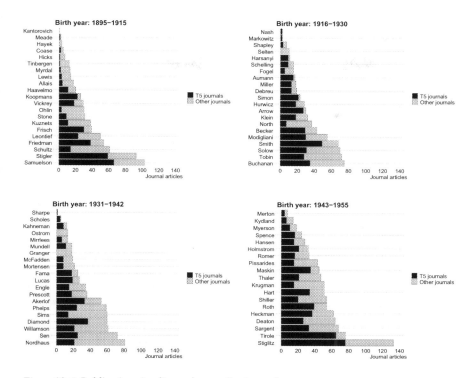

Figure 12.5 Publications in elite and non-elite journals

Nobel Laureates thus appear – much like their fellow economists – to be hyperaware of the top five's ability to make or break their career. To receive a Nobel Prize in economics without any T5 publications is not an unseen phenomenon (see the case of Soviet mathematician and economist Leonid V. Kantorovich), but the dominant route to tenure at a leading economics department or to the Nobel Prize in economics is clearly via publications in T5 journals.

7 Economics: a hierarchical discipline with homogenous elite careers

This contribution tried to shed some light on a group of Nobel Laureates in economics whose ideas have significant repercussion in the academic world, and in some cases, outside of it. Kenneth Arrow, for example, helped transform economic theory into a mathematical science, created modern social choice theory, and established most of the major findings in general equilibrium theory (Maskin, 2019). While highly influential in the discipline, the Nobel Laureate Arrow reached less recognition outside the discipline than, for example, Amartya Sen or Paul Krugman (Prinz, 2017). Flip through the past year's issues

222 *Philipp Korom*

of the *New Republic*, the *New York Review of Books*, or the *New York Times* and you will find many references to these two economists. Others, like Milton Friedman, provided the intellectual foundation for public policies. Friedman's influence on the anti-inflation, tax-cutting, and antigovernment policies of Ronald Reagan or Margaret Thatcher is difficult to overstate (Forder, 2019).

Using prosopographical tools, I have shown that the academic careers of Nobel Laureates in economics have enough in common for connections to be uncovered. More specifically, I have laid bare institutionalized pathways to the Nobel Prize, implying that individuals follow similar routes shaped by the overall intellectual structure of the discipline. This macrostructure is hierarchically organized with five top departments and (their in-house) journals dominating the discipline. While my analysis *cannot* reveal whether economists pursue some rational "master plan" to win the Nobel Prize,[13] it becomes apparent that most of them pursue their careers through the same "institutional elite channels": Nobel Laureates in economics are either hired by one of the top five departments, and/or they work towards a visiting professorship at MIT, Harvard, Stanford, Princeton, or University of Chicago. To enter these elite circles, they regularly publish in the T5 journals whose editors are mostly affiliated with one of the T5 departments. Furthermore, I can empirically show that in many cases there exist master-apprentice relationships between Nobel Laureates (that were formed at one of the T5 departments). A prominent example is Kenneth Arrow, who taught at Harvard and Stanford and mentored graduates who became Nobel Laureates themselves: John C. Harsanyi, Eric S. Maskin, Roger B. Myerson, A. Michael Spence, and Joseph E. Stiglitz.

These results point to a relatively homogenous elite that is shaped by an elite subset of American institutions rather than by departments across the United States or the world. The dominance of few departments goes hand in hand with a unitary disciplinary structure. While other social science disciplines like sociology are fractious with many specialties and few interlinkages between them, economics is found to have a "sizeable [intellectual] core that incorporates a number of major subfields" (Crane & Small, 1992). Mathematical models – commonly recognized as the "golden standard" (Rodrik, 2016) – build bridges between specialties and hold economics as a discipline together.

Now, consensus implies control as well. The relationship between disciplinary consensus (of what constitutes good science) and control is, as Fourcade et al. (2015, p. 96) argue, an intricate one:

> there might be more consensus because there is more control (for instance if a consistent view of what constitutes quality research is promoted by those who control the top journals); conversely, control might be more effective and enforceable because there is more consensus.

Whatever the case, in the end the unitary and hierarchical structure leads to few pathways to the uppermost levels of prestige in economics, with powerful gatekeepers affiliated with the T5 departments of the discipline. As the Nobel

Pathways to the Nobel Prize in economics? 223

committee decided not to stray too far away from the discipline's internal prestige rankings (Offer & Söderberg, 2016), the majority of all Nobel Laureates reveal similar pathways connected with top departments and top journals.

Finally, it should be noted that my findings – that there are institutionalized pathways to the Nobel Prize in economics – do not allow me to explain why some who were at the pinnacle of economics, such Joan Robinson or John K. Galbraith, did not receive the prize, nor to make reasonable predictions of who will join the group of Laureates in the future. However, the conceptual model for analyzing typical career pathways put forward in this contribution can be put to use in a different way. What can be "tested" is whether a new Laureate fits or deviates from the picture presented in this chapter. Recurrent "fits" tell us that economics has not changed, while recurrent "misfits" hint, most likely, to a *de*-institutionalization of elite careers that stem from major changes from within the discipline.

Notes

1 Acknowledgement: This study was financially supported by the Austrian Science Fund (FWF, project number: P29211).
2 Research became the preeminent marker of academic prestige around the end of the 19th century, as reflected in psychologist James McKeen Cattell's (1860–1944) early endeavors to measure scientific eminence. Cattell asked leading representatives of 12 disciplines (e.g. anatomy) to rank the most eminent scientists (e.g. anatomists) in their respective background disciplines by giving priority to the scientists' contributions to research (Cattell, 1906).
3 Friedrich August von Hayek's speech at the Nobel Banquet, December 10, 1974. (www.nobelprize.org/prizes/economic-sciences/1974/hayek/speech/, 5th of July, 2019).
4 Milton Friedman's speech at the Nobel Banquet, December 10, 1976 (www.nobelprize.org/prizes/economic-sciences/1976/friedman/speech/, 5th of July, 2019).
5 Institutions are here understood to be the building blocks of social order representing "collectively enforced expectations with respect to the behavior of specific categories of actors or to the performance of certain activities" (Streeck & Thelen, 2005, p. 9). In this sense, chairs of elite departments (e.g. Harvard University) must recruit strong faculty members, and editors of top journals (e.g. *American Economic Review*) are expected to publish cutting-edge research. It is these social pressures that organize the behavior of actors in academia into rather predictable patterns.
6 Editors of all five journals are usually associated with one of the T5 departments. Currently, Esther Duflo (MIT) is the editor of the *AER*, Joel Sobel (UC San Diego) of *Econometrica*, Harald Uhlig (University of Chicago) of the *JPE*, Andrei Shleifer (Harvard University) et al. of the *Quarterly Journal of Economics*, Jerome Adda (Bocconi University) et al. of the *Review of Economic Studies*.
7 This compound term is inspired by the concept of the "institutionalized life course" that was first coined by Kohli (1985). It presupposes an institutional pattern that shapes lives both in terms of movement through positions and of biographical plans. The concept is frequently used in the social sciences, as there is an abundance of evidence that individual trajectories are shaped by meso- and macro-level institutional conditions.
8 In some cases, however, it is impossible to know the exact length of stay. The curriculum vitae of Christopher A. Sims, for example, reveals that he was a visiting professor at Yale University in 1974. I can only assume that such information implies that Sims spent at least one semester at Yale (and not less time).

224 *Philipp Korom*

9 Please note that John Nash could not be included because he is the only Laureate with no full professorship.
10 A visit to a host institution was only counted once per scholar. To give an example: The economist Peter A. Diamond was a visiting fellow at Harvard University twice throughout his career. In the analysis, however, I establish only a single link between MIT (home institution) and Harvard University (host institution) based on this information.
11 In social network analysis the term "indegree" stands for the number of arcs coming into a vertex.
12 Friedrich Hayek, for example, is mostly known for his contributions to the philosophy of science, and Reinhard Selten is considered one of the fathers of experimental economics.
13 The chosen research design does not allow me to investigate scholars' intentions and motives. To understand the "internal mechanism" of the detected institutionalized pathways, qualitative in-depth studies are warranted (see also Becker (2017) on evidence in the social sciences). To most economists the Nobel Prize comes, at least partly, as a surprise (see, for example, Alvin E. Roth's reactions to the prize on YouTube. The YouTube video was uploaded by Stanford University on October 15, 2012, with the title "Stanford Visiting Professor Al Roth Reacts to Winning the 2012 Nobel for Economics").

References

Amir, R., & Knauff, M. (2008). Ranking Economics Departments Worldwide on the Basis of PhD Placement. *The Review of Economics and Statistics*, *90*(1), 185–190.

Becker, H. S. (2017). *Evidence*. Chicago and London: The University of Chicago Press.

Bjork, S., Offer, A., & Söderberg, G. (2014). Time Series Citation Data: The Nobel Prize in Economics. *Scientometrics*, *98*(1), 185–196.

Blaug, M. (1999). *Who's Who in Economics* (3rd ed.). Cheltenham and Northampton, MA: Edward Elgar.

Boettke, P. J., Fink, A., & Smith, D. J. (2012). The Impact of Nobel Prize Winners in Economics: Mainline vs. Mainstream. *American Journal of Economics and Sociology*, *71*(5), 1219–1249.

Booth, W. C. (1982). Between Two Generations: The Heritage of the Chicago School. *Profession*, 19–26.

Breit, W., & Hirsch, B. T. (Eds.). (2009). *Lives of the Laureates: Twenty-Three Nobel Economists*. Cambridge, MA: MIT Press.

Bürgin, R., & Ritschard, G. (2014). A Decorated Parallel Coordinate Plot for Categorical Longitudinal Data. *The American Statistician*, *68*(2), 98–103.

Card, D., & DellaVigna, S. (2013). Nine Facts about Top Journals in Economics. *Journal of Economic Literature*, *51*(1), 144–161.

Carstensen, M. B., & Schmidt, V. A. (2016). Power through, over and in Ideas: Conceptualizing Ideational Power in Discursive Institutionalism. *Journal of European Public Policy*, *23*(3), 318–337.

Cattell, M. J. (1906). *American Men of Science: A Biographical Directory*. New York: The Science Press.

Chan, H. F., & Torgler, B. (2012). Econometric Fellows and Nobel Laureates in Economics. *Economics Bulletin*, *32*, 3365–3377.

Charle, C. (2015). Prosopography (Collective Biography). In J. D. Wright (Ed.), *International Encyclopedia of the Social and Behavioral Sciences* (pp. 256–260). Amsterdam: Elsevier.

Colussi, T. (2018). Social Ties in Academia: A Friend Is a Treasure. *The Review of Economics and Statistics*, *100*(1), 45–50.

Pathways to the Nobel Prize in economics? 225

Crane, D., & Small, H. (1992). American Sociology since the Seventies: The Emerging Identity Crisis in the Discipline. In T. C. Halliday & M. Janowitz (Eds.), *Sociology and its Publics: The Forms and Fates of Disciplinary Organization* (pp. 197–234). Chicago: University of Chicago Press.

David, S. V., & Hayden, B. Y. (2012). Neurotree: A Collaborative, Graphical Database of the Academic Genealogy of Neuroscience. *PLoS ONE, 7*(10), e46608.

Forder, J. (2019). *Milton Friedman.* New York: Springer.

Fourcade, M., Ollion, E., & Algan, Y. (2015). The Superiority of Economists. *Journal of Economic Perspectives, 29*(1), 89–114.

Gauthier, J.-A., Bühlmann, F., & Blanchard, P. (2014). Introduction: Sequence Analysis in 2014. In P. Blanchard, F. Bühlmann, & J.-A. Gauthier (Eds.), *Advances in Sequence Analysis: Theory, Methods, Applications* (pp. 1–17). New York: Springer.

Hallett, T., Stapleton, O., & Sauder, M. (2019). Public Ideas: Their Varieties and Careers. *American Sociological Review, 84*(3), 545–576.

Han, S.-K. (2003). Tribal Regimes in Academia: A Comparative Analysis of Market Structure across Disciplines. *Social Networks, 25*(3), 251–280.

Heckman, J. J., & Moktan, S. (2018). Publishing and Promotion in Economics: The Tyranny of the Top Five. *INET Working Papers, No. 82.*

Heinze, T., Jappe, A., & Pithan, D. (2019). From North American Hegemony to Global Competition for Scientific Leadership? Insights from the Nobel Population. *PLOS ONE, 14*(4), e0213916.

Hermanowicz, J. C. (2005). Classifying Universities and Their Departments: A Social World Perspective. *The Journal of Higher Education, 76,* 26–55.

Horowitz, I. L. (1983). Toward a Nobel Prize for the Social Sciences. *PS: Political Science & Politics, 16*(1), 57–58.

Jencks, C., & Riesman, D. (1968). *The Academic Revolution.* Garden City, NY: Doubleday & Co.

Kohli, M. (1985). The Institutionalization of the Life Course: Historical Findings and Theoretical Arguments. *Kölner Zeitschrift Für Soziologie Und Sozialpsychologie, 37*(1), 1–29.

Lebaron, F. (2006). "Nobel" Economists as Public Intellectuals: The Circulation of Symbolic Capital. *International Journal of Contemporary Sociology, 43*(1), 88–101.

Light, D. W., Maresden, L. R., & Corl, T. C. (1973). *The Impact of the Academic Revolution on Faculty Careers.* Washington, DC: ERIC Clearinghouse on Higher Education.

Lindbeck, A. (1985). The Prize in Economic Science in Memory of Alfred Nobel. *Journal of Economic Literature, 23*(1), 37–56.

Lindbeck, A. (2001). The Sveriges Riksbank (Bank of Sweden) Prize in Economic Science in Memory of Alfred Nobel 1969–2000. In A. W. Levinovitz & N. Ringertz (Eds.), *The Nobel Prize. The First 100 Years* (pp. 197–217). London and Singapore: Imperial College Press and World Scientific Publishing.

Long, J. S. (1978). Productivity and Academic Position in the Scientific Career. *American Sociological Review, 43*(6), 889–908.

Maesse, J. (2015). Economic Experts: A Discursive Political Economy of Economics. *Journal of Multicultural Discourses, 10*(3), 279–305.

Maskin, E. S. (2019). The Economics of Kenneth J. Arrow: A Selective Review. *Annual Review of Economics, 11,* 1–26.

McClelland, C. E. (1980). *State, Society and University in Germany 1700–1914.* Cambridge: Cambridge University Press.

Menand, L., Reitter, P., & Wellmon, C. (2017). *The Rise of the Research University.* Chicago: The University of Chicago Press.

226 *Philipp Korom*

Musselin, C. (2010). *The Market for Academics*. New York: Routledge.

Nobelstiften (1972). *Nobel: The Man and his Prizes*. New York: American Elsevier.

Offer, A., & Söderberg, G. (2016). *The Nobel Factor: The Prize in Economics, Social Democracy, and the Market Turn*. Princeton, NJ: Princeton University Press.

Pieters, R., & Baumgartner, H. (2002). Who Talks to Whom? Intra- and Interdisciplinary Communication of Economics Journals. *Journal of Economic Literature*, *40*(2), 483–509.

Prinz, A. (2017). Memorability of Nobel Prize Laureates in Economics. *Applied Economics Letters*, *24*(6), 433–437.

Rodrik, D. (2016). *Economics Rules: The Rights and Wrongs of the Dismal Science*. New York: Norton.

Rothstein, B. (2015, October 11). Ekonomipriset i strid med andan i Nobels testamente. *Dagens Nyheter*.

Samuelson, P. A., & Barnett, W. A. (Eds.). (2007). *Inside the Economist's Mind: Conversations with Eminent Economists*. Malden, MA: Blackwell.

Streeck, W., & Thelen, K. A. (Eds.). (2005). Introduction: Institutional Change in Advanced Political Economies. In *Beyond Continuity: Institutional Change in Advanced Political Economies* (pp. 1–39). Oxford ; New York: Oxford University Press.

Tol, R. S. J. (2018). Rise of the Kniesians: The Professor-student Network of Nobel Laureates in Economics. *University of Sussex Working Paper, No. 05*.

Vane, H. R., & Mulhearn, C. (2005). *The Nobel Memorial Laureates in Economics: An Introduction to their Careers and Main Published Works*. Cheltenham: Elgar.

Weinberg, B. A., & Galenson, D. W. (2019). Creative Careers: The Life Cycles of Nobel Laureates in Economics. *De Economist*. https://doi.org/10.1007/s10645-019-09339-9

Zuckerman, H. (1977). *Scientific Elite: Nobel Laureates in the United States*. New York: Free Press.

13 Forms of social capital in economics

The importance of heteronomous networks in the Swiss field of economists (1980–2000)

Thierry Rossier and Pierre Benz

1 Introduction[1]

In June 2017, Marion Fourcade gave a keynote lecture at the annual congress of the Swiss Society of Economics and Statistics in Lausanne, insisting in particular on the importance of ideological and political issues in guiding research in economics. During the time dedicated to questions, someone in the audience argued against Fourcade's statements:

> I think there is a lot of heterogeneity in economics, and much of what you've said would maybe apply to some subfields of economics, but not so much to others. Think of pure series with equilibrium refinements, there is not much ideology there. Or also . . . if you think of the resource curse and conflict[s], and development, and these kinds of things, there are very few people holding ideological views on whether oil is good, or bad. . . . It's more like a technical question that you try to analyse with statistical methods. Or also the randomised control trials, for example. Very often, actually, the margin of manoeuvre . . . where ideology comes in, in some fields, it's relatively small.[2]

This professional economist was arguing for economics to be of a "pure" nature. Economists often believe in the autonomy of the discipline, especially toward political issues.[3] However, some scholars have stressed the importance of ideology and political orientation in guiding economists' preferences for research specialisations and methodologies, and being related to their departmental affiliation (Beyer & Pühringer 2019; Horowitz & Hughes 2017; Fourcade 2018). This denegation of politics and, more generally, of "power" (Lebaron 2000: 243) has been identified as a specific feature of the discipline. Being much more heteronomous than economists would often state, economics is in fact strongly embedded in the field of power (i.e. the field[4] of the dominant of all the other fields; Bourdieu 1996a, 2005). Consequently, controversies at stake are not solved like in the most autonomous sciences, such as natural and life sciences

DOI: 10.4324/9780367817084-17

(Benz 2019), but rather depend on recognition and consecration tied to the field of power (Lebaron 2018: 217). As a "trans-epistemic" field, economics has roots in academia, politics, business and the media, and economists located at different intersections of these fields often diverge in their accounts of what is good economics (Maesse 2015). In a more historical perspective, economics has been close to political and economic decision-makers for a long time (Fourcade 2009), but its autonomy might have increased in the more recent period due to the professionalisation and the internationalisation of the discipline, and the related dissociation from the nationally anchored public administration and political class (Schmidt-Wellenburg & Lebaron 2018: 17–18; Fourcade 2006).

Economists differ regarding their internal (e.g. ties to other academic economists) and external (e.g. ties to actors in the political and private sectors) networks. The type, form and size of these networks are constitutive of a specific hierarchy between individuals and participate to structure the discipline. This perspective has only received little attention until now and only a few studies (Denord et al. 2011; Eloire 2014; Godechot & Mariot 2004; Serino et al. 2017; Lunding et al. 2020) have focused on the power provided through network relations or, said otherwise, on *social capital* within fields. To our knowledge, except Klüger (2018; and in this volume), no research has systematically investigated the role of social capital in the economics profession and its effects on the relative autonomy of the field.

This chapter aims to investigate the structure and evolution of social capital within the field of economists in Switzerland, where the discipline is particularly internationalised (Rossier & Bühlmann 2018) and where different elite groups are particularly close, cohesive and connected (Bühlmann et al. 2012). It relies on an original prosopographical database of all professors of economics at Swiss universities between 1980 and 2000 (n = 200), who constitute the dominant agents in the discipline and concentrate the most dominant resources in the field (Rossier 2017). In a first empirical part, we focus on the distinction and hierarchy between autonomous (i.e. internal) and heteronomous (external) forms of social capital. By means of multiple correspondence analysis (MCA), we identify two main oppositions of resources and profiles among economists. The principal opposition is based on the volume of extra-disciplinary network resources, and the secondary opposition is related to the volume of intra-disciplinary configurations of social capital. In a second part, we centre on the evolution in the structure of the field from 1980 to 2000. Through class-specific MCA, we show that, despite the fact that intra-disciplinary social capital gains in importance in the recent period, extra-disciplinary social capital decidedly constitutes the key structuring logic along time. The chapter is organised as follows. First, we develop the notions of scientific field and social capital. Second, we present our sample and data, our methodology and our indicators of social capital. Third, in an empirical part, we focus on the structure of the field according to social capital logics and on the historical evolution of these dynamics. Finally, we summarise our main findings and open on new research perspectives.

2 Internal and external forms of social capital in the field of economists

A scientific (or disciplinary) field such as economics is very often structured around an opposition between a *scientific pole*, linked to scientific capital[5] – a symbolic capital associated with internal scientific prestige and recognition – and a *society* (or *worldly*) *pole*, related to external – academic (i.e. at the university level), political and economic – capitals. The overall volume of capitals detained also matters in these fields (Bourdieu 2004). Insights on economics show that this discipline often follows these two modes of structuration (Lebaron 2001; Schmidt-Wellenburg 2018). In scientific fields, the role of social capital must not be underestimated (Gingras 2012; Bühlmann et al. 2017), but, until now, this particular resource has been given little attention.

Bourdieu (1986: 248–249) defines social capital as follows:

> Social capital is the aggregate of the actual or potential resources which are linked to possession of a durable network of more or less institutionalized relationships of mutual acquaintance and recognition – or in other words, to membership in a group – which provides each of its members with the backing of the collectivity-owned capital, a "credential" which entitles them to credit, in the various senses of the word.

Bourdieu considers social capital as the most important resource in *any* social space together with economic and cultural capitals. From a quantitative perspective, social capital depends on the size of the network of an individual and on the volume of capitals detained by other members of the network, understood as their more or less important integration to the field of power (Bourdieu 1996a). From a qualitative perspective, social capital is characterised by the nature of the capitals detained by the linked individuals. A high volume of social capital puts individuals in a rather favourable position within a given field since it tends to multiply the other detained capitals (Eloire 2018). While reflecting the importance of maintaining connections between members of certain fractions of the dominant class (Lenoir 2015), social capital can be considered as a resource that may generate symbolic capital within a field (De Nooy 2003), including a scientific field such as economics as a scientific discipline. In order to provide a better understanding of the structure of social capital in economics, this chapter differentiates between *intra-* and *extra-disciplinary* forms of social capital.

Intra-disciplinary social capital can be obtained through networks *within* the disciplinary field of economics. At the *institutional level*, social capital can be acquired through positions occupied at the top of powerful institutions, where individuals are linked to other powerful individuals. In scientific fields, it corresponds to the executive committee of disciplinary institutions or deanship in disciplinary departments (Bourdieu 2004). At the *inter-personal level*, social capital can be acquired through more or less intricate and institutionally formalised

230 *Thierry Rossier and Pierre Benz*

relations with other individuals engaged in the field of economists. These relations can be developed over a longer period of time and allow individuals to mobilise strong ties. Two types are of particular concern to us: relations developed through doctoral supervision of future economics professors (Bühlmann et al. 2018) and through research collaborations (Larivière et al. 2010; Gingras 2012). At the *departmental level*, social capital can be acquired through institutional affiliations during the career. Since, as stated before, international experiences seem to situate an individual closer to the autonomous pole of the scientific field, having been related to researchers in other countries also constitutes a form of intra-disciplinary social capital and a sign of belonging to a transnational scientific community (Bühlmann et al. 2013). In particular, stays at US departments lead to a large volume of important scientific resources in economics (Fourcade 2006). Finally, at the *scientific production level*, citations create a (more or less loose) directed tie between researchers (Kaplan 1965). If a scientist's work is cited, it denotes some sort of recognition among peers which can be activated and facilitates the creation of a more bonding connection (or not). Moreover, the works cited are published in a certain type of medium (i.e. scientific reviews, book collections, etc.). Being published in an "international" journal, for example, denotes the belonging to particular invisible colleges (Crane 1969), where one is able to gain certain scientific dispositions (i.e. scientific practices and know-how), which allowed this type of publication.

Extra-disciplinary social capital can be acquired through similar channels *outside* the disciplinary field of economics. At the *institutional level*, it can be obtained by sitting on more or less powerful boards and being tied to elites from different sectors of society (Mills 1956). In academia, social capital relates to executive boards of important (transdisciplinary) academic organisations or universities (Bourdieu 1988). Outside academia, positions occupied in the higher state administration, the parliament or the board of large companies allow individuals to develop strong ties to political and economic powers (Rossier et al. 2017; Larsen & Ellersgaard 2018). At the *inter-personal level*, the supervision of the doctorate of future administrative, political and economic elites is another very strong tie to groups coming from outside the discipline and to the field of power. At the *departmental level*, having links to the same (Swiss) department, where some individuals have remained for most of their career, favours the insertion within a local community, which is often related to external logics (Wagner 2010). Consequently, individuals with local profile will tend to own extra-disciplinary forms of social capital.

In this chapter, we investigate the structure of social capital within the field of economists and its historical and institutional dynamics, paying particular attention to the relative importance of intra- and extra-disciplinary networks.

3 Research strategy and methods

3.1 Data

Our data stem from a historical database on Swiss elites[6] and were collected as part of the research project "Academic Elites in Switzerland 1910–2000:

Between Autonomy and Power".[7] Our empirical analyses rely upon all the associate and full professors in economics (including financial economics) at all the ten Swiss universities and the two federal institutes of technology between the dates of 1980 and 2000 ($n = 200$). The choice of these dates allows us to study our object historically, but without focusing on a too-long time period which would prevent us from having comparable indicators. We stop at the date of 2000 in order to have rather complete biographical information on these professors' careers (the youngest professor of the group was 50 years old when data were collected in 2015). The names of the professors were collected using Swiss university directories (*Annuaires des universités suisses*) published yearly, which contain the complete list of the Swiss academic personnel at that time, as well as activity reports from the 12 universities. We then collected biographical information on these professors on the basis of diverse sources, such as the *Swiss Historical Dictionary*, the *Who's Who in Switzerland*, several university anniversary monographs, databases and other material provided by university archives, university activity reports, newspaper archives, online curricula, doctoral dissertations, the website moneyhouse.ch for the commerce register of Swiss companies and the "P3" database of the Swiss National Science Foundation for the funding of research from this institution.

3.2 Methods: MCA and CSA

In a first step, to visualise how forms of social capital vary between the 200 economics professors, we conduct a *multiple correspondence analysis*. MCA is a multivariate geometrical method aiming at reducing the complexity among a large set of categorical variables. It allows us to visualise this information based on the logic of several dimensions (or axes) of opposition between *active* (in the sense that they construct "actively" the space) variables. The first axis represents the most dominant opposition of resources and profiles, the second axis the second most dominant, etc. The closer individuals are in the space, the more they tend to share a common profile. Conversely, the closer the modalities of variables (i.e. resources) are situated in the space, the larger is the group of individuals who tend to share them. A set of *illustrative* variables, which do not contribute to construct the space, can be projected. Modalities and variables with a contribution above the average contribution are emphasised in the interpretation of the axes. Various measures of the part of the explained variance ("inertia") are projected onto an axis. Since these rates are usually low, they are recalculated in *modified rates* to better appreciate the importance of the first axes. Generally, we retain the number of axes, which represent at least 80% of the cumulated modified rates (Hjellbrekke 2018; Le Roux & Rouanet 2010).

In a second empirical step, to grasp the historical evolution of the capitals among the field, we propose to use *class specific MCA* (CSA). After having separated the space among a certain number of sub-clouds based on illustrative variables (here, each year of professorship between 1980 and 2000), CSA searches for new axes within the given sub-clouds, while keeping the distances between individuals from the initial space. Thanks to that technique, we are

232   *Thierry Rossier and Pierre Benz*

able to measure the degree of similarity between individuals in every sub-cloud and in the whole space. The principal axes of the sub-clouds of individuals are compared to the initial axes. To assess their association, the cosines of the angle between the "old" and the "new" axes are recalculated in a standardised correlation coefficient between −1 and 1 (Hjellbrekke & Korsnes 2016). By comparing the axes of each year to the axes of the whole space, we are able to assess historical evolutions within the field of economists. Our analyses are realised through the *R* package *soc.ca* (Larsen et al. 2016).

3.3   Indicators of social capital

In this part, we specify the indicators we use as active variables in our MCA in order to focus on the forms of social capital described earlier. We also specify our illustrative variables.[8]

We measure *intra-disciplinary social capital* with the following indicators:

- **Scientific institutional positions**, through executive affiliations within scientific and disciplinary hierarchies, are considered by being a member of the *executive board of the Swiss Society of Economics and Statistics*, the main disciplinary association in Switzerland, and through *department dean positions*.
- **Scientific inter-personal networks** are twofold. First, to study the particular ties of professors to other (economics) university professors, which can be considered as the "elites" of the academic field, we investigate social capital through PhD supervision, by the *number of PhD student members of the Swiss academic elites (university professors) and the number of PhD "brother"/"sister"[9] members of the academic elites*. Second, we focus on links through research projects funded by the Swiss National Science Foundation (SNSF), the main public provider of scientific funding. Researchers can apply (as sole applicant or as co-applicants) for funding and receive money to conduct research during a given period of time (usually between one and four years). We are interested in their *degree in scientific collaborations*, i.e. their total number of co-applicants, and the *number of years of scientific collaborations*, i.e. the total number of years they have been involved in a project with at least one co-applicant.[10]
- For **international departmental networks**, we indicate if they have been involved, first, in an *at least one-year stay outside Switzerland*, and, second, *in the US*.
- Finally, to consider social capital through **scientific production**, we focus on the *number of citations of the 10 most cited publications in the Web of Science*. The Web of Science, run by Clarivate Analytics, compiles the citations since the year 1900 of around 12 000 (mostly English-speaking) journals considered as the most "important" for each discipline. This indicator constitutes a good measure for prestige and recognition at the international (or at least Anglo-American) level, and for involvement in transnational scientific networks.

Forms of social capital in economics 233

We focus on **extra-disciplinary social capital** with the following indicators:

- **Academic institutional positions** are measured through membership in *boards of important academic organisations* (i.e. science "mandarins"), which encompass several disciplines, i.e. the social sciences and humanities and all the disciplines. We retain the following positions: member of the two leading organs of the Swiss National Science Foundation, the executive committee of the University Teachers Association, the Academy of Humanities and Social Sciences, the Commission for Technology and Innovation, and the Swiss Science Council. We also retain *university vice-chancellors*.
- **Economic institutional positions** are measured by three indicators: through *economic elite positions*, defined as CEOs or non-executive board members of the 110 largest Swiss companies, or executive committee member of the major business interest groups; through membership in *the executive board of a firm*; and in *the non-executive board of a firm* (no matter the size, total turnover, or the market capitalisation).
- **State institutional positions** relate to *political* or *administrative elite positions*. Political elites are members of the federal government and the federal parliament. Administrative elites are the governing board members of the Swiss central bank or heads of a federal office. Aside from these influential political positions, we also take into account *members of federal expert committees*, which are institutionalised expert groups whose main task is to advise the federal government and administration.
- **Administrative, political and economic inter-personal networks**, i.e. their links to economic, political and administrative elites, are again measured through PhD supervision: *number of PhD student members of the Swiss extra-academic elites* (according to the same definition as before) and *number of PhD "brother" / "sister" members of the extra-academic elites*.
- Finally, **local departmental networks** are measured through a process of *local reproduction*, by linking the university where professors obtained their doctorate and the university where they were appointed professors. If a professor teaches in the same university where he or she obtained his/her PhD, it shows a particular local involvement.

Aside from these diverse forms of social capital, in order to work on subgroups based on time-periods, we project variables regarding the *21 years between 1980 and 2000* as illustrative variables to have each time a subgroup of people who were professors during a particular year.[11]

4 The structure of social capital in economics

We proceed to the analysis of the structure of social capital in the Swiss field of economists. In a first empirical part, we uncover the overall structure of the diverse forms of social capital by identifying dimensions of opposition among resources through MCA. In a second part, we test the evolution of this structure between 1980 and 2000 through CSA.

234 Thierry Rossier and Pierre Benz

4.1 External and internal social capitals

In this part, we proceed to a multiple correspondence analysis to highlight the principal oppositions within the structure of social capital of economics professors between 1980 and 2000 ($n = 200$). The analysis relies on 19 active variables (47 active modalities), which measure different forms of social capital (see Table 13.1 for the contributions and frequencies of the active variables and modalities; the ones contributing to each axis above the average contribution are highlighted in grey). The first two axes account for 81% of the cumulated

Table 13.1 Contributions and frequencies of the active variables and modalities

Form of social capital	Dimension	Variable	Modality	Dim.1	Dim.2	Freq.
Intra-disciplinary social capital	Scientific institutional positions	Board member of Swiss Society of Economics and Statistics	No	0.6	2.2	158
			Yes	2.2	8.1	42
			Total	2.8	10.3	200
		Department dean	No	0.9	1.4	124
			Yes	1.4	2.2	76
			Total	2.3	3.6	200
	Scientific interpersonal networks	PhD student member of academic elites	0	1.2	1.0	123
			1–2	0.7	0.0	58
			3+	1.7	5.1	19
			Total	3.6	6.1	200
		PhD "brother"/"sister" member of academic elites	0	6.2	1.6	93
			1–3	2.6	1.8	88
			4+	4.0	0.0	19
			Total	12.8	3.4	200
		Degree in scientific collaboration (SNSF)	0	1.6	5.0	79
			1–5	0.0	0.1	78
			6–10	2.2	9.3	29
			11+	0.2	2.8	14
			Total	4.0	17.2	200
		Years of research collaboration (SNSF)	0	1.7	4.6	104
			1–5	0.0	0.3	46
			6–10	1.8	2.6	36
			11+	1.1	5.5	14
			Total	4.6	13.0	200
	International departmental networks	Stay in other country	No	4.1	10.3	47
			Yes	1.3	3.2	153
			Total	5.4	13.5	200
		Stay in the US	No	0.1	3.9	118
			Yes	0.2	5.7	82
			Total	0.3	9.6	200

Form of social capital	Dimension	Variable	Modality	Dim. 1	Dim. 2	Freq.
	Scientific production	Number of citations in Web of Science (10 most cited publications)	0	1.6	6.9	66
			1–200	0.0	0.3	91
			201–500	0.9	2.2	28
			501+	0.7	4.1	15
			Total	**3.2**	**13.5**	**200**
Extra-disciplinary social capital	Academic institutional positions	Academic organisation board (science "mandarins")	No	0.3	0.1	184
			Yes	3.7	1.4	16
			Total	**4.0**	**1.5**	**200**
		University vice-chancellor	No	0.3	0.1	187
			Yes	4.6	0.9	13
			Total	**4.9**	**1.0**	**200**
	Economic institutional positions	Economic elite members	No	0.4	0.0	186
			Yes	4.7	0.1	14
			Total	**5.1**	**0.1**	**200**
		Executive board of company	No	0.2	0.1	172
			Yes	1.2	0.3	28
			Total	**1.4**	**0.4**	**200**
		Non-executive board of company	No	1.5	0.4	141
			Yes	3.6	0.9	59
			Total	**5.1**	**1.3**	**200**
	State institutional positions	Political or administrative elite members	No	0.1	0.0	191
			Yes	2.2	0.0	9
			Total	**2.3**	**0.0**	**200**
		Expert committee member	No	3.0	0.0	137
			Yes	6.6	0.1	63
			Total	**9.6**	**0.1**	**200**
	Administrative, political and economic inter-personal networks	PhD student member of extra-academic elites	0	1.2	0.0	169
			1+	6.3	0.0	31
			Total	**7.5**	**0.0**	**200**
		PhD "brother"/"sister" member of extra-academic elites	0	3.2	0.2	142
			1–3	4.6	0.3	42
			4+	3.3	0.1	16
			Total	**11.1**	**0.6**	**200**
	Local departmental networks	Local reproduction (professor in university of PhD)	No	3.8	1.9	121
			Yes	5.9	3.0	79
			Total	**9.7**	**4.9**	**200**

modified rates (Table 13.2), therefore we only retain those for our analyses. Figure 13.1 displays the cloud of modalities and Figure 13.2 the cloud of individuals. We see a concentration of individuals on the lower and left parts, while the cloud is sparser in its upper and right parts. This less dense zone

Table 13.2 Inertia rates of the 11 first axes of the MCA

Axis	1	2	3	4	5	6	7	8	9	10	11
Eigenvalue	0.18	0.12	0.10	0.09	0.08	0.07	0.07	0.06	0.06	0.06	0.05
Variance (%)	12.4	8.2	6.5	6.0	5.6	5.0	4.7	4.3	4.2	3.9	3.7
Modified rates (%)	63.3	17.7	7.2	5.0	3.2	1.6	1.1	0.5	0.3	0.1	0.0
Cumulated modified rates (%)	63.3	81.0	88.2	93.2	96.4	98.0	99.1	99.6	99.9	100.0	100.0

Figure 13.1 Axes 1 and 2. Cloud of modalities

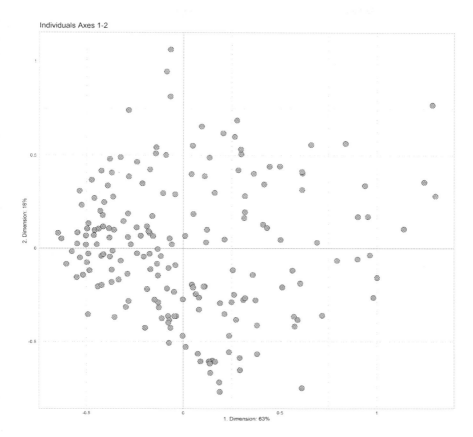

Figure 13.2 Axes 1 and 2. Cloud of individuals

corresponds to a small group of individuals with powerful resources situated on the right pole of Axis 1 and the upper pole of Axis 2, while the majority of individuals detains less important resources in the space.

Axis 1 represents 63.3% of the adjusted inertia rates. Six variables contribute to this factor above the contributions average (i.e. 5.3%), for a total of 56.1%: PhD "brother"/"sister" members of the academic elites (12.8%), PhD "brother"/"sister" members of the extra-academic elites (11.1%), local reproduction (9.7%), expert committee (9.6%), PhD students members of extra-academic elites (7.5%) and stay in other country (5.4%). Nineteen modalities contribute to this axis above the contributions average (i.e. 2.1%), for a total of 76.8%. On the negative coordinates (west of the graph), we find PhD "brother"/"sister" members of the academic elites: 0 (6.2%), local reproduction: no (3.8%), PhD "brother"/"sister" members of the extra-academic elites: 0 (3.2%) and expert committee: no (3.0%). On the positive coordinates (east of

238   *Thierry Rossier and Pierre Benz*

the graph), we find expert committee: yes (6.6%), PhD students members of the extra-academic elites: 1+ (6.3%), local reproduction: yes (5.9%), economic elite: yes (4.7%), vice-chancellor: yes (4.6%), PhD "brother"/"sister" members of the extra-academic elites: 1–3 (4.6%), stay in other country: no (4.1%), PhD "brother"/"sister" members of the academic elites: 4+ (4.0%), academic organisation: yes (3.7%), non-executive board of company: yes (3.6%), PhD "brother"/"sister" members of the extra-academic elites: 4+ (3.3%), PhD "brother"/"sister" members of the academic elites: 1–3 (2.6%), political or administrative elite: yes (2.2%), Swiss Society of Economics and Statistics: yes (2.2%) and degree in scientific collaborations: 6–10 (2.2%).

The first axis is structured by the volume of social capital, but of a particular kind. On the one hand, we see economists with extra-academic affiliations (members of an expert committee for the Swiss federal administration, member of the Swiss political and economic elites, member of the non-executive board of a company) and large external networks (they have the same supervisor as a large number of other political, administrative and economic elites, and have themselves supervised the doctorate of such elite members). At the same time, they have an important influence in the higher circles of academia outside their discipline (they have occupied the position of vice-chancellor of a university and have been a member of the directing board of important interdisciplinary academic organisations, such as the SNSF) and have a certain amount of academic networks, having the same supervisor as a large number of other university professors (but they have *not* supervised the PhD of future professors themselves).[12] Finally, they are involved in local circles (having obtained their PhD in the same university in which they are teaching) and detain no tie outside Switzerland. Opposed to these individuals who are endowed with a large amount of mundane networks, largely outside their discipline,[13] we see, on the other hand, professors of economics without academic and extra-academic networks in the form of having the same supervisor of other elite members, without local social capital, and without political affiliations, in the form of membership in an expert committee. In summary, this factor, which is by far the most important in the space, corresponds to an axis of *volume of extra-disciplinary social capital* (in its academic, political and economic forms, mostly organised at the local level, and without international ties), divided between those who own this form of capital and those who do not.

Powerful individuals detaining very important external social capital are situated on the right pole of this first axis (see Figure 13.3), such as Joseph Deiss (professor of economic policy in Fribourg), a member of the federal parliament who became part of the Federal Council (the federal government) between 1999 and 2006. We can also mention Niklaus Blattner (professor of labour market and economic industry in Basel) who was the executive secretary of the Swiss Bankers Association, one the most important business interest groups, and member of the governing board of the Swiss central bank, and Gaston Gaudard (professor of international and regional economics in Fribourg and Lausanne) who was vice-chancellor of the University of Fribourg, member of one of the two leading boards of the SNSF and member of the board of

Forms of social capital in economics 239

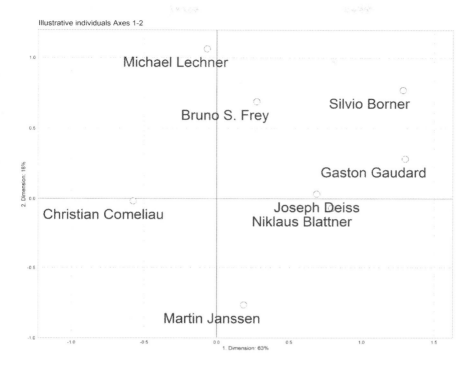

Figure 13.3 Axes 1 and 2. Illustrative individuals.

the *Société de banque suisse*, one of the country's three major banks at the time. On the other pole (left side of the axis), we see individuals with few network resources in Switzerland, such as the Belgian and French professor Christian Comeliau who taught economic development in Geneva, after having occupied teaching positions in Louvain, Kinshasa and Paris. Comeliau detained no important resources in Swiss extra-academic circles whatsoever.

Axis 2 only accounts for 17.7% of the cumulated modified rates. The opposition represented through Axis 1 is therefore 3.5 times more important than the one through Axis 2. Seven variables contribute to this axis above average (for a total of 83.2%): degree in scientific collaborations (17.2%), citations in Web of Science (13.5%), stay in other country (13.5%), years of research collaborations (13.0%), board of Swiss Society of Economics and Statistics (10.3%), stay in the US (9.6%), and PhD students members of academic elites (6.1%). Eighteen modalities contribute to this factor above average (for a total of 86.7%). On the negative coordinates (south of the graph), we find stay in other country: no (10.3%), citations in Web of Science: 0 (6.9%), degree in scientific collaborations: 0 (5.0%), years of research collaborations: 0 (4.6%), stay in the US: no (3.9%), local reproduction: yes (3.0%) and Swiss Society of Economics and

240   *Thierry Rossier and Pierre Benz*

Statistics: no (2.2%). On the positive coordinates (north of the graph), we find: degree in scientific collaborations: 6–10 (9.3%), Swiss Society of Economics and Statistics: yes (8.1%), stay in the US: yes (5.7%), years of research collaborations: 11+ (5.5%), PhD students members of academic elites: 3+ (5.1%), citations in Web of Science: 501+ (4.1%), stay in other country: yes (3.2%), degree in scientific collaborations: 11+ (2.8%), years of research collaborations: 6–10 (2.6%), dean: yes (2.2%) and citations in Web of Science: 201–500 (2.2%).

This second axis displays another opposition. It shows, on one side, economics professors owning a large amount of intra-disciplinary social capital: members of the board of the disciplinary association, university department deans, a great number of co-applicants in the SNSF network, a large number of collaboration years and a lot of citations in the Web of Science. These networks are organised at the national (SNSF) and international (Web of Science) levels at the same time. They also own international social capital, having stayed for scientific research for at least one year outside Switzerland, in particular in the USA. They detain a large share of academic networks, having supervised the doctorate of future Swiss economics professors. Regarding "elite" PhD networks, the division is clear and the powers associated with both dimensions of opposition in the space have to be differentiated: Individuals with a large amount of capitals associated with Axis 1 have the same supervisor as other academic and extra-academic elite members and have supervised *extra-academic elites* only, meanwhile individuals with a lot of resources coming from the second dimension of the space solely supervise the PhD of *academic elites*. On the other side, we see economics professors without scientific networks (no citations, no collaborations, no positions in the board of the association), without international networks, but in the process of local power reproduction (doctorate in the teaching university). This dimension summarises then a *volume of intra-disciplinary social capital* (organised at the national and international levels), divided again between those who detain it and those who do not (but do own local social capital).

On the upper pole of Axis 2, we see individuals with powerful scientific and international networks such as the "superstar" Bruno S. Frey (professor of theoretical and practical economics in Basel, Konstanz, Zurich and Warwick) who is one of the most cited European economists (more than 5000 citations of his ten most cited publications in Web of Science) and collaborated in numerous research projects; or Michael Lechner (professor of econometrics in St. Gallen, after occupying positions in Harvard and Mannheim), member of the board of the Swiss Society of Economics and Statistics and dean in St. Gallen, with a fair record of citations (more than 200) and numerous research collaborations. On the lower pole, we observe individuals with a more local profile and no scientific network resources whatsoever, such as Martin Janssen, who did his PhD in Zurich before becoming professor of financial economics in the same university and sat in numerous company boards, but with no insertion in intra-disciplinary networks whatsoever.

Forms of social capital in economics 241

In summary, our results show how the space is structured according to two dimensions: the first displays the volume of extra-disciplinary social capital and the second of intra-disciplinary social capital. Both those dimensions are structured according to the overall volume of resources, dividing the dominant, who detain a large amount of social capital, and the dominated, who do not. Particularly dominant economists are to be found in the north-east quadrant of the space where the volume of both forms of social capital is high, such as Silvio Borner (professor of economic policy in St. Gallen and Basel), a well-known expert for the federal administration, dean in both universities, member of the board of the disciplinary association and of the insurance company Helvetia (one of the most important in the country). Borner, who is one of the most influential actors in the field, became in the 1990s very active within the so-called neoliberal coalition (Mach 2002), which advocated drastic policy reforms that would eventually lead to the liberalisation of the Swiss economy.

It is to be noted that the first opposition has much more weight in the space than the second (63.3% of the inertia rates against 17.7%). Economics is thus a much more heteronomous discipline than economists would say it is. Indeed, our results show the importance of external logics, whether in the form of political, economic or (transdisciplinary) academic networks. Nonetheless, we can still wonder if, despite this overall trend, there has been some historical changes regarding the importance of these two dimensions. Some could even hypothesise a reversing movement in the importance of both these logics during the very recent period. We investigate the historical evolution of this structure between 1980 and 2000.

4.2 Importance of heteronomous networks during the 1980–2000 period

In this second part, we assess the importance of the two main dimensions of social capital (and thus the robustness of our analyses) during the historical period on which we focus. To do so, we proceed to a class-specific MCA (CSA) on each group of professors separated by year (i.e. whether they occupy a professor position at a Swiss university in each given year). Figure 13.3 shows the association (calculated by standardising the cosine) between the first axis of the MCA for the entire group, and the first axis of the CSA for each year between 1980 and 2000 (i.e. "Dimension 1"), and between the second axis of the MCA and the second axis of the CSA for each group respectively (i.e. "Dimension 2"). By doing so, we are able to see whether there are variations across time in the intensity of both dimensions identified in the previous part, or if the structure stays stable during the whole period, and thus social capital reproduces itself across time.

We observe that for the first axis, the association between Axis 1 of the MCA and of the CSAs by year is very high and does not vary a lot (correlation coefficients: $\mu = 0.97$, sd $= 0.01$). Therefore, the first dimension, related to the volume of extra-disciplinary social capital, remains particularly stable.

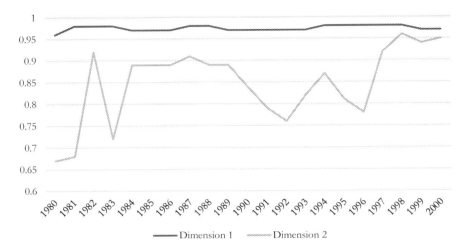

Figure 13.4 Correlation coefficients (absolute values) between axes of the MCA and the CSA by year

Heteronomous networks are, for the whole period, the most important source of distinction in the field of economists. For the associations between Axis 2 of the MCA and of the CSAs, a larger variance of the correlation coefficients can be observed ($\mu = 0.85$, sd $= 0.09$). By calculating the slope of the line which represents the evolution of the association among these axes, we observe, despite some variations, a relative (but significant) increase in importance of the association between the second axis of the MCA and of the CSAs for each year between 1980 and 2000.[14] Intra-disciplinary social capital has more weight in the recent period. This increase could explain, to some extent, the belief in the autonomy of the field. However, this process cannot hide the fact that the structure of social capital remains very stable during the whole period, and, consequently, the main logics of structuration of the field do not lose in importance. Extra-disciplinary social capital (such as sitting in academic, expert or company boards) has proven to be of an important value in economics for the whole period.[15]

5 Conclusions

The main aim of this chapter was to focus on the structure of social capital within the Swiss field of economists by relying on the sociological profile of 200 economics professors between 1980 and 2000. In a first part, we showed that the space was structured according to two dimensions. The main one was organised around the volume of extra-disciplinary social capital through academic, economic and political affiliations, as well as extra-academic and

Forms of social capital in economics 243

local networks. The secondary opposition was organised around the volume of intra-disciplinary social capital: scientific affiliations, personal scientific and international ties, and networks of citations. In economics heteronomous logics are the most prevalent in order to detain power defined as the ability to use one's own personal network composed of the collective resources owned by all the other individuals a professor is directly connected to. This type of power mostly consists in being able to influence the outcome of public and academic policy or the economy, therefore primarily *outside* the discipline. Nonetheless, a secondary type of power can be identified, consisting in being able to influence other economists with one's own writings and research, thus *within* the discipline. In a second part, we showed that the importance of extra-disciplinary social capital remained stable across the whole period. At the same time, intra-disciplinary social capital varied more and experienced a slight, but significant, increase in importance between 1980 and 2000. Despite this evolution, mundane networks constitute the main form of opposition for the whole period, which stresses the porosity of the field to external logics.

These network affiliations and resources configurations also have repercussions outside of the positional structure of the field. They influence position-takings in economics, measured through theoretical and methodological preferences, as well as research domains. Based on qualitative insights we have developed in the previous parts through illustrative profiles of professors, we have observed different teaching and research specialisation. On the first axis, economic, political and administrative elites as well as academic "mandarins" (right of the axis) teach very "practical" topics, such as economic, industry or labour market policy, while on the pole of the have-nots (left side of the axis), research domains are less close to the state and economic powers (Christian Comeliau for example is a "heterodox" economist working on economic development). On the second axis, renowned scientists (top of the axis) use mathematical models and experimental and statistical methods, linked to "autonomous" practices in economics, and work on a variety of scientific objects (in his own words, Bruno S. Frey applies economics in "non-economic fields"[16]). On the bottom of the axis, the "scientific" have-nots work on more applied topics, such as finance. Network and capital configurations are critical in influencing how economics is defined and how scientific practice is done.

In this chapter, we have focused on structural, institutional and historical processes related to the forms of social capital in the field of economists. These networks of economists have to be situated in a wider context. Scholars have noted important transformations since Bourdieu's seminal work on the field of power in the 1970s–1980s (1996a). First, the boundaries among economic and cultural capital are much blurrier than before, because cultural capital accumulation is increasing at the economic pole of the field, and, second, neoliberalism has renewed oppositions by submitting politics and the higher civil service to the aims of the private companies (Denord & Lagneau-Ymonet 2016: 46). The historical role of economists in this process must not be underestimated, since their scientific apparel and tools are particularly efficient in spreading the

244 *Thierry Rossier and Pierre Benz*

"economic belief" within the whole society (Lebaron 2000; Denord 2016). It is thus needed to explore the modalities and forms of networks of the economists in the field of power in order to unveil their role in the recent process of concentration of (economic and cultural) power within the hands of the economic fraction of the dominant class.

Notes

1 We would like to thank Philip Korom and Stephan Pühringer for their very relevant comments and their deep reading of a former version of this chapter, which greatly contributed to improve it.

2 "SSES Annual Congress 2017 – Marion Fourcade", www.youtube.com/watch?v=yR-9Fe3cW9E (58:16–59:08).

3 We can find similar statements regarding the objectivity of economics at the very top of the discipline. Nobel Prize laureate Robert Schiller stated in an interview, "The Nobel Prize is designed to reward those who do not play tricks for [public and media] attention, and who, in their sincere pursuit of the truth, might otherwise be slighted", cited in Ötsch et al. (2018: 37).

4 A field is a more or less autonomous space, where individuals struggle for its specific capital, which enables them to occupy dominant positions (Bourdieu 1996b).

5 A capital is a form of powerful resources involved in systemic processes allowing their garnering (Savage et al. 2005; Bourdieu 1986).

6 The "Swiss Elite Database", developed by the Swiss Elite Observatory (www.unil.ch/obelis/en/home.html), where elites are defined according to their position (Mills 1956). Elite members are the individuals occupying executive or top positions within the hierarchies of power institutions in several Swiss fields.

7 This project (100017_143202) was funded by the Swiss National Science Foundation and was supervised by Felix Bühlmann, André Mach and Thomas David.

8 To look all those variables summarised in a table (as well as their contributions to the first two axes of the MCA), see Table 13.1.

9 We name that way individuals with the same *Doktorvater* (i.e. Ph.D. supervisor) to mark the analogy with family ties.

10 To have comparable data among all the professors, we decided to measure this number of years *before* the age of 51, since the youngest professor was 50 during our data collection.

11 We will not address gendered considerations in this chapter because of lack of space. Women are under-represented within this group of professors: only eight women out of 200 professors. However, given the variety of profiles of these eight women, we were not able to observe a gendered differentiation between their social capital configurations and male professors' profile. A deeper research on women professors in economics is currently ongoing. Preliminary results can be found in Rossier (2019).

12 Given our empirical findings, it seems quite unexpectedly that having the same supervisors as other university professors belongs more to external logics rather than internal ones.

13 Two other modalities, which contribute above average to Axis 1, correspond more to disciplinary scientific networks and powers rather than to extra-disciplinary social capital: member of the board of the disciplinary Swiss Society of Economics and Statistics: yes, and number (degree) of collaborations in the scientific network funded by the SNSF: 6–10. To a certain extent, they are related to academic and external powers. Indeed, the disciplinary association is at the same time the scientific centre of the discipline, and the interface between economics and political powers (Jost 2016). The SNSF collaboration network mostly corresponds to a network motivated by scientific

Forms of social capital in economics   245

logics, but at the same time some "big" projects with a large amount of funding and co-applicants can follow a public agenda and be intricately related to political powers (Benninghoff & Leresche 2003). Nonetheless, these modalities contribute both to the axis just above average (= 2.2%), contrary to their contribution to the second axis, which is very important.

14 The equation y = a * x + b, where a corresponds to the slope: y = 0.0066x + 12.308 (R^2 = 0.23).
15 It is to be noted that we do not have comparable data for the more recent period (2001–2020) on social capital, since economics professors appointed after that tend to have experienced shorter academic careers (and their Ph.D. students have not already had the time to be part of the elite). One could hypothesise that the importance of those two dimensions has reversed during the very recent period. However, given the historical stability of the prevalence of heteronomous networks in the field of economists, we can suppose that the structure of the field has not moved quickly in this direction since 2001.
16 Such as "happiness, politics. . . , environment, family, conflict, history and art" (Bruno S. Frey's CV: www.bsfrey.ch/cv/EN_2019_CV_Bruno_Frey_Long.pdf).

References

Benninghoff, M., & Leresche, J.-P. (2003). *La recherche, affaire d'Etat. Enjeux et luttes d'une politique fédérale des sciences.* Lausanne: PPUR.

Benz, P. (2019). *Des sciences naturelles aux sciences de la vie. Changements et continuités des élites académiques de la biologie et de la chimie en Suisse au xxe siècle.* PhD dissertation, University of Lausanne.

Beyer, K., & Pühringer, S. (2019). Divided We Stand? Professional Consensus and Political Conflict in Academic Economics. *ICAE Working Paper Series* (94).

Bourdieu, P. (1986). The Forms of Capital. In J. G. Richardson (Ed.), *Handbook of Theory and Research for the Sociology of Education* (pp. 241–258). New York: Greenwood.

Bourdieu, P. (1988). *Homo Academicus.* Palo Alto, CA: Stanford University Press.

Bourdieu, P. (1996a). *The State Nobility: Elite Schools in the Field of Power.* Cambridge: Polity Press; Oxford: Blackwell Publishers Ltd.

Bourdieu, P. (1996b). *The Rules of Art: Genesis and Structure of the Literary Field.* Palo Alto, CA: Stanford University Press

Bourdieu, P. (2004). *Science of Science and Reflexivity.* Chicago: The University of Chicago Press.

Bourdieu, P. (2005). *The Social Structures of the Economy.* Cambridge: Polity Press.

Bühlmann, F., Benz, P., Mach, A., & Rossier, T. (2017). Mapping the Power of Law Professors: The Role of Scientific and Social Capital. *Minerva: A Review of Science, Learning and Policy, 55*(4), 509–531.

Bühlmann, F., David, T., & Mach, A. (2012). Political and Economic Elites in Switzerland: Personal Interchange, Interactional Relations and Structural Homology. *European Societies, 14*(5), 727–754.

Bühlmann, F., David, T., & Mach, A. (2013). Cosmopolitan Capital and the Internationalization of the Field of Business Elites: Evidence from the Swiss Case. *Cultural Sociology, 7*(2), 211–229.

Bühlmann, F., Rossier, T., & Benz, P. (2018). The Elite Placement Power of Professors of Law and Economic Sciences. In O. Korsnes, J. Hjellbrekke, M. Savage, J. Heilbron, & F. Bühlmann (Eds.), *New Directions in Elite Studies* (pp. 247–264). Oxford & New York: Routledge.

246 *Thierry Rossier and Pierre Benz*

Crane, D. (1969). Social Structure in a Group of Scientists: A Test of the "invisible college" Hypothesis. *American Sociological Review, 34*(3), 335–352.

De Nooy, W. (2003). Fields and Networks: Correspondence Analysis and Social Network Analysis in the Framework of Field Theory. *Poetics, 31*(5–6), 305–327.

Denord, F. (2016). *Le néo-libéralisme à la française. Histoire d'une idéologie politique.* Marseille: Editions Agone.

Denord, F., Hjellbrekke, J., Korsnes, O., Lebaron, F., & Le Roux, B. (2011). Social Capital in the Field of Power: The Case of Norway. *The Sociological Review, 59*(1), 86–108.

Denord, F., & Lagneau-Ymonet, P. (2016). *Le concert des puissants.* Paris: Editions Raison d'agir.

Eloire, F. (2014). Qui se ressemble s'assemble? Homophilie sociale et effet multiplicateur: les mécanismes du capital social. *Actes de la recherche en sciences sociales, 205,* 104–119.

Eloire, F. (2018). The Bourdieusian Conception of Social Capital: A Methodological Reflection and Application. *Forum for Social Economics, 47*(3–4), 322–341.

Fourcade, M. (2006). The Construction of a Global Profession: The Transnationalization of Economics. *American Journal of Sociology, 112*(1), 145–194.

Fourcade, M. (2009). *Economists and Societies: Discipline and Profession in the United States, Britain, and France, 1890s to 1990s.* Princeton: Princeton University Press.

Fourcade, M. (2018). Economics: The View from Below. *Swiss Journal of Economics and Statistics, 154*(5).

Gingras, Y. (2012). Le champ scientifique. In F. Lebaron, & G. Mauger (Eds.). *Lectures de Bourdieu* (pp. 279–294). Paris: Ellipses.

Godechot, O., & Mariot, N. (2004). Les deux formes du capital social: Structure relationnelle des jurys de thèses et recrutement en science politique. *Revue française de sociologie, 45*(2), 243–282.

Hjellbrekke, J. (2018). *Multiple Correspondence Analysis for the Social Sciences.* Oxford & New York: Routledge.

Hjellbrekke, J., & Korsnes, O. (2016). Women in the Field of Power. *Sociologica, 2,* 1–28.

Horowitz, M., & Hughes, R. (2017). Political Identity and Economists' Perceptions of Capitalist Crises. *Review of Radical Political Economics, 50*(1): 173–193.

Jost, H. U. (2016). *Von Zahlen, Politik und Macht. Geschichte der schweizerischen Statistik.* Zurich: Chronos Verlag.

Kaplan, N. (1965). The Norms of Citation Behavior: Prolegomena to the Footnote. *American Documentation, 16*(3), 179–84.

Klüger, E. (2018). Mapping the Inflections in the Policies of the Brazilian National Economic and Social Development Bank during the 1990s and 2000s within Social Spaces and Networks. *Historical Social Research, 43*(3), 274–302.

Larivière, V., Macaluso, B., Archambault, É., & Gingras, Y. (2010). Which Scientific Elites? On the Concentration of Research Funds, Publications and Citations. *Research Evaluation, 19*(1), 45–53.

Larsen, A. G., & Ellersgaard, C. H. (2018). A Scandinavian Variety of Power Elites? Key Institutional Orders in the Danish Elite Networks. In O. Korsnes, J. Hjellbrekke, M. Savage, J. Heilbron, & F. Bühlmann (Eds.), *New Directions in Elite Studies* (pp. 133–149). Oxford & New York, Routledge.

Larsen, A. G., Ellersgaard, C. H., & Andrade, S. (2016). Package 'soc.ca'. Link: https://cran.r-project.org/web/packages/soc.ca/soc.ca.pdf.

Le Roux, B., & Rouanet, H. (2010). *Multiple Correspondence Analysis.* Los Angeles: SAGE Publications Inc.

Lebaron, F. (2000). *La croyance économique. Les économistes entre science et politique.* Paris: Editions du Seuil.

Lebaron, F. (2001). Economists and the Economic Order. The Field of Economists and the Field of Power in France. *European Societies*, *3*(1), 91–110.

Lebaron, F. (2018). Economie, science et champ du pouvoir. Propos recueillis par Alizé Papp et Jules-Rémy Sarant. *Regards croisés sur l'économie*, *22*(1), 215–223.

Lenoir, R. (2015). La notion de capital social dans l'œuvre de Pierre Bourdieu. *Regards Sociologiques*, *47–48*, 109–132.

Lunding, J. A., Ellersgaard, C. H., & Larsen, A. G. (2020). The Established and the Delegated: The Division of Labour of Domination among Effective Agents on the Field of Power in Denmark. *Sociology*, online first: https://journals.sagepub.com/doi/full/10.1177/0038038520928220.

Mach, A. (2002). Economists as Policy Entrepreneurs and the Rise of Neoliberal Ideas in Switzerland during the 1990s. *Economic Sociology: European Electronic Newsletter*, *4*(1), 3–16.

Maesse, J. (2015). Economic Experts: A Discursive Political Economy of Economics. *Journal of Multicultural Discourses*, *10*(3), 279–305.

Mills, C. W. (1956). *The Power Elite*. New York: Oxford University Press.

Ötsch, W. O., Pühringer, S., & Hirte, K., 2018, *Netzwerke des Marktes: Ordoliberalismus als Politische Ökonomie*. Wiesbaden: Springer VS.

Rossier, T. (2017). *Affirmation et transformations des sciences économiques en Suisse au XXe siècle*. PhD dissertation, University of Lausanne.

Rossier, T. (2019). Prosopography, Networks, Life Course Sequences, and so on. Quantifying with or beyond Bourdieu? *Bulletin of Sociological Methodology*, *144*: 6–39.

Rossier, T., & Bühlmann, F. (2018). The Internationalisation of Economics and Business Studies: Import of Excellence, Cosmopolitan Capital or American Dominance? *Historical Social Research*, *43*(3), 189–215.

Rossier, T., Bühlmann, F., & Mach, A. (2017). The Rise of Professors of Economics and Business Studies in Switzerland: Between Scientific Reputation and Political Power. *European Journal of Sociology*, *58*(2), 295–326.

Savage, M., Warde, A., & Devine, F. (2005). Capitals, Assets, and Resources: Some Critical Issues. *British Journal of Sociology*, *56*(1), 31–47.

Schmidt-Wellenburg, C. (2018). Struggling over Crisis. Discoursive Positionings and Academic Positions in the Field of German-Speaking Economists. *Historical Social Research*, *43*(3), 147–188.

Schmidt-Wellenburg, C., & Lebaron, F. (2018). There Is No Such Thing as "the Economy". Economic Phenomena Analysed from a Field-Theoretical Perspective. *Historical Social Research*, *43*(3), 7–38.

Serino, M., D'Ambrosio, D., & Ragozini, G. (2017). Bridging Social Network Analysis and Field Theory through Multidimensional Data Analysis: The Case of the Theatrical Field. *Poetics*, *62*, 66–80.

Wagner, A.-C. (2010). Le jeu de la mobilité et de l'autochtonie au sein des classes supérieures. *Regards sociologiques*, *40*, 89–98.

14 Paths of international circulation

How do economists and economic knowledge flow?[1]

Elisa Klüger

1 Introduction

This chapter draws upon the Brazilian case and weaves a narrative about the patterns and effects of international circulation of economists, economic knowledge and expertise. The text is divided into two sections preceded by methodological considerations. The first section examines *how economists and economic ideas flow*. It shows how the structure of the Brazilian space of economists was articulated historically and highlights the establishment of connections with foreign experts and institutions. The second section focuses on the patterns of knowledge transposition in order to discuss *how dissimilar ideas spread and (re)shape a structured space of economists*. The conclusion underlines how internationalization, besides being a source of cosmopolitan capitals for peripheral elites, works as a conduit for ideas and expertise that impact their economies and societies.

Elites[2] from peripheral countries[3] have widely relied on internationalization as a strategy to accumulate cosmopolitan assets, which are highly valued in struggles to occupy the dominant positions in local fields of power (Dezalay and Garth, 2002). Cosmopolitan assets are credentials and dispositions resulting from international socialization. To become cosmopolitan, peripheral elites import goods from overseas; mimic manners and fashions; are educated according to foreign standards; and translate and incorporate specialized knowledge, ideas and ideals coming from abroad. Above all, they keep moving around the world. Besides gaining familiarization with foreign landscapes, languages, habits and ideas, international circulation fosters the creation and reinforcement of ties between economic, political and cultural elites from different countries, enlarging the surface of their influence and power (Wagner, 2007).

Contemporaneously, among the most prestigious cosmopolitan qualifications are international academic and professional experiences. The process of modernization of the bureaucracies of peripheral states was accompanied by a strong search for technical credentials, which enhanced the hunt for imported knowledge and expertise. The circulation of knowledge operated both ways: professionals from the center were sent by their governments, universities and philanthropic foundations to peripheral countries while specialists from these

DOI: 10.4324/9780367817084-18

Paths of international circulation 249

nations went abroad to receive advanced training. Economics was among the core fields of expertise which benefitted from these circulations, being strategic for those exporting as well as those importing, in a progressively intertwined world economy (Montecinos and Markoff, 2009).

Early in the 20th century, economic experts from the center traveled around, offering formulas aiming at making peripheral economies open and solvent for their creditors. From the 1940s onwards, the United States consolidated its position as the leading source of economic experts and expertise. The dissemination of economic knowledge led by the US operated differently: they provided technical and financial aid as counterparts to political and military alignments, diffusing, withal, their perspectives on the economy and society. From a peripheral perspective, these ties with foreign experts and the experiences abroad were major sources of technical legitimacy and social status (Drake, 1994; Malan et al., 1980).

General statements about the foreign influence over the constitution of the peripheral fields of economics, nonetheless, cannot account for important variations. First, the circulation through different countries fosters diverse perspectives on the economy and streams of economics. Second, each country exporting economic knowledge is permeated by internal struggles, with multiple orientations competing for prestige and international diffusion. Third, political preferences and intellectual configurations in peripheral countries influence how welcomed imported ideas will be. Fourth, the social characteristics of the agents and social networks shape how economic ideas will spread over each space of economists. Focusing on Brazil allows illustrating these variations in a context where international entanglements were decisive since the constitution of its space of economists.

2 Data and methods

This chapter is based on a historical reconstruction of the establishment of international bridges through which economists and economic knowledge circulate. These are represented in a network displaying Brazilian economists and liberal professionals who occupied prestigious functions within the public economic administration and in the academic field of economics. It depicts the connections established with foreign agents and institutions, illustrating patterns of internationalization and displaying how these ties are distributed in the Brazilian space[4] of economists.

The data used to build the network was collected in biographical dictionaries, biographies, CVs, newspapers, pre-existing interviews and interviews conducted by me, between 2012 and 2018, for two different projects: "Meritocracy of Ties: Genesis and Reconfigurations of the Space of Economists in Brazil" and "Theoretical, Political and Social Influences from Exile: The Case of Brazilian Intellectuals in Chile from 1964 to 1973". These research projects are prosopographic and aim at building a social portrait of several generations of Brazilian economists. The individuals and institutions that integrate the network were selected through a "historical" snowball sampling, that is, a qualitative and non-probabilistic technique in which agents and their connections become part of the database when mentioned in interviews, documents and narratives about the Brazilian space of economists.

This network is formed by 440 agents, including individuals, universities, governmental institutions and governments. The ties in the network are bidirectional and non-weighted and indicate connections between agents and institutions or between agents. These are of multiple natures, such as friendship, marriage, professional interactions, political affiliations and association with schools, research centers, governmental bodies or governments. The representation of a wide variety of ties and the simultaneous inclusion of every link that an agent has or had in his or her trajectory derives from the premise that every one of these bonds helps to shape their worldview, practices and position taking and, thus, the institutions they are associated with. Moreover, the number of ties and the social surface reached by an agent are indicators of its volume of social capital, an asset that enhances the ability of an agent to connect agents and groups, currently employed in struggles for influence, power and prestige.

The distances between agents and institutions in the network express the totality of their affiliations, which are the structuring forces of the space and of its polarities. Network analysis is a relational technique that allows representing geometric distances between agents and institutions resulting precisely from the outline of their connections. The network displayed in this chapter was generated using the software *Gephi* and the distribution of agents and institutions in a bi-dimensional space results from the use of the *Force Atlas 2* algorithm. The network is produced by "nodes [that] repulse each other like charged particles, while edges attract their nodes, like springs. These forces create a movement that converges to a balanced state. This final configuration is expected to help the interpretation of the data" (Jacomy et al., 2014, p. 2). This method is relational since the positions of the nodes only acquire meaning in their relation to all others, and its goal is to turn "structural proximities into visual proximities" (*idem*, p. 2).

Even if space and fields, as conceived by Pierre Bourdieu, and networks are associated with divergent theoretical traditions (Bourdieu, 2000; Becker and Pessin, 2006), current research combines these two frameworks following their common goal of producing spatial representations in which the distances between the unities are relationally defined (Nooy, 2003; Denord, 2003; Serino et al., 2017; Klüger, 2017b). I argue here that the distances in networks – as well as distances in fields – allow representing polarized structures in which the relative position of agents depends on how they are situated vis-à-vis each other in what Bourdieu defines as struggles for determining the dominant principles of domination. Here, however, structural proximity and polarizations are not a direct expression of similarity of habitus and capital composition[5] of agents that do not necessarily meet – as in a Bourdieusian social space – but are altered repeatedly by their interactions. Therefore, the network has the advantage of displaying concrete ties that can be mobilized at the daily operation of the

Paths of international circulation 251

space, "unraveling the processes in which a field is being restructured and symbolic values are (re)produced" (Nooy, 2003, p. 325).

3 How do economists and economic ideas flow? Learning from the Brazilian case

The Brazilian space of economists relied on international cooperation since its establishment in the 1940s. The patterns of collaboration with foreign experts and institutions varied according to geopolitical interests and engagement of agents and universities in foreign exchanges. This section illustrates how internationalization influenced the constitution of a Brazilian space of economists and its transformations over time.

3.1 International cooperation at the genesis of the space of economists – 1940s and 1950s

The first Brazilians who acquired specialized credentials in economics were, in general, diplomats who studied abroad and public administrators trained in Europe and the United States. By the 1940s, the Brazilian state started to deem economic skills as essential for modernizing and rationalizing economic management. Soon the first departments of economics – which were created by lawyers and engineers – began to recruit foreign professors and establish agreements with universities abroad in order to transfer specialized knowledge on the subject (Loureiro, 1997).

Eugênio Gudin, an engineer with an elite background and vast cosmopolitan capitals, was the main person responsible for the creation, in 1946, of the two major schools of economics in Rio de Janeiro: the National Faculty of Economics (FNCE[6] later renamed Federal University of Rio de Janeiro, UFRJ – E2[7]) and the Getúlio Vargas Foundation (FGV – B2). After taking part at the Bretton Woods conference, in 1944, Gudin visited Harvard accompanied by Octavio de Bulhões, a lawyer with a specialization in economics and also a member of the elites. Subsequently, they wrote a report to the Minister of Education stating that the teaching of economics in Brazil should follow Harvard's model – which separated economics from administration and accounting – and recommending hiring North American professors (Gudin, 1979; Silveira 2009).

Gudin managed to recruit some foreign specialists who fled Europe during the World Wars, such as the Czech Alexandre Kafka, the Polish Richard Lewinson and some temporary French, South African, Belgian, Dutch and German professors, causing the FGV to look like a "tower of Babel". Gudin also fostered international connections by inviting foreign professors to give short courses and lectures on contemporary topics and techniques. Among them were the well-known economists Lionel Robbins, from the London School of Economics, Gottfried Haberler, from Harvard, Ragnar Nurkse, from Columbia/Princeton, and Jacob Viner, from Chicago (D'Araújo, 1999).

252   Elisa Klüger

Simultaneously, North American specialists were sent to Brazil as part of governmental agreements for economic cooperation. The tonality of the Brazil-US economic diplomacy changed several times during the second half of the 20th century, influencing the rhythm and intensity of the establishment of these connections. Closer interactions and cooperation increased every time that proximity with Latin America became politically strategic, either following the need for supplies and military support during wars or as a strategy for combating the spread of communist ideas within the subcontinent (Malan et al., 1980).

In the 1950s, the outbreak of the Korean War was followed by the promulgation of the Act of International Development, which voiced the intention of making available scientific innovations and technical-industrial progress to the Third World. Based on this act, the Mixed Commission Brazil-US was created (CMBEU – **B1**). This mission engaged Brazilian and American specialists in preparing projects of infrastructure – mostly energy and transportation – to be financed jointly. The Commission also gave birth to the National Bank of Economic Development (BNDE, later National Bank of Economic and Social Development BNDES – **E2**), which would be responsible for managing the funding. They recruited qualified personnel and incorporated the knowledge and techniques bequeathed by the CMBEU, becoming the epicenter of development planning in Brazil (Campos, 1994; Sola, 1998).

The CMBEU agreement was terminated in 1953, and a period of diplomatic negligence followed. As the US withdrew from its position of knowledge provider, Brazil went looking for different sources of expertise and sought help from the United Nations' Economic Commission for Latin America (CEPAL – **F3**). Following up on the great repercussion of Raul Prebisch's manifesto, *El desarrollo económico de América Latina y sus principales problemas* (1949), CEPAL and its thesis about the necessity of planning and governmental guided industrialization were put on the spot (Garcia, 2005). The BNDE, willing to engage in broader economic planning, convenes with CEPAL to receive a team led by the Sorbonne (**F2**) trained economist Celso Furtado, the only Brazilian at the Commission. Furtado worked at the BNDE, from 1953 to 1955, to prepare a diagnostic of the productive sector in Brazil for subsidizing an integrated planning of the economy. Furtado's analysis was an important source for Juscelino Kubitschek's Plano de Metas, Brazil's largest experience of state-led economic planning, which focused on the energy, transportation and transformation industry sectors (Furtado, 2014).

This first cooperation led to a follow-up agreement, for the import of CEPAL's "Intensive Training in Problems of Economic Development". The first edition of this course happened in Rio de Janeiro, in 1956, and was inaugurated by President Kubitscheck himself. This course offered a specialization in planning, aiming to prepare bureaucrats and intellectuals for understanding economic activity within a geographical and historical frame and to intervene accordingly to local specificities. The course had 21 editions, in 12 different cities, and lasted until 1967, spreading economic knowledge to regional

Paths of international circulation 253

bureaucracies and universities all over the country. In 1960, CEPAL inaugurated an office in Rio de Janeiro, in cooperation with the BNDE, assuming the direction of the courses and centralizing research on Brazil's economy. The CEPAL-BNDE office incorporated young Brazilian economists, notably Maria da Conceição Tavares, Carlos Lessa and Antonio Barros de Castro and influenced a generation of specialists in economics (Klüger et al., 2019, *under review*).

3.2 The export of US's economic expertise during the Cold War – 1960s and 1970s

While the CEPAL became a leading influence in the formation of public administrators, North American-based mainstream economic knowledge reached the universities. At the beginning of the 1960s, troubled by an increasing anti-Americanism in the region and the proximity between Cubans and Soviets, Kennedy's administration reclaimed a cooperative attitude towards the subcontinent. The rationality subjacent to his "Alliance for Progress" was that the best way to avoid the spread of communism would be to enhance social and economic development, ameliorating well-being. The Alliance promised to foster direct economic investments, transfer modern industrial techniques and agricultural equipment, as well as send experts to areas with a scarcity of qualified professionals to participate in the development of local scientific communities. The United States Agency for International Development, which coordinated these investments, and some non-governmental foundations, such as the Ford Foundation and the Rockefeller Foundation, engaged especially in strengthening scientific fields seen as strategic, including economics (Ribeiro, 2006; Miceli, 1993).

The scientific cooperation comprised investments in university infrastructures, funding of visiting professors and invitations to train local academics, as well as the granting of scholarships to Brazilians who would study economics in the US. These initiatives organized and intensified an international flow of scientists that until this point was unsystematic. Aiming to facilitate these circulations, the Brazilian schools of economics established partnerships and started to prepare the students to apply for positions abroad.

In the 1950s, the School of Administration of the Getúlio Vargas Foundation (EAESP – **E5**), located in São Paulo, established an exchange program with the Michigan State University (**D5**) to qualify recently hired professors, like Luiz Carlos Bresser Pereira, who would lead the creation of a school of economics in close connection with studies of public administration (D'Araújo, 1999). In 1960, the FGV-RJ created a Center for Advancement of Economists, which offered supplementary training in mathematics and macro- and microeconomics, as well as three weekly hours of English lessons, preparing their students to pursue graduate courses in the US. They managed to send 16 students overseas until 1964, mostly funded by Rockefeller Foundation scholarships, with their main destinations being Yale **(B4)**, Vanderbilt **(B4)**, and Berkeley **(C3)** (D'Araújo, 1999; Simonsen, 1966).

254   *Elisa Klüger*

In the mid-1960s, Vanderbilt and Yale established direct agreements with the largest Brazilian schools of economics: FGV and the Faculty of Economics and Administration of the University of São Paulo (FEA-USP – **D4**). These were intermediated by Alexandre Kafka, who worked at FGV before moving to the International Monetary Fund, and by Werner Baer, a specialist in Latin American Development who had taught at Yale and Vanderbilt and worked as a visiting professor at FGV and USP (Baer, 1998; Kafka, 1998). At that time, Yale's Economic Growth Center master's and Ph.D. programs had a quota for international students. Simultaneously, the USAID financed a cooperation between the FGV and the USP with Vanderbilt's graduate program in economic development, encompassing circulations in both directions. Vanderbilt sent teachers to coach the local professors and offered scholarships for newly graduated Brazilians to pursue their masters and Ph.Ds. in Nashville. Besides, the Ford Foundation provided additional funding for both FGV and USP, fostering a quick professionalization of the graduate training in economics in Brazil (Rocca et al., 1984).

The University of California at Berkeley, in its turn, took part in a different sort of agreement. In 1965, the USAID sent to Rio de Janeiro a technical mission integrated by Berkeley professors and young doctors in economics. Their goal was to help establish the Office for Applied Economic Research (EPEA, later IPEA – **C3**), a state institution created a year before and directed by João Paulo dos Reis Velloso – who studied at the CAE and was returning from his master's at Yale. Coordinated initially by Howard Ellis and later by Albert Fishlow, the California Mission carried studies of the Brazilian economy and conceived a decennial plan for Brazil's industry, agriculture, infrastructure, as well as education and health. Fishlow simultaneously taught an economic development course at the FGV, sewing ties with the academy. The mission was terminated in 1968 because of political disagreements with the Brazilian government, motivated by the promulgation of the dictatorship's Institutional Act 5 (AI-5), which suspended human rights and deepened censorship and political repression. Fishlow argued that UC Berkeley's progressive political orientation was incompatible with state violence and the suspensions of civil rights, ending the agreement. Nevertheless, the links between Brazil and Berkeley persisted since he took in several Brazilian students, starting with his former assistants at IPEA: Pedro Malan and Regis Bonelli (D'Araújo et al., 2005).

3.3 *The circulations of exiled economic experts – 1960s and 1970s*

The AI-5 also increased the volume of forced international circulation of leftist economists, which were happening since the military takeover of 1964. The exile differed from other circulations of intellectuals given that the accumulation of cosmopolitan dispositions, international credentials and foreign knowledge was an unintended consequence. After the coup, some economists managed to get scholarships in North American universities willing to shelter those facing dangerous situations in Brazil, for instance, Cornell (**E5**). In

Europe, the heart of the exile of intellectuals was France, but there were far more social scientists than economists, with very weak links to the Sorbonne (**F2**) and Nanterre (**F3**). Some other economists, among which was Celso Furtado, ended up in England, working in Cambridge (**F3**) and/or Oxford (**D3**) (Klüger, 2017a).

However, until the mid-1970s, the main destination of the exiled economists was neither Europe nor the US, but Latin America, which led to the establishment of a path for intra-periphery circulations. A large group of intellectuals went to Uruguay right after the military coup, others to Mexico. The epicenter of this reallocation was, nonetheless, Chile. There were political affinities between segments of the exiled community and the Chilean Cristian Democrat administration of Eduardo Frei Montalva and/or the Socialist government of Salvador Allende. These affinities led to the incorporation of Brazilians in both administrations, where they took part in the elaboration of plans for land reform, alphabetization, and economic planning. Finally, Santiago was populated by a dense network of international organizations (including the CEPAL as well as UN's Food and Agriculture Organization and the International Labor Organization) and quartered graduate programs oriented towards the study of Latin American economy and society (Klüger, 2017c).

CEPAL incorporated many of the exiled economists, not only those previously working in its Brazilian office, but also a large share of employees of the Superintendence for the Development of the Northeast (SUDENE – **F2**), an organization created and coordinated by Celso Furtado, which was under severe surveillance by the military (Furtado, 2014). The graduate programs of the Latin American School of Social Sciences (FLACSO) and of the Latin American School of Economics (ESCOLATINA – **G3**) received dozens of Brazilian students. ESCOLATINA, during those years, was fairly aligned with CEPAL's economic perspective, as many of the Commission's researchers taught at the school. Both graduate programs were built with North American funds, recruited foreign professors at the beginning and prioritized the building of quantitative analysis skills until the end of the 60s. Following the political radicalization and polarization during Salvador Allende's government, the programs moved towards qualitative frameworks of analysis and became highly politicized. The school of economics advocated for a modern political economy,[8] with its professors and students engaging in struggles for economic transformations leading to more inclusive and egalitarian societies (Beigel, 2009, Montecinos and Markoff, 2009; Valdés, 1995).

ESCOLATINA, FLACSO and CEPAL were highly affected by the military coup that took place in Chile in 1973. Many among their researchers and professors were dismissed and the critical perspectives that prevailed in the 1960s and early 1970s replaced by highly quantitative models of economics and social sciences that claimed to be universal and politically neutral. The dominant force at the Chilean space of economists were, henceforth, the so-called Chicago Boys, who implemented policies deeply inspired by Milton Friedman's neoliberal ideas. In the following years, Chicago's school of economics' (**A3**) influence spread all over the subcontinent. Even if Brazil had no direct cooperation with Chicago (as was the case for Chile, Argentina and Colombia), professors from Chicago visited Brazil, and students, such as Carlos Geraldo Langoni, were sent to Illinois for their PhDs. They obtained Ford Foundation or USAID scholarships, after attending, at the end of the 1960s, courses offered by IPEA's Center of Training in Economic and Social Development (CENDEC). Headed by an economist with a master's diploma from Chicago, Og Francisco Leme, CEDEC sent students to several universities abroad, notably Chicago, John Hopkins (**B3**) and Stanford (**B5**) (Valdés, 1995; Biglaiser, 2002; D'Araújo et al., 2005; Friedman, 2012).

By the end of the 1960s, the exclusive agreements with Vanderbilt, Yale and Berkeley gave place to diversified circulations, with students pursuing their international paths individually. Besides the already mentioned universities of Cornell, Chicago, John Hopkins and Stanford, young Brazilian economists were to be found at the Massachusetts Institute of Technology (**C2**), Harvard (**B2**), Princeton (**C2**) and New York University (**D1**), among other US universities. The frequency of exchanges with British institutions also rose, including connections with the University of London (**C3**) and Sussex (**G2**).

According to Maria Rita Loureiro and Gilberto Tadeu Lima (1994), in 1991, 60% of the Brazilian professors in economics obtained a PhD abroad, 46% in North American universities, 7.5% in France and 5.5% in England. The universities with a larger number of graduates were, in order, Vanderbilt, Chicago, Berkeley, Harvard, Michigan and Illinois (Loureiro and Lima, 1994, p. 38). These numbers are a partial expression of the patterns of international circulation, including only those who stayed at the universities and not those who worked in the government and private sector. Regarding the strong connection with Chile, absent of the data, it should be indicated that those who attended ESCOLATINA obtained only their master's degrees in Chile. Besides, many abandoned the program after the rise of Pinochet's dictatorship. Finally, CEPAL's influence has no expression in PhD diplomas, with stronger effects on the public administration, given that state bureaucrats were the largest group among those attending the Commission's training program and the exiled working at CEPAL.

4 How do dissimilar ideas spread and (re)shape a structured space of economists?

The first step in discussing how international circulation impacted the constitution of the Brazilian space of economists is to map the space and represent the connections between Brazilian and foreign agents and institutions. To do so, I built a synthetic network based on a historical reconstruction of the space of economists in Brazil from the 1940s to the first decade of the 2000s (Klüger, 2017a). The network is inserted into a grid that allows locating and comparing agents' and institutions' positions, and the size of the nodes increases with the number of connections shared by an agent.

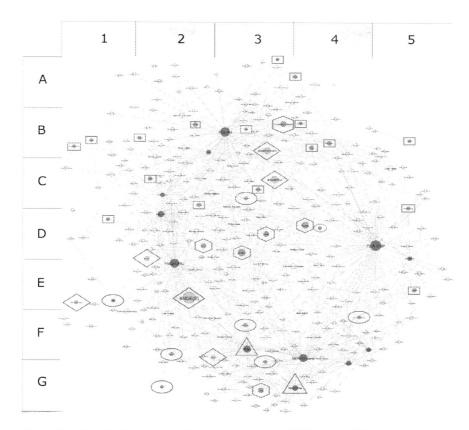

Figure 14.1 The Brazilian space of economists from the 1940s to the 2000s

Triangle: Latin American connections. Circle: European connections. Square: North-American connections. Diamond: governmental economic institutions. Hexagon: presidential administrations from 1964 to 2010. Grey color and no frame: Brazilian schools of economics.

In the network, the horizontal division mirrors regional partitions. Zones **1** and **2** include mostly economists from Rio de Janeiro and institutions located in Rio, as well as several specialists from the northeast of the country and Minas-Gerais. Zones **4** and **5** are mainly populated by economists from the state of São Paulo and institutions located in São Paulo, while the central zone **3** has a more balanced regional composition. The distribution also expresses age divisions, with the elderly usually located at the margins of the network, that is zones **1** and **5**, and connected with peers from the same regions.

Along the vertical axis are displayed the patterns of international circulation of economists and economic knowledge. Sectors **A**, **B** and **C** form the zone of North American influence. The European connections spread from **C** to **G**, but are concentrated in area **F**. Latin American affiliations figure at the sectors

258 *Elisa Klüger*

F and **G**. The center of the network is mostly restricted to national connections. To understand the impact of different circulations on the configuration of space, it is important to look at the degree of connectivity, represented by the size of the nodes. The average number of connections of a node in the network is 8.26. There are 17 US institutions represented, averaging 8,235 connections (140 total). Among these, Harvard and Yale have almost twice the average of connections. The European institutions are less amalgamated, with eight institutions averaging 5,875 in degree (47 total). Latin America has only two institutions present in the network, but their connectivity is rather strong, averaging 34 in degree (68 total). Even if Latin American links have an average impact of four times the mean weight of US institutions, the sum of the ties with the US is twice the amount of bonds with other Latin American countries. Furthermore, US institutions are more spread over the network, reaching from sectors **A** to **E**, while Latin Americans are limited to sectors **F** and **G**.

The path that goes from **A** to **G** can be read as a gradient that starts with the most orthodox versions of economics and goes up to the most heterodox ones. Orthodox or monetarist versions of economics can be characterized by their opposition to state interventionism, assuming that the free market would necessarily lead to growth and an optimal distribution of resources. In this view, fiscal austerity, economic stability, openness to foreign trade and no external control were conditions for respecting the market and letting it work at its best (Campos, 1996). This approach usually relies on formalized economic models that taint, with attempts of scientific objectivity and neutrality, the behavioral and ideological fundaments of its analysis (Lebaron, 2000).

Latin American heterodoxy, at the other end of the network **F** and **G**, combines several streams of the modern political economy, including Karl Marx, John M. Keynes, Michal Kalecki, CEPAL's ideas and dependency theory. Against the highly mathematized models of the orthodoxy, they mix economics with historical and sociological analysis, arguing that the historical inequalities that shaped the international division of labor block the economic development of peripheral areas. Therefore, they recommended active economic planning and state-guided industrialization to ensure coordinated efforts of development and reduction of international disparities.

There is a large spectrum of positions between these two extremes. Sectors **B** and **C** are under the influence of North American mathematized and pro-market economics. The schools represented at these sectors incorporate, nevertheless, critiques of the natural aptitude of the markets, trying to seize its imperfections (as the limited distribution of information, shared externalities, free-riding). Contrary to orthodoxy, they sustain the importance of government intervention to correct some biases, to administrate the offer of public goods and even to invest in strategic sectors that are unattractive to the private market, such as infrastructure and scientific/technologic development.[9]

Sectors **D** and **E** are predominantly national, and sectors **E** and **F** are under some European influence, including institutionalist versions of economics, Keynesian economics, studies of industrial organization and of innovation and technologic policies. The Brazilian economists studying in Europe between the 1960s and the 1980s were mostly engaged in economic history, history of economic thought or economic and technological development, and many of them were also exiled intellectuals.

Once the gradient of positions is described, the next step is to look at the international connections prevailing in each sector of the Brazilian space of economists.

4.1 The north of the network – Sectors A and B

The University of Chicago is represented at the peak of sector **A**, alongside Virginia and John Hopkins. The Brazilian economists trained in Chicago worked mainly at the FGV and Brazil's Central Bank (SUMOC, later BACEN – **B3**), both located in **B** sector. FGV was slightly pluralist at the beginning, including some professors with nationalist and heterodox perspectives, even though led by liberals like Gudin and Bulhões. After the constitution of its graduate school, the mainstream and mathematized perspectives prevailed and were radicalized when its director, Mario Henrique Simonsen, joined the military administration in the 1970s, being replaced by the Chicago PhD Carlos Langoni. He invited several monetarists, such as Edy Kogut, José Luiz Carvalho, Antonio Lemgruber and José J. Senna, to join him at FGV, and they also attained leadership positions at the Central Bank in the early 1980s (D'Araújo, 1999).

The BACEN is located in the middle of sector **B**, recruiting directors from all regions of the country. Regarding the Central Banker's highest diploma, only eight of 34 specialists got their diploma in Brazil, three of them at the FGV. Among the others, there are two from British and 24 from North American universities, including four from Harvard, three from MIT, three from Chicago, three from Berkeley, and three from Princeton. The BACEN oscillates, thus, between orthodoxy and some softer versions of mainstream economics.

The National University of Brasília (UNB – **B2**) is also at sector **B**, between the FGV and the Faculty of Economic Sciences of the Federal University of Minas Gerais (FACE-UFMG – **C2**). A recurrent educational trajectory was to be an undergraduate at FACE and a master's student at FGV, and then to pursue a PhD abroad before teaching at the UNB. The UNB recruited most of its economists when they were returning from PhD programs at Berkeley, Vanderbilt, Yale, MIT and Harvard, universities which are located near the network. Their goal was to establish a mainstream economics department, regarding theory and methods, while being politically critical towards the military and FGVs monetarism (Cunha et al., 2014).

4.2 The center of the network – Sectors C, D and E

Sector **C** is also under the influence of North American mainstream economics. The IPEA is next to Berkeley, as a result of the circulation promoted by the

260 *Elisa Klüger*

California Mission. The IPEA recruited specialists from diverse backgrounds and different regions of Brazil, spreading its influence widely. Regarding its international connections, the PUC-RJ (**D2**) is quite similar to the UNB, since many of its professors – Pedro Malan, Chico Lopes, Edmar Bacha – previously taught in Brasília. The PUC-RJ hired doctors trained in the US and eventually in Europe. At this school predominated a market-oriented perspective, however critical of the notion of a self-regulating market. For instance, concerning inflation, even if they agreed that fiscal control was important to reach a monetary equilibrium, they perceived behavioral trends that pushed people to inflate prices while assuming that everyone else would do the same. In this case, no monetarist solution could coordinate expectations and settle prices (Bacha, 2012).

The agency for Funding of Studies and Projects (FINEP – **D2**), located in Rio, designs policies for science/technology and innovation and welcomed several specialists returning from England with expertise on the economic effects of science, technology, and innovation. The University of São Paulo (**D4**) is situated on the São Paulo side of sector **D**, at the middle point of the gradient since embracing professors with diversified views of economics. Alongside Delfim Netto and his Delfim Boys, who led the economic administration during the dictatorship, there were younger economists trained in moderate mainstream schools – notably Vanderbilt, Yale and Cornell – and some graduates who identified with Keynesian and/or Marxist ideas.

The EAESP appears close to USP in zone **5**, both recruiting most of its professors in the state of São Paulo. As its location on sector **E** reveals, EAESP economics differed from that of its Rio *alma mater*, drawing inspiration from Keynesian and developmentalist ideas. The main international connections of the EAESP are with Michigan and Cornell, located in sector **D** and **E** respectively. On the Rio de Janeiro side of sector **E**, there are two large institutions, the FNCE-UFRJ and the BNDES, both inspired by developmentalist perspectives. Many of the Bank cadres and directors have connections with UFRJ, enhancing their proximity in the network. UFRJ has also several ties with institutions located at the south of the network, exchanging several professors with the University of Campinas (UNICAMP).

4.3 *The south of the network – Sectors F and G*

The CEPAL (**F3**) is a major influence for UFRJ, BNDES and UNICAMP. The BNDE and the CEPAL had a joint office for several years, many of the Banks' bureaucrats attended CEPAL's courses and CEPAL's economists such as Castro, Lessa, and Conceição worked at the Bank. These three senior economists and other experts trained by CEPAL participated in the creation of UNICAMP's economics department, alongside with graduates from the ESCOLATINA who moved to the Campinas after Chile's 1973 military coup (Klüger, 2017c). UNICAMP became the anti-mainstream school of the Brazilian space of economists, combining Marxism, Keynesianism, CEPAL's ideas

Paths of international circulation 261

and some conceptions derived from Soviet planning. When UNICAMP's professors pleaded to join the Economics Graduate Association, FGV denied them access, saying that their approach to economics was not "scientific". This battle ended with the FGV leaving the Association, in 1974, because all others backed the UNICAMP's admission (Haddad, 1997).

The UNICAMP was one of the main sources of professors for the Catholic University of São Paulo (PUC-SP – **G4**) and shared researchers with the Brazilian Center for Analysis and Planning (CEBRAP – **G4**). The CEBRAP also welcomed researchers returning from exile, some who had worked at the CEPAL or studied at the ESCOLATINA. Professors from Campinas often published in CEBRAP's journal and attended conferences and debates at the Research Center (Belluzzo, 2011). The proximity between CEBRAP, UNICAMP and PUC-SP is based not only on shared personnel but also on compatible ideas. Their economics is open to interdisciplinarity, considering historical, social and geopolitical specificities (Borges et al., 1998).

4.4 *The governments and their economists*

The gradient of positions in the network expresses, thus, the main opposition within the Brazilian space of economists and allows one to observe how diverse sources of foreign economic knowledge spread over the space. Correlations between positions in the space and political position taking, in its turn, can be spotted through the locations of the dots representing the governments from 1964 to 2010. The distances between these reveal how divergent political orientations led to the recruitment of economists with different perspectives.

The military governments appear at the north of the network (**B3**), recruiting from the conservative segments of USP, represented by the Delfim Netto and his students, and from FGV, including several of the Chicago-trained economists. All the democratic governments from 1985 until 2002 are located in the center of the network. José Sarney's government (**D4**) shifted its economic orientation several times. In the beginning, it counted mostly on economists from the FGV, but unsatisfied with their results, recruited an economic team encompassing economists from UNICAMP, USP and PUC-RJ. Fernando Collor de Mello's administration (**D3**) relied mostly on economists from USP, combined with some professionals from the PUC-RJ, PUC-SP and UFRJ. If Sarney's and Collor's administrations leaned towards São Paulo, their successor, Itamar Franco, was slightly closer to Rio de Janeiro and Minas Gerais (**D2**). Fernando Henrique Cardoso was Itamar's Minister of Finance, and the anti-inflationary plan he launched was key for his victory at the following presidential elections. Once elected (**D3**), Cardoso kept most of his former economic team, integrated by economists from the PUC-RJ and the USP. Finally, Lula's administration (**G3**) opposed the military governments diametrically, having assembled heterodox economists from UNICAMP and neighboring schools with strong Latin American connections.

262 *Elisa Klüger*

5 Conclusion

This chapter focused on the Brazilian case in order to analyze the international flow of economists and economic ideas, and how they (re)shape a structured space of economists. The historical reconstruction of its international connections cast light on strategies of technical legitimation of local elites and the effects of their international engagements over the national struggles for prestige and political/administrative power. From the discussion, it is possible to say that there are correspondences between the structure of polarities observed at the national and international levels. As Dezalay and Garth (2002) indicate, these affinities result from a double movement: on the one side, the local elite looks abroad for legitimated sources of knowledge, cosmopolitan capitals and strategic connections; on the other side, internationally dominant forces reinforce their positions geopolitically when sending their experts abroad, exporting ideas and setting a favorable economic agenda worldwide.

The structure of the space expresses an opposition between dominant North American schools of economics and a strong Latin American influence at a scattered heterodox position. The degrees of connections indicate that even if the US has the most extensive influence over the Brazilian space of economists, the connections with CEPAL and ESCOLATINA are the single largest sources of economic knowledge. Between these extremities, there is a myriad of intermediate positions in which mainstream ideas and oppositions to it coexist and recombine. Most of the governments also appear in the center of the network, mixing expertise from several schools.

Further investigation could address the spillover effect of the internationalization of Brazilian economists on the regions where they circulate, inquiring if the ideas emanating from peripheral areas also impact the center. Supplementary research should be conducted to evaluate if those who circulate between the center and the periphery; those who circulate between peripheries and those who do not circulate have different social profiles and compositions of economic, cultural and cosmopolitan capitals. Thus, it will become possible to observe if international circulation led to changes in the social profiles of the elites or if it reinforces inequalities, offering additional cultural, social and symbolic resources to those already affluent.

Notes

1 This chapter combines results from two research projects: a Ph.D. thesis, funded by CNPQ and CAPES-PSDE grants, conducted at the Department of Sociology of the University of São Paulo, and as visiting researcher at the Université de Picardie Jules Verne and University of California – Berkeley and a postdoc at the Brazilian Center for Analysis and Planning and Princeton University, supported by São Paulo Research Foundation (FAPESP) grants: 2017/13937–1 e 2018/09487–7. I wish to thank the editors for all the helpful remarks and Johanna Gautier, Pierre Benz and Thierry Rossier for their detailed comments and recommendations.

2 Economists were able to make of their expertise a source of prestige that surpassed the academic field, becoming a key to access positions of decision and influence at the state and private sector.

Paths of international circulation 263

3 In this chapter, the division between center and periphery is not restricted to the economic aspects that distinguish industrialized countries and those relying on the export of primary goods (Prebisch, 1949). Economic domination is frequently combined with broader cultural dependency, including reliance on foreign technology, knowledge and expertise. Therefore, in this chapter the term periphery indicates dependency on both material and immaterial resources.

4 The use of Bourdieu's amplified notion of space, instead of his concept of field, allows comprising not only the relatively autonomous field of economics but also the governmental institutions responsible for the economic administration and agents that circulate between the academic, public and private sectors.

5 Even though Bourdieu didn't operationalize the links between social affinity and social connections, he and Monique Saint-Martin make clear that the orchestration of habitus and similarity of lifestyles are at the base of the establishment of all kinds of ties, and all achievements in a field that depend on the existence of personal relations (1978, p. 37). Thus, it can be inferred that according to this logic the ties at a network express social similarities/differences.

6 For all institutions, the name has been translated but the acronym will be kept in Portuguese.

7 When a new institution is mentioned, a code indicating its position at the network is added.

8 Modern political economy can be differentiated from mainstream economics based on its interdisciplinary attitude; its critics "against the extensive use of methodological individualism, of equilibrium and harmony concepts, of marginalism, against the exogenous and static character of psychological and sociological assumptions, and against the neglect of historical and dynamic factors"; and its focus on the historical and geographically specific aspects of the economies. It considers that economic outcomes vary accordingly to different cultures and political priorities, which requires studies to be localized and empirical, instead of general models based on predetermined assumptions about the human behavior (Rotschield, 1989, p. 4).

9 David Colander and Arjo Klamer conducted a survey at the graduate schools in economics at the beginning of the 1980s, which helps to differentiate the schools located at points **A** and **B**. The results show that MIT and Harvard students are usually in strict opposition to Chicago. Yale appears in the middle, usually closer to MIT/Harvard. For instance, 70% of Chicago graduates believed that minimum wage increased unemployment of young and unqualified workers, while only 24% of the MIT students and 15% of Harvard graduates agreed. No one from Chicago disagreed with the idea that inflation was purely a monetary phenomenon, 84% of them agreeing strongly. On the other hand, only 7% of MIT students and 15% of Harvard's agreed strongly with that. Finally, only 6% of Chicago's graduates agreed strongly that "The distribution of income in developed nations should be more equal", against more than 50% of MIT, Harvard and Yale students (Colander and Klamer, 1987, pp. 103–104).

References

Bacha, E. (2012). *Belíndia 2.0: fábulas e ensaios sobre o país dos contrastes*. Rio de Janeiro: Editora Civilização Brasileira.

Baer, W. (1998). Explorando o mundo real. *Economia Aplicada*, 2(4), 767–770.

Becker, H., & Pessin, A. (2006). A Dialogue on the Ideas of 'World' and 'Field'. *Sociological Forum*, 21(2), 275–86.

Beigel, F. (2009). La FLACSO chilena y la regionalización de las ciencias sociales en América Latina (1957–1973). *Revista Mexicana de Sociología*, 71(2), 319–349.

Belluzzo, L. G. (2011). Luiz Gonzaga Belluzzo por Ricardo Ismael, Rosa Freire D'Aguiar, Alexandre de Freitas Barbosa e Bernardo Ricupero. *Cadernos do Desenvolvimento*, 6(9), 420–441.

264 *Elisa Klüger*

Biglaiser, G. (2002). The Internationalization of Chicago's Economics in Latin America. *Economic Development and Cultural Change*, 50(2), 269–286.

Borges, M. A., Mello, C. H. P., Galvani, C., & Gomes, W. P. (1998). *Memória do Departamento de Economia: a fala de alguns de seus chefes*. São Paulo: EDUC.

Bourdieu, P. (2000). *Les Structures Sociales de l'économie*. Paris: Éditions du Seuil.

Bourdieu, P., & Saint-Martin, M. (1978). Le patronat. *Actes de la Recherche en Sciences Sociales*, 20–21, 3–82.

Campos, R. O. (1994). *A Lanterna na Popa*. Rio de Janeiro: Topbooks.

Campos, R. O. (1996). Entrevista com Roberto Oliveira Campos. In C. Biderman, L. F. Cozac, & J. M. Rego (Eds.). *Conversas com Economistas Brasileiros*. São Paulo: Editora 34.

Colander, D., & Klamer, A. (1987). The Making of an Economist. *Journal of Economic Perspectives*, 1(2), 95–111.

Cunha, L. R., Leopoldi, M. A., & Raposo, E. (2014). *Dionísio Dias Carneiro, um humanista cético: uma história da formação de jovens economistas*. Rio de Janeiro: Editora PUC-Rio/LTC.

D'Araújo, M. C. (1999). Fundação Getúlio Vargas: concretização de um ideal. Rio de Janeiro: Editora FGV.

D'Araújo, M. C., Farias, I. C., & Hippolito, L. (2005). *IPEA 40 anos apontando caminhos: depoimentos ao CPDOC*. Brasília: IPEA.

Denord, F. (2003). Genèse et institutionnalisation du néo-libéralisme en France (années 1930 – années 1950) Ph.D. diss. Paris: EHESS.

Dezalay, Y., & Garth, B. (2002). *La Mondialisation des Guerres de Palais: la restructuration du pouvoir d'État en Amérique Latine, entre notables du droit et "Chicago boys"*. Paris: Éditions du Seuil.

Drake, P. W. (1994). *Money Doctors, Foreign Debts, and Economic Reforms in Latin America from the 1890s to the present*. Wilmington: Jaguar Books on Latin America.

Friedman, M. (2012). Bases para un desarrollo económico, conferencia en el Edificio Diego Portales de Santiago, el 26 de marzo de 1975. In A. Soto. (Ed.). *Un Legado de Libertad: Milton Friedman en Chile* [Kindle]. Instituto Democracia y Mercado/Atlas Economic Research Foundation/Fundación para el Progreso.

Furtado, C. (2014). *Obra autobiográfica: A Fantasia Organizada, A Fantasia Desfeita, Os Ares do Mundo*. São Paulo: Companhia das Letras.

Garcia, A. (2005). Circulation internationale et formation d'une "école de pensée" latino-americaine (1945–2000). *Information sur les sciences sociales*, 44 (2/3), 521–555.

Gudin, E. (1979). Carta ao Ministro Gustavo Capanema, 21 de agosto de 1944. In P. E. B. Carneiro (Ed.). *Eugênio Gudin visto por seus contemporâneos*. Rio de Janeiro: Editora da Fundação Getúlio Vargas.

Haddad, P. R. (1997). Itaipava 30 anos depois: Seminário da USP – Cinquenta Anos de Ciência Econômica no Brasil. FEA-USP, agosto de 1996. In M. R. Loureiro (Ed.). *50 Anos de Ciência Econômica no Brasil: pensamento, instituições e depoimentos*. Petrópolis: Editora Vozes.

Jacomy, M., Venturini, T., Heymann, S., & Bastian, M. (2014). ForceAtlas2, a Continuous Graph Layout Algorithm for Handy Network Visualization Designed for the Gephi Software. *PLOS ONE*, 9(6).

Kafka, A. (1998). *Depoimento Alexandre Kafka*. Brasília: Secretaria de Relações Institucionais do Banco Central do Brasil.

Klüger, E. (2017a) *Meritocracia de laços: gênese e reconfigurações do espaço dos economistas no Brasil*. Ph.D. diss. São Paulo: Universidade de São Paulo.

Klüger, E. (2017b). Espaço social e redes: contribuições metodológicas à sociologia das elites. *Tempo social – Revista de sociologia da USP*, 29(3), 83–110.

Paths of international circulation 265

Klüger, E. (2017c). Circulations périphériques: les effets sur l'espace politique brésilien de l'exil des intellectuels de gauche au Chili entre 1964 et 1973. *Revue internationale des études du développement*, 230(2), 29–56.

Klüger, E., Wanderley, S., & Barbosa, A. F. (2019). The CEPAL-BNDE Center and the Building of a Generation of Intellectuals Engaged in Planning the Brazilian Development. *Under review*.

Lebaron, F. (2000). *La Croyance Économique: les économistes entre science et politique*. Paris: Éditions du Seuil.

Loureiro, M. R. (1997). *Os Economistas no Governo: gestão econômica e democracia*. Rio de Janeiro: Editora Fundação Getúlio Vargas.

Loureiro, M. R., & Lima, G. T. (1994). A internacionalização da ciência econômica no Brasil. *Revista de economia política*, 14(3), 31–51.

Malan, P., Abreu, M., Bonelli, R., & Pereira, J. E. C. (1980). *Política econômica externa e industrialização no Brasil 1939/1952*. Rio de Janeiro: IPEA/INPES.

Miceli, S. (1993). *A Fundação Ford no Brasil*. São Paulo: Editora Sumaré.

Montecinos, V., & Markoff, J. (2009). *Economists in the Americas*. Cheltenham, MA: Edward Elgar.

Nooy, W. (2003). Fields and Networks: Correspondence Analysis and Social Network Analysis in the Framework of Field Theory. *Poetics*, 31, 305–327.

Prebisch, R. (1949). O desenvolvimento econômico da América Latina e alguns de seus problemas principais. *Revista Brasileira de Economia*, 3(3), 47–11.

Ribeiro, R. A. (2006). *A Aliança para o Progresso e as relações Brasil-EUA*. Ph.D. diss. Campinas: UNICAMP.

Rocca, C. A., Ceotto, E., & Rizzieri, J. A. B. (1984). O Instituto de Pesquisas Econômicas e a Fundação Instituto de Pesquisas Econômicas. In A. P. Canabrava (Ed.). *História da Faculdade de Economia e Administração da Universidade de São Paulo (1946–1981)*. São Paulo: FEA-USP.

Rotschield, K. W. (1989). Political Economy or Economics? *European Journal of Political Economy*, 5, 1–12.

Serino, M., D'Ambrosio, D., & Ragozini, G. (2017). Bridging Social Network Analysis and Field Theory through Multidimensional Data Analysis: The Case of the Theatrical Field. *Poetics*, 62, 66–80.

Silveira, P. B. A. (2009). *O estado da ciência e a ciência do Estado: a Fundação Getúlio Vargas e a configuração do campo das ciências econômicas no Brasil*. Master thesis. Rio de Janeiro: UFRJ.

Simonsen, M. H. (1966). O Ensino de Economia em nível de Pós-Graduação no Brasil. *Revista Brasileira de Economia*, 20(4), 19–30.

Sola, L. (1998). *Ideias econômicas, decisões políticas: desenvolvimento, estabilidade e populismo*. São Paulo: Editora da Universidade de São Paulo/Fapesp.

Valdés, J. G. (1995). *Pinochet's Economists: The Chicago School in Chile*. Cambridge: Cambridge University Press.

Wagner, A. (2007). *Les classes sociales dans la mondialisation*. Paris: Éditions la découverte.

Index

Page numbers in *italic* indicate a figure and page numbers in **bold** indicate a table on the corresponding page. Page numbers followed by 'n' indicate a note.

Academic Family Tree 216
academic institutional positions of economists 233
academic inter-personal networks of economists 233
academic revolution 209
Ackley, G. 137
Act of International Development 252
affective economies 113
Agamben, G. 132
Ahmed, S. 113, 114
Alderson, Wroe 102, 104
Allende, Salvador 255
Alliance for Progress 253
Amariglio, Jack 80
Amir, R. 214
Anderson, B. 113
Andreatta, Beniamino 138
Arbeitskreis Steuermythen 199
Arendt, Hannah 93
Arrow, Kenneth 220, 221, 222
Åsbrink, Per 212
Association for the Industry in the South (SVIMEZ) 135
Aumann, Robert J. 220
austerity policies 87; and Brexit 25; in Germany 150; Greek economic crisis 109, 116; in Italy 134, 135, 138

Bach, Stefan 196
Badiou, Alain 81
Baer, Werner 254
Bank of International Settlements (BIS) 176
Bank of Mexico 177
Bäuerle, Lukas 7, 53

Baumgartner, H. 213
Beck, U. 103
Becker, Gary S. 61, 67n7, 111, 210
Bellofiore, R. 94
Benz, Pierre 1, 11, 227
Berman, E. P. 148
Bernanke, Ben 48, 55, 58, 61, 64–65
Beyer, Karl M. 9, 147
Binkley, S. 114
biology 79, 82
biopolitics of economic expertise 129–132
Birken, Lawrence 80
Bjerke, Flemming 4, 8, 90
Blattner, Niklaus 238
Bockman, J. 129
Bofinger, Peter 195, 199
Böhm von Bawerk, Eugen 216
Bologna reform 60
Boltanski, Luc 10, 171, 172
Bonelli, Regis 254
Borner, Silvio 241
Bourdieu, Pierre 10, 250, 263n5; notion of space 263n4; on power 19, 22, 23; on production of dominant ideology 171, 172; on social capital 229
Bradlow, D. D. 170
Brady Plan 180–181, **180**
Brazilian Center for Analysis and Planning (CEBRAP) 261
Bresser Pereira, Luiz Carlos 253
Brexit discourse 7, 24; discursive formation of expert positions as political identities 28–31; institutional relations and place of UK in EU field 24–28; reputation and legitimacy of economic experts 31–32; workers category 26–28

Index 267

Brown, Wendy 82
Buchanan, James M. 74, 75–76, 84, 85, 86, 87, 216
Buira, Ariel 177
Bulhões, Octavio de 259
Burda, M. 150
Bürgin, R. 216
business economists 8, 90, 98, 104, 105
Butterwegge, Christoph 197

Callon, M. 22, 97
Calomiris, Charles 175
Camdessus, Michel 179
Cantinflas 173
Cardoso, Fernando Henrique 261
Carli, Guido 137
Carvalho, José Luiz 259
Cassa per il Mezzogiorno 135, 136, 140
Castro, Antonio Barros de 253, 260
Cattell, James McKeen 223n2
Center of Training in Economic and Social Development (CENDEC) 256
Central Bank of Brazil (BACEN) 259
Central Bank of Sweden 212
Chicago Boys 127, 255–256
Chile 255, 256
Ciampi, Carlo Azeglio 138, 140
circular cumulative causation 93
citations, and social capital 230, 232, 240
classical liberalism 8, 78, 80
classical political economy 8, 73–74; epistemic structure of 81, 83; *homo economicus* 81, 82; and neoclassical economics 78, 79, 81
class-specific multiple correspondence analysis (CSA) 231–232, 241–242, *242*
Coase, Ronald H. 216, 218
Coats, A. B. 2
Codice Camaldoli 134
Colander, D. 194, 263n9
Collor de Mello, Fernando 261
Cologne dispute over method (*Kölner Methodenstreit*) 150–151
Comeliau, Christian 239
competition 8, 90; and collusion, difference between 95; dispositive 8, 99–101, *100*, 102, 103; domination of society 101–102; as exercise of power 94–97; general competition and risk 103; growth and differentiation 102–103; overlapping of targets 96; rationalizing business economists 104

competitive power principle 95–97, *96*, 99, 100, 104
competitive power technologies 97; competitive rationality, construction of 98–99; soft power in marketing management 97–98
Conceição Tavares, Maria da 253, 260
constitutional political economy 75, 76, 87
converted conservatism 172–173
Corl, T. C. 215
cosmopolitan assets, and internationalization 248
Costantini, O. 25
counter-hegemonic organic intellectuals 188, 191, 195, 199, 200
cultural political economy (CPE) 190
cultural turns 189–190

Davies, W. 102
Davignon, Étienne 139
Davou, B. 109
Dean, J. 112
Deiss, Joseph 238
Delfim Netto, Antônio 260, 261
Demertzis, N. 109
Dezalay, Y. 128, 262
Diamond, Peter A. 218
discipline dispositive 94, 98
discourse 1, 3, 4, 6–8, 130–131; Brexit 24–32; discourses of excellence 32; economic expert discourses 1, 3, 7, 19–33; economics textbook 54–66; frames 56; Greek bank advertising 109, 114–121; and Italian disciplinary economics 126, 132–140; Lacanian discourse theory 23, 29; negative emotional discourse 109, 114; sociology of knowledge approach to discourse 7, 53; *see also* public discourses, role of economists in
discursive power 6–7, 19–20; imaginary power 23, **23**, 28–31; and Nobel Prize 210; performative power 22–23, **23**, 24–28; in social studies of economics 20–22; symbolic power 23–24, **23**, 31–32
division of labour: within German economists 151, 153, 159, 164; socio-technical 126, 127, 130, 131, 132, 140
dominant ideology 5, 10, 171, 172–175, **173**, 181; *see also* Mexican default debt crisis (1982)
Dunn, Jeffrey 104

268 Index

Echeverría Álvarez, Luis 173

Economic Council of the Christian Democratic Union (Wirtschaftsrat der CDU e.V.) 199

economic expert discourses 1, 3, 7, 19; Brexit discourse 24–32; dispositif analytical approach for analysing 21–22; forms of discursive power 22–24, **23**; forms of power in social studies of economics 20–22

economic expertise 9, 126–127, 140–141; biopolitics of 129–132; discursive practices 126, 127, 129, 130–131, 132, 135, 140; Foucault on 131; internationalization of state apparatuses 128–129; laboratories of 127–129, 132; lay perspective on Italian disciplinary economics 132–140; profanation 132; propriety, relations of 126, 127, 130, 131, 132, 134; socio-technical division of labour 126, 127, 130, 131, 132, 134, 140; transnational networks 128, 129, 130, 131, 135; and United States 249; *see also* Italian disciplinary economics

economic imaginaries 1, 190

economic institutional positions of economists 233

economic inter-personal networks of economists 233

economic naturalists 58, 64–65

economics 3, 6; autonomy of 11, 227, 228, 242, 243; Buchanan on 76; business economists 8, 90, 98, 104, 105; channels of influence 20; denaturalization of 81; discipline, emergence of 130; epistemic field of 130, 131, 141; existential crisis of 182n4; as expert knowledge 76, 79, 84; as a field 5, 11–12; Foucault on 73, 77; German, current state of 149–151; and governmentality 3–4, 8–9; hierarchies in 2; language 25, 26–28; laws and principles 57–58, 59, 60, 65, 66; as a means of strengthening individual empowerment 76; as a mental science 81, 82; and neoliberal governmentality 73, 74; network structures in 4–5, 9–11; and politics 147–148, 227; and power 1–2, 3, 5, 147–149, 227; power of 87, 126, 127–129, 131; as public science 77; reasons for studying 57–58; research, ideological and political orientation in 227; schools of thought 194, 216; as a scientific discipline 147–148; as

trans-epistemic field 228; truths of 58, 63, 66; *see also* macroeconomics, academic; Nobel Laureates; social capital in economics; social studies of economics (SSE); textbooks, economics

Economics (McConnell) 55

Economics (Samuelson) 54

economists 1–2, 19; abstract tools of 64; authority, and cognitive infrastructure of polity 20; business economists 8, 90, 98, 104, 105; Catholic, in Italy 134, 135; and dominant ideology 173; field, social capital in 229–230; field-specific habitus of 5; Foucault on 77; and political economy 58–59; professional jurisdiction of 128; as public intellectuals 2, 148; rationalizing business economists 104; role in public debates 148; transnational networks of experts 128, 129, 130, 131, 135; as universal intellectual 201n5; *see also* German newspapers, wealth/ inheritance taxation in; Germany, influential economists in; space of economists, Brazilian; Swiss field of economists, social capital in

economized economic education 62

Einaudi, Luigi 134–135

Ellis, Howard 254

Ely, Richard T. 216

Engels, Friedrich 172

entrepreneurship: entrepreneurial self 62, 64; and neoclassical economics 83–84

Erhard, Ludwig 149

European Central Bank (ECB) 25

European Round Table of Industrialists 139

European Single Act 139–140

European Union (EU) 24–28, 138–140

euro-pessimism 139

euro-sclerosis 139

extra-disciplinary social capital in economics 11–12, 230, 233, 237–239, *239*, 241, 242–243

Eyal, G. 129

Faculty of Economics and Administration, University of Sao Paulo (FEA-USP) 254

Faculty of Economic Sciences, Federal University of Minas Gerais (FACE-UFMG) 259

Fama, Eugene F. 218

Federal Open Market Committee (FOMC) 7, 36–37, 48–49n1; autonomy of 47–48;

Index 269

and new classical economics 38–44; voting members of 40; and Willes 40–44
Federal Reserve (Fed) 7, 36, 38, 44–47, 170, 175
Federal Reserve Bank of Minneapolis 38–40
Federal Reserve Bank of St. Louis 38, 44
Federal University of Rio de Janeiro (UFRJ) 260, 261
Feld, Lars 195, 199
Fellesson, M. 98
field 1, 5, 11–12, 129, 155, 250; epistemic field of economics 130, 131, 141; place of economics in field of power 5, 128, 227–228; scientific, economics as 1–2, 5, 229; -specific habitus, of economists 5; and symbolic power 23–24, 32; trans-epistemic 32, 148, 149, 228; *see also* Nobel Laureates; space of economists, Brazilian; Swiss field of economists, social capital in
Financiadora de Estudos e Projetos (FINEP) 260
Fishlow, Albert 254
Flaubert, G. 171
Ford Foundation 137, 253, 254
Foucault, Michel 3, 29, 58, 65, 76, 87; on economic expertise 131; on economics 73, 77; on governmentality 76, 97–98; on knowledge 76–77; on knowledge structure of human sciences 79; on liberal governmentality 8, 73–74, 78, 80, 83; marginalism 74, 80, 81; on neoclassical economics 78, 80, 83; on party governmentality 86; on power 8, 19, 22, 63, 90, 91, 92, 101; study of neoliberalism 84; use of archeological method 80, 81
Fougère, M. 98
Fourcade, Martin 2, 128, 148, 222, 227
Four Freedoms 25, 27
Franco, Itamar 261
Frank, R. H. 55, 58, 61, 64–65
Frankfurter Allgemeine Zeitung (FAZ) 151, 155, 193, 196, 198
Franz, Wolfgang 195
Fratzscher, Marcel 195, 197
freedom: and Greek bank advertising 117–118; and power 91–94; and public choice theory 75, 85
Frei Montalva, Eduardo 255
Freud, Sigmund 79, 81

Frey, Bruno S. 240
Friedman, Milton 37, 111, 210, 218, 222, 255; monetarism 38, 45; and Nobel Prize 209
Fuest, Clemens 195, 197, 198–199
Furtado, Celso 252, 255

Galbraith, John K. 91, 92, 223
Garth, B. G. 129, 262
Gaudard, Gaston 238
Gautier Morin, Johanna 10
gender bias, in German economics 153, **153**, 164
general equilibrium theory 39, 221
German Confederation of Trade Unions (DGB) 199
German Council of Economic Experts 150, 195, 201n6
German Federal Republic 149
German newspapers, wealth/inheritance taxation in 10–11, 188–189; and book publications 197–198; mainstream economists 194–195, 198–199; methodology 192–195, **192**; occurrence of economists over time *197*; ordoliberalists 194–195, 198–199; ownership 192–193; paradigmatic orientation of economists 194–195, 198, **198**; plural mainstream economists 195, 198; political affinities of economists 198–199, 200; political orientation of newspapers 193, 197, 200; post-Keynesian and heterodox economists 195, 198, 199; quantitative appearance of economists 195–198, **196**, 200; reference to economic experts 197
Germany, influential economists in 9–10, 147–149; affiliations with research institutes/academic think tanks 156–157, **157**, 164; co-authorship network 162, *163*; connections with governmental bodies/international organizations/central banks 157–159, **159**, 164; institutional-personal network 160, *161*; linkages to ideological/advocacy think tanks, foundations and institutions 157, **158**; media presence of 148; media ranking 151, 153, 155; non-university activities 156–159; and ordoliberalism 149–151, 164; personal details **153–154**, 153–155; place of PhD 154–155, **155**, 164; political impact ranking 151, 153, 155; professional networks among 160,

270   Index

161, 162, *163*, 164–165; public policy
petitions by economists 159; research
data and methodological approach
151–152, **152**; research profile 155–156,
156; research ranking 151, 152, 155;
top-level research *vs.* policy advice 151,
159, 164
Getúlio Vargas Foundation (FGV) 251,
253, 254, 259, 261
governmentality 3–4, 8–9, 22, 97, 131,
138; Foucault on 76, 97–98; internal
76, 86; in marketing management
98; neoliberal 73–87, 109, 112; party
governmentality 86
Grabka, Markus 196
Gramsci, Antonio 10, 188, 190, 200n4
Greek bank advertising, emotional/affective
strategies of 9, 114–121; austerity
politics 109, 116; budget stories 120;
economic potential 115–116, 117;
freedom 117–118; individuality 117,
118; individual meaning 116, 117; living
indicators 118–120; negative emotional
discourse 109, 114; stability 120–121
grounded theory analysis 49n1
Gudin, Eugênio 251, 259
Gürkan, Ceyhun 8, 73
Gurría, José Ángel 176
Gwartney, J. D. 55, 60, 61, 62, 64

Haber, Stephen 175
Haberler, Gottfried 251
Hall, P. A. 2, 20
Hansen, Lars P. 218
hard power 90, 91, 92
Harsanyi, John C. 222
Harvard University 258, 263n9
Haucap, J. 148, 151
Hayek, Friedrich A. 63, 85, 110,
111–112, 209
Heckman, James J. 213, 220
hegemonic organic intellectuals 188,
190–191, 195, 199, 200
Hermanowicz, J. C. 212
Hernández Cervantes, Héctor 177
heterodox economics 91, 194, 258
Hickel, Rudolf 197, 199
Hirschel, Dierk 197
Hirschman, A. O. 92
Hirschman, D. 20, 148
Hoffmann, Andreas 196
Homburg, Stefan 197
homo economicus 64, 81–82, 83, 85, 112

homo politicus 85
Horn, Gustav 199
human capital theory 60, 61–63
human existence, and economic
principles 58
human sciences 79, 80, 81
Hüther, Michael 195, 197, 198

imaginary power 7, 19, 23, **23**, 28–31
impact loans 135
inflation targeting 48
inheritance taxation 189, 200n2
Institute for Applied Economic Research
(IPEA) 254, 256, 259–260
Institutional Act 5 (AI-5) 254
institutional positions of economists
232, 233
Institutional Revolutionary Party
(PRI) 175
Instituto Nazionale di Economia Agraria
(National Institute of Agrarian
Economics) 133
internal governmentality 76, 86
international departmental networks of
economists 232
International Monetary Fund (IMF)
138, 181; bailout, Mexican debt
crisis (1982) 171, 175, 176, 177,
179; legitimacy of 170
inter-personal networks of economists:
academic, political and economic 233;
scientific 232
intra-disciplinary social capital in
economics 11, 229–230, 232, 239–241,
239, 242, 243
invisible hand 82, 101
Istitutio Nazionale di Statistica (National
Institute of Statistics) 133
Istituto per la Riscostruzione
Industriale (Institute for Industrial
Reconstruction) 133
Italian Communist Party (PCI) 134, 138
Italian disciplinary economics 9, 132–133,
140–141; Catholic economists 134, 135;
crisis as governing expertise 136–138;
deflationary therapy 136–137, 138;
econometric models 137, 138; economic
experts as an EU constitutional force
138–140; making of Italian model of
development 133–136; monetarism
134–135; *Servizio Studi* 133, 134, 135,
137, 138, 140; state-cadres 136, 137;
trade unions 136, 137, 138

Index   271

Janssen, Martin 240
Jencks, C. 209
Jessop, Bob 10, 190
Johnson, Peter A. 44
Johnston, L. 55, 58, 61, 64–65
journals, publication in: Nobel Laureates
213, 220–221, *221*, 222; and social
capital 230

Kafka, Alexandre 251, 254
Kahneman, Daniel 210
Kant, Immanuel 76, 81, 86
Kennedy, John F. 253
Keynes, J. M. 147
Keynesian economics 74–75
Kichline, James L. 42
Klamer, Arjo 263n9
Klein, N. 170
Klüger, Elisa 12, 228, 248
Knauff, M. 214
Knies, Karl Gustav A. 216
Knight, Frank 216
knowledge: economic expert knowledge
3, 6, 20–22, 24, 33, 73, 76, 79;
economics textbook 58, 59, 60, 65;
episteme 80–81, 82, 83; Foucault
on 76–77; and governmentality 98;
informal 3; international circulation of
248–262; knowledge-power 77, 78, 82;
monetary policy making and academic
macroeconomics as domains of 7, 47–48;
production 36, 43, 79, 137; sociology
of knowledge approach to discourse 7,
53; structure, of human sciences 79; of
subjectivity 63
Knox, David 176, 180
Kogut, Edy 259
Kohli, M. 223n7
Korom, Philipp 11, 209
Kraft, Joseph 176
Krugman, Paul 55, 61, 160, 195, 197,
210, 221
Kubitschek, Juscelino 252
Kurunmäki, L. 96

Labini, Sylos 138
Lacan, J. 23, 29
laissez-faire economics
78–79
Langoni, Carlos Geraldo 255, 259
Larosiere, Jacques de 172, 175–176
Latin American School of Economics
(ESCOLATINA) 255, 260, 261

Latin American School of Social Sciences
(FLACSO) 255
Latour, B. 93, 129
Lebaron, F. 2, 148
Lechner, Michael 240
Lee, F. S. 194
Leipold, Alexander 193
Leme, Og Francisco 256
Lemgruber, Antonio 259
Lessa, Carlos 253, 260
Lewinson, Richard 251
Lewis, Arthur W. 218
Light, D. W. 215
Lima, Gilberto Tadeu 256
Lindbeck, Assar 211
Lindholm, R. W. 170
Lindsey, D. E. 45
local departmental networks of
economists 233
Loureiro, Maria Rita 256
Lucas, Robert E. 38–39, 40, 216
Lucas Critique 38, 44
Lukes, S. 91
Lula da Silva, Luiz Inácio 261
Lutz, Vera 135

MacLaury, Bruce 39
Macroeconomic Policy Institute (IMK) 199
macroeconomics, academic 7, 36–38; as
autonomous domain of knowledge and
power 47–48; knowledge production 32;
and practical monetarism 44–47; rational
expectations macroeconomics 7, 37,
38–44; and Willes 40–44
Madrid, Miguel de la 174, 177
Maesse, Jens 1, 6, 19, 148, 191, 201n5
Maingueneau, D. 29
Malan, Pedro 254
Mancera Aguayo, Miguel 174, 177, 178
Mankiw, Gregory 53, 55, 57, 61–62, 64,
67n11
Marangos, J. 170
Maresden, L. R. 215
marginalist economics 74, 80, 81;
epistemic structure of 81–82, 83; and
governmental reason 82
market analysis 103
Market Economy Foundation (Stiftung
Marktwirtschaft) 199
marketing 8; management, soft power in
94, 97–98; and power 90–91, 104, 105;
see also competition
Markoff, J. 173

Index

Marshall, Alfred 79
Marshall Plan 135
Marx, Karl 172
Maskin, Eric S. 222
Massachusetts Institute of Technology
(MIT) 263n9
Massumi, B. 113
master-apprentice relationships between
Nobel Laureates 216, 222
McConnell, Campbell 55
media economists in Germany 164;
affiliations with research institutes/
academic think tanks 156–157, **157**;
average age of 154; connections with
governmental bodies/international
organizations/central banks 157–159,
159; linkages to ideological/advocatory
think tanks, foundations and institutions
157, **158**; nationality of 154; networks
165; ordoliberal references in
publications 156; place of PhD 155;
primary affiliations of 153; public policy
petitions signed by 159; research profiles
155, **156**; *see also* German newspapers,
wealth/inheritance taxation in
Meltzer, A. H. 40, 45
Mexican default debt crisis (1982)
10, 170–171; Brady Plan 180–181,
180; changes in political and
administrative staff 177–178; failures
and experimentations 178–181; global
convergence in economic rationale
176–178; production of dominant
ideology 172–175; as a proxy to unveil
information mechanisms 175–176;
redefinition of social positions 173;
renewal of elites 174; research data and
method 171–172; restructuration of
national economy 179
Michigan State University 253
Mill, John S. 81
Miller, G. William 42
Miller, Merton H. 218
Miller, P. 96
Miller, R. 55, 65
Minford, Patrick 28, 29, 30, 31, 32
Mirowski, P. 2
Mishkin, F. S. 49n5
Mixed Commission Brazil-US
(CMBEU) 252
Modigliani, Franco 137, 138, 139
Modigliani Controversy 138
Mödl, M. 151
Moktan, Sidharth 213, 220

monetarism 37, 38, 43, 75, 182n4, 258; in
Italy 134–135; practical 38, 44–47
monetary policy of central banks 7, 36–38;
as autonomous domain of knowledge
and power 47–48; Federal Reserve
Bank of Minneapolis 38–40; practical
monetarism 44–47; rational expectations
macroeconomics 38–44
Montecinos, V. 173
Montes de Oca, Luis 178
Monti, Mario 132, 139
Mont Pelerin Society (MPS) 110, 178
Morgan, M. S. 2
Morin, Johanna Gautier 170
Moss, M. 91
Mudd, Michael 95, 100
Mudge, S. L. 25
Müller-Armack, Alfred 149
multiple correspondence analysis (MCA)
11, 165, 228, 231, 234–241, **234–236**,
236–237
Muniesa, F. 97
Myerson, Roger B. 222
Myrdal, Gunnar 93

Nash, John 11
National Bank of Economic and Social
Development (BNDES) 252, 253, 260
National Faculty of Economics
(FNCE) 251
nationality of German economists
153–154, **154**
National University of Brasília (UNB) 259
neoclassical economics 5, 8, 73, 74,
87, 194; criticism of 77–78; and
entrepreneurial subject 83–84; epistemic
structure of 81; Foucault on 78, 80,
83; and governmental reason 79, 81;
homo economicus 82; and neoliberal
governmentality 73, 74, 77–84; rise of
79, 81
neoliberal governmentality 8, 9, 73, 87,
109, 112; constructivist and active
governmentality 84; Foucault on 73–74;
homo economicus 81–82, 83; internal
governmentality 76, 86; labour power
84; and marginalism 82; neoclassical
economics as foundation of 77–84;
problem and method 74–77; and public
choice theory 84–86; shift from classical
liberal governmentality to 83
neoliberalism 4, 8–9, 78, 109–110, 243;
affects 113–114; bank advertising,
emotional/affective strategies

Index 273

114–121; and economic reasoning 63; emotional and affective states in 111–112; emotional logic of 114; and entrepreneurial subject 84; feelings 113; *homo economicus* 82; philosophical background of 110–112

network analysis 250

networks 1, 4–5, 9–11, 22, 228, 250; academic, political and economic inter-personal networks 233; and discourses of excellence 32; German influential economists 149, 156–157, **157**, 160, *161*, 162, *163*, 164–165; heteronomous 241–242, *242*, 243; local departmental networks 233; professor-student networks of Nobel Laureates 215–216, *217*; scientific inter-personal networks 232; and social capital 229–230; social power structures in academic economics 4–5; and symbolic power 32; transmission of economic knowledge into politics 4; transnational networks of experts 128, 129, 130, 131, 135; visiting professorship of Nobel Laureates 219–220, *219*, 222; *see also* German newspapers, wealth/inheritance taxation in; Mexican default debt crisis (1982)

new classical macroeconomics 37, 47, 48; Federal Reserve Bank of Minneapolis 38–40; and practical monetarism 46; Willes's efforts at persuading FOMC to adopt rational expectations macroeconomics 40–44

new Keynesian economics 36, 47, 48

Nicoletta, Gerardo Costabile 4, 9, 126

Nobel, Alfred 211

Nobel Laureates: disciplinary strand of career 215; elite departments 212–213; external strand of career 215; institutional strand of career 215; journals, publications in 213, 220–221, *221*, 222; main career pathways 216, 218–219, *218*; PhD-granting institutions 215–216; professor-student networks 215–216, *217*; prosopographical approach 212; prosopographical database 213–214, **214–215**; public ideas 210; visiting networks 219–220, *219*, 222

Nobel Prize 11, 23, 209–210, 211, 244n3; critiques of 209; interdependencies 210–211, *211*; political undertone

to 212; prize-worthy contributions 211–212; selection procedures of 211

Nordhaus, W. 58, 64

Nurkse, Ragnar 251

Offer, A. 212

Office for Applied Economic Research (EPEA) 254

O'Neill, D. 190

optimistic evolutionism 172, 173

ordoliberalism 84, 149–151, 165n2, 194

organic intellectuals, economists as 188, 190–191, 195, 199–200; *see also* German newspapers, wealth/inheritance taxation in

Organisation for Economic Co-operation and Development (OECD) 139

Organization of American States (OAS) 180

Ötsch, W. O. 191

Pahl, Hanno 7, 36, 55

parallel coordinate plot 216

Partee, J. Charles 42, 43

party governmentality 86

pastoral power, and governmentality 97

performative power 7, 19, 22–23, **23**, 24–28

performativity studies 19, 21

performativity theory 21

Pieters, R. 213

Piketty, Thomas 160, 195, 197, 198

Pinochet, Augusto 256

Piraeus Bank 115–120

Plano de Metas 252

policy advice economists in Germany 164; affiliations with research institutes/academic think tanks 156–157, **157**; average age of 154; connections with governmental bodies/international organizations/central banks 157–159, **159**; linkages to ideological/advocacy think tanks, foundations and institutions 157, **158**; nationality of 154; networks 165; ordoliberal references in publications 156; place of PhD 155; primary affiliations of 153; public policy petitions signed by 159; research profiles 155, **156**

political economy 58–59, 63, 81; classical 8, 73–74, 75, 76, 78, 79, 81, 82, 83, 87; constitutional 75, 76, 87; cultural 190; deontological turn in 76; and Mill 81; modern 255, 258, 263n8; and

274 *Index*

performativity approaches 21; role of intellectuals in 188, 190, 195, 200

political institutional positions of economists 233

political inter-personal networks of economists 233

politics: austerity politics 87, 109, 116; biopolitics of economic expertise 129–132; Buchanan on 76; collective politics 84, 85, 86; and economics 147–148, 227; transmission of economic knowledge into 4

Pontifical Catholic University of Rio de Janeiro (PUC-RJ) 260, 261

Pontifical Catholic University of Sao Paulo (PUC-SP) 261

Popp Berman, E. 20

Porter, M. E. 102–103

post-Keynesian economics 194

post-Marxism 188, 189–190

Poulantzas, N. 200n3

power 6–7, 19; competition as exercise of 94–97; competitive power principle 95–97, *96*, 99, 100, 104; competitive power struggle 93, 101, 102; competitive power technologies 97–99; as a complex phenomenon 2–5; and determination 93, **93**; disciplinary 86; and economics 1–2, 3, 5, 147–149, 227; of economics 87, 126, 127–129, 131; of economics textbooks 57; exercise by business economists 104; forms, in social studies of economics 20–22; forms of **92**; Foucault on 22, 63, 73, 76, 90, 91, 92, 101; and freedom 91–94; hard 90, 91, 92; imaginary 7, 19, 23, **23**, 28–31; knowledge-power 77, 78, 82; labour power 84; market power 90–91, 92, 93; Marxian and Bourdieusian approaches to 20–21; monetary policy making and academic macroeconomics as domains of ˙47–48; and neoclassical economics 77; of Nobel Laureates 210; performative 7, 19, 22–23, **23**, 24–28; performativity theory 21; power principle (Alderson) 102; role of competitive power in market society 101–104; security-management modality of 73; and social capital in Swiss economics 243; social power structures in academic economics 4–5; soft 90–92, 94, 95, 97–98; symbolic 7, 19, 23–24, **23**, 31–32; technologies of 93, 95, 97–99, 104; Weber's theory of 20

practical monetarism 44–47

Prebisch, Raul 252

prestige ranks of Nobel Laureates 214, 216, 218, *218*

primary affiliations of German economists 153, **154**

Principles of Economics (Mankiw) 55, 57

professorships of Nobel Laureates 216, 218–219, *218*

psychology 79, 81, 82

Psyllakou, Elena 4, 8–9, 109

public choice theory 74, 75; ethical dimension of 76; and neoliberal governmentality 8, 73, 74, 84–86

public discourses, role of economists in 10, 188; cultural turns 189–190; media economists 191; organic intellectuals 190–191; political affiliations and ideological convictions 191–192; *see also* German newspapers, wealth/inheritance taxation in

public intellectuals, economists as 2, 148

Pühringer, Stephan 1, 9, 147, 193

rational expectations macroeconomics 7, 37, 49n5; and Federal Reserve Bank of Minneapolis 38–40; Willes's efforts at persuading FOMC to adopt 40–44

rationality: competitive 98–99; governmental 77, 79, 83

Reagan, Roanld 46, 75

real business cycle models 44

Regan, Donald 175

regulation theory 188, 189–190

Reis Velloso, Joao Paulo dos 254

representative democracy, and public choice theory 84, 86

research economists in Germany 164; affiliations with research institutes/ academic think tanks 156–157, **157**; average age of 154; co-authorship network 162; connections with governmental bodies/international organizations/central banks 157–159, **159**; linkages to ideological/advocacy think tanks, foundations and institutions: 157, **158**; nationality of 154; networks 162, 164–165; ordoliberal references in publications 156; place of PhD 154–155; primary affiliations of 153; public policy petitions signed by 159; research profiles 155, **156**

Resnick, Stephen 77

Ricardo, David 80, 81

Riesman, D. 209
Ritschard, G. 216
Robbins, Lionel 251
Robinson, Joan 223
Rockefeller Foundation 133, 253
Rogoff, Kenneth 195
Rosenstein-Rodan P. 135
Rossier, Thierry 1, 11, 227
Roth, Alvin E. 218

Saint-Martin, Monique 263n5
Salinas de Gortari, Carlos 180
Samuelson, Paul A. 54, 58, 64, 218
Sanger, Stephen 95, 100
Sargent, Thomas 39–40
Sarney, José 261
Schabas, Margaret 81
Schiller, B. 55, 60
Schiller, Karl 149
Schiller, Robert 244n3
Schmidt, C. M. 151, 195
School of Administration, Getulio Vargas Foundation (EAESP) 253, 260
Schumpeter, Joseph 84
scientific collaborations of economists 232
scientific institutional positions of economists 232
scientific inter-personal networks of economists 232
scientific production of economists 230, 232
security-management modality of power 73
Seelkopf, L. 200n1
Seikel, D. 25
self-regulation, and discipline 94
semiosis 190
Sen, Amartya 221
Senna, Jose J. 259
Sennett, Richard 75
sequence analysis (SA) 214
Sharpe, William F. 218
Shouse, E. 113
Silva Herzog Flores, Jesus 174, 175, 176, 177, 178
Simmel, Georg 101, 103
Simon, Herbert 11, 98, 220
Simonsen, Mario Henrique 259
Sims, Christopher A. 223n8
Sinn, Hans-Werner 195, 197
Skålén, P. 98
Slobodian, Q. 112
Smith, Adam 101

social capital in economics 11, 227–228, 229; at departmental level 230; extra-disciplinary 11–12, 230, 233; at institutional level 229, 230; at inter-personal level 229–230; intra-disciplinary 11, 229–230, 232; research strategy and methods 230–233; at scientific production level 230; social capital, definition of 229; *see also* Swiss field of economists, social capital in
Social Democratic Party (SPD), Germany 199
social network analysis (SNA) 4–5, 9, 12, 151, 152
social studies of economics (SSE) 2, 6, 12, 19, 20–22, 126, 129
sociology of knowledge approach to discourse (SKAD) 7, 53
Söderberg, G. 212
soft power 90–92, 94, 95, 97–98
Solow, Robert M. 218
Soziale Marktwirtschaft (social market economy) 149
space of economists, Brazilian 12, 248, 249, 257; circulations of exiled economic experts 254–256; distances between agents and institutions 250; European institutions 257, 258–259, 260; export of US's economic expertise during Cold War 253–254; governments 261; gradient of positions 258–259; impact of international circulation 256–261; international cooperation 251–253; Latin American institutions 257–258, 260–261; North American institutions 257, 258, 259–260; research data and methods 249–251
Sparsam, Jan 7, 36
Spence, A. Michael 222
Spiegel, Der (newspaper) 193, 197, 198
Stability and Growth Pact 25
stagflation 44, 45
Stavrakakis, Y. 109
Stigler, George 216
Stiglitz, Joseph E. 150, 160, 195, 222
subjectivation 63
Süddeutsche Zeitung (newspaper) 193, 197, 198
Sum, N. L. 190
Summers, Larry 147
Superintendence for the Development of the Northeast (SUDENE) 255
supervision, and discipline 94
SVIMEZ 137

276 *Index*

Swiss field of economists, social capital in 11, 228; cloud of individuals *237*; cloud of modalities *236*; contributions and frequencies of active variables and modalities **234–235**; extra-disciplinary social capital 233, 237–239, *239*, 241, 242–243; heteronomous networks 241–242, *242*, 243; indicators 232–233; intra-disciplinary social capital 232, 239–241, *239*, 243; research data 230–231; research methods 231–232; teaching and research specialisation 243
Swiss National Science Foundation (SNSF) 232, 244–245n13
symbolic capital 20–21, 23, 148
symbolic power 7, 19, 23–24, **23**, 31–32

Tangentopoli 140
Taylor, Mark 53, 64
taz (newspaper) 192, 193, 197, 198
tenure, and publications in journals 210, 213, 220, 221
textbooks, economics 7–8, 53–54; capitalization of economics education 59–62; and decision making 60; design of 60–61; discourse 54–59; entrepreneurial self 62; and human capital theory 61–63; identity offerings 54, 56, 57, 62, 63, 64, 65, 66; income-orientated perspective 60, 61; political economy 58–59, 63; power of 57; production process 55–56, 61, 65; profitable application of knowledge 60; as public mass media 55; reasons for studying economics 57–58; research strategy and methods 56–57; scientific discourse 55; semi-public discourse 55; shift of mindset of readers 64; subjectivation 63, 65, 66; subject positions 58, 63, 64
Thaler, Richard H. 215
Theine, Hendrik 10, 188
think tank economists in Germany 153
Thomas, T. 148
Tol, R. S. J. 215–216
transnational networks of economic experts 128, 129, 130, 131, 135
Truger, Achim 201n6
Tversky, Amos 210

United Nations Economic Commission for Latin America (CEPAL) 252–253, 255, 256, 260, 261
United States: dissemination of economic knowledge by 249; export of economic

expertise to Brazil 253–254, 262; Marshall Plan 135; and Mexican default debt crisis (1982) 176; Mixed Commission Brazil-US (CMBEU) 252; *see also* monetary policy of central banks
United States Agency for International Development (USAID) 253, 254
University of California, Berkeley 254
University of Campinas (UNICAMP) 260–261
University of Chicago 259, 263n9
University of Cologne 151
University of São Paulo (USP) 254, 260, 261
US Treasury 170, 171

Vanderbilt University 254
Vauchez, A. 25
Veblen, Thorstein B. 78, 79, 81, 82
Viner, Jacob 251
visiting professorship of Nobel Laureates 214, 219–220, *219*, 222
Volcker, Paul 37, 38, 44–46, 172, 175, 178

Wagner, G. G. 148
Wallace, Neil 39
Washington consensus 174, 181
Wayne, M. 190
wealth inequality in Germany 189
wealth taxation: and capital classes 189; in Germany 189, 200n1
Weber, Max 19, 20, 22
welfare capitalism 78
Wells, R. 55, 61
Welt, Die (newspaper) 193, 197, 198
Welt am Sonntag (newspaper) 193, 197, 198
Wicksell, Knut 74
Willes, Mark H. 39, 40–44, 47, 49n11
Wolff, Richard 77
Wolter, P. 193
World Bank 170, 181

Yale University 254, 258, 263n9
Yellen, Janet 48

Zeit, Die (newspaper) 193, 197, 198
Zimmermann, Klaus 147, 153
Zuidhof, P.-W. 65

Printed in the United States
by Baker & Taylor Publisher Services